Uelsmann Untitled

University Press of Florida

Florida A&M University, Tallahassee
Florida Atlantic University, Boca Raton
Florida Gulf Coast University, Ft. Myers
Florida International University, Miami
Florida State University, Tallahassee
New College of Florida, Sarasota
University of Central Florida, Orlando
University of Florida, Gainesville
University of North Florida, Jacksonville
University of South Florida, Tampa
University of West Florida, Pensacola

A Retrospective

Jerry Uelsmann

With an essay by Carol McCusker

University Press of Florida

Gainesville · Tallahassee · Tampa · Boca Raton

Pensacola · Orlando · Miami · Jacksonville · Ft. Myers · Sarasota

Uelsmann Untitled

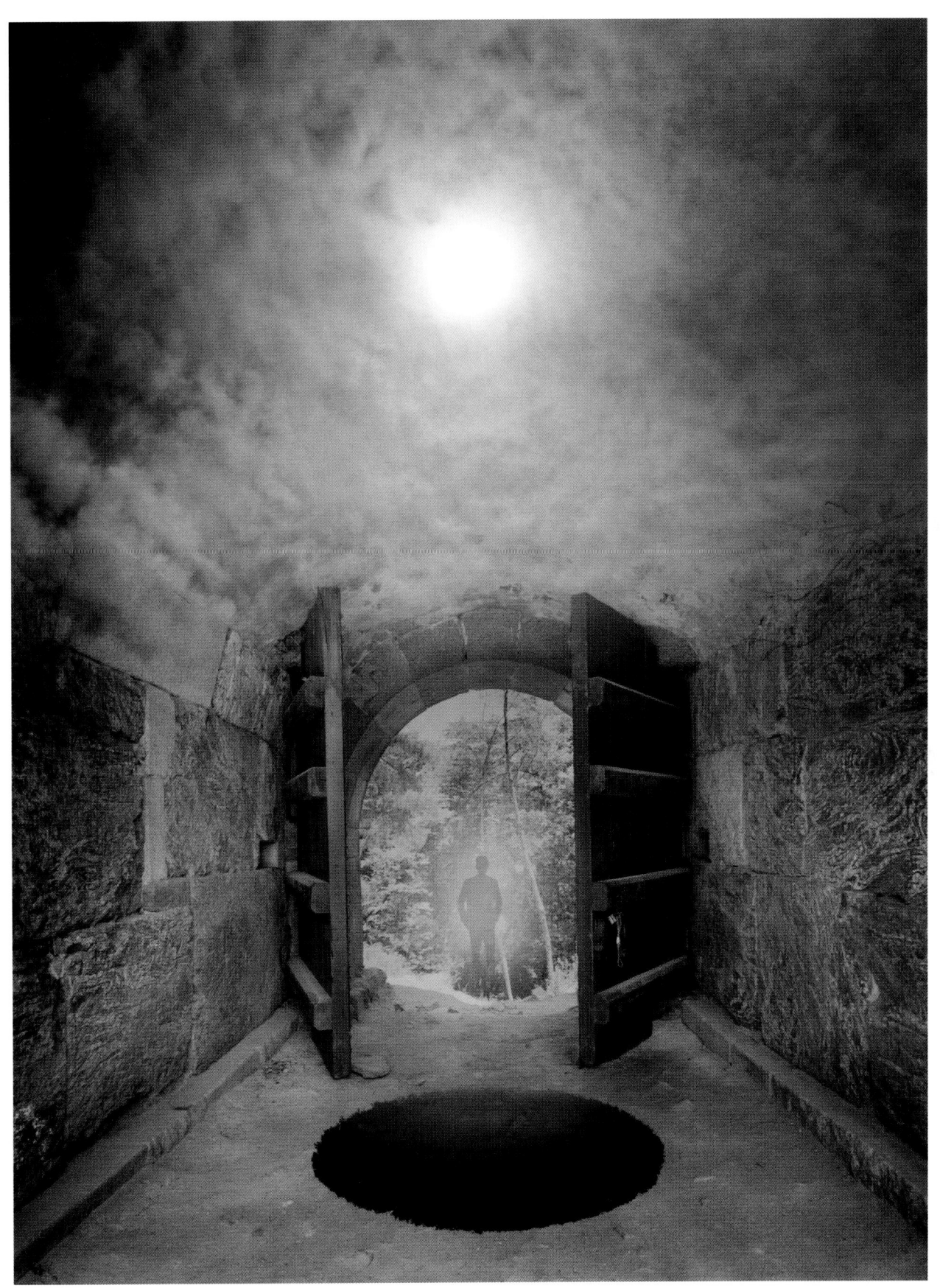

Frontispiece: The Portal 2013
Front cover: Journey into Night 2006
Back cover: 2011

19 18 17 16 15 14   6 5 4 3 2 1

Library of Congress Cataloging-in-Publication Data
Uelsmann, Jerry, 1934– author.
Uelsmann untitled : a retrospective / Jerry Uelsmann ; with an essay by Carol McCusker.
pages cm
ISBN 978-0-8130-4949-6
    1. Uelsmann, Jerry, 1934– 2. Photography, Artistic. 3. Photographers—Florida—Gainesville. 4. Photomontage. 5. Art and photography. I. McCusker, Carol. II. Title.
TR655.U33 2014
770.92—dc23   2013034790

The University Press of Florida is the scholarly publishing agency for the State University System of Florida, comprising Florida A&M University, Florida Atlantic University, Florida Gulf Coast University, Florida International University, Florida State University, New College of Florida, University of Central Florida, University of Florida, University of North Florida, University of South Florida, and University of West Florida.

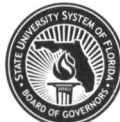

University Press of Florida
15 Northwest 15th Street
Gainesville, FL 32611-2079
http://www.upf.com

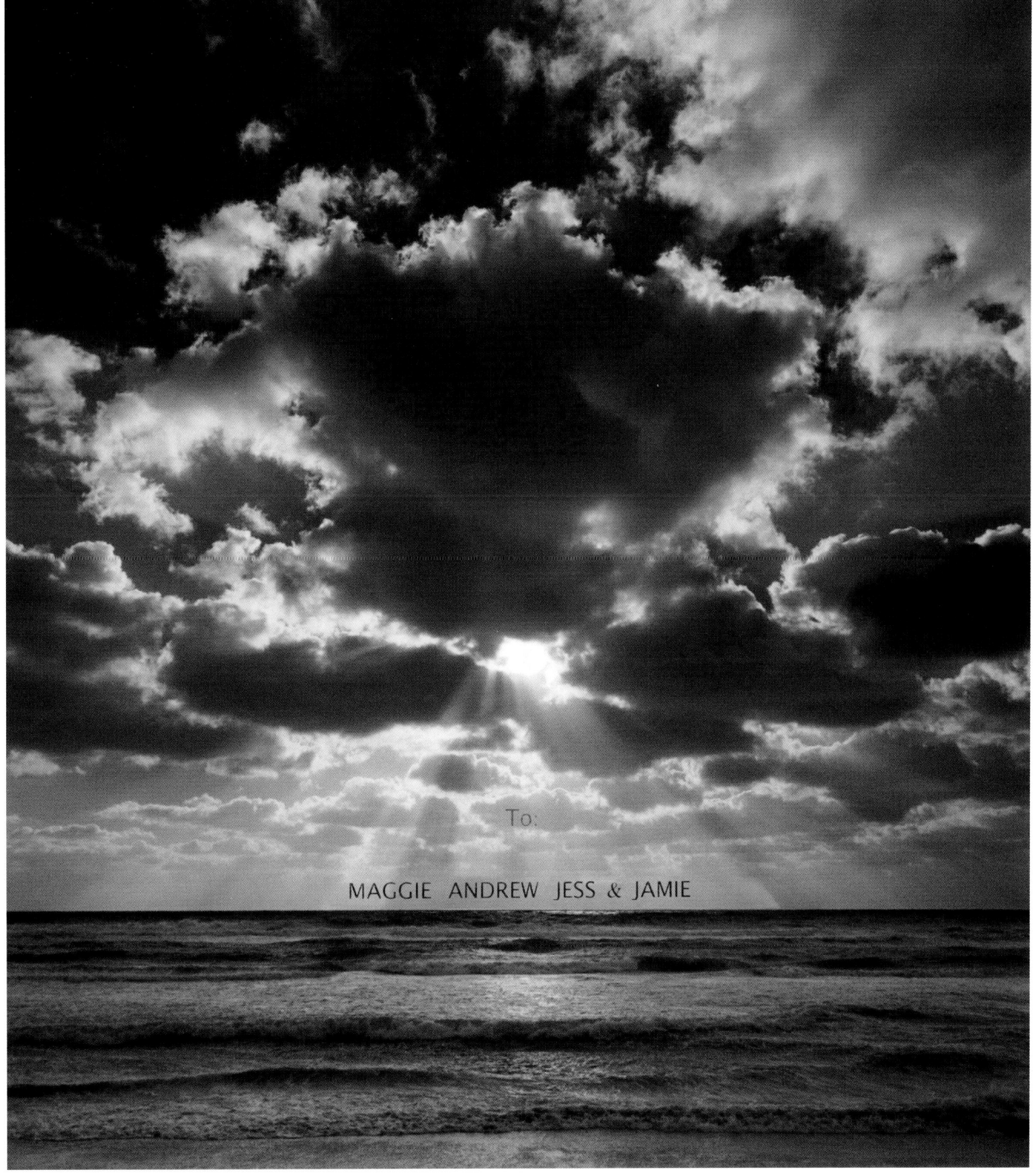

To:

MAGGIE ANDREW JESS & JAMIE

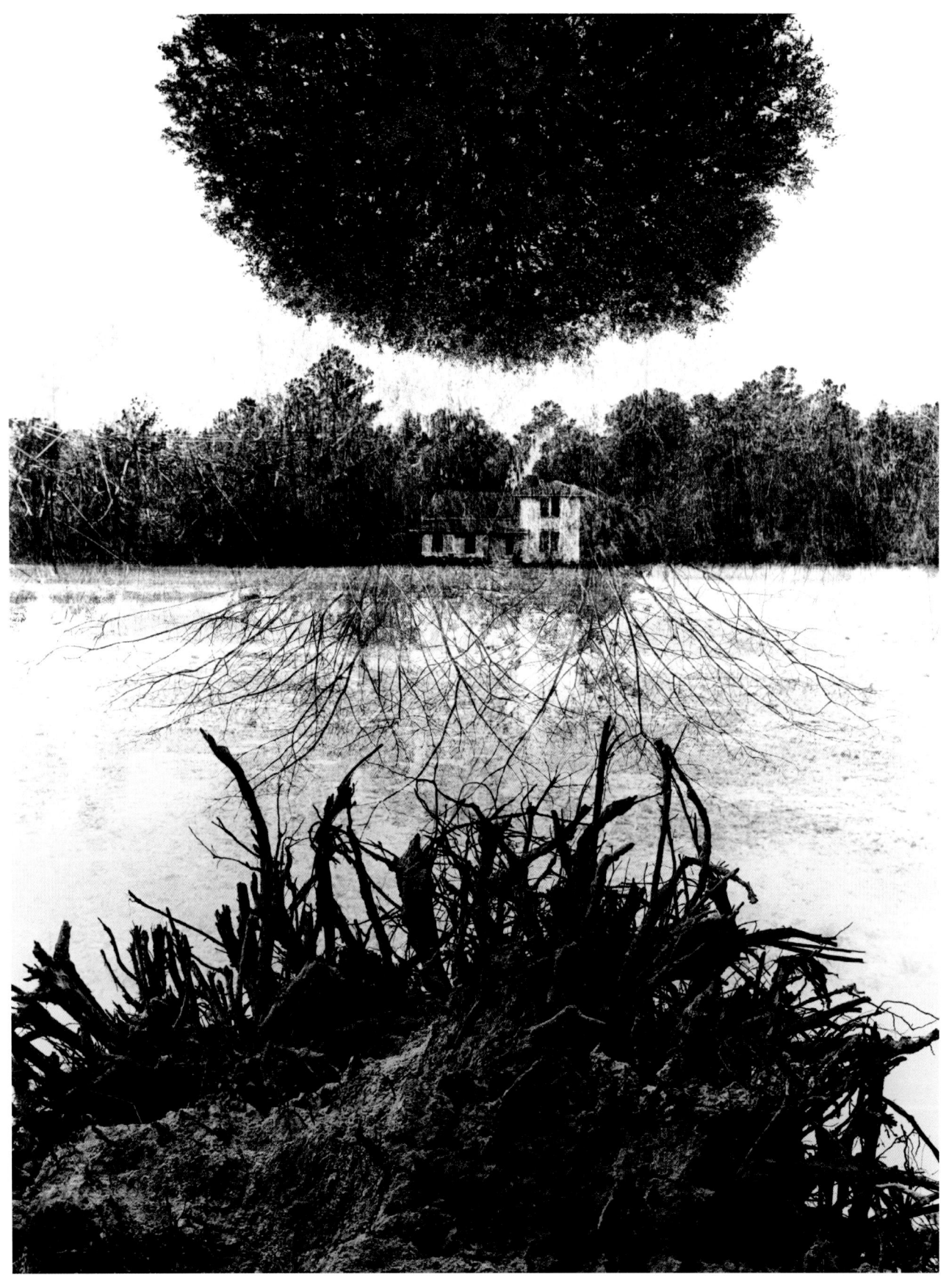

Poet's House 1965

PRIMAL SCENE

Carol McCusker

A conversation with Jerry Uelsmann is a spirited experience punctuated with historical asides, humor, and equal doses of insight into and irritation with politics, human nature, and the art world. For Uelsmann, life is a series of synchronous encounters that he embraces with enthusiasm. An overall optimism beams from his puckish countenance, seeming to electrify even his unruly hair. It is not a feigned attitude, and it is especially noteworthy since disappointment and loss have also been his lot. Along the road of his seventy-nine-year journey, he has learned wisdom and acceptance in keeping with the Buddhist teachings he declares essential to his life. Uelsmann has established his own way and his own spiritual hermitage, a southern outpost in Gainesville, Florida, that has nurtured his soul for decades.

Uelsmann's haven, far from the cultural centers of New York or Los Angeles, is a modernist house built after WWII and shared with his wife, photographer Maggie Taylor. It is a series of straight lines and plate glass fenestrations. Two picture windows make up the walls of their living room, merging interior with exterior spaces. Looming above and enveloping the house are four 300-year-old live oaks draped in Spanish moss. Their massive trunks and cascading branches touch the ground and extend back up beyond sight, creating canopies of light and shadow. On the lawn beneath them sits a sculpture of a rabbit five times the normal size. With the scene lit at night, the effect is magical: gathered in the living room, guests feel they are sitting inside a Uelsmann or Taylor photograph—architecture defines one space, nature floats in the other, Alice is tumbling down the rabbit hole. The rest of their home is stippled with natural light and art hung salon-style that almost exclusively depicts alternative realities. The effect is pure enchantment.

Uelsmann is a people person who also covets solitude. In the company of others, he is quick to laugh and a storyteller as well as a listener. He attentively observes not only what a person is saying but also how the speaker says it. He is nourished by a life of examining human nature—what is said or left unspoken—in himself and those close to him. Yet an evening at his home is likely to end with him or Taylor at their player piano, pumping its recalcitrant pedals into melody—a favorite: Queen's "Bohemian Rhapsody" ("Is this the real life? Is this just fantasy?"). The euphoric oxygen rush induced by this group sing-along is exactly the effect he wants. Uelsmann has internalized a lesson from the Laughing Buddha: through laughter (or singing) one exits suffering and enters bliss.

A similar exuberant mood unfolds (visually instead of aurally) during a walk through his three-room studio, which could be misconstrued as the prop room for the Quay Brothers or Tim Burton. Its walls are pinned with cartoons, dolls' heads, strange toys that move or talk, 3-D sculptures of Hieronymus Bosch paintings, and nineteenth-century Victoriana. Its myriad shelves and recessed spaces hold camera memorabilia from the history of photography, mug shots from the age of Alphonse Bertillon, scribbled drawings from friends and fans, and gifts from fellow artists. It is the lair of a collector amused by absurdist gizmos spanning a period from the dawn of the Industrial Revolution to the present. These riotous fantasies, double entendres, and tokens of affection are a record of Uelsmann's life. Their effect on him is talismanic; they constitute a chorus that silently encourages or inspires his next creation. An essay by William Anderson, which Uelsmann returns to often, says the offering of such creative gifts changes "the state of being of the enjoyer," who then transfers "the effects of this energy" into "happiness, awareness, tranquility or a willing surrender of our private concerns to a universal experience."[1] Uelsmann carries this energy into the darkroom. His finished photographs of fantastic realities are mined from the world that exists in him as much as the world that surrounds him.[2]

Lining Uelsmann's darkroom are seven enlargers and the respective sinks, chemicals, and processing trays essential to the work of a prolific analog photographer. Each photograph is made from three to five negatives meticulously aligned in the exposure process to make a single, composite print. Watching him produce such prints is akin to viewing a choreographed dance. Moving in measured succession from enlarger to enlarger (each holds a negative that is one piece of the final image), he waves his hand or a shaft of paper like a composer on a rostrum, each movement having the desired dodging or burning effect on the paper below. It is precise work, demanding patience, vision, and long hours. Unequivocally, this is Uelsmann's realm; he is alive in it. He is a virtuosic printer, creating silver-based paper imagery that Photoshop cannot quite mimic. Like a shaman, he conjures images that "allude to the fragile and mysterious quality of life itself," says the artist of his work. Why Uelsmann chooses to make photographs of the intangible through a medium that records only fact is best understood in light of the teachers he studied with, the historical moment into which he stepped as an artist, and the geography he lives in.

*

"A man's work is nothing less than the slow trek to rediscover, through the detours of art, those two or three great and simple images in the presence of which his heart first opened."

—Albert Camus

In 1946, at the age of twelve, Jerry Uelsmann took drawing lessons at the Detroit Institute of Arts. Walking the galleries one day, he was transfixed by a portrait painting. The portrait had a marked effect on him, though he didn't notice the artist's name. Years later, while attending art history classes at Indiana University (art historical references can be found in many of his photographs), he encountered the portrait again. It was Van Gogh's *Self-Portrait* (1887), owned by the Detroit Institute of Arts. What in Van Gogh's portrait "opened" Uelsmann? Given Uelsmann's own "detour" away from commercial toward fine art photography, perhaps he found a kindred spirit in the nineteenth-century painter, whose decision to confront convention with non-traditional free expression went against the grain of then-accepted, marketable painting practices. As other artists and writers have noted before, Uelsmann's photographic practice and his theory of "post-visualization" could "be seen to have altered the language, the substance, and the direction of [the medium itself]."[3] Indeed, Uelsmann's photographs aren't dependent upon the actual world in the traditional sense. Photo-historian Bill Jay notes that while many in his generation were aspiring to be street photographers in the style of Robert Frank, Uelsmann "disrupted the cozy assumptions prevalent in the 1960s. [He] was disrespectful to the agreed One True Path to Photographic Enlightenment: the socially concerned document." Instead, Uelsmann offered "the artist's vision, the interior world of creation . . . [that] swept away the old order and signaled a new era. A photograph was no longer *of* something, it was *about* something."[4]

Uelsmann's path began at the Rochester Institute of Technology (RIT), where he would receive a B.F.A. in 1957. His initial intention was to become a commercial photographer. Two influential teachers changed that course. Ralph Hattersley, who taught at RIT, wrote *Discover Yourself through Photography,* which was based on his teaching. "Art is a prime means for studying and achieving oneness in self," he told his students. "Man sees both the world and himself as composed of opposites—conflicts, polarities. . . . We are making photographs to understand what our lives mean to us."[5] The psychology of creativity was new territory for his young acolytes; the point for Hattersley was to open photography up to new possibilities.

This personal approach toward the medium was expanded by Minor White, also teaching at RIT. White's philosophy, manner, and appearance were uniquely charismatic. He might slip references to the I Ching or the Tao into classes on composition or urge his students to subvert the dominant documentary trend by first "being still with yourself until the object of your attention affirms your presence." The camera was a tool for self-transformation, for finding the equivalent of "personal feeling through objects in the real world." His most resonant quote, "One does not photograph something simply for what it is, but for what else it is," took inspiration from Zen meditation and the teachings of G. I. Gurdjieff and P. D. Ouspensky.[6] Like Van Gogh's portrait, Hattersley and White tapped into something elemental in Uelsmann's relationship to life. A few of Uelsmann's photographs survive from this period. They are straight images (combination printing would come later), yet the temperament that would inform his future work is there, "humanistic, introspective, and a touch of melancholy."[7] Also present in the early work is Uelsmann's extraordinary technical expertise. A rich chiaroscuro of light and shadow, texture and depth defines the finished print, the physical means to a transcendent end.

In 1958, Uelsmann moved to Bloomington for graduate school at Indiana University, enrolling in a Master of Science program for audiovisual communication, as very few universities offered advanced degrees in fine art photography. He received his MS, yet dissatisfied with the mere mechanical application of his craft, he transferred over to Indiana University's art department to earn a second Master's, this one in fine arts. This studio emphasis in photography allowed Uelsmann to study design and art history and, most important, brought him in contact with Henry Holmes Smith, another major innovator in photography teaching at that time. Smith favored abstract, camera-less photograms in the style of László Moholy-Nagy and the German Bauhaus. His advanced courses and prolific writings, like those of Hattersley and White, emphasized self-discovery and experimentation over documentation. Elimination of prescribed ways of looking meant personal freedom and creativity. A photographer and former student of Smith, Jack Welpott, noted that Smith's strength as a teacher came from "an awareness that the photographic image is central to our visual language, and that literacy in this language is of tremendous sociopolitical importance." Later, Uelsmann recalled, "Henry has always been a prolific reader and thinker constantly seeking new connections and new questions. . . . [He] was a walking 'mind bomb.' On occasions too numerous to mention, a passing comment would serve as a spark for an amazing explosion of ideas and possibilities."[8]

Concurrent with the radical ideas advanced by Hattersley, White, and Smith was the forceful vision of Edward Steichen, who from 1947 to 1961 was the influential director of photography at the Museum of Modern Art (MoMA) in New York. His exhibitions and writing championed (although not exclusively) photojournalism and documentary photography. His mammoth 1955 blockbuster exhibition, *The Family of Man*, which toured thirty-seven countries for eight years, consisted of 503 documentary photographs by 273 photographers depicting humankind at work and play from birth to death. For many photographers coming out of WWII or coming of age in the Cold War ethos of 1950s America, socially concerned photography dominated their attention, especially as the streets of U.S. cities heated up to become sites of civil rights and anti-war protests.

Uelsmann's developing sympathies were both in step and out of step with conformist America. He understood its practical, "plan-for-the-future" ethos (he trained to be a commercial photographer to create educational visual materials for schools). Yet once in the company of Hattersley, White, and Smith, he turned toward the "be-here-now" spirit of Zen meditation, improvisation, and new experiences (equally valued by the Beat writers, jazz musicians, and Method actors of the era). Zen practice also revered the natural world. The environment—its trees, roots, seasons, and open vistas—could be symbolically connected to the ever-shifting subterranean psychological and spiritual depths of human existence. The unseen realms—of thought and feeling, of sexual awakening and dream states—often enclosed in nature began to emerge as dominant themes in Uelsmann's practice as the 1960s unfurled.

In 1960, Uelsmann was offered a teaching position at the University of Florida in Gainesville by photographer and historian Van Deren Coke.[9] The cumulative influence of Uelsmann's teachers shaped his curriculum as it did his vision and made the University of Florida, through Uelsmann's efforts, a renowned school for the study of non-traditional photographic practice. In the following decade, photographers Doug Prince, Todd Walker, and Evon Streetman would join Uelsmann on the faculty.[10] This fecund period was the beginning of Uelsmann's accumulation of thousands of negatives, which he still uses, featuring recurring motifs—trees, hands, nudes, architecture, water—all charged with symbolic import.

During his first two years in the South, two experiences weighed heavily on Uelsmann—segregation and the death of his father. As a native of working-class Detroit, Uelsmann found racism incomprehensible and fought with colleagues to end segregation in the university. It was a long and bitter struggle. His reflections on racism could be seen to inform his consistent use of anonymous (male) figures who portray a universal, "every man" quality, with race and age erased. His photographs imagine a more democratic, humanistic world where "difference" does not exist. During the same time period, his father, a grocer in Detroit, died suddenly of a heart attack. The loss devastated Uelsmann. Knowing death from this personal place undoubtedly informs several Uelsmann photographs that picture figures dematerializing or in the process of leave-taking. His images also depict worlds that exist alongside this one, suggesting the possibility of an afterlife.

Although humor rarely enters Uelsmann's work, it is prominent in personal interactions with the artist. In Zen philosophy, humor is a vehicle for understanding; it helps one reach enlightenment and removes attachment to the world. But as photo-historian and friend Peter Bunnell observes, though humor may be absent from Uelsmann's imagery, "one cannot escape the belief that his comedy conceals an intensity of concern for life and personal doubt that Jerry harbors about life's meaning."[11] His photographs deconstruct codified expectations about the human condition by loosening his and our ideas of want and need. Concepts of love and loss, permanence and change, realized by a decidedly buoyant point of view, shape his personal pursuit of meaning.

In 1967, John Szarkowski, successor to Steichen at MoMA, offered Uelsmann a solo exhibition (a coveted imprimatur for every photographer). Shortly after, Ansel Adams invited Uelsmann to lecture on the West Coast—it was an interview of sorts. Subsequently, Adams invited him to teach at his annual photography workshops in Carmel and Yosemite. Uelsmann did so for the next fifteen years. Adams saw in Uelsmann a great craftsman, even as he expressed reservations about images not made "whole-clothed" from reality. From 1967 into the 1970s, Uelsmann was the subject of numerous exhibitions and publications.[12] His work was championed by Bunnell, curator at MoMA and Princeton, and Uelsmann began to place his art in relation to a deepening appreciation for Jungian psychology and universal myths. Several years would pass, however, before an encouraging, authoritative voice would grant combination printing its proper place within the history of photography and bestow on it an insightful appreciation.

In 1976, photography critic A. D. Coleman wrote "The Directorial Mode," an influential essay that champions interpretive photography. A major hurdle for this kind of imagery, according to Coleman, is "to free itself from the imperative of realism."[13] His text explores the philosophical differences between photographic purists like Ansel Adams, Edward Weston, Paul Strand, and Walker Evans and those who intervene in the straight process through montage or staged tableaux. Coleman asserts that almost *all* photography interrupts reality, from Alexander Gardner's Civil War staging of a rebel sharpshooter to Edward Weston's pepper: "The substantial distinction, then, is between treating the external world as a given, to be altered only through photographic means (point of view, framing, printing, etc.), or, the world as raw material, to be itself manipulated."The latter approach he termed the *directorial mode*.[14]

A rift, often contentious, emerged in the 1960s between straight photography and the directorial mode as practiced by Uelsmann, Edmund Teske, Clarence John Laughlin, Robert Heinecken, Betty Hahn, Duane Michals, Robert Fichter, and others. "It is not the viability of either stance, since both are equal in the length of their traditions," says Coleman. "Rather, it is the presumption of moral righteousness which has accrued to purism." Coleman roundly chastises the photo history books as well as some curators for omitting directorial photographers from their pages or exhibitions "in what seems a deliberate attempt to break the movement's back."[15]

In the 1970s, this was a bold declaration in defense of the manipulated image. Today, with the successes of Gregory Crewdson, Cindy Sherman, and scores of others, one wonders what all the fuss was about. Yet Coleman's essay was integral to expanding our appreciation for the tableau and combination print and paved the way for the directorial mode so prevalent today. As Bunnell states, "Contemporary photography is not the same as it would have been without Uelsmann"[16]; through his contributions as a photographer, teacher, lecturer, and writer, he anticipated much of what is happening today.

Indeed, Uelsmann has been credited as one of the forefathers of the digitally manipulated image that plays with or questions the medium's relationship to reality through the effects of manipulation or staged tableaux, which present us with a view into the artist's mind. Throughout his career, Uelsmann has invented such imagery, albeit in the darkroom (and not with Photoshop, as the digital generation frequently assumes). His conceptual approach to time and space and his arrangement of imaginative narratives, produced through trial and error in the darkroom, are the lush, organic antecedents to works by many digital artists dominating the photography world today.

*

Currently, Uelsmann is fascinated with the work of David Eagleton, a neuroscientist who studies and writes about the subjectivity of the brain. Eagleton raises questions about the nature of consciousness by examining how genetics and subjective experience might shape the brain's chemistry, fears, desires, and ideas. Regarding Uelsmann, how might the embrace of Zen philosophy combined with kudzu vines, sinkholes, primordial creatures, and erratic weather influence the creative landscape of an artist who has lived in northern Florida for over fifty years?

Florida offers a yin-yang experience—dark waters in its rivers, turquoise light in its springs—opposites that are equal and constitute a single reality. As a kind of hideaway in the wilderness, the South provides Uelsmann with a slow-paced, focused retreat in which to work (his output is prolific). At the same time, the state of Florida is and has been a sociopolitical hotbed with escalating environmental problems. Combined with Uelsmann's esoteric pursuits, the conflicting fabric of Florida and the South may subconsciously inform his imagery, in which nothing is assured or known and layers of contradictory realities coexist.

Interesting things happen on the margins of landmasses—one has only to think of Tasmania, Nepal, Alaska—or Florida. Located at the southeast edge of the North American continent, it is a peninsula that separates the Atlantic Ocean from the Gulf of Mexico, generating weather across its width that can be quick and unpredictable (a clergyman in the 1840s once described Florida as "self-willed and unreasonable"[17]). Home to the Calusas and Seminoles, it also hosted pirates and mavericks; historically, it has been a place where only the tough and resourceful survive. Florida's limestone bedrock consists of eons of dead sea creatures. Over millennia it has been riddled by acidic rainwater that permeated the ground and carved out underground caverns and streams[18]—formations that occasionally cause the earth above them to collapse. Its landscape is contradictory: lush, verdant, and soft to look at, it camouflages primal elements beneath (alligators, pythons, sinkholes) that are the stuff of nightmares. Extensive swampland makes solid footing uncertain. Shadows and mist can obscure vision, eliding reality and perception. It is a place where humans are launched into the cosmos (NASA) and fantasylands thrive (Disney).

Native Americans referred to the sudden loss of lakes into newly formed sinkholes as the "disappearing waters." Ancient burial mounds would pop up abruptly just as whole trees and dwellings sank beneath the earth. An overarching geological truth—and one that mirrors Uelsmann's focus on subterranean psychological states or spiritual aspirations—is that "what happens on the surface of the earth is closely connected to what happens underground. And the relationship runs in both directions."[19] Another form of yin-yang.

And just as Florida's land and sea life took millennia to form, a timelessness suffuses Uelsmann's photographs. Ouspensky, the mystic who inspired Minor White, observed how his spiritual path brought him to find "a strange meaning" in the timelessness "of old fairy-tales. Woods, rivers, mountains, became living beings; mysterious life filled the night; with new interests and new expectations I began to dream. . . ."[20] The symbolic fusion of earth with man (or the man-made) is no accident in Uelsmann's photography; he emphasizes connections between our greater aspirations and nature as an ally or foil in a timeless struggle for meaning or contentment. Elevated figures and trees, hands holding worlds, land masses colliding with coastlines—their fluidity as well as their impermanence illustrate Uelsmann wrestling with the "I" or ego in his life as well as in his photography.

Geography is a kind of mapping. Yet most maps are made only of land rather than of people and emotions. Uelsmann changes this equation. His photographs are maps of the human heart that include terra firma alongside terrains of passion and yearning. As with all maps, they are multi- and nondirectional all at once. His figures stand at the intersection of psychological states and external worlds—human galaxies every bit as complex and unfathomable as the cosmos. His layered, symbolic tableaux map human alienation or connection, sensuality, lost history, and humor. Through these organic, often enigmatic photographs, the author engages viewers in a conversation about life, the universe, and the universal. Their constructed-ness underscores their impermanence—in time they too will pass or metamorphose into something else; there is no need for attachment. Uelsmann might find the summary of his art, career, and lifestyle in the words of Joseph Campbell, a fellow seeker, storyteller, and teacher, who wrote, "People say that what we're all seeking is a meaning for life. What we're really seeking is an experience of being *alive*, so that our life experiences on the purely physical plane will have resonance within our innermost being and reality, so that we can actually *feel* [and, Uelsmann might add, *see*] the rapture of being alive."[21]

NOTES

1. William Anderson, "The Central Man of All the World," *Parabola: The Magazine of Myth and Tradition*, Spring 1988, 8–9.

2. Jerry Uelsmann, paraphrased from *The Mind's Eye: Photographs by Jerry Uelsmann* (San Francisco: ModernBook Editions, 2010), 34. The direct quote is "I believe that the world exists *in* us as much as it does around us."

3. Peter C. Bunnell, "Jerry N. Uelsmann: Silver Meditations," in *Inside the Photograph: Writings on Twentieth-Century Photography* (New York: Aperture Foundation, 2006), 197. "Postvisualization" was Uelsmann's definition of the creative process that ensued *after* one's film exposures had been made and discoveries had emerged in the darkroom, as opposed to Ansel Adams's "pre-visualization," which required "the ability to anticipate a finished image before making the exposure."

4. Bill Jay, "Book of Revelations," in *Approaching the Shadow*, by Jerry N. Uelsmann (Portland: Nazraeli Press, 2000), unpaginated.

5. The first quote is from Ralph Hattersley, review of *Aesthetic Realism: We Have Been There—Six Artists on the Siegel Theory of Opposites*, by David Bernstein, Lou Bernstein, Anne Fielding, Chaim Koppelman, Dorothy Koppelman, Ted van Griethuysen, with essay by Eli

Siegel, *Popular Photography*, November 1969; the second is from Ralph Hattersley, *Discover Yourself through Photography* (New York: Association Press, 1971).

6. These are often-repeated quotes of Minor White's on the practice of photography; I have heard them in conversation with John Upton, Fred Sigman, and Jerry Uelsmann, all former White students. White's phrases came from theories of Chinese artists of the Sui Dynasty such as Xie He's Six Principles of Painting, which codified Confucius's thinking on the use of art to better one's self. Thanks to photographer and art historian Fred Sigman for his insight on non-traditional spiritual teachings in relation to White.

7. Phillip Prodger, "Photography through the Kaleidoscope," in Uelsmann, *Mind's Eye*, 33.

8. Jack Welpott and Jerry Uelsmann quotes are from www.henryholmessmith.com.

9. Van Deren Coke would go on to found the distinguished photography department at the University of New Mexico, Albuquerque, hiring Uelsmann's colleagues and friends Tom Barrow and Betty Hahn, and he became director of photography at the George Eastman House and San Francisco Museum of Modern Art. The narrative of his influence on this period of the history of photography remains to be written.

10. Each artist was experimental in his own way, making three-dimensional plexiglass photo boxes or multinegative silver prints, adding objects to the print surface, using the Sabattier effect, introducing expressive color, and using photo lithography and photo silk-screening.

11. Bunnell, "Jerry N. Uelsmann," 193.

12. Among these were several solo shows including the Philadelphia Museum of Art, the George Eastman House, the Art Institute of Chicago, the American Cultural Center in Paris, and a traveling exhibition from MoMA. See Peter C. Bunnell's "Timeline" in *Jerry Uelsmann: Silver Meditations*, by Jerry N. Uelsmann (Dobbs Ferry, N.Y.: Morgan & Morgan, 1975).

13. All subsequent quotes are from A. D. Coleman, "The Directorial Mode: Notes toward a Definition," in *Light Readings: A Photography Critic's Writings, 1968–1978* (Albuquerque: University of New Mexico Press, 1998).

14. The "directorial mode" existed in photography from the very beginning with Hippolyte Bayard's 1840 fictional "drowned man" and in America in the twentieth century with the work of Frederick Sommer, Clarence John Laughlin, Ralph Eugene Meatyard, and Arthur Tress, among others, all of whom Uelsmann either knew or was aware of.

15. Although there was still vocal resistance to combination printing in the 1970s, photo-historian and curator Keith Davis asserts, "this rift, which began much earlier, was beginning to heal, as the 'other history' that Uelsmann represents was embraced, however cautiously, by the field at large. . . . By the mid- to late '70s, constructed or staged imagery was rising rapidly." Keith Davis, in notes to the author, April 2013.

16. Bunnell, "Jerry N. Uelsmann," 196.

17. David Owen, "Notes from Underground: Florida's Sinkhole Peril," *New Yorker*, March 18, 2013, 36–41.

18. Ibid.

19. Ibid.

20. P. D. Ouspensky, *A New Model of the Universe*, as quoted online: goodreads.com/work/quotes/1954150-a-new-model-of-the-universe.

21. Joseph Campbell, interviewed by Bill Moyers, *Joseph Campbell and the Power of Myth with Bill Moyers,* PBS, 1988.

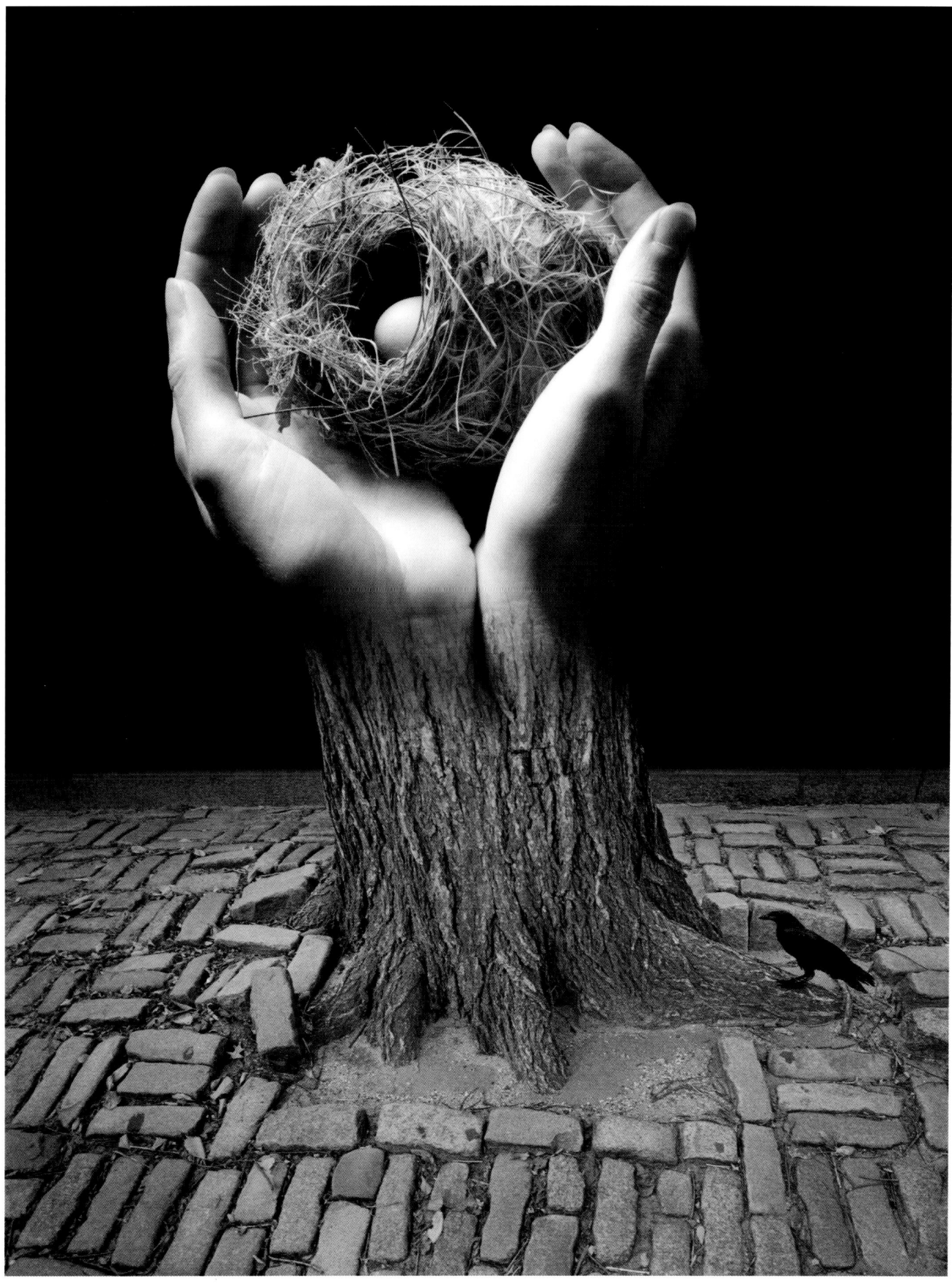

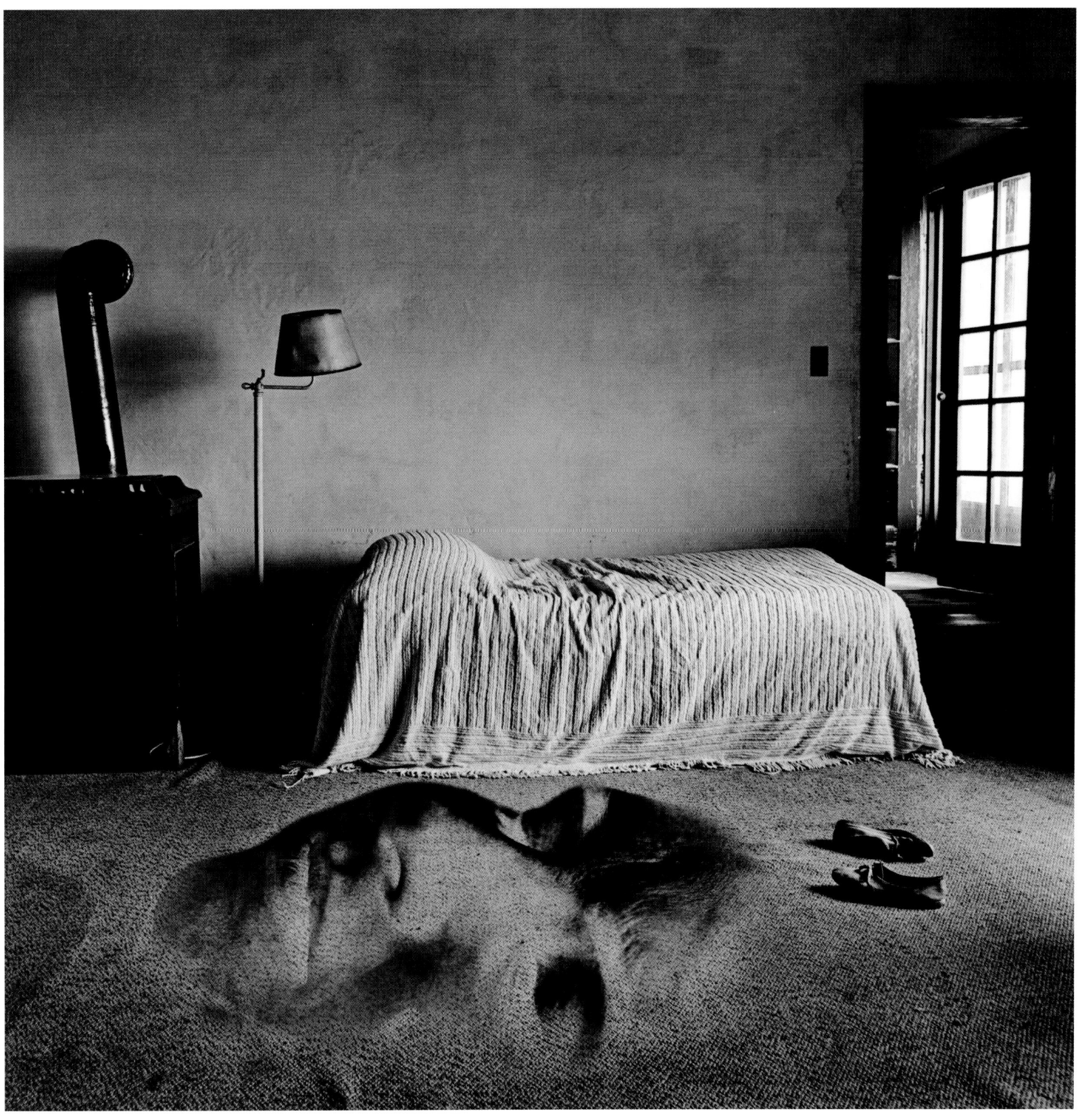

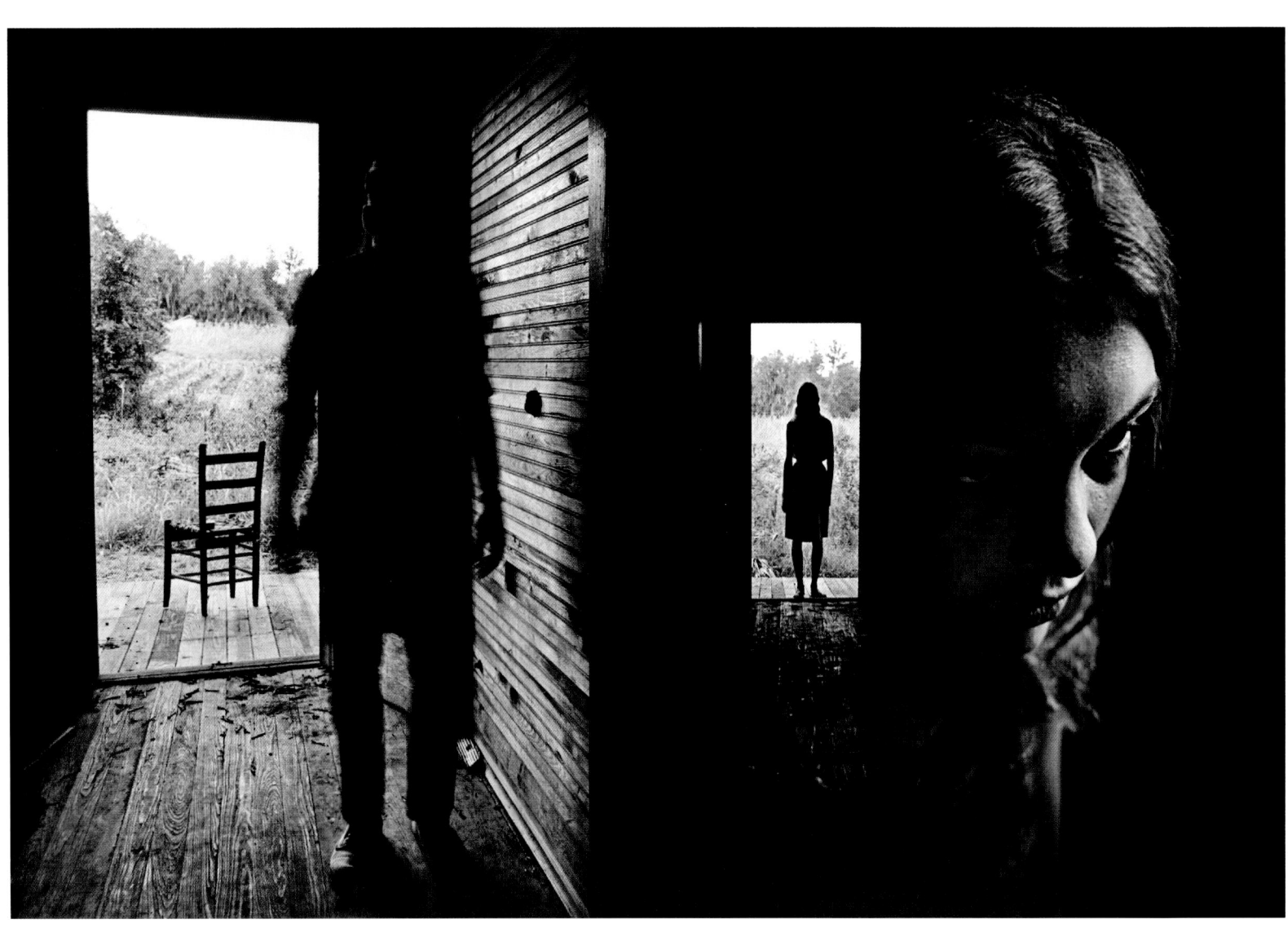

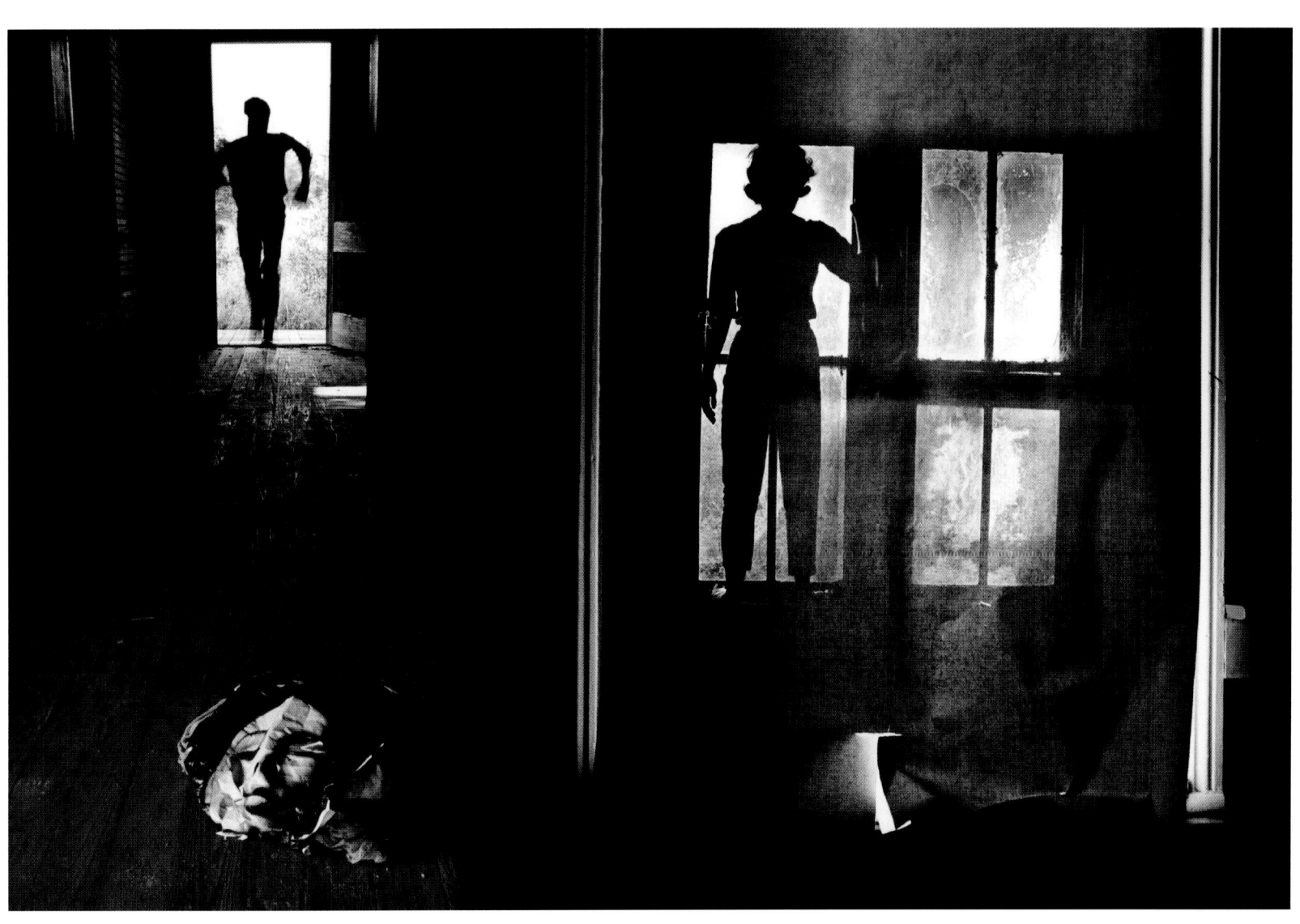

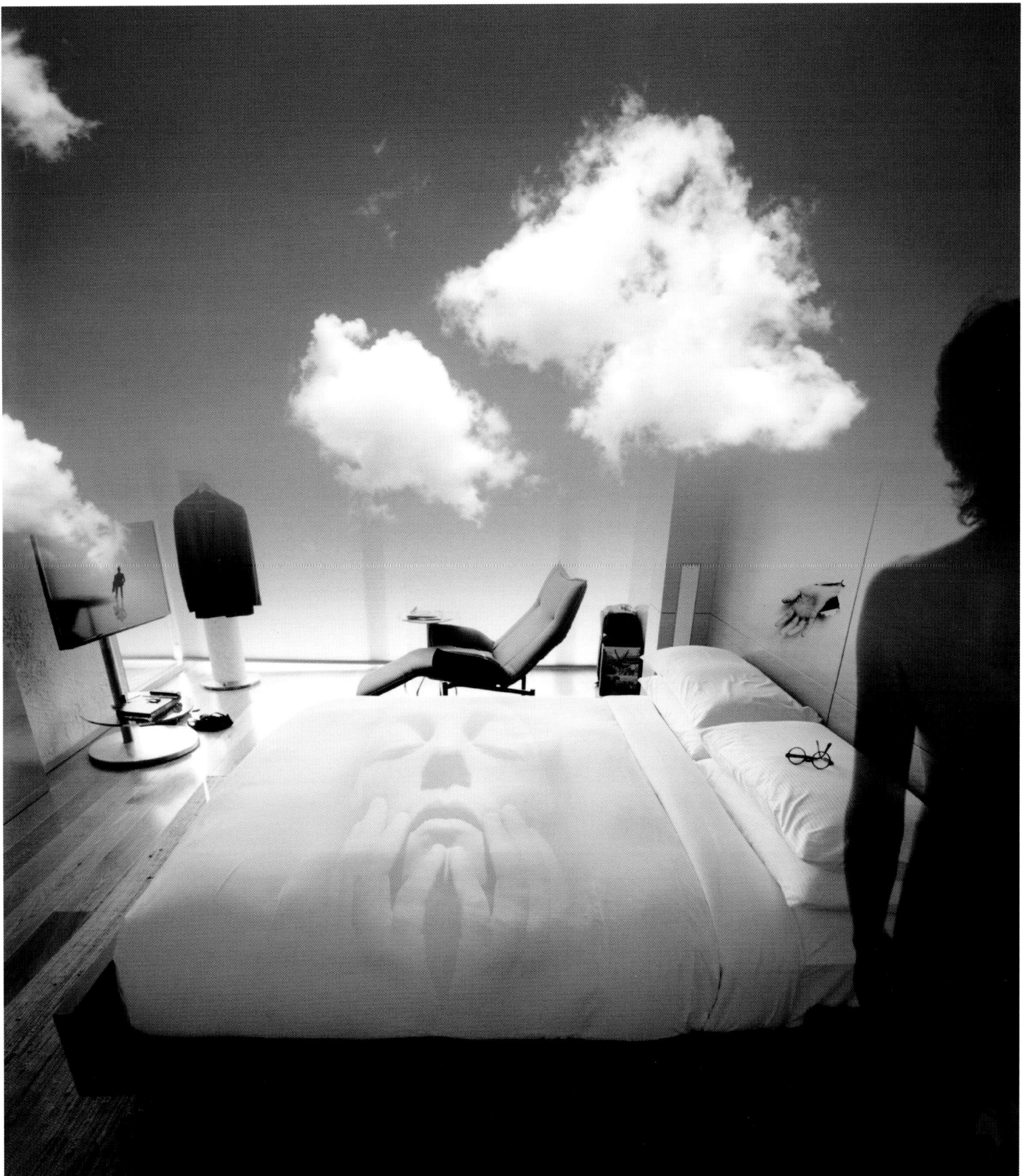

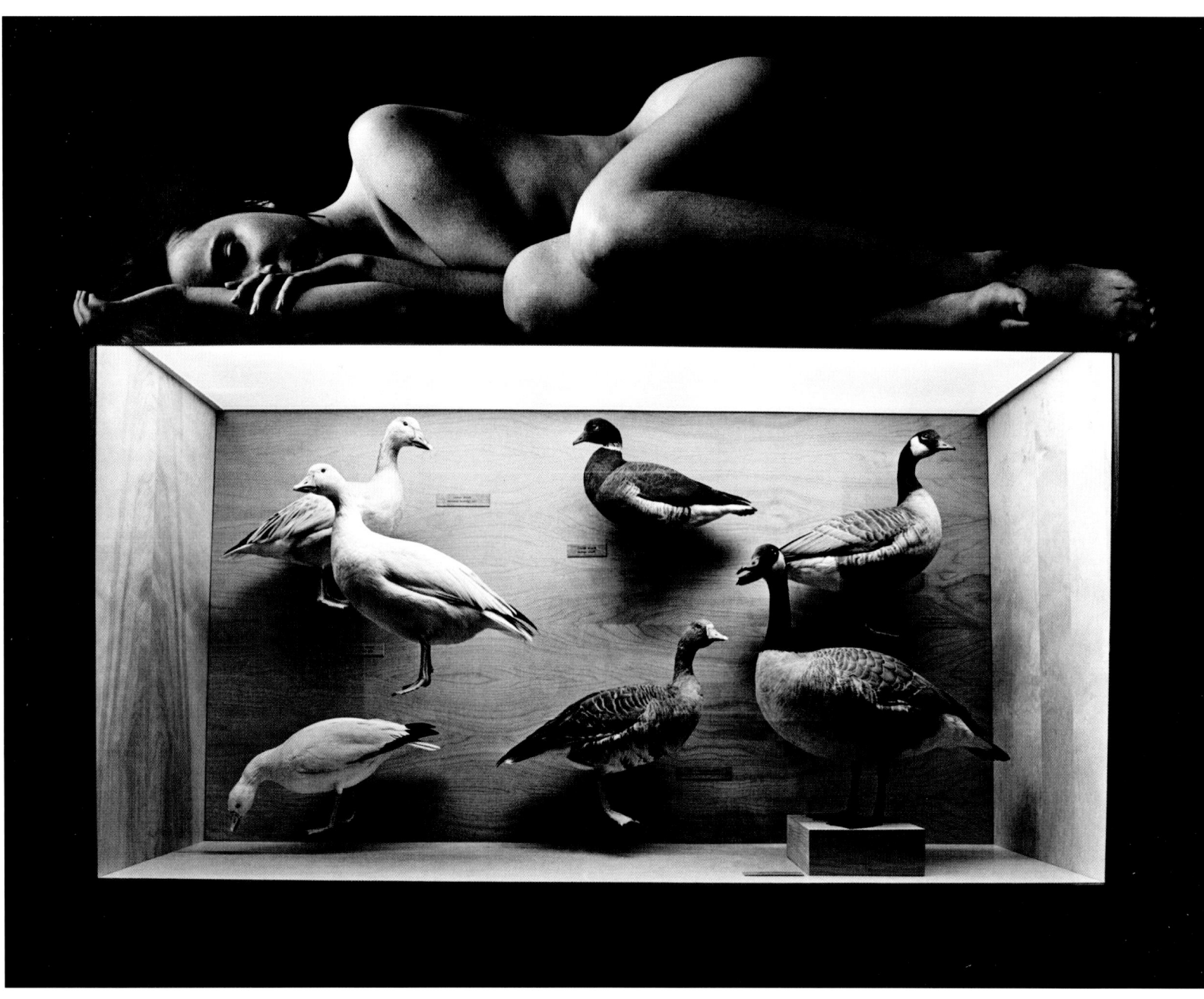

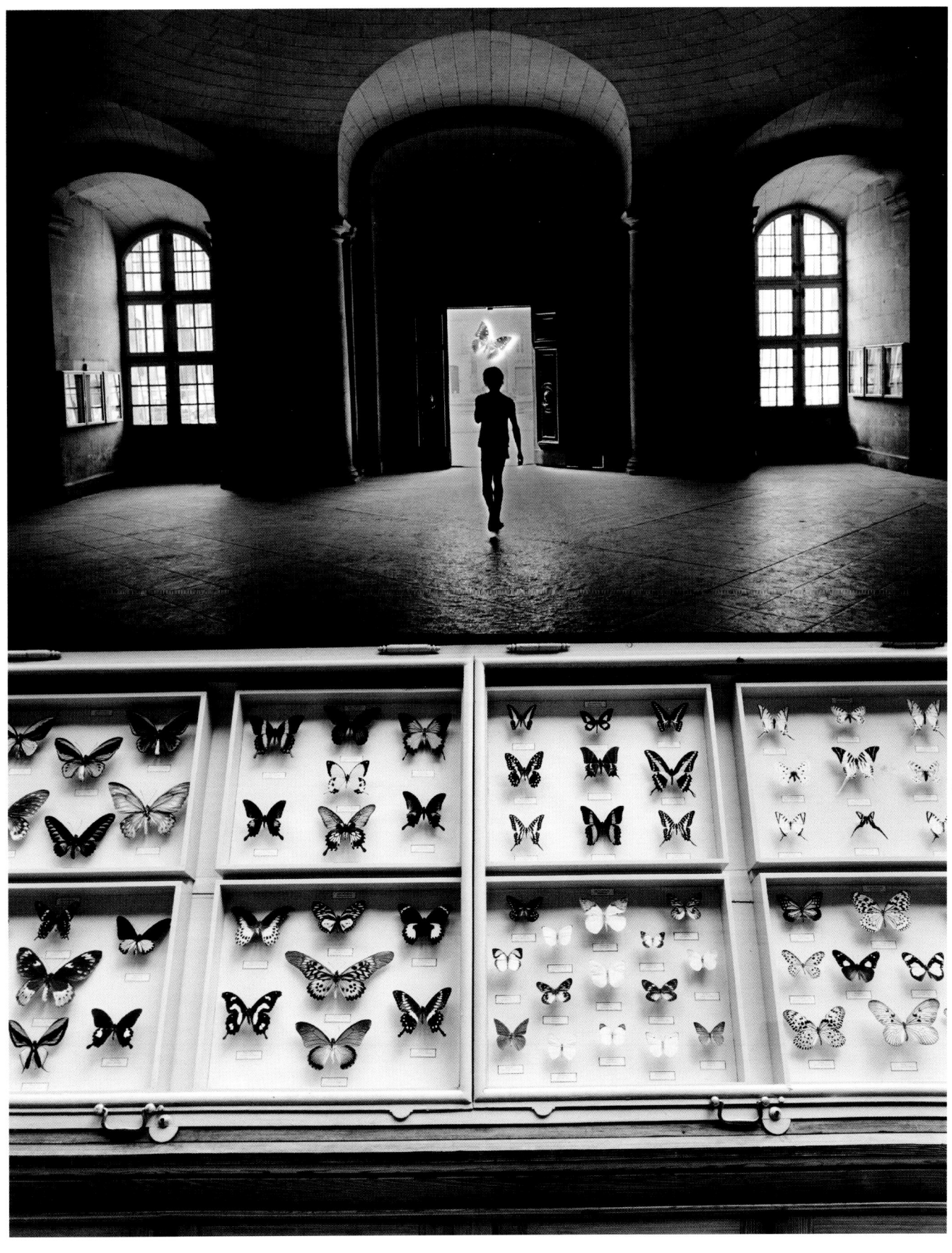

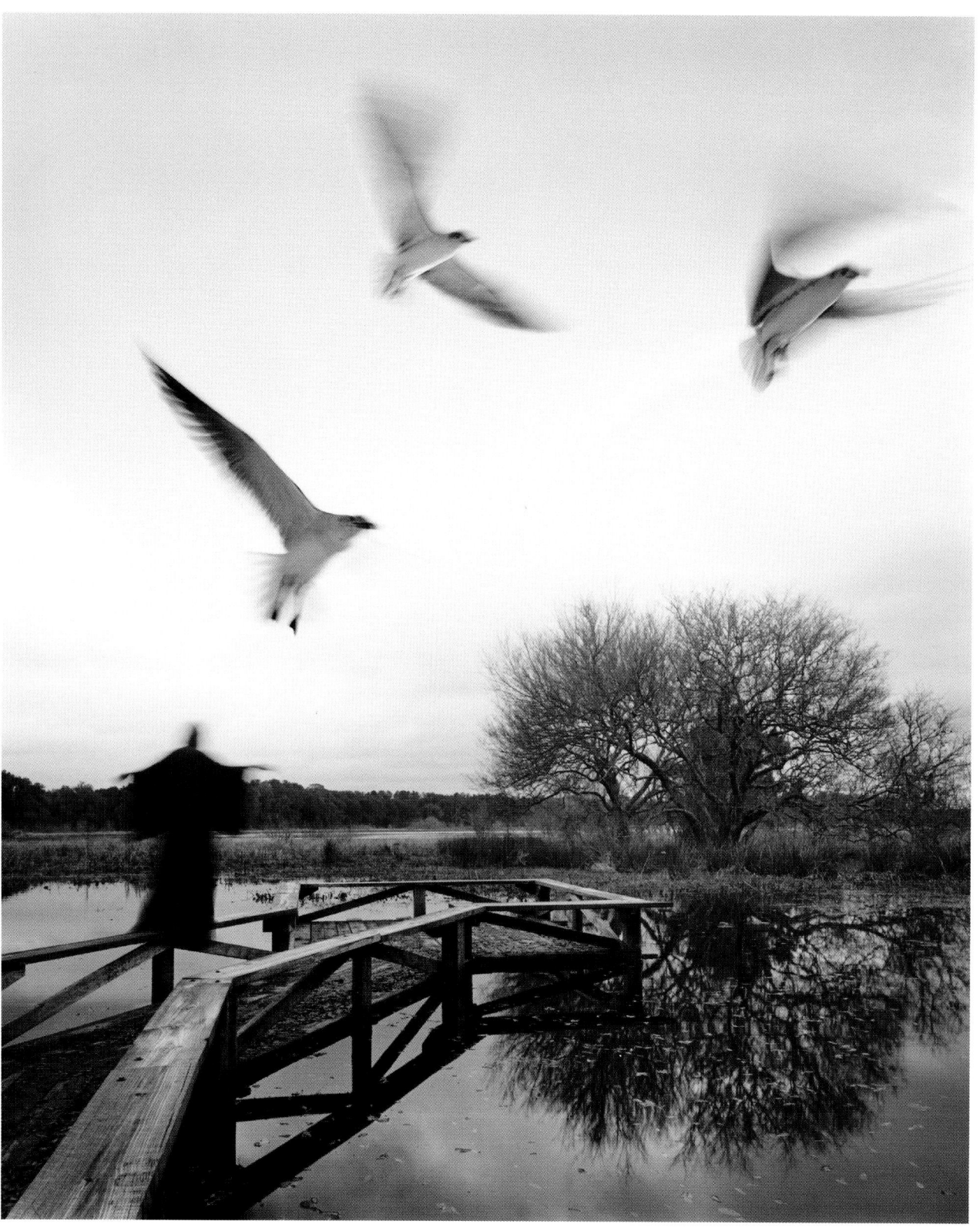

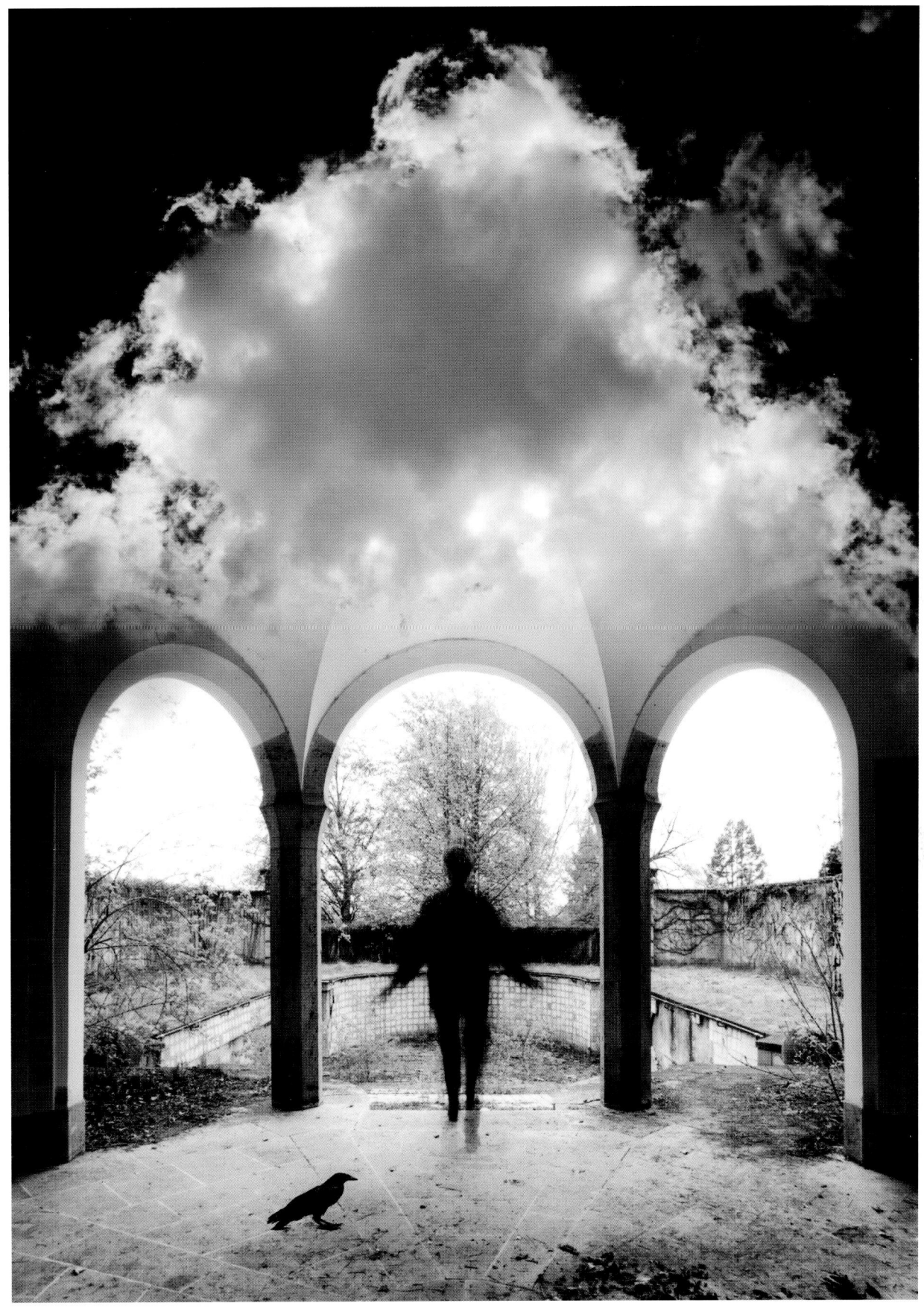

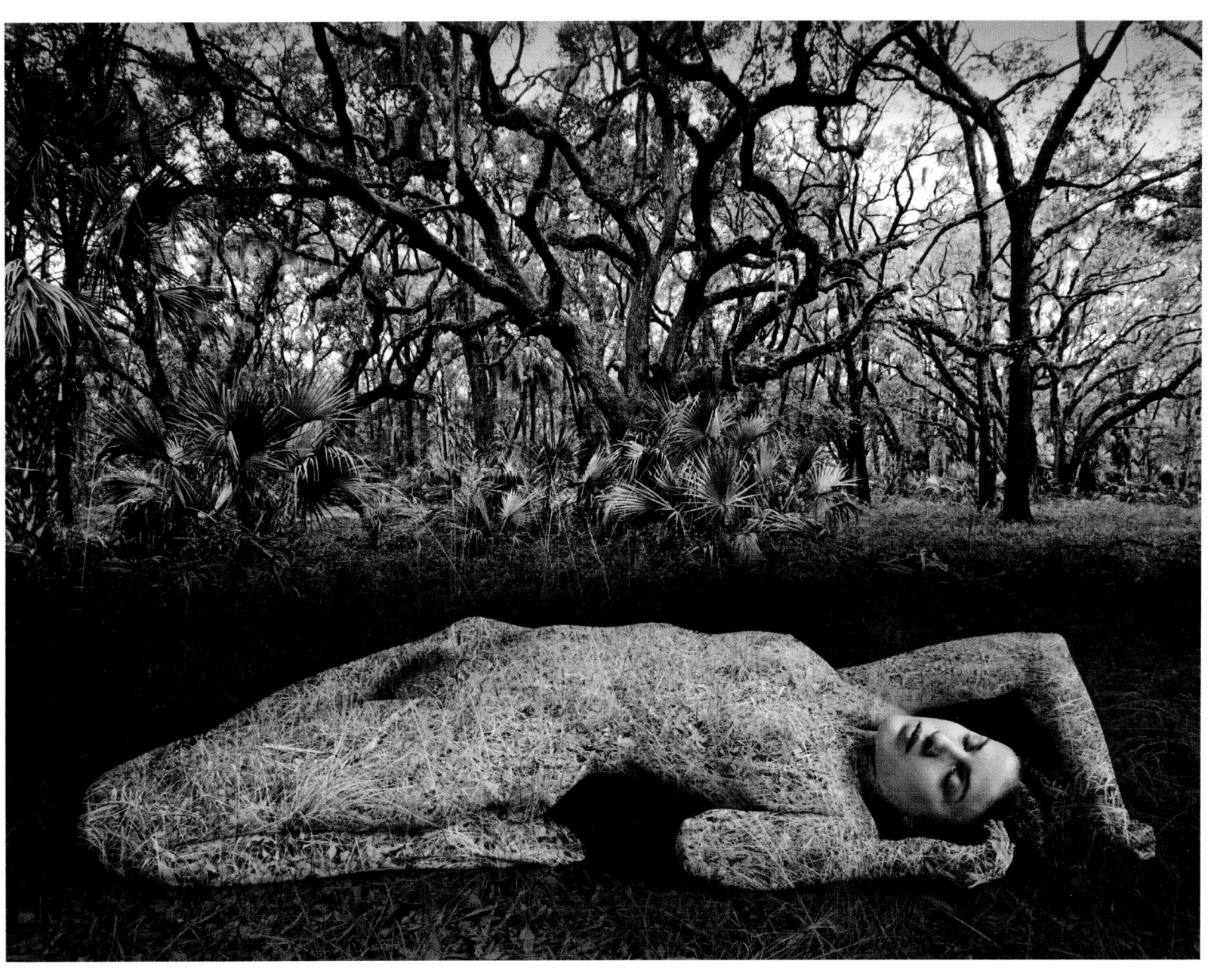

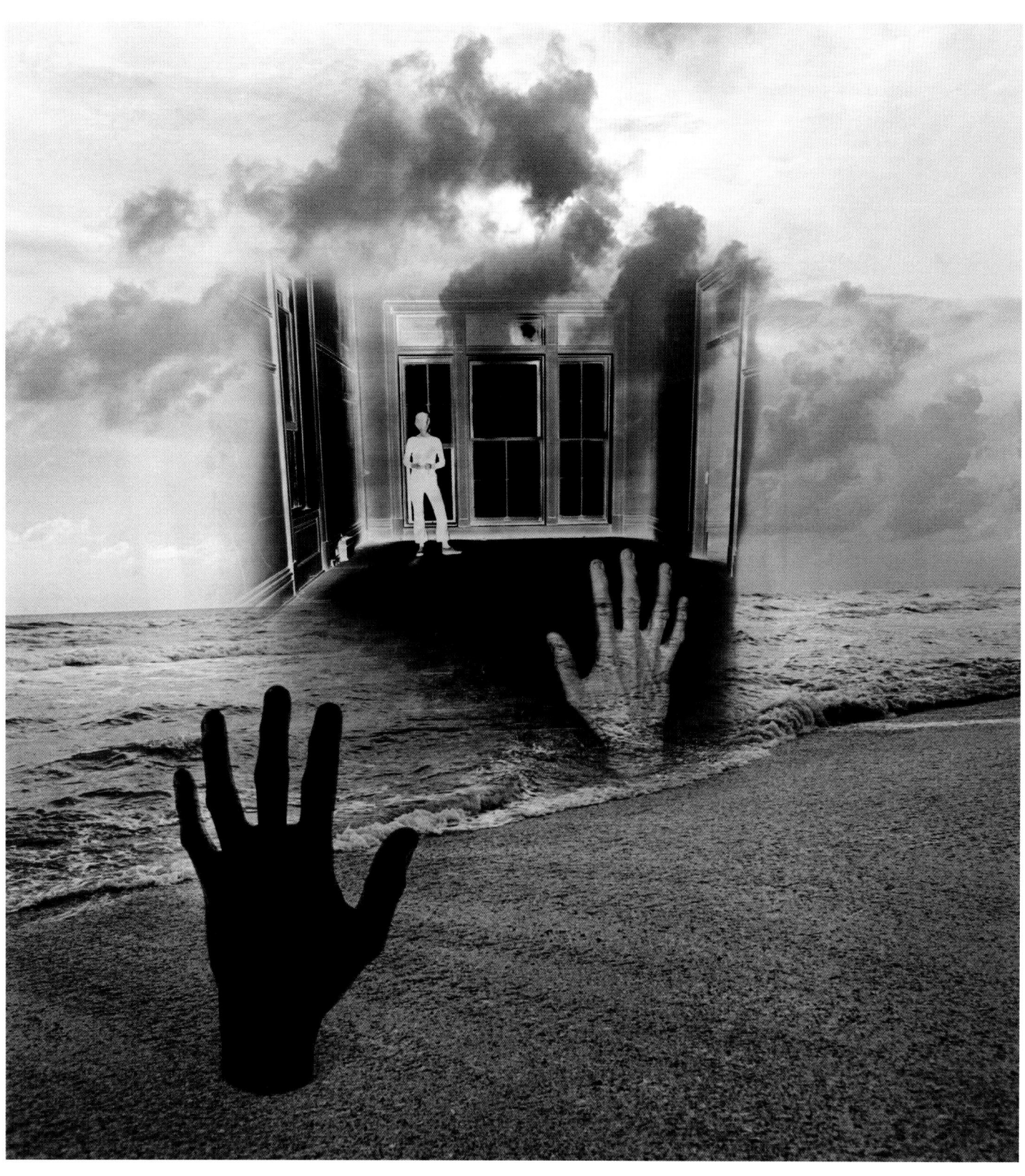

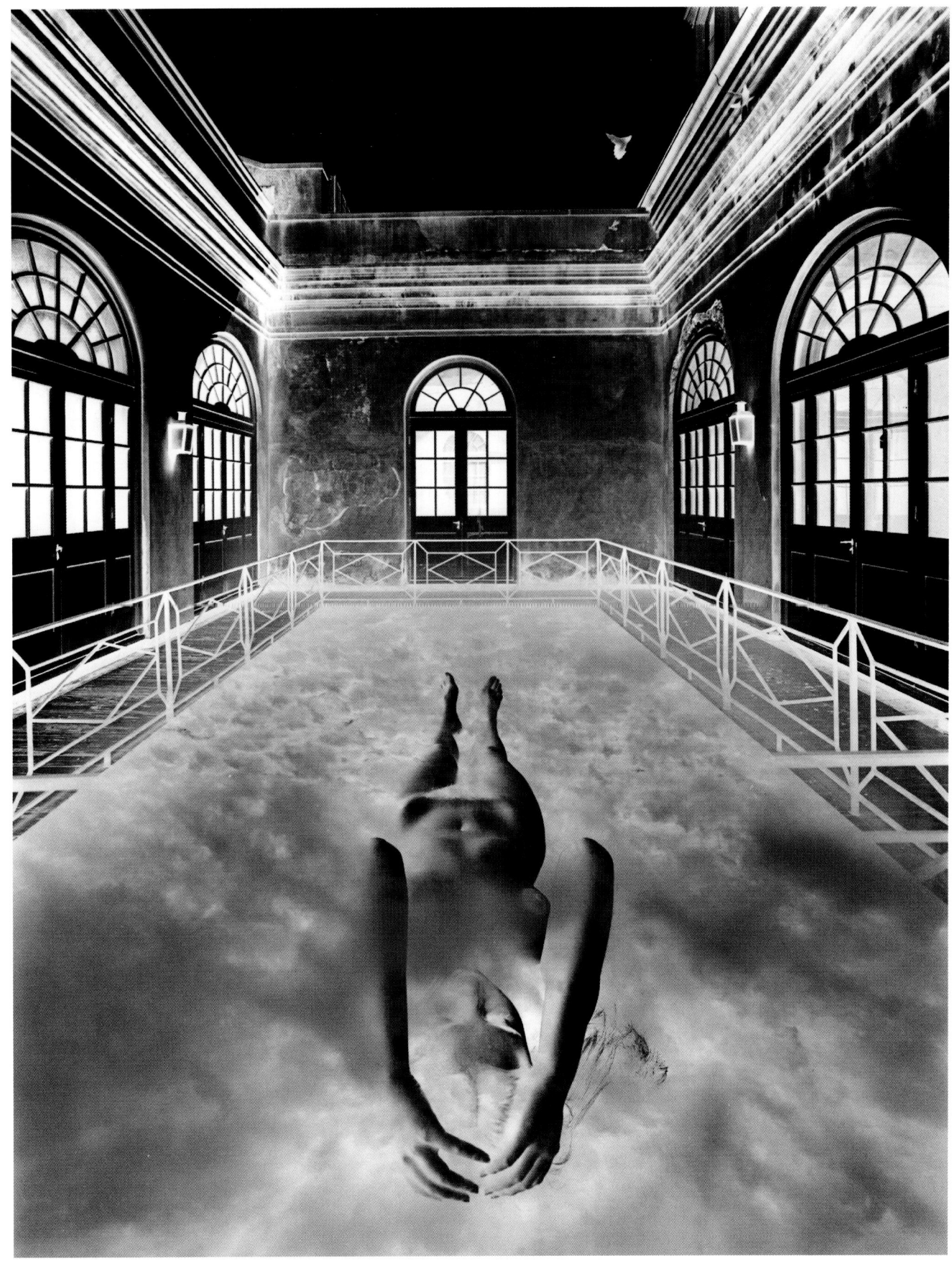

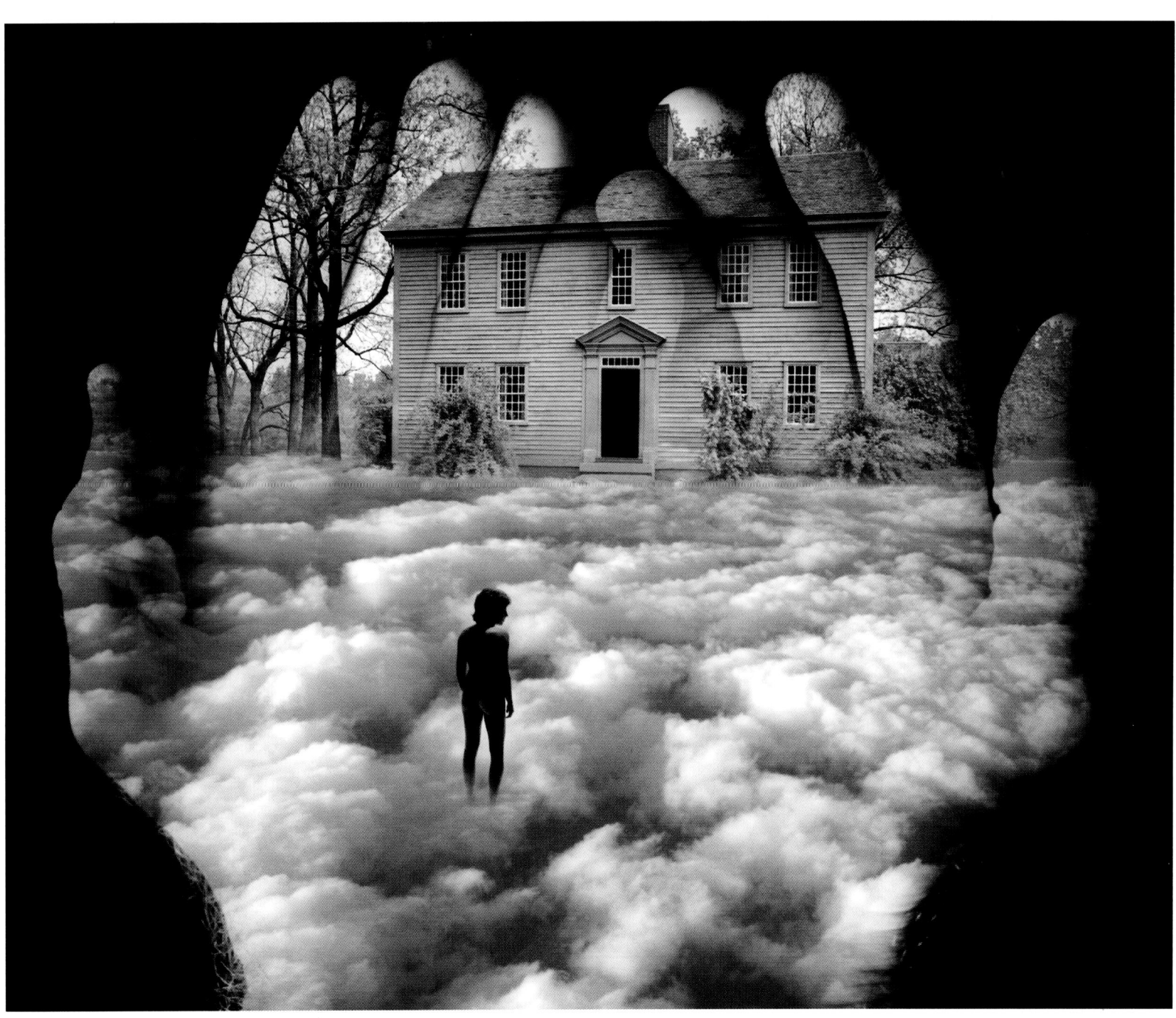

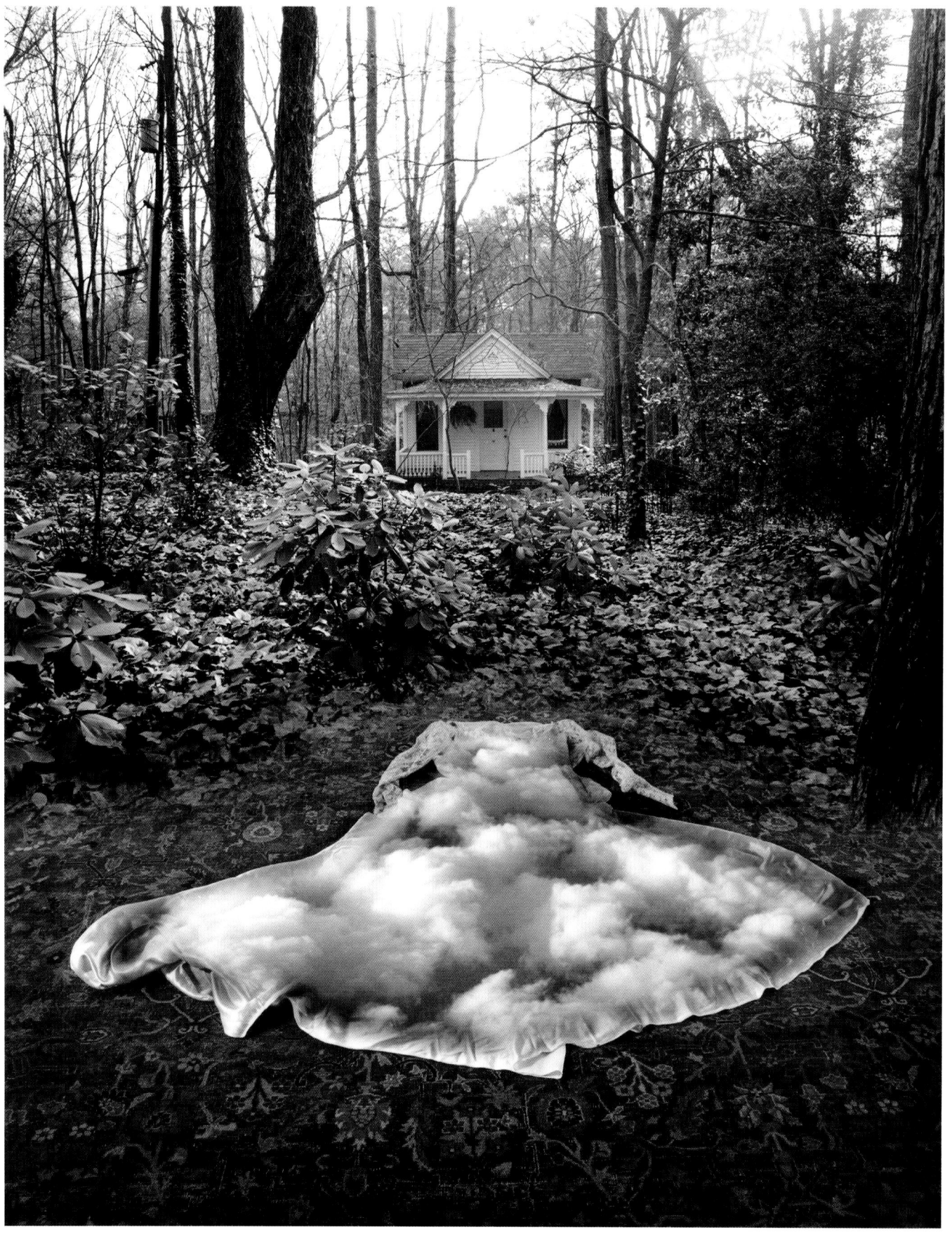

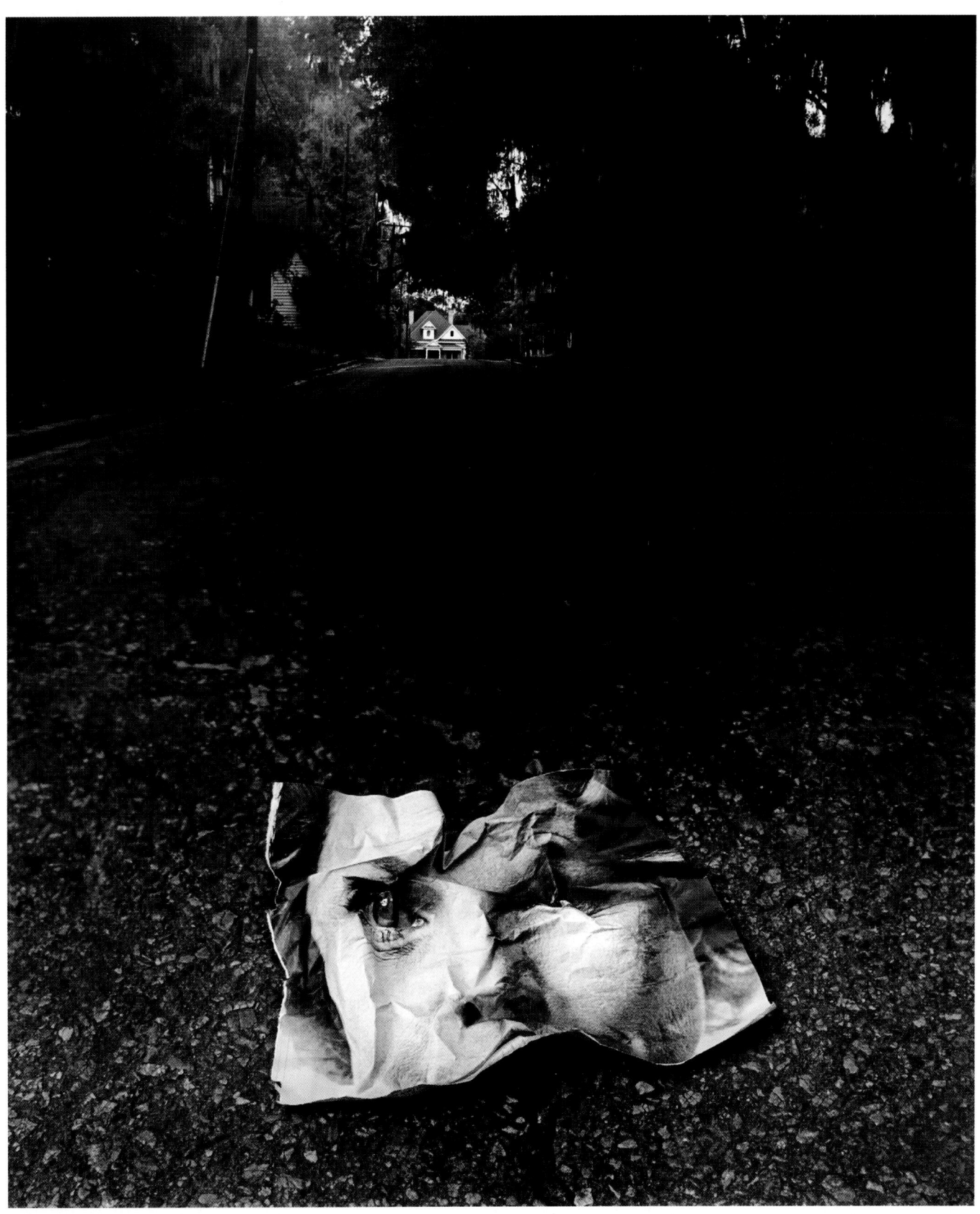

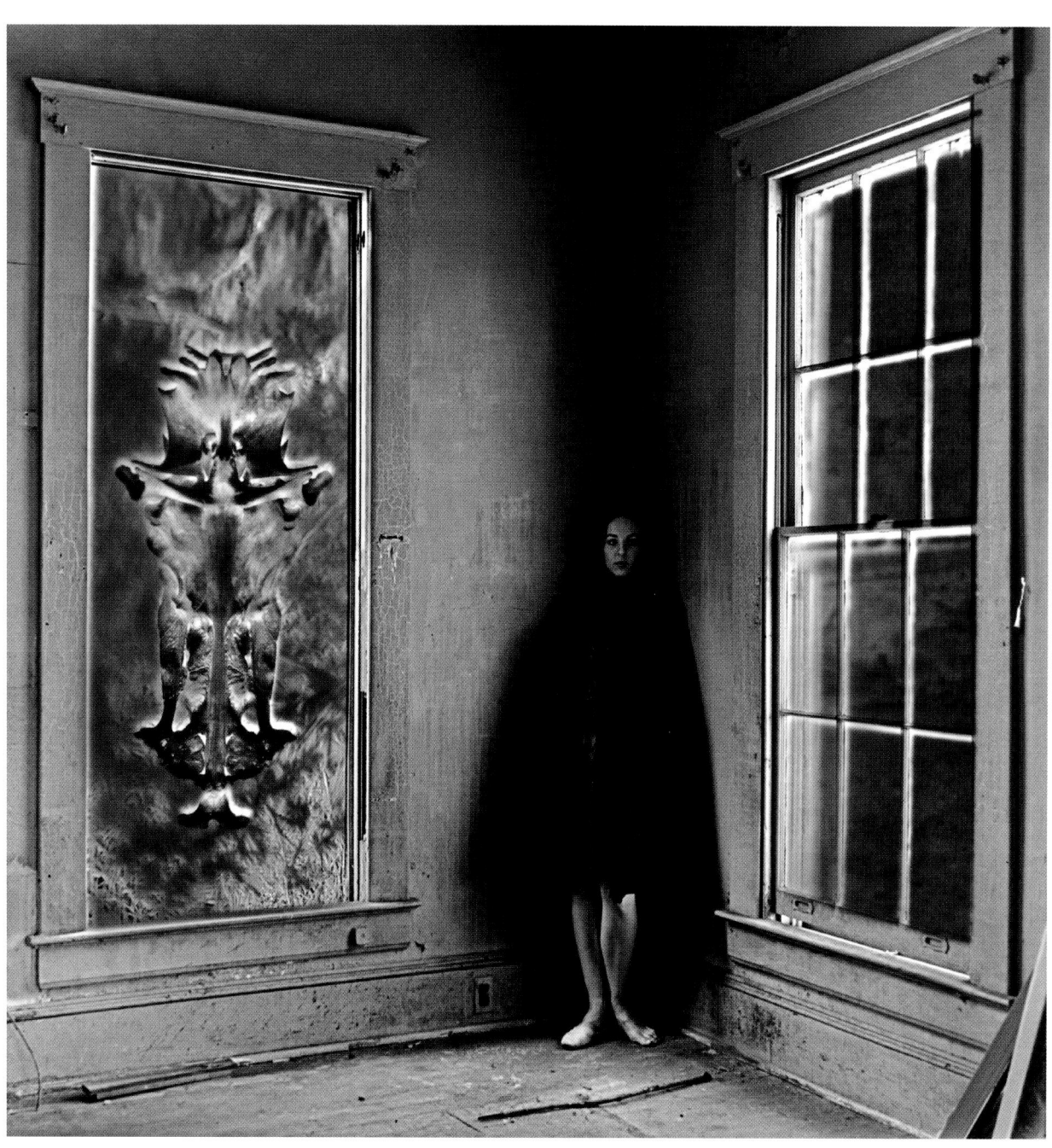

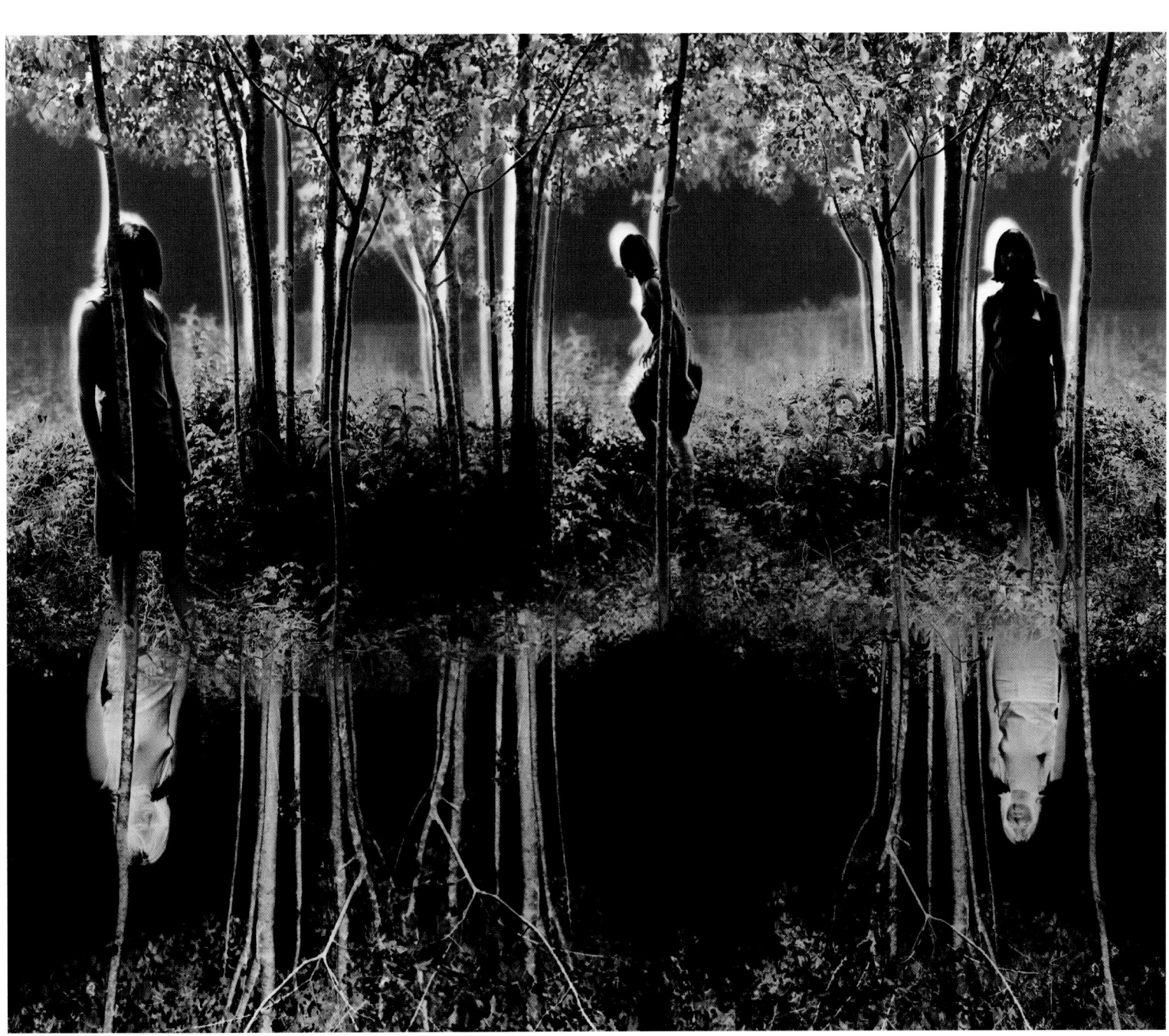

33 | Small Woods Where I Met Myself (final version) 1967

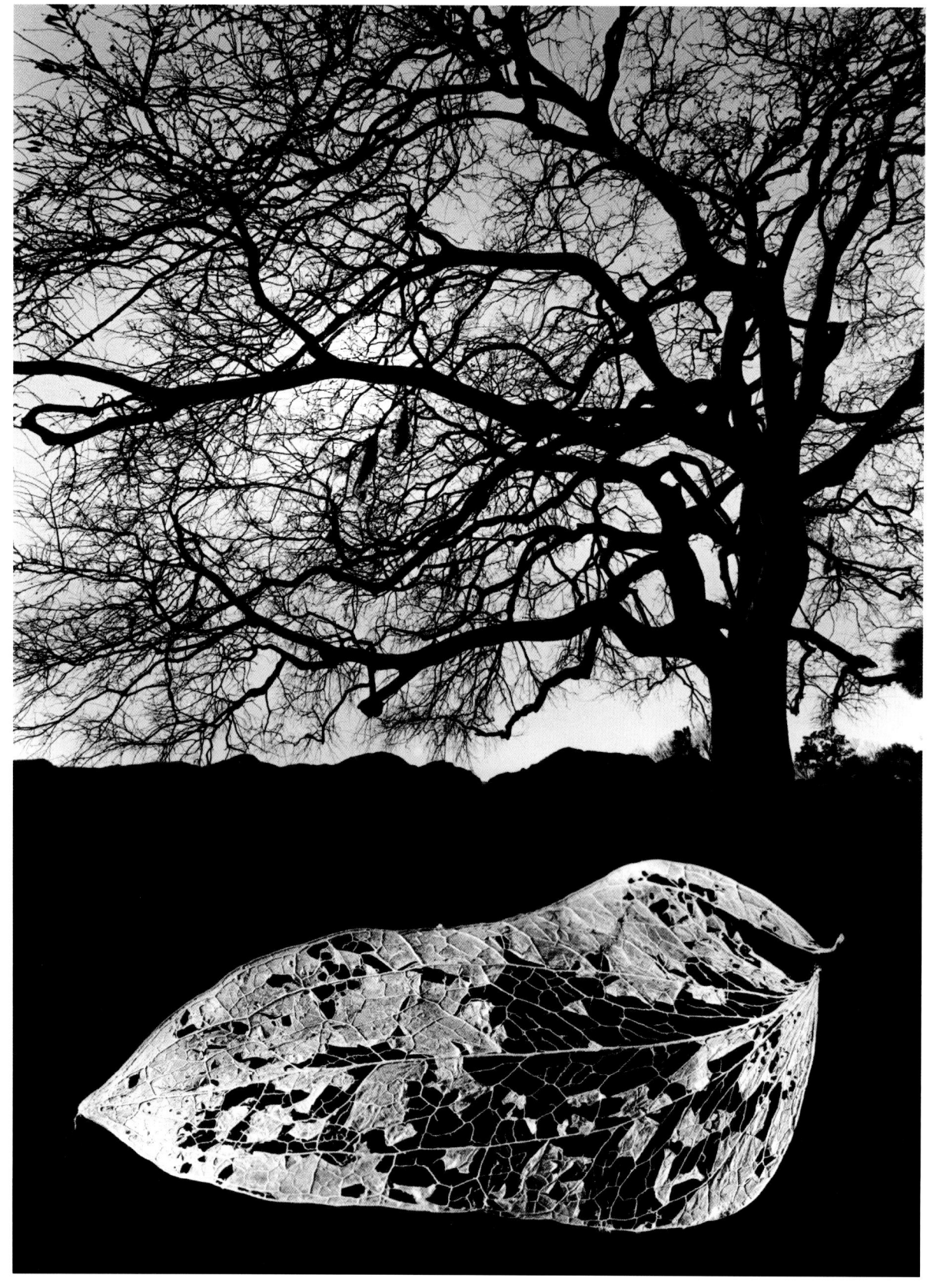

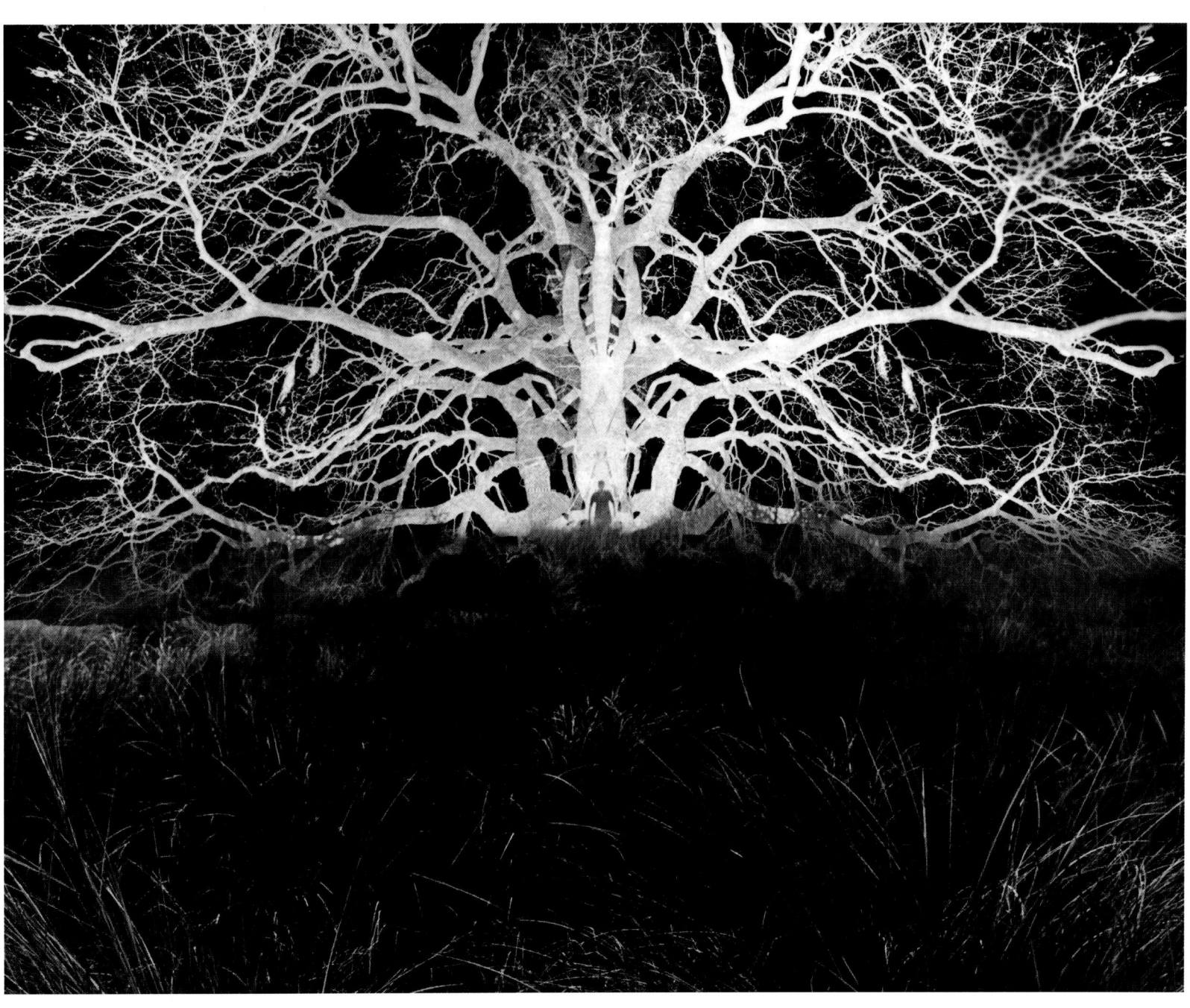

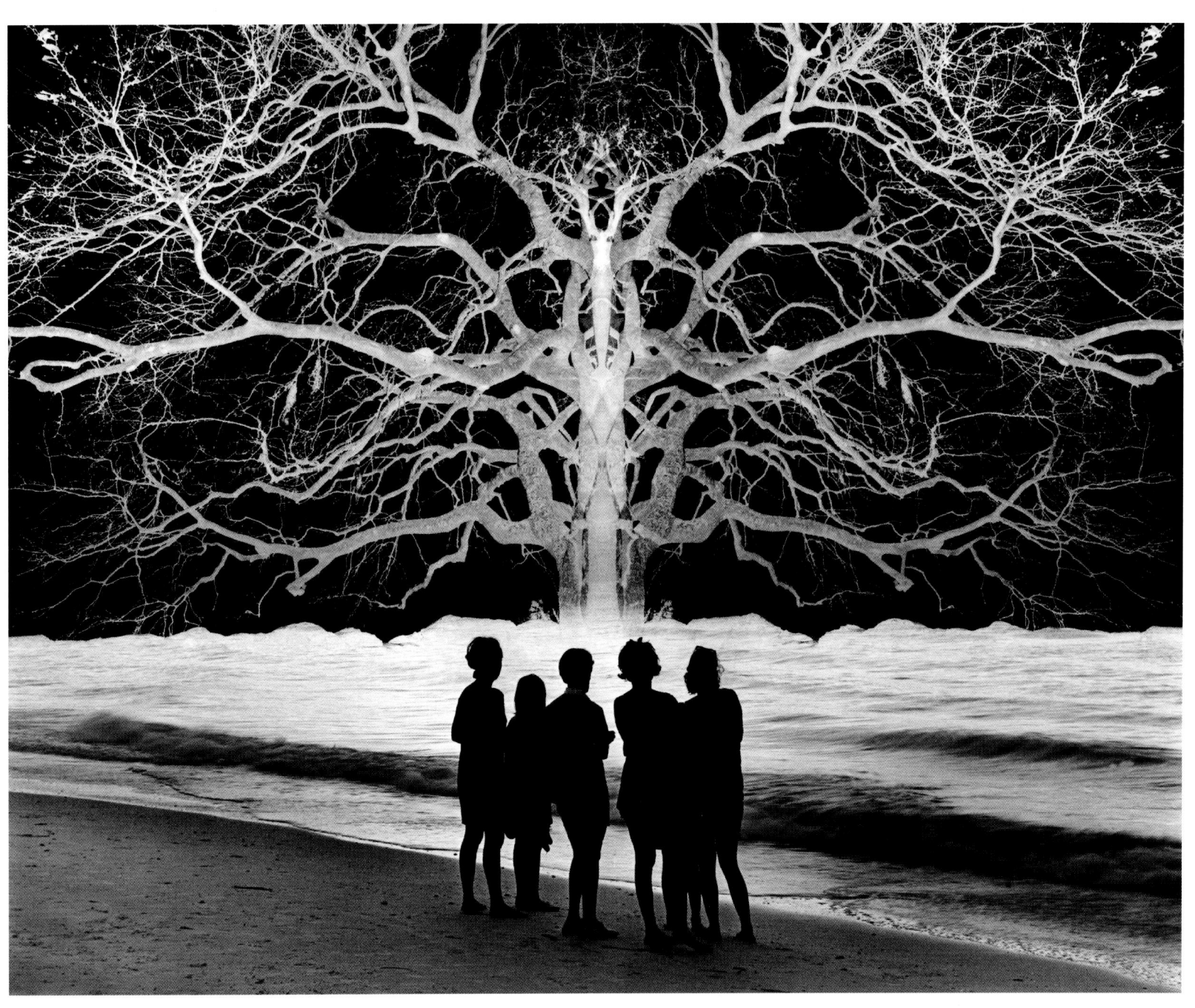

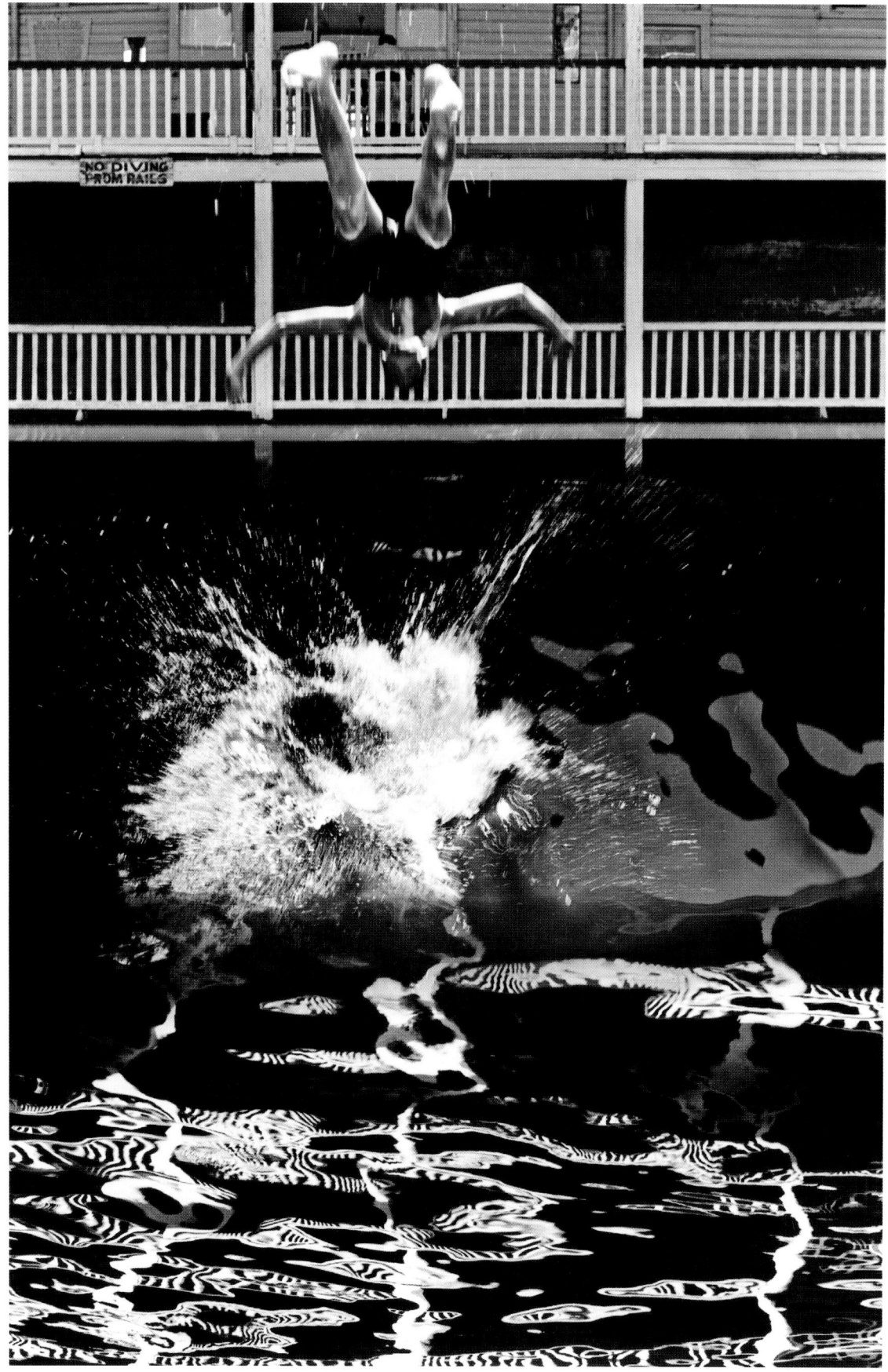

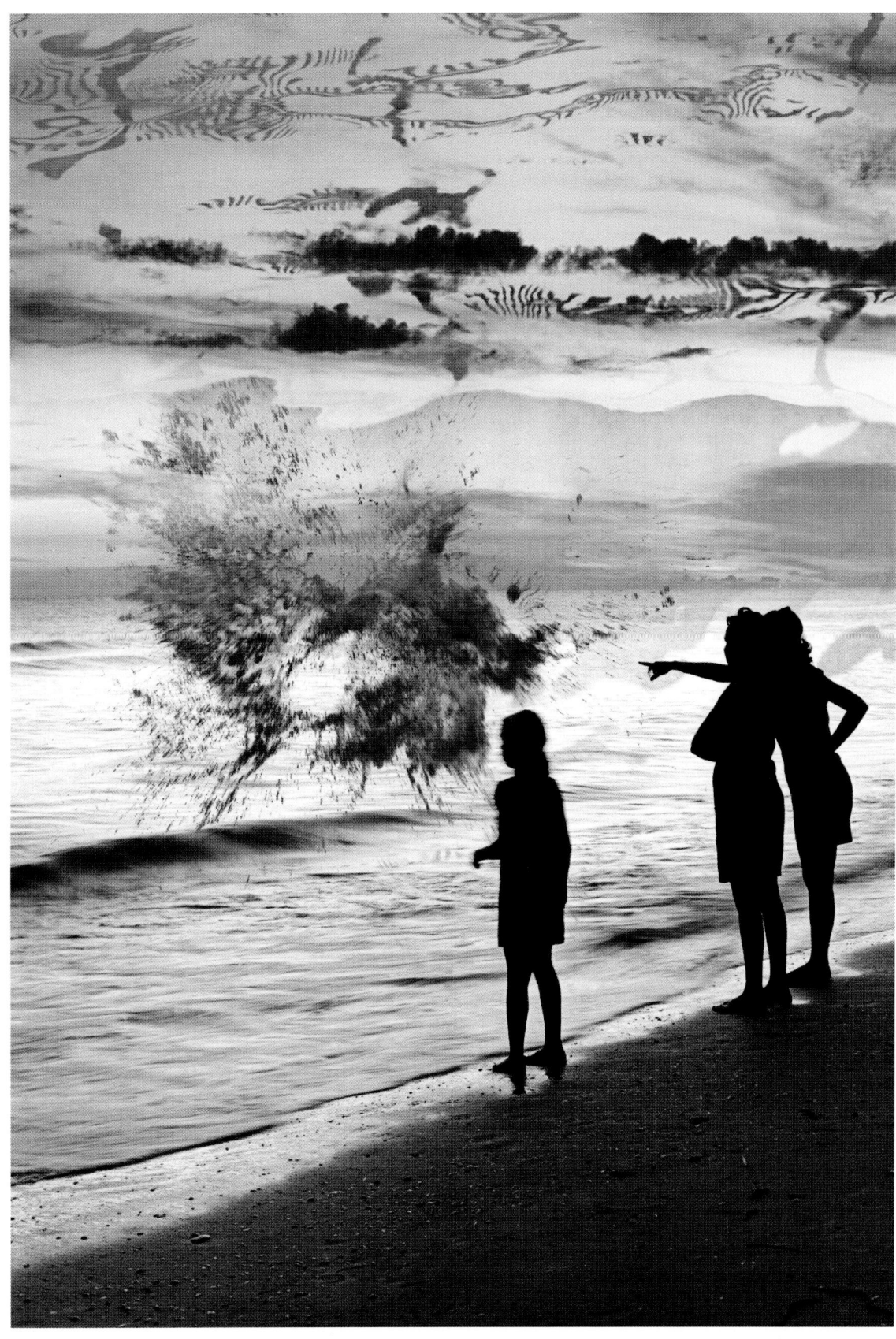

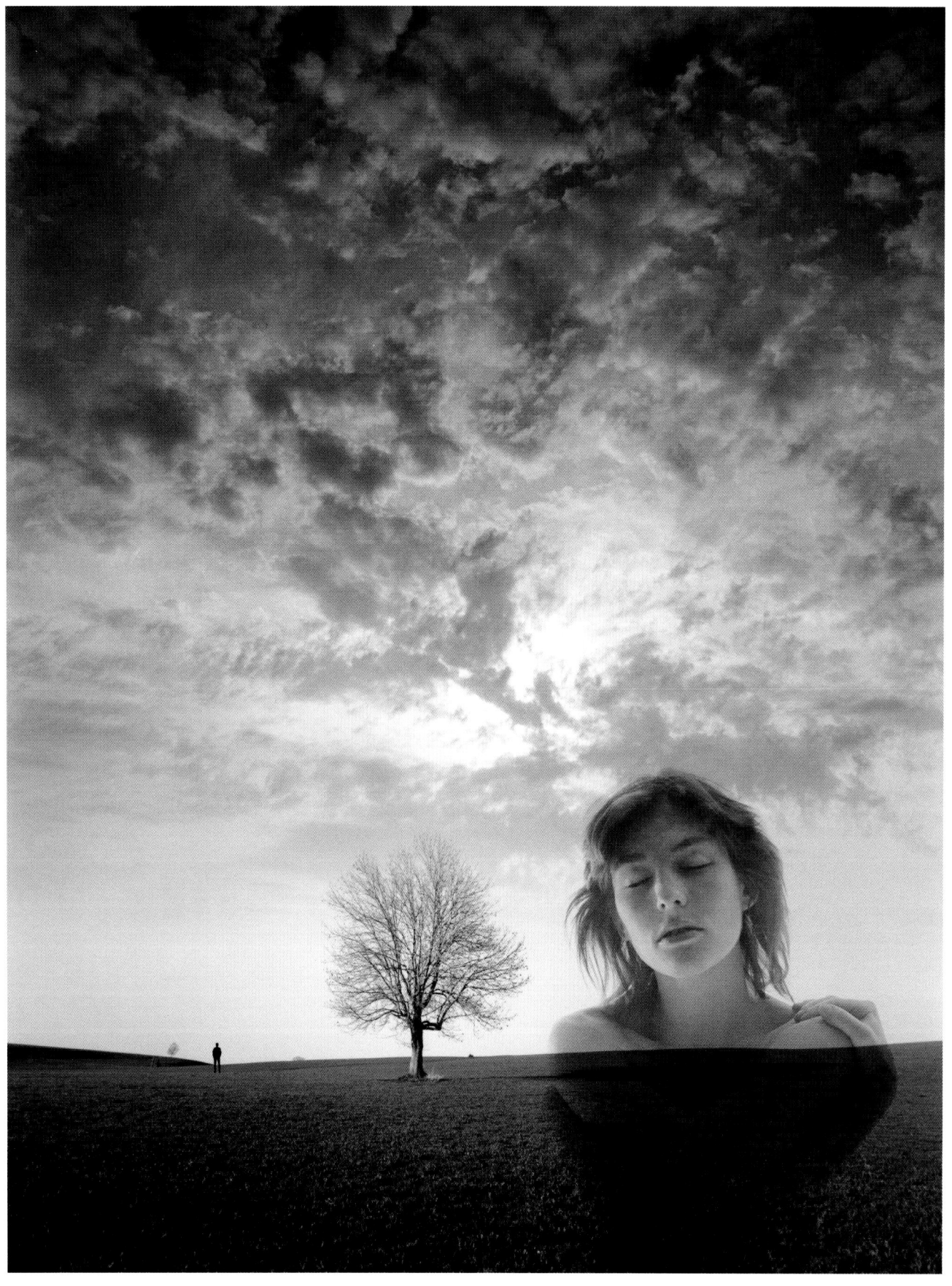

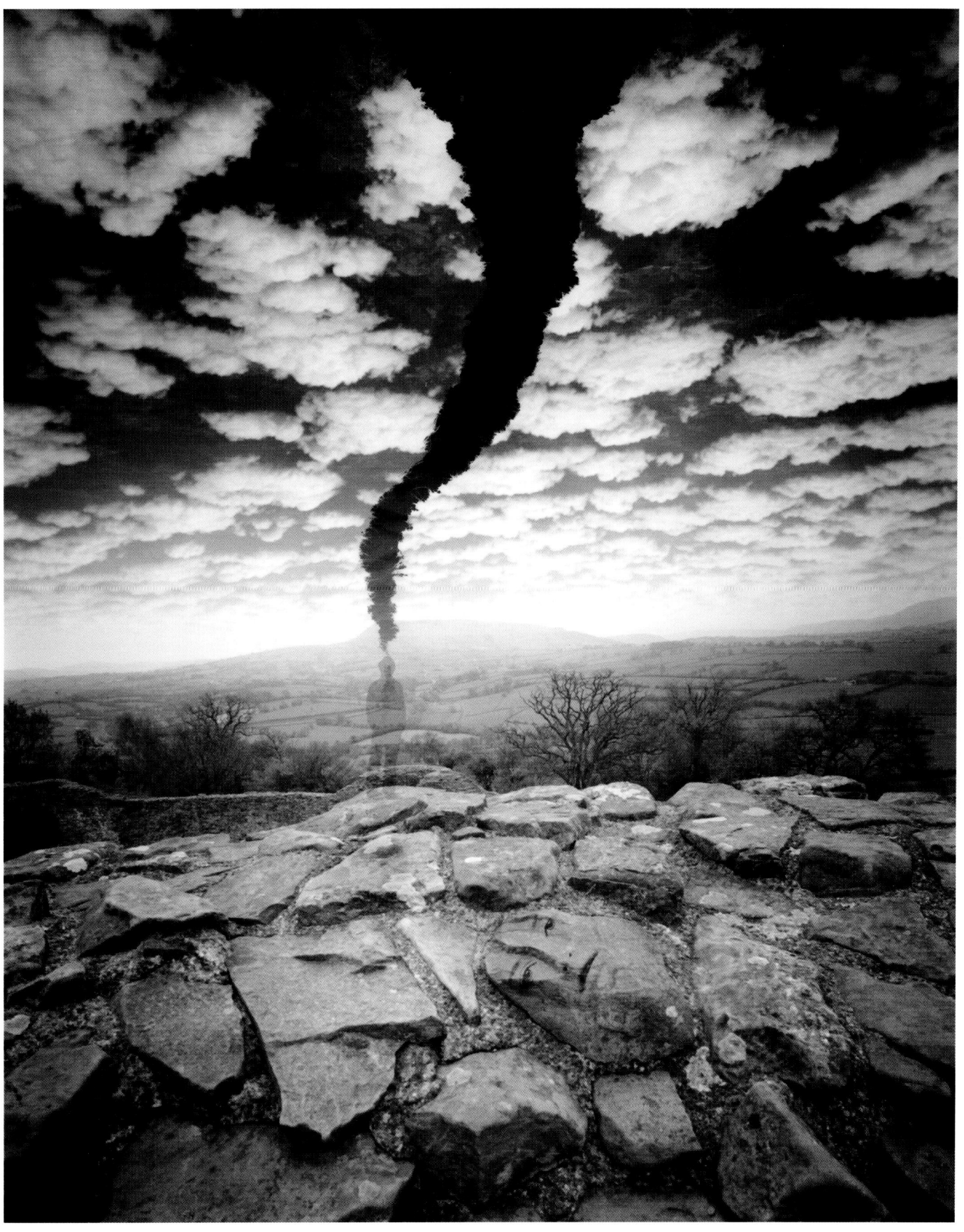

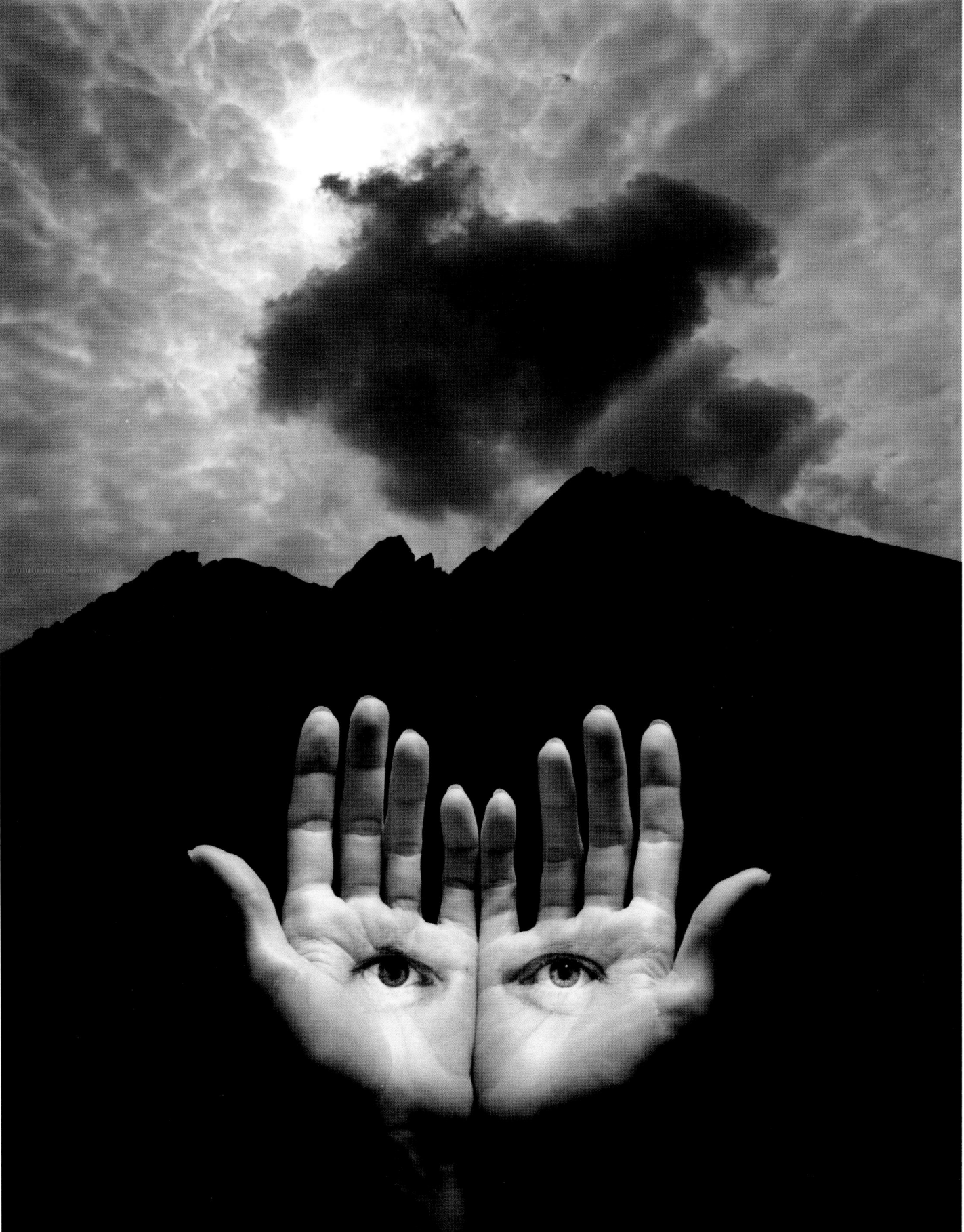

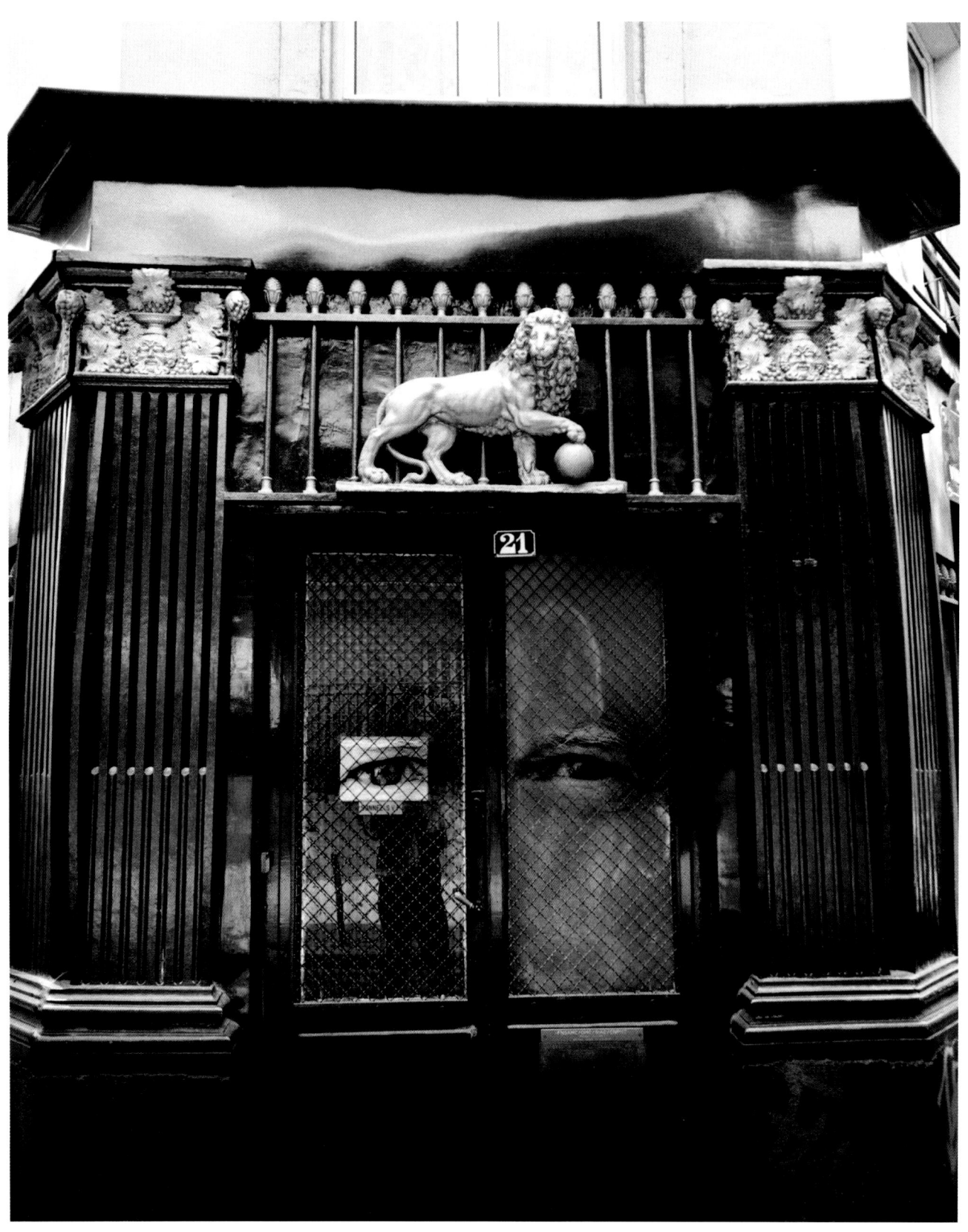

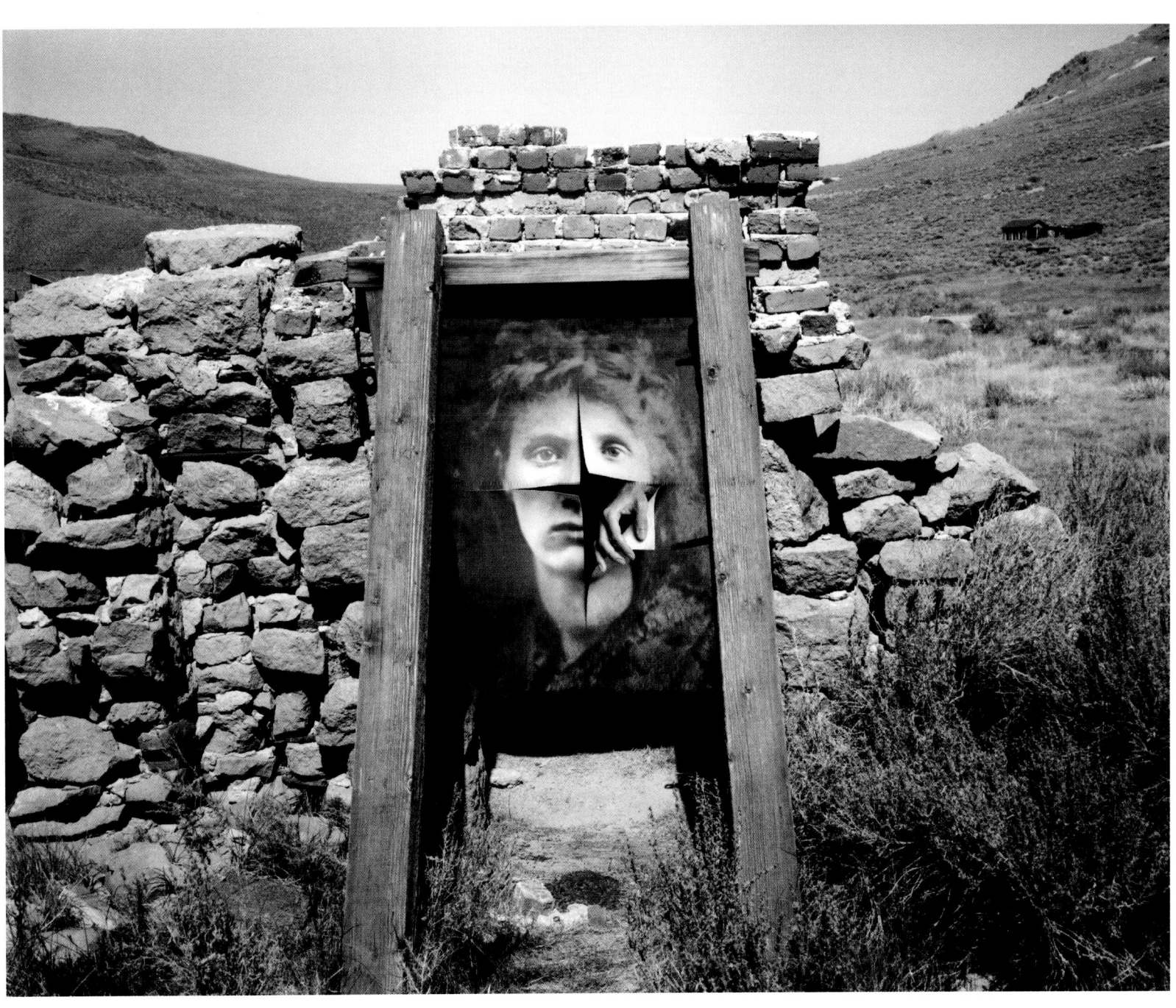

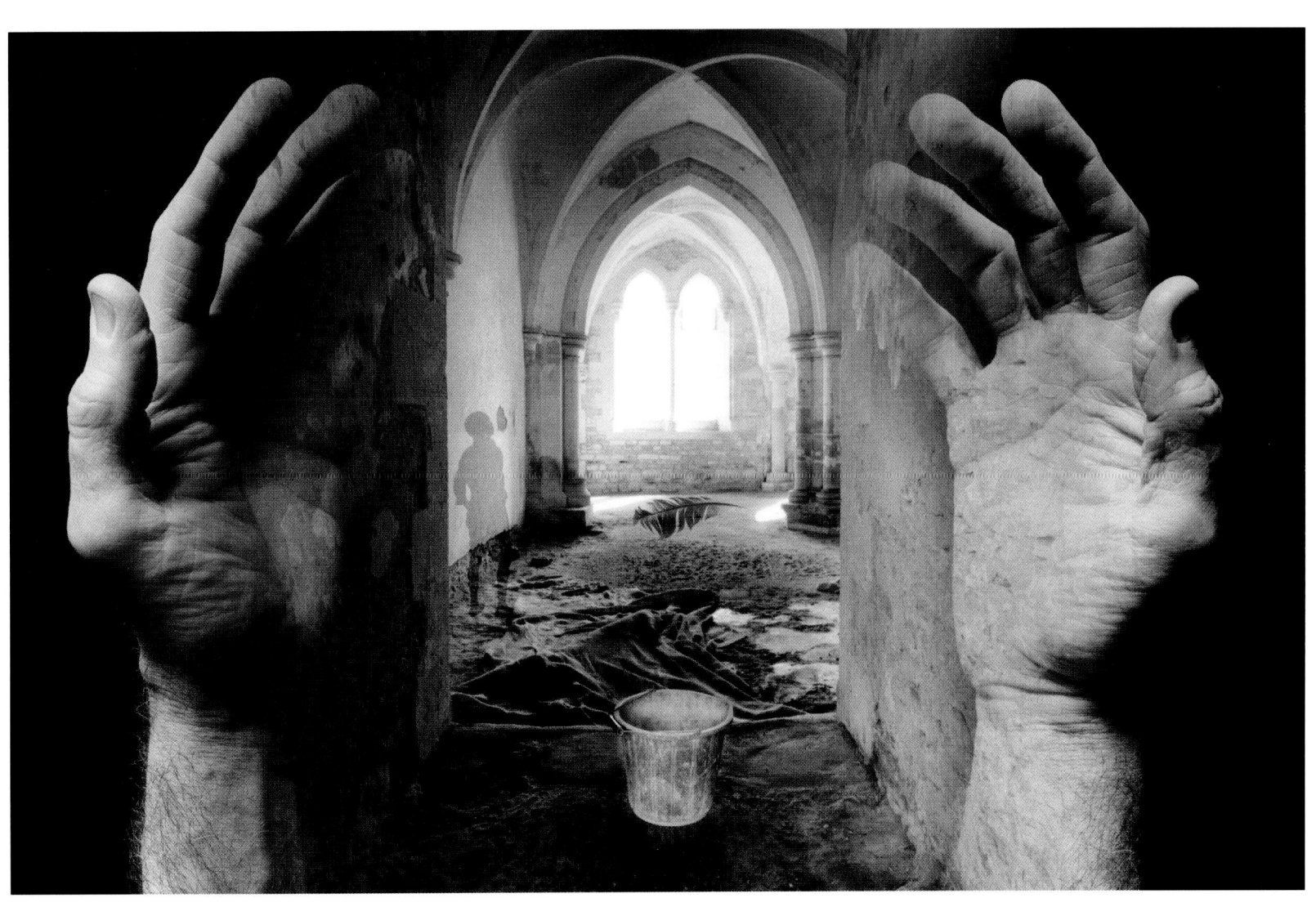

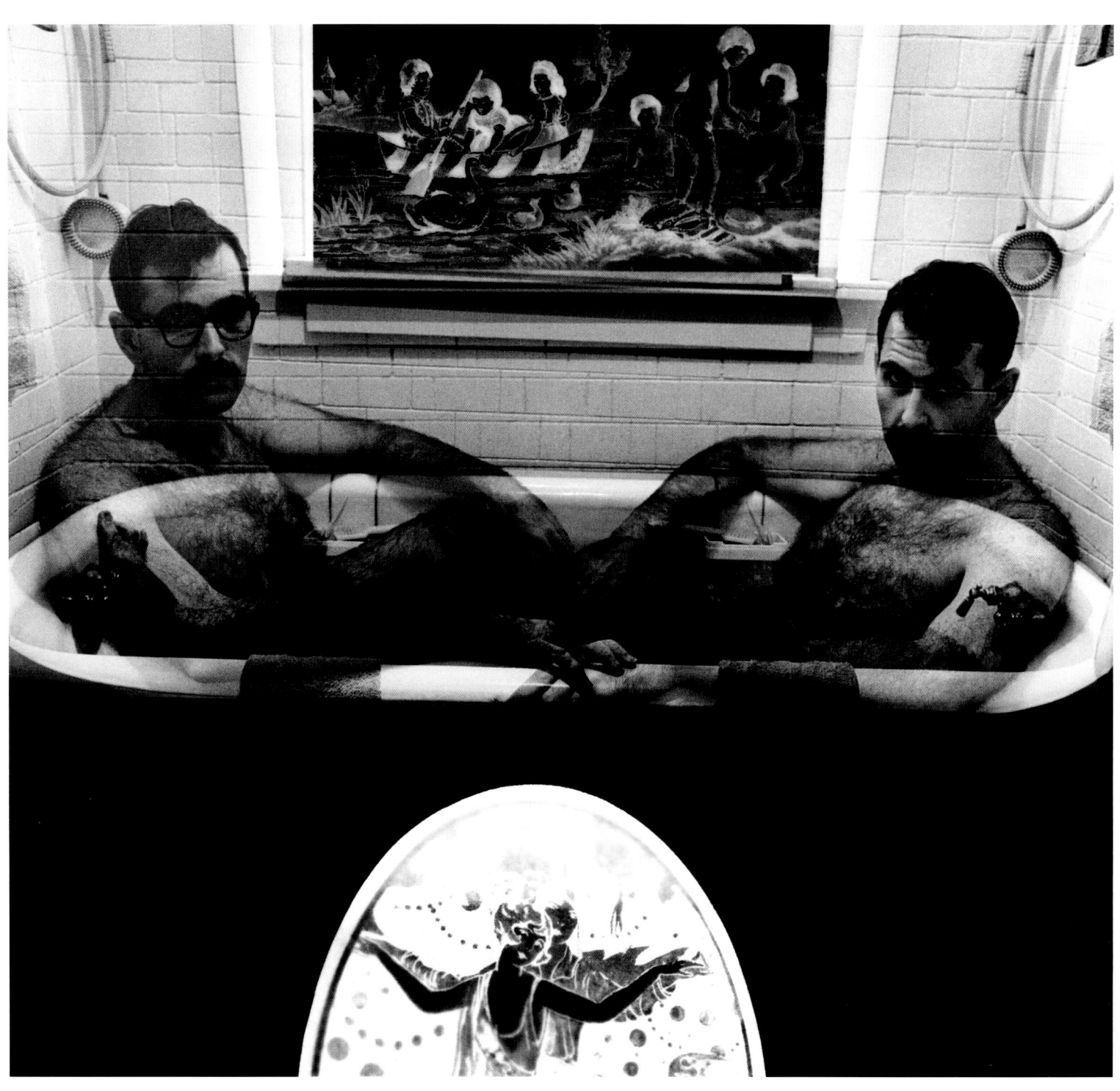

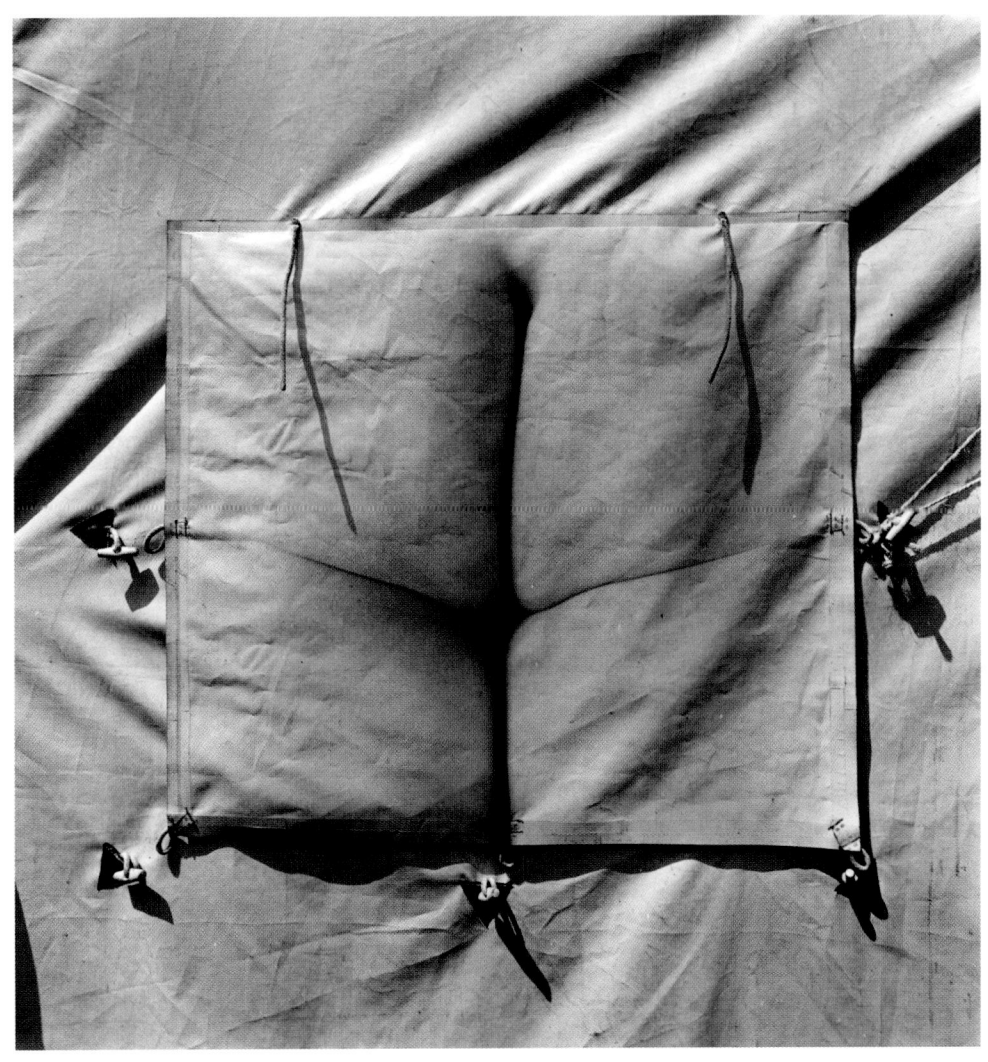

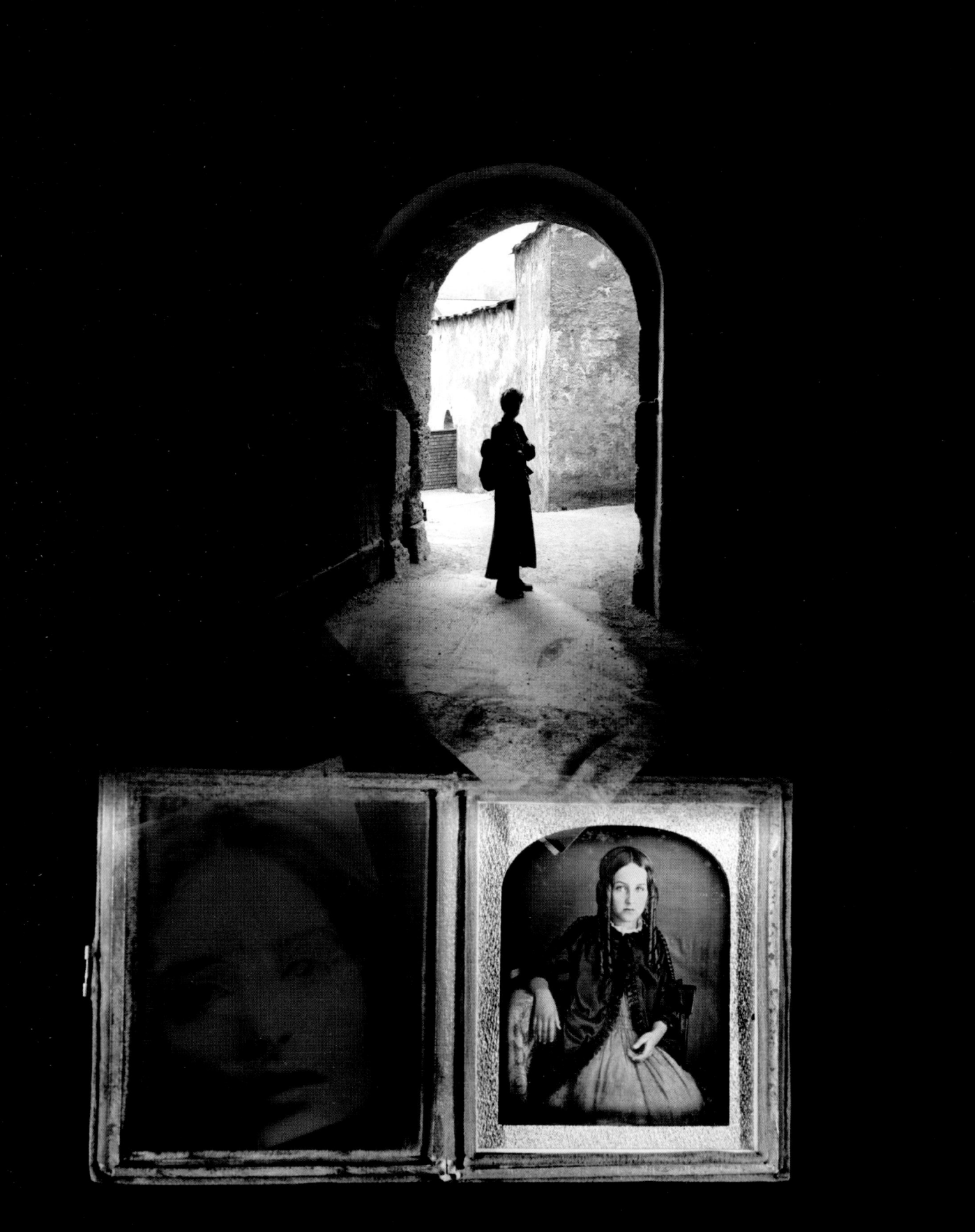

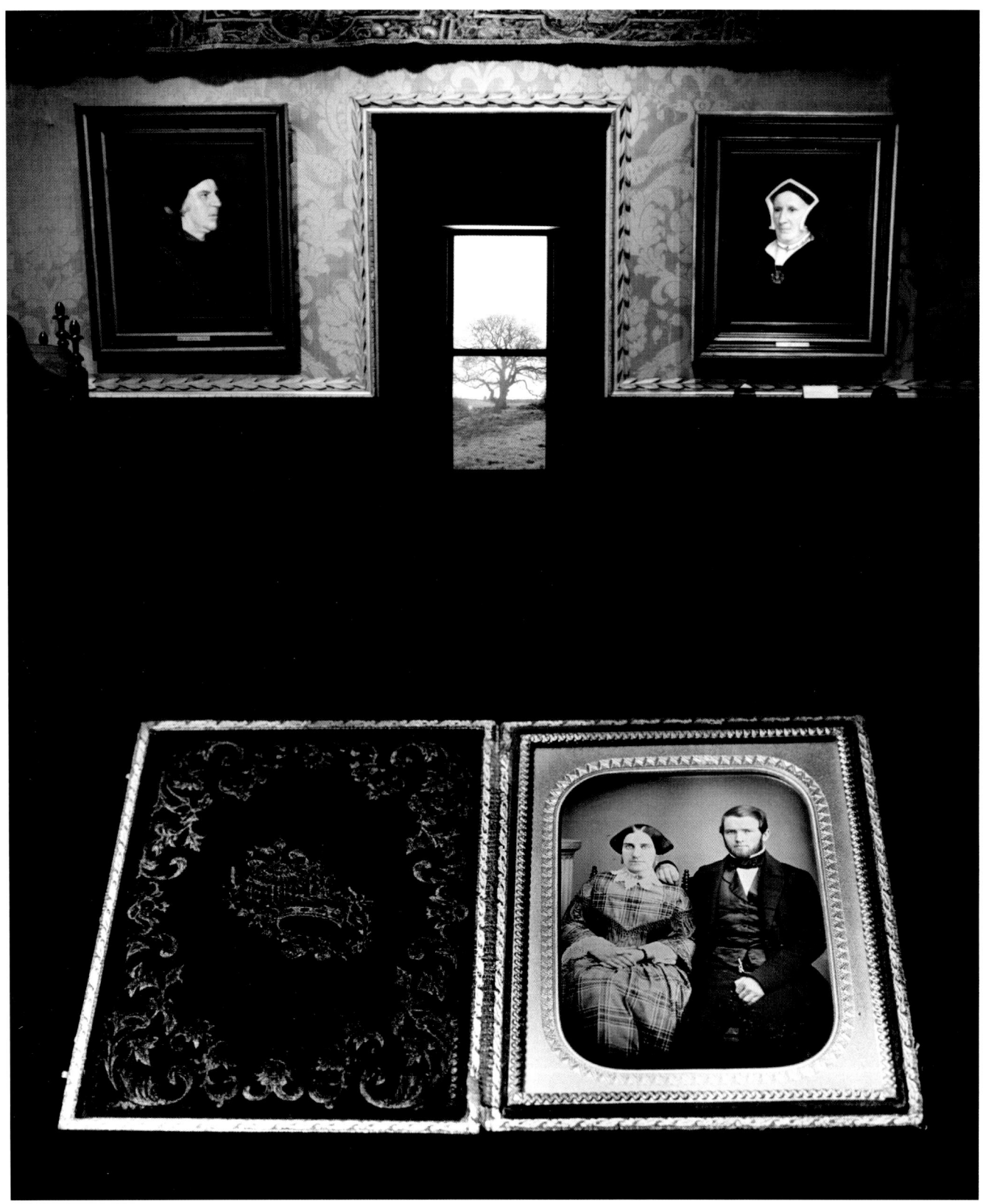

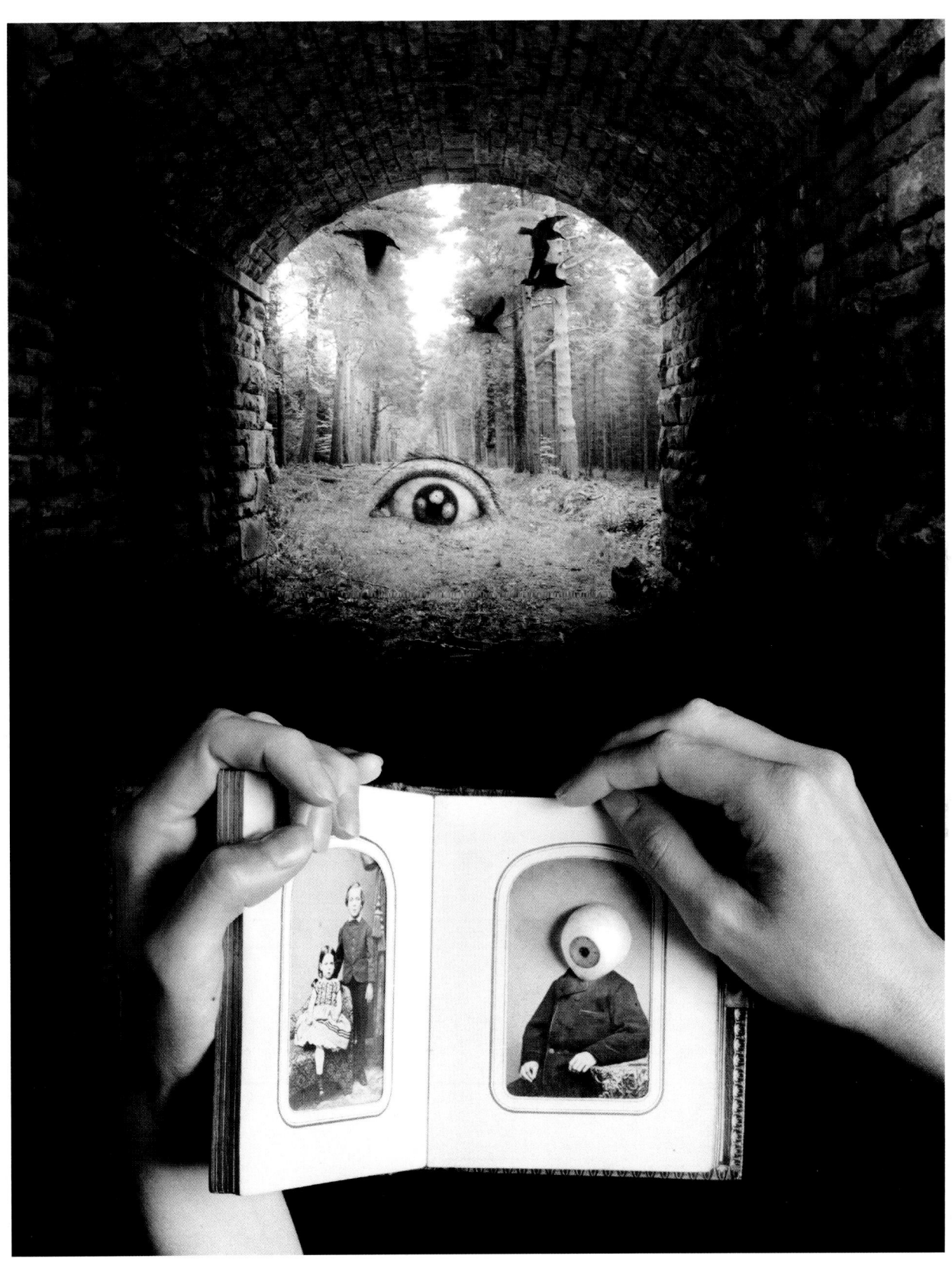

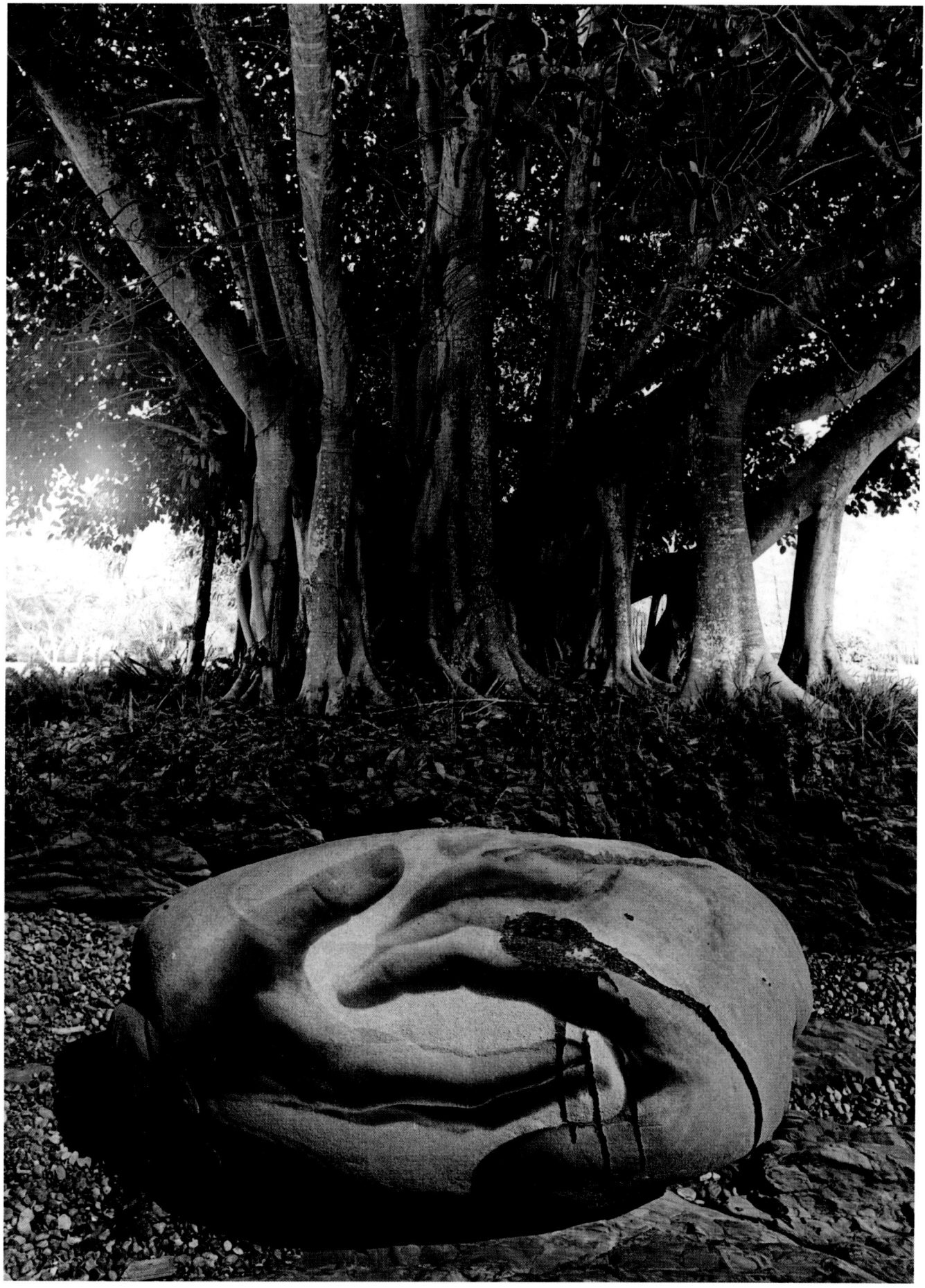

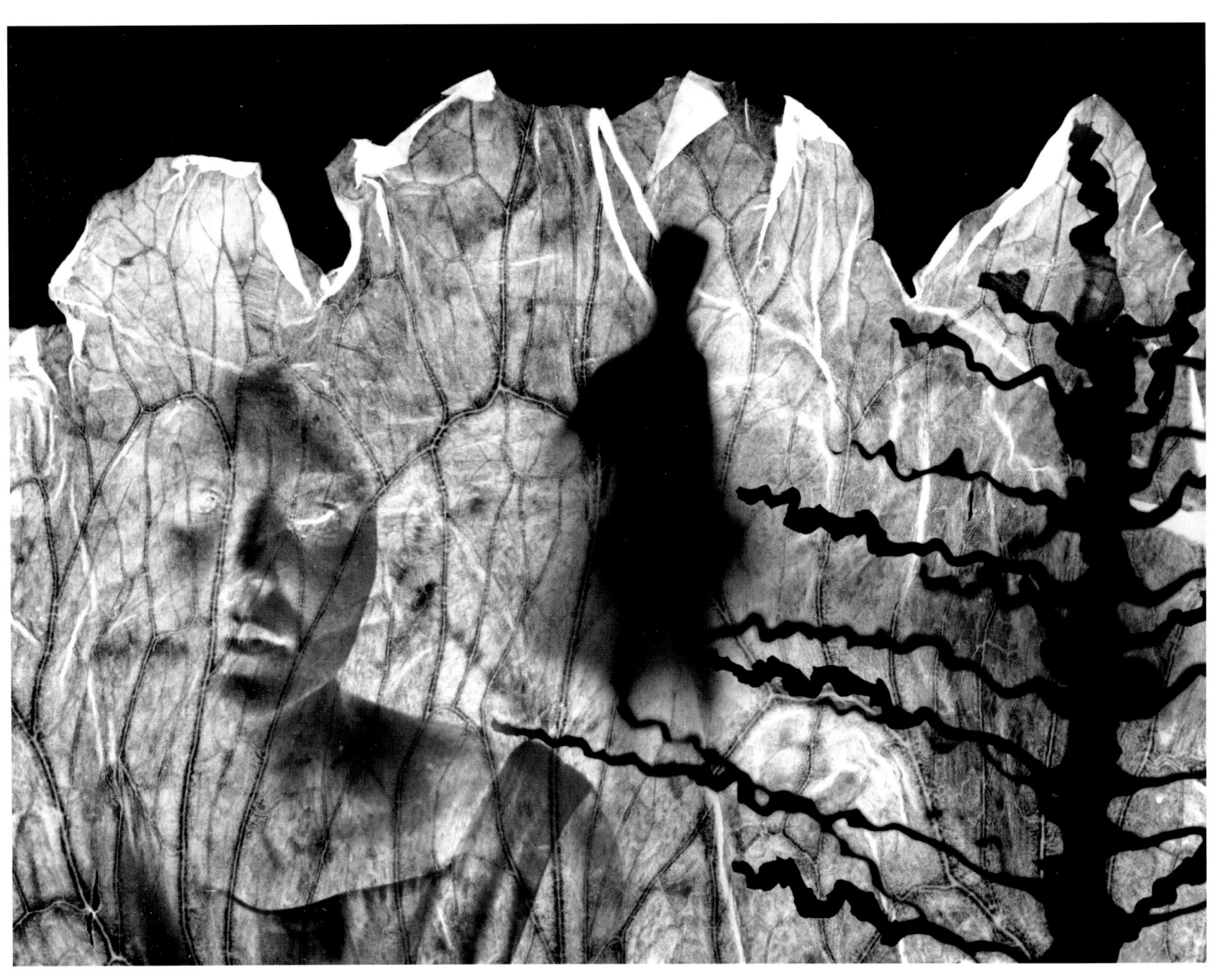

Conjecture of a Time 1964 | 56

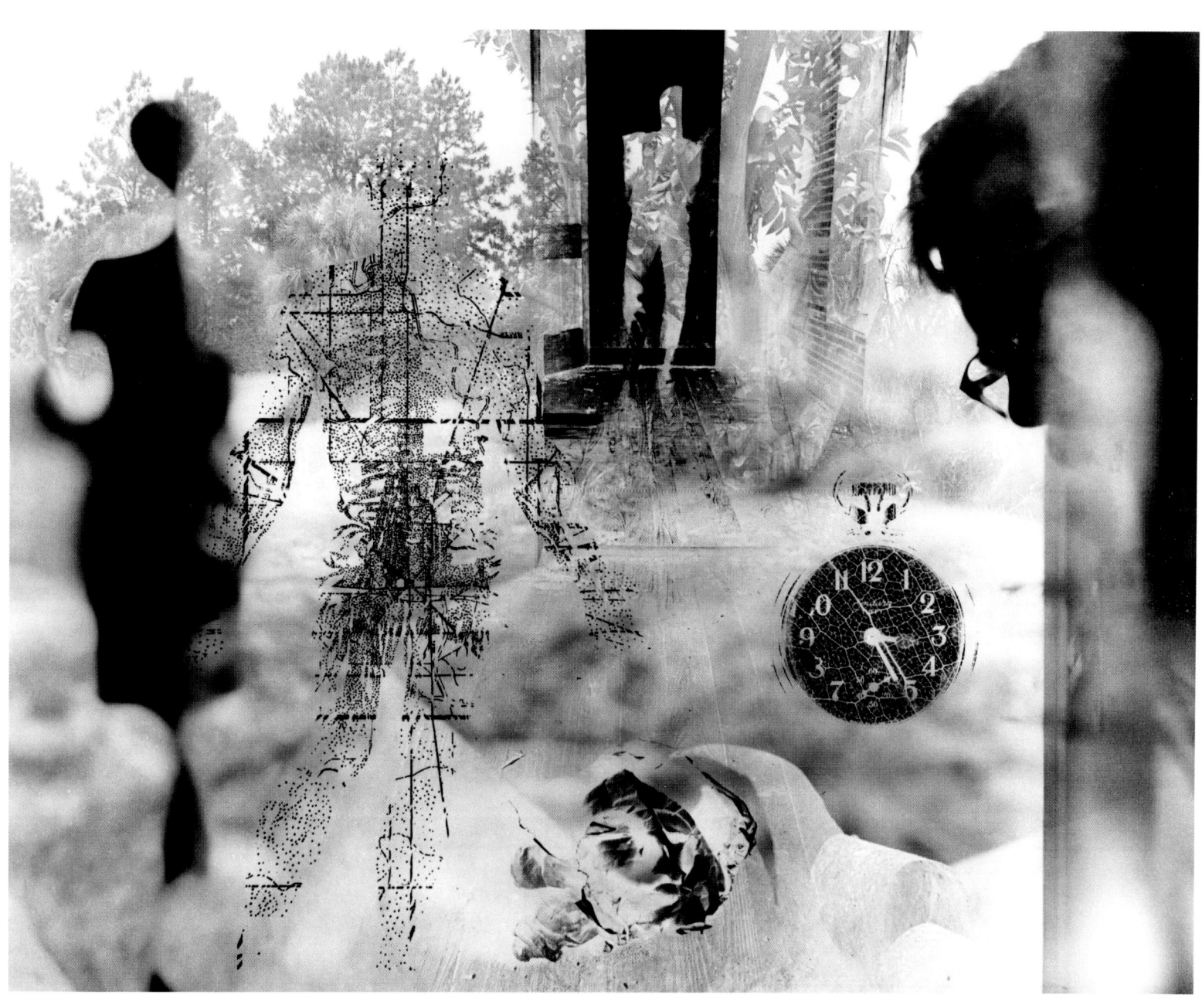

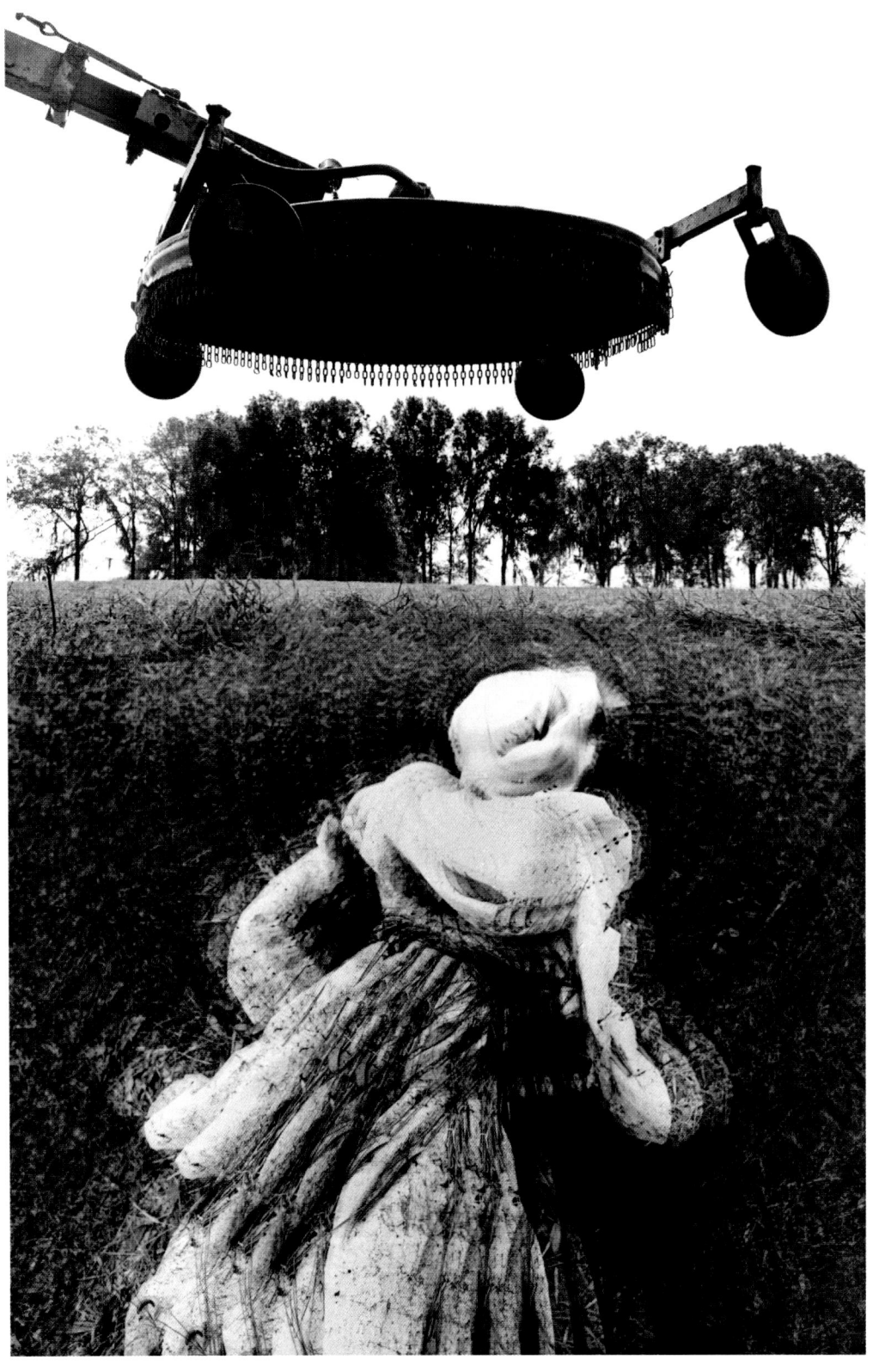

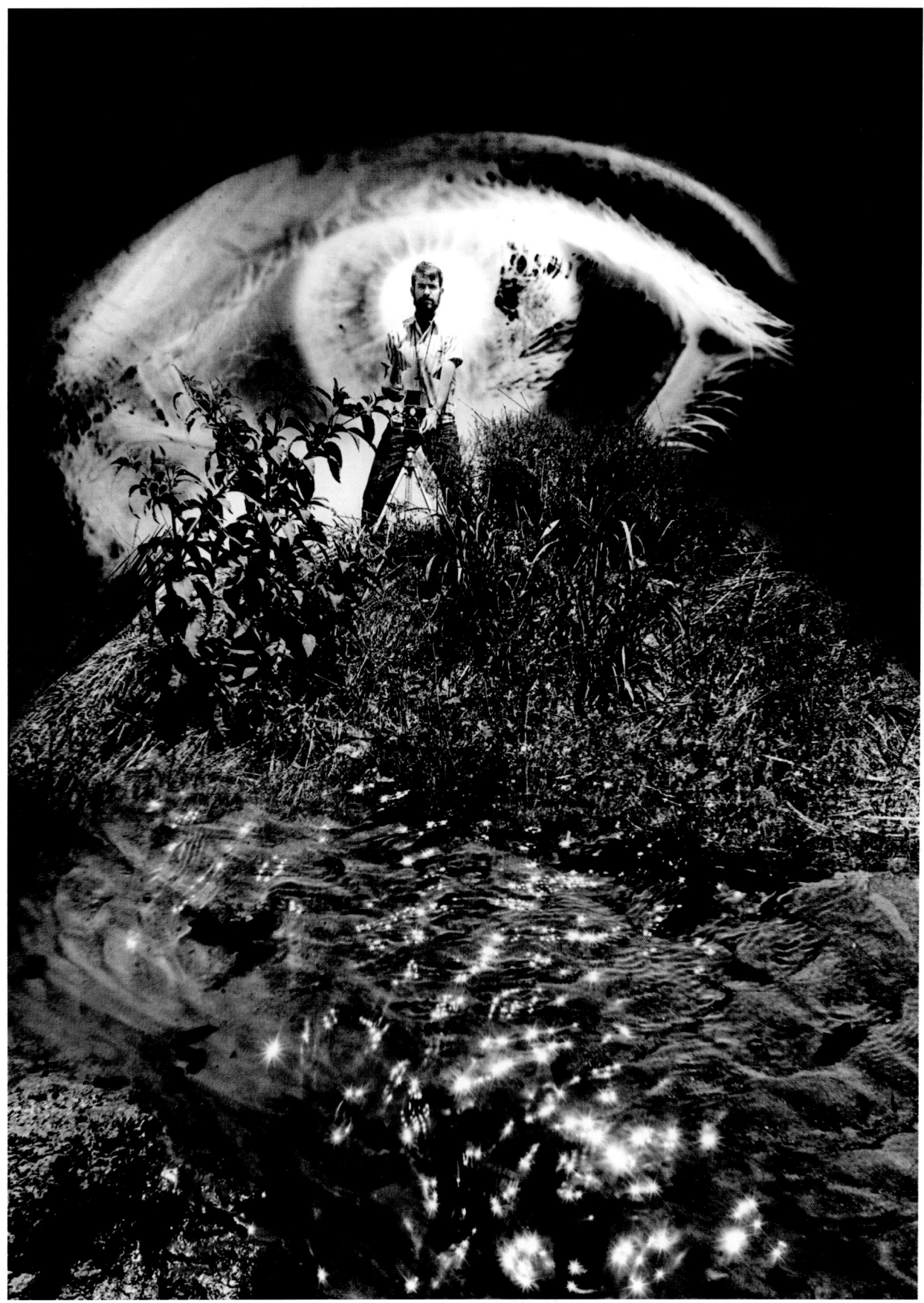

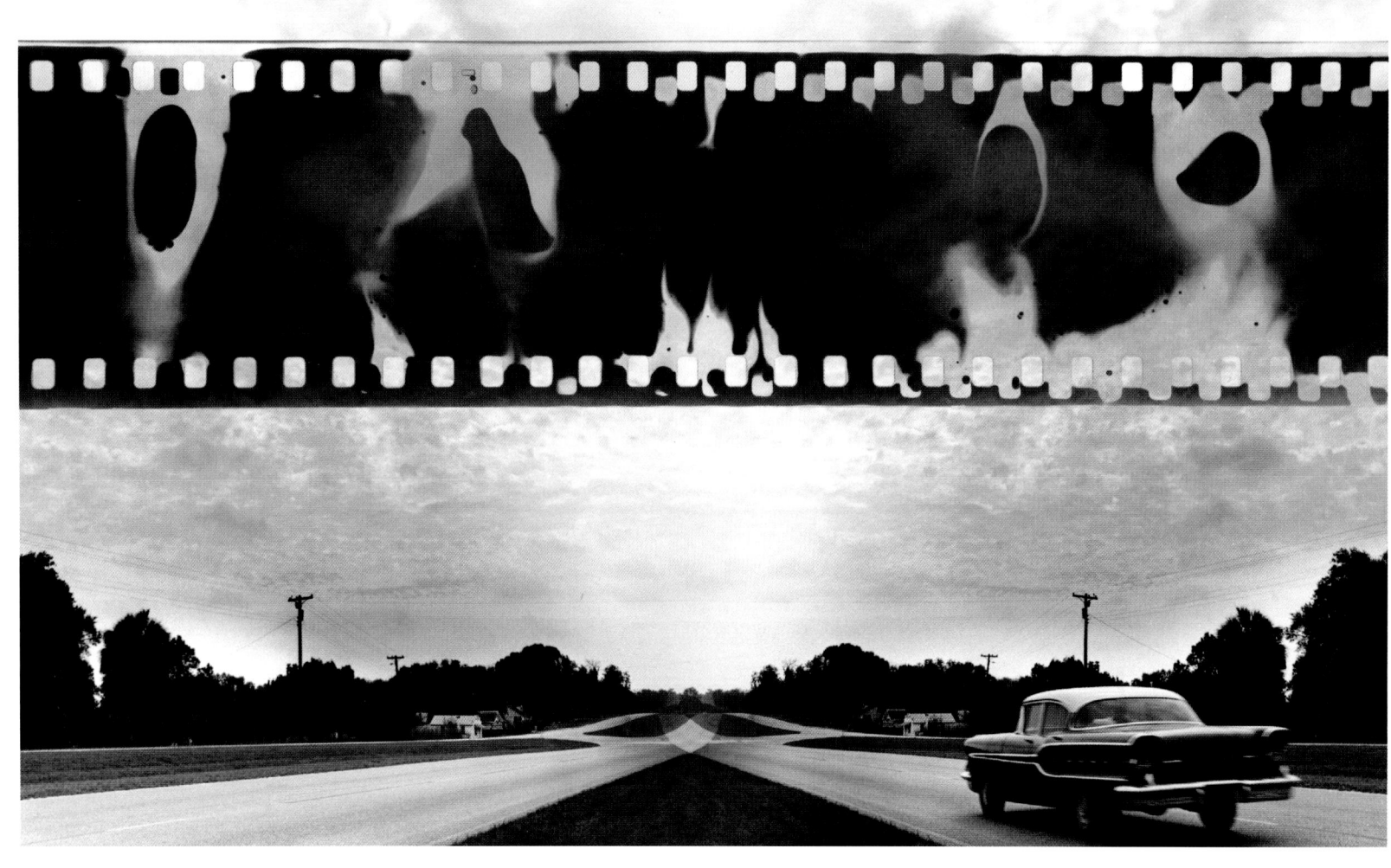

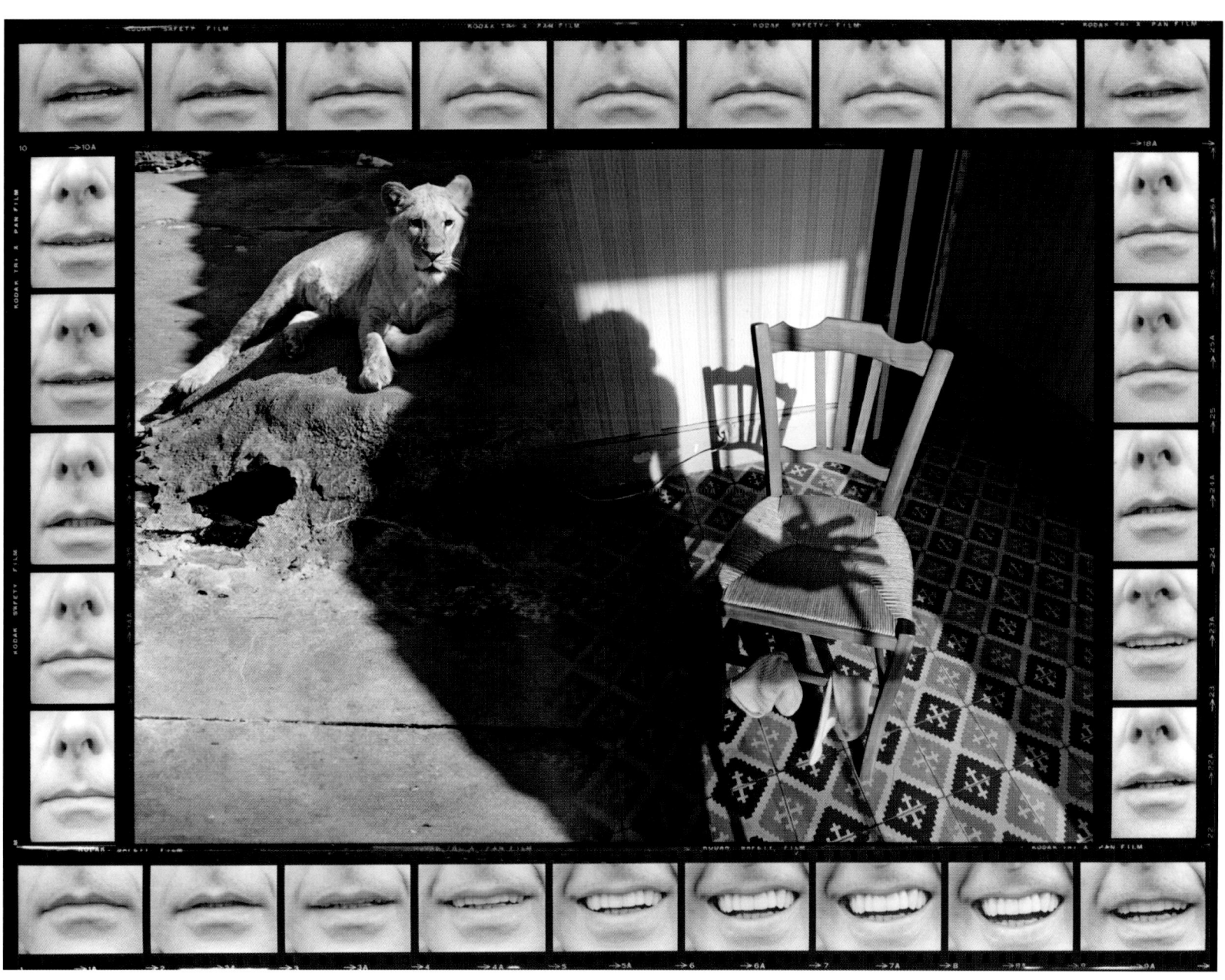

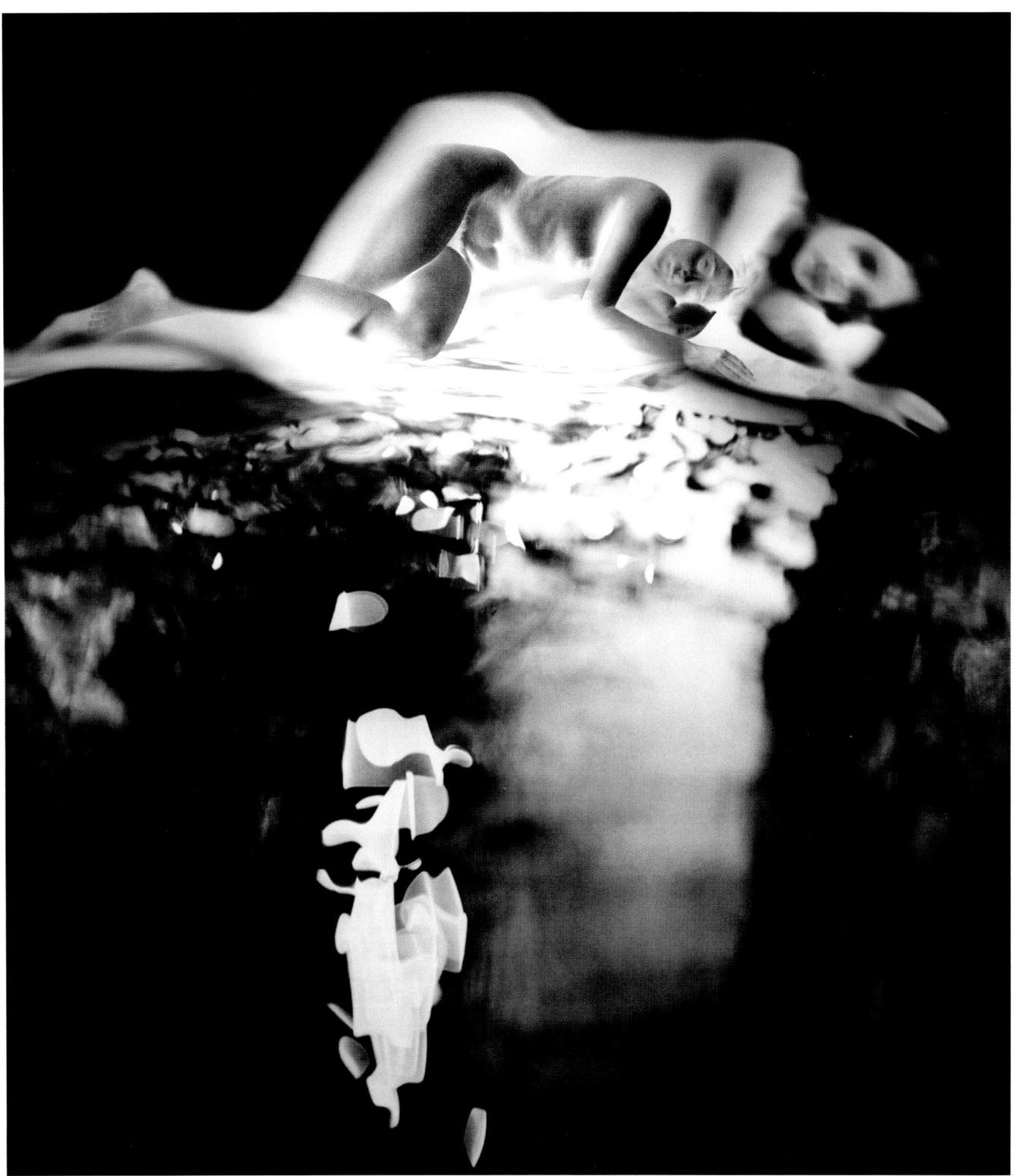

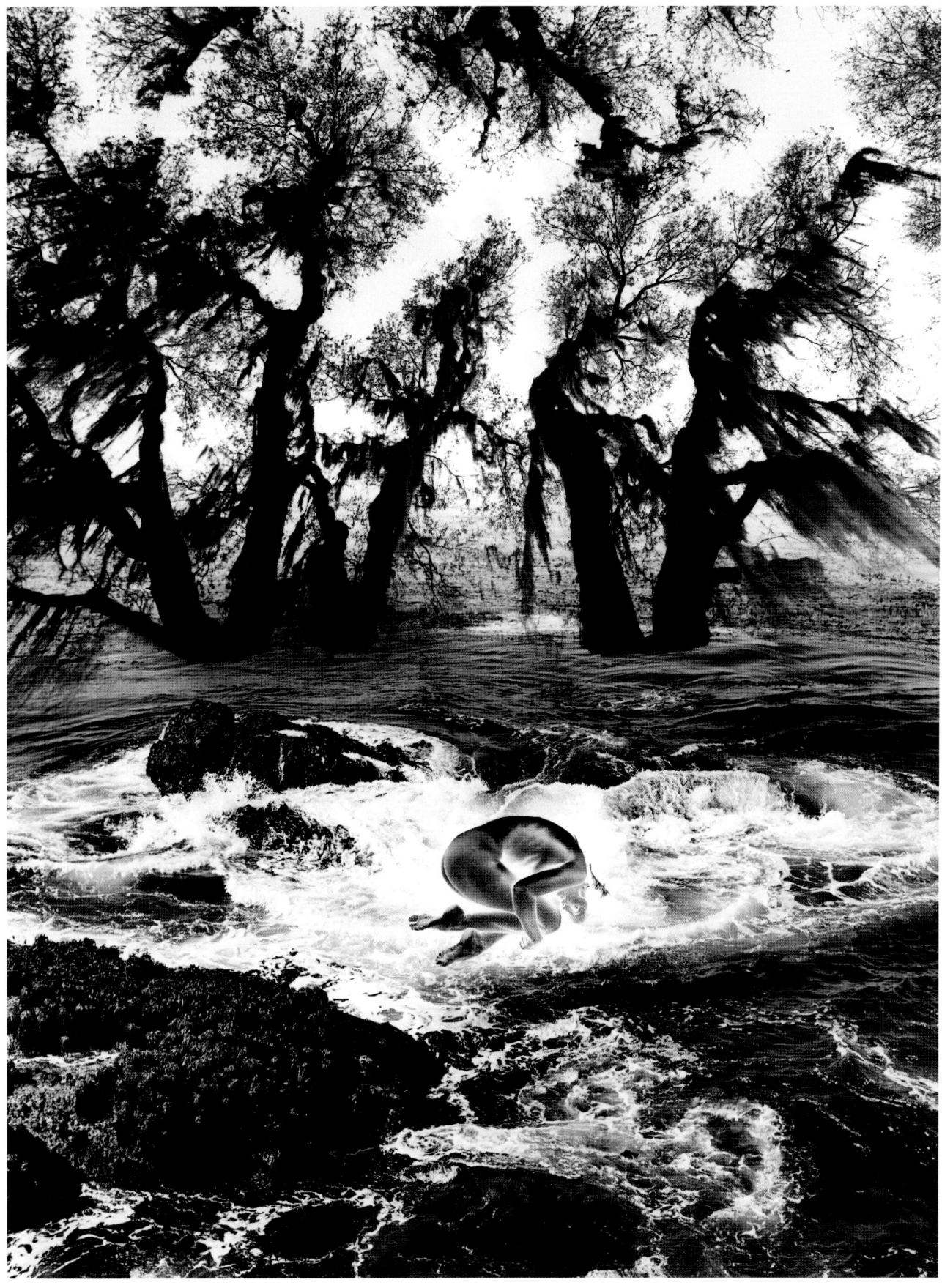

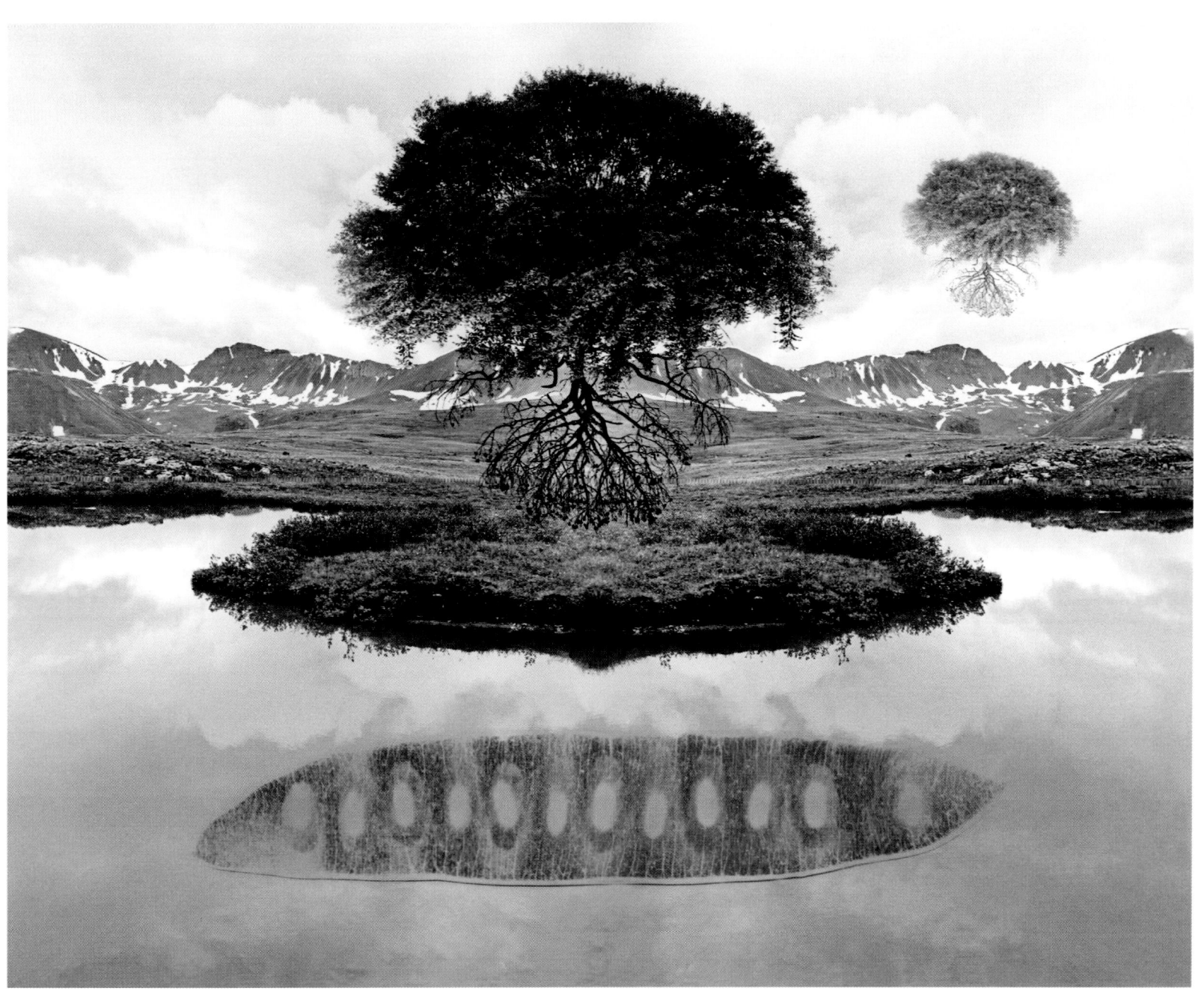

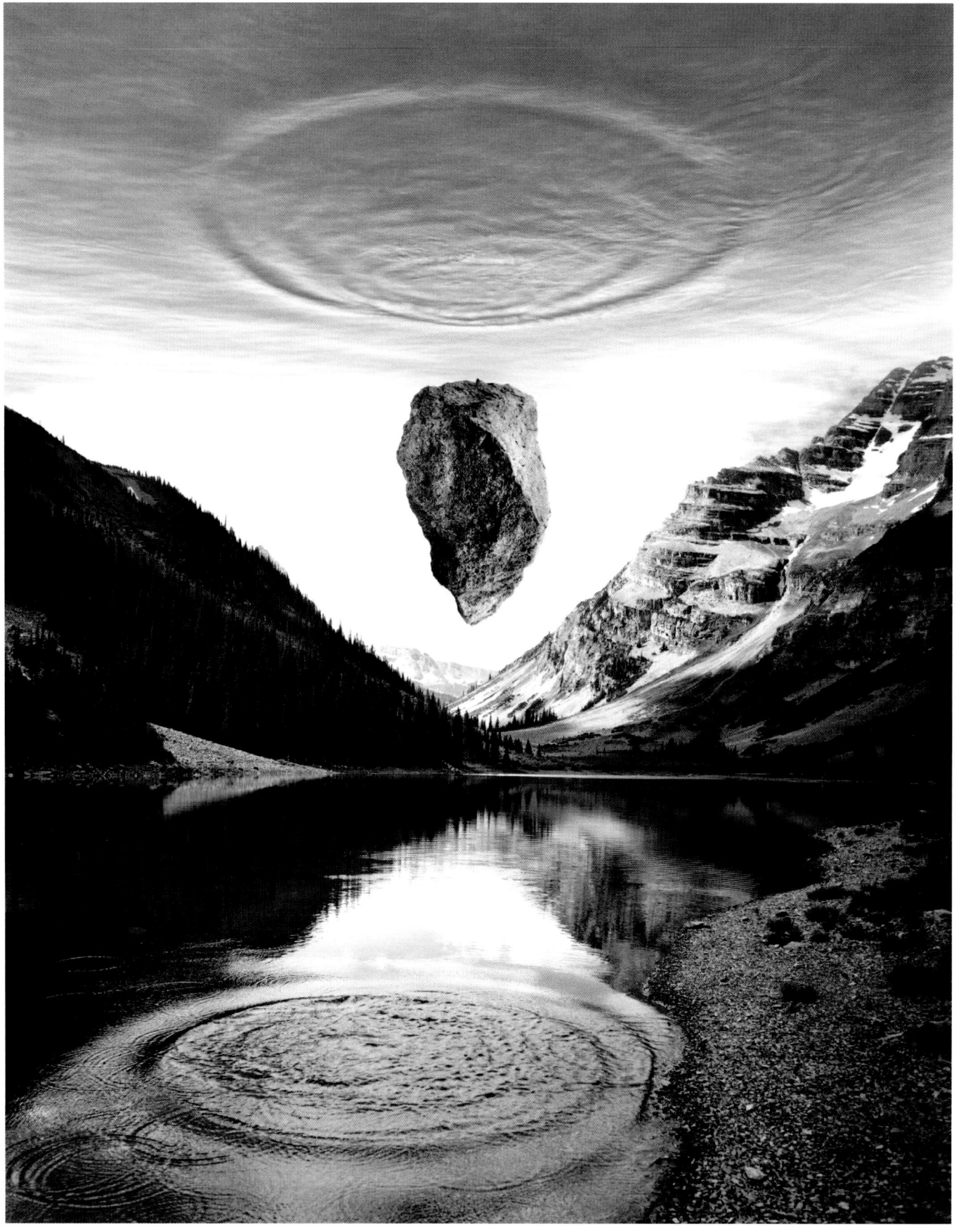

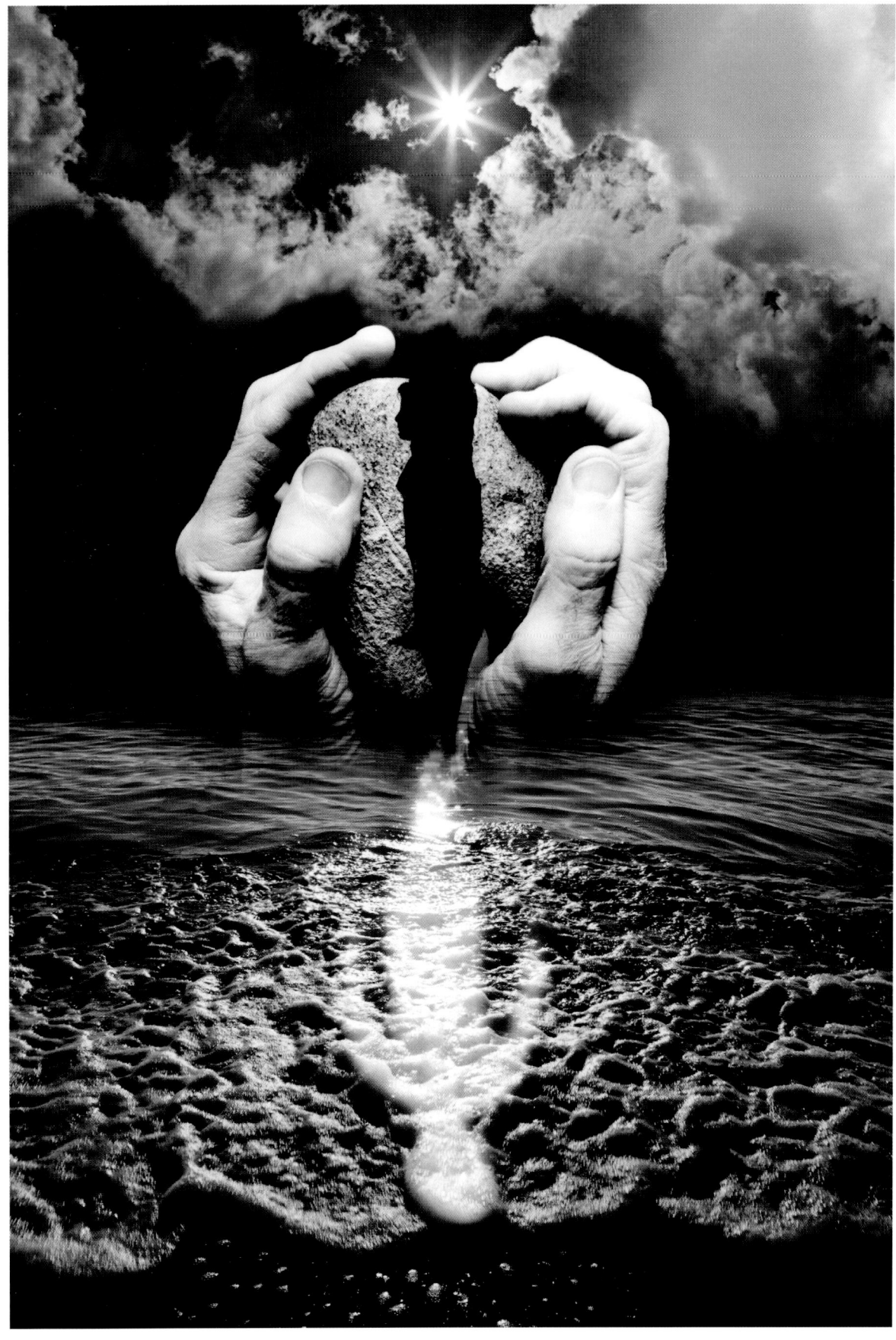

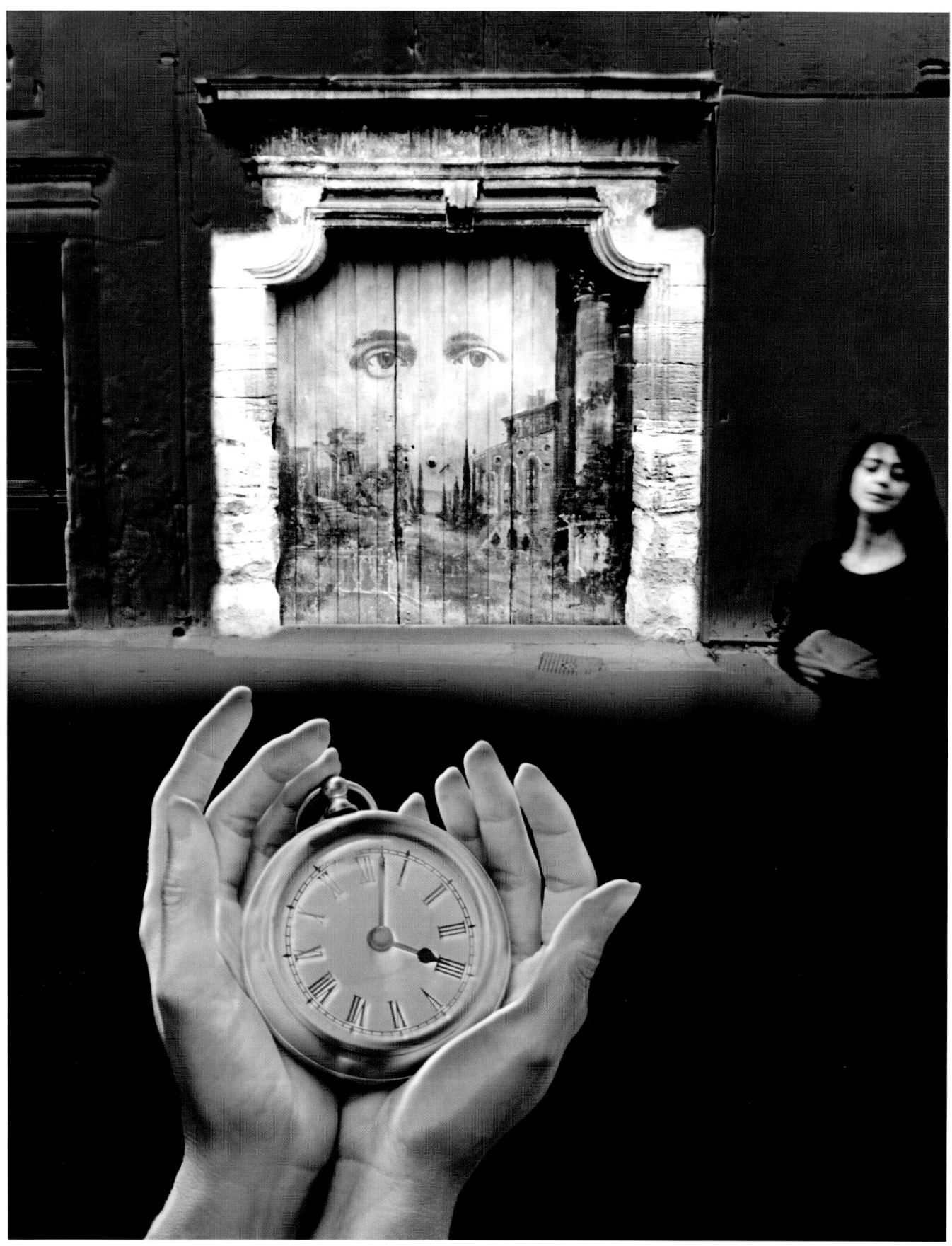

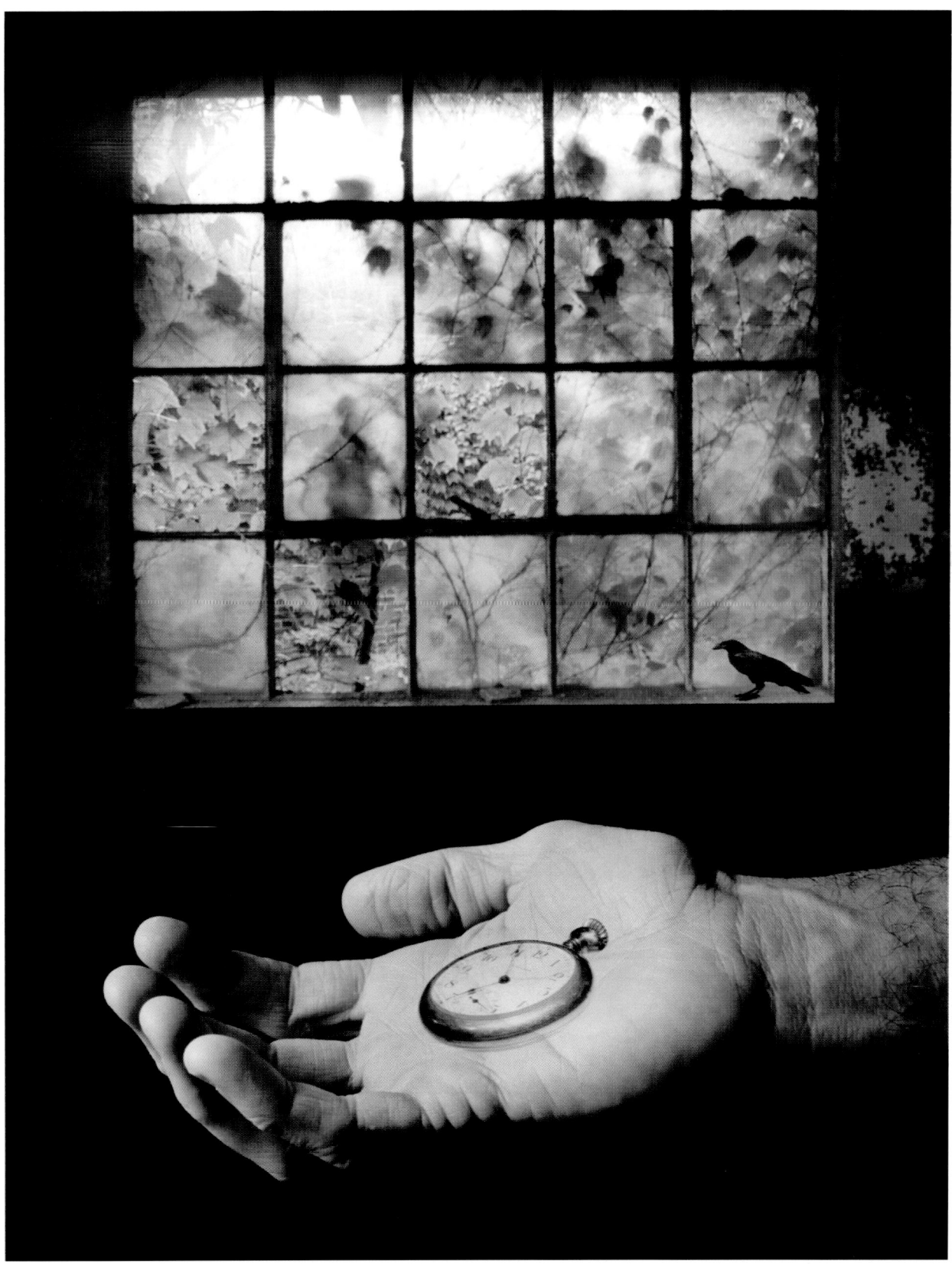

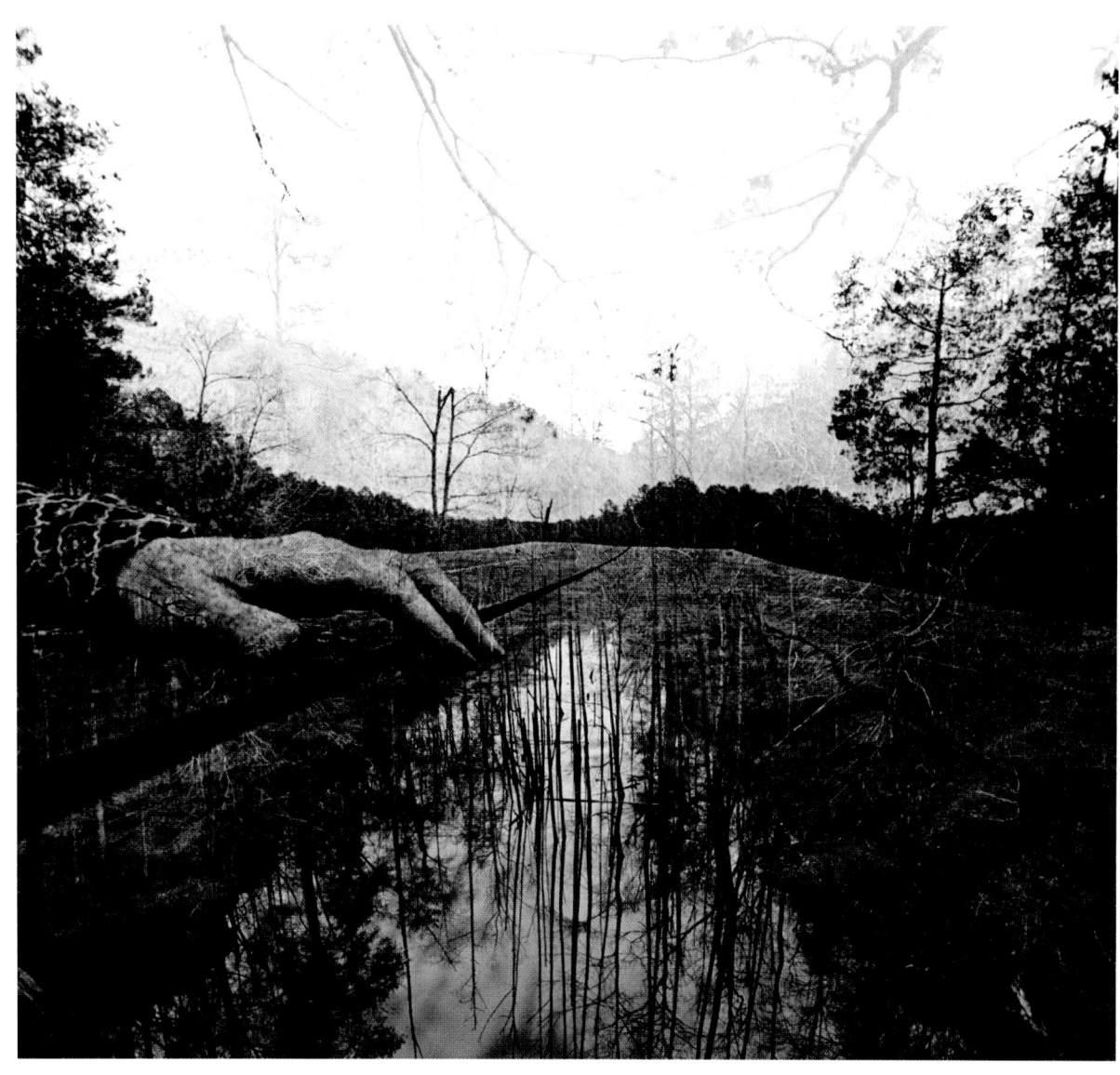

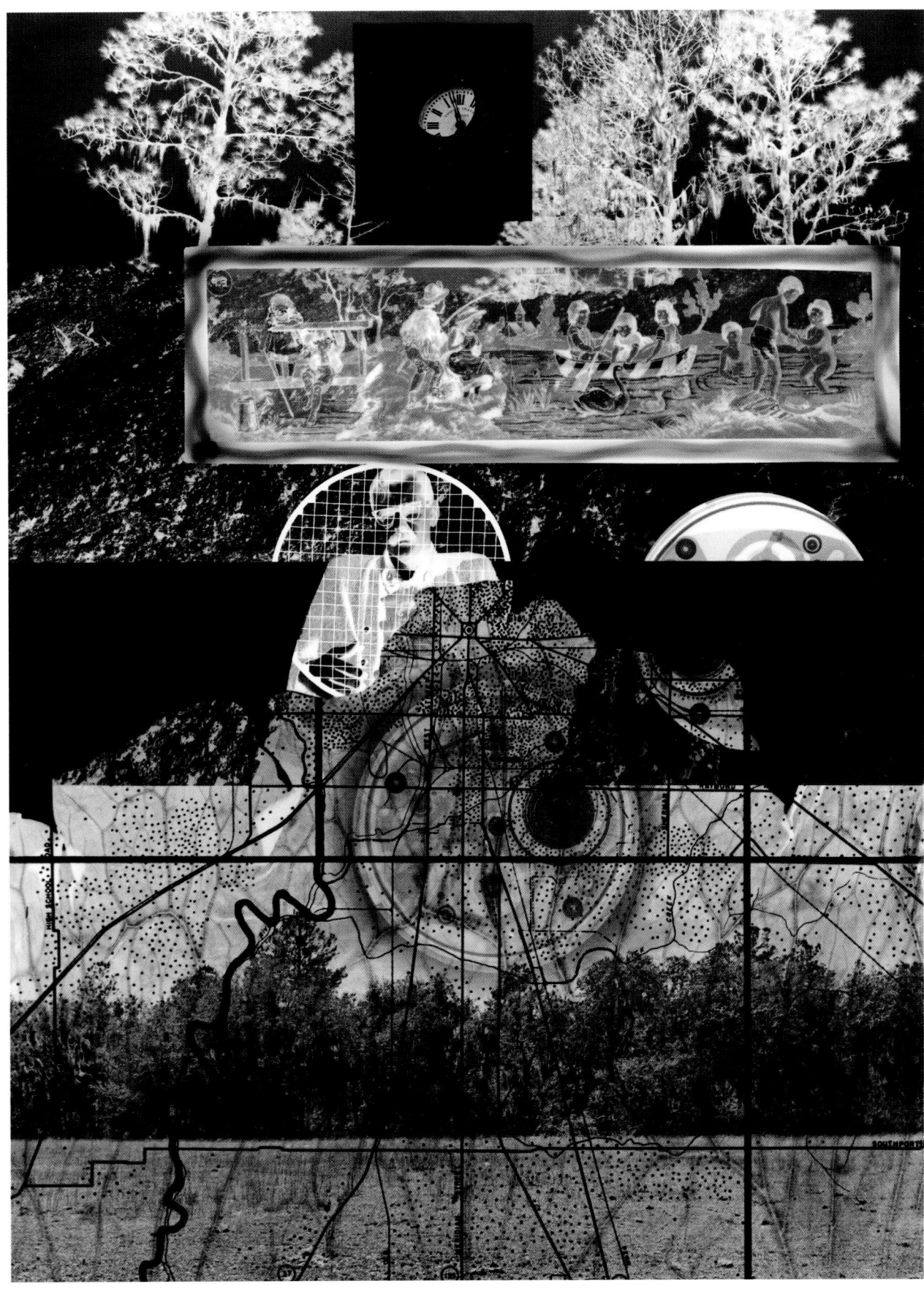

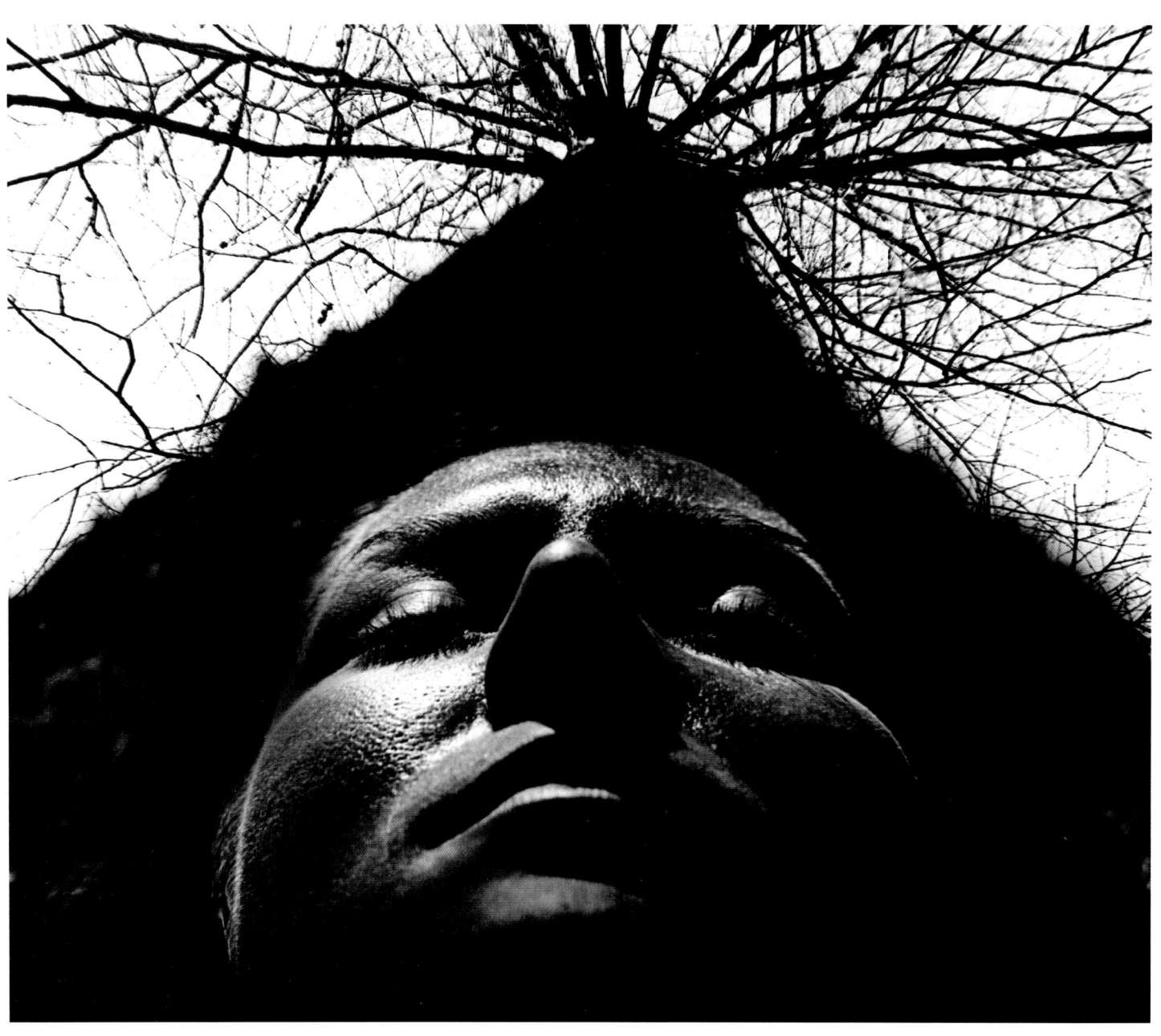

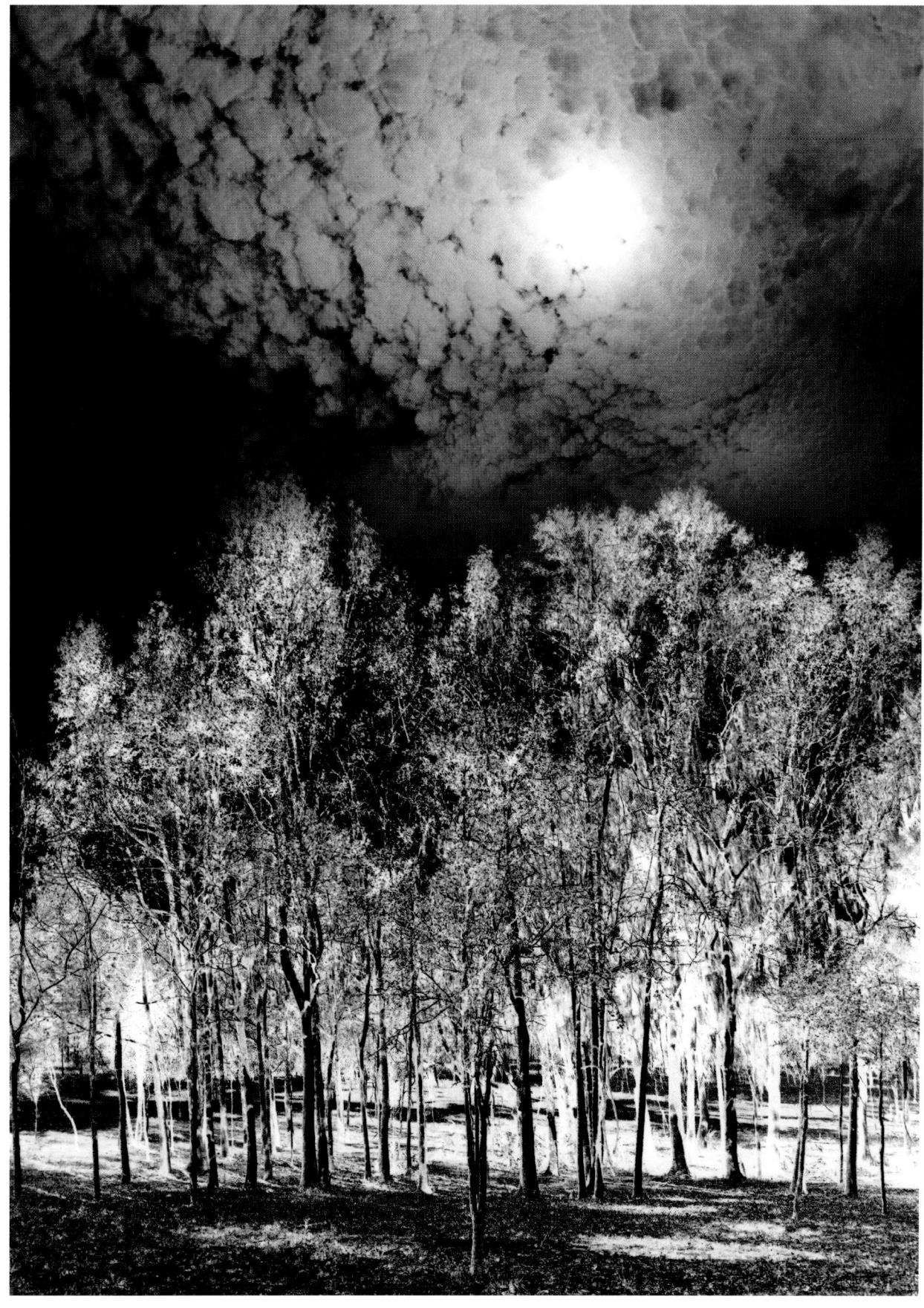

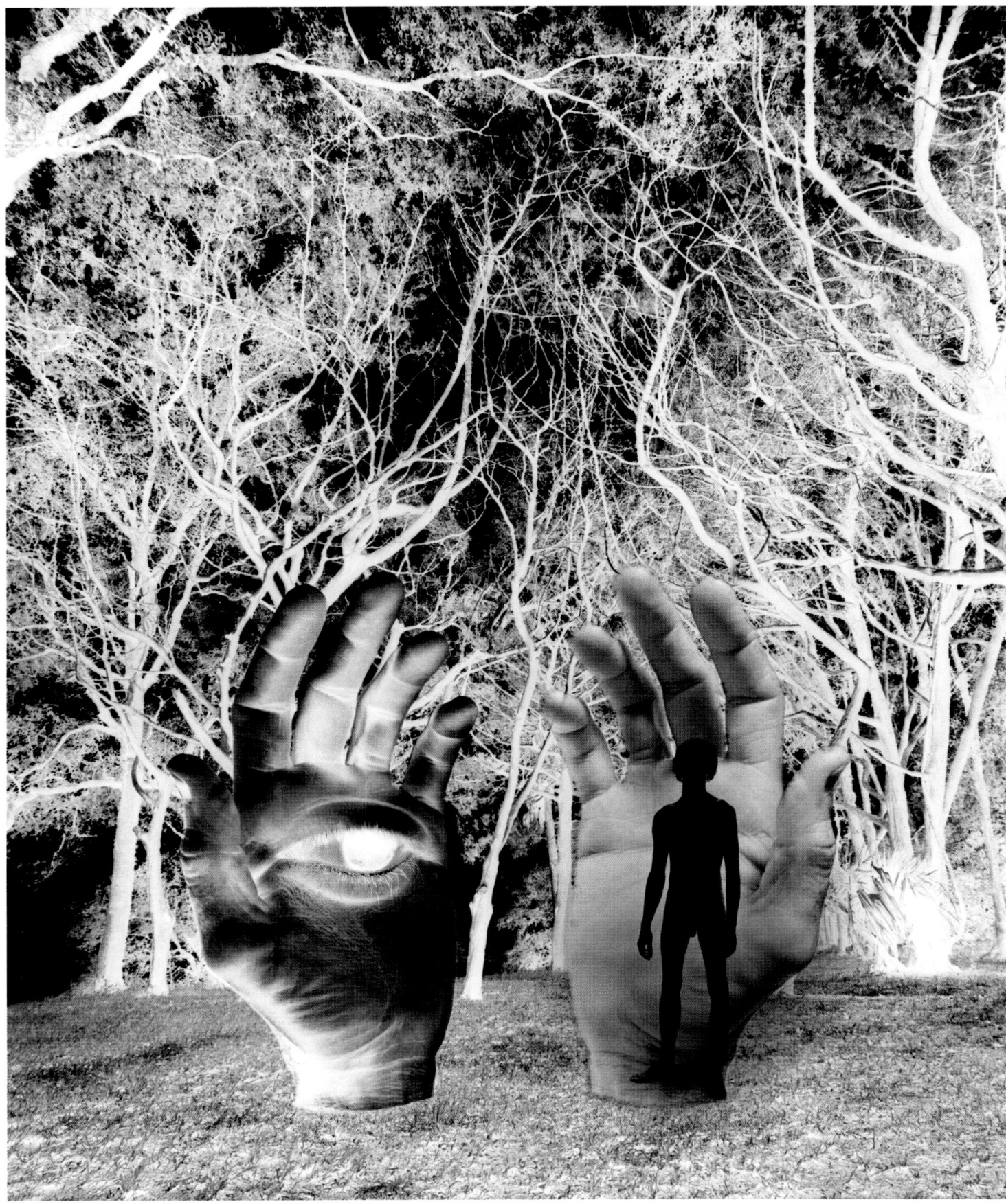

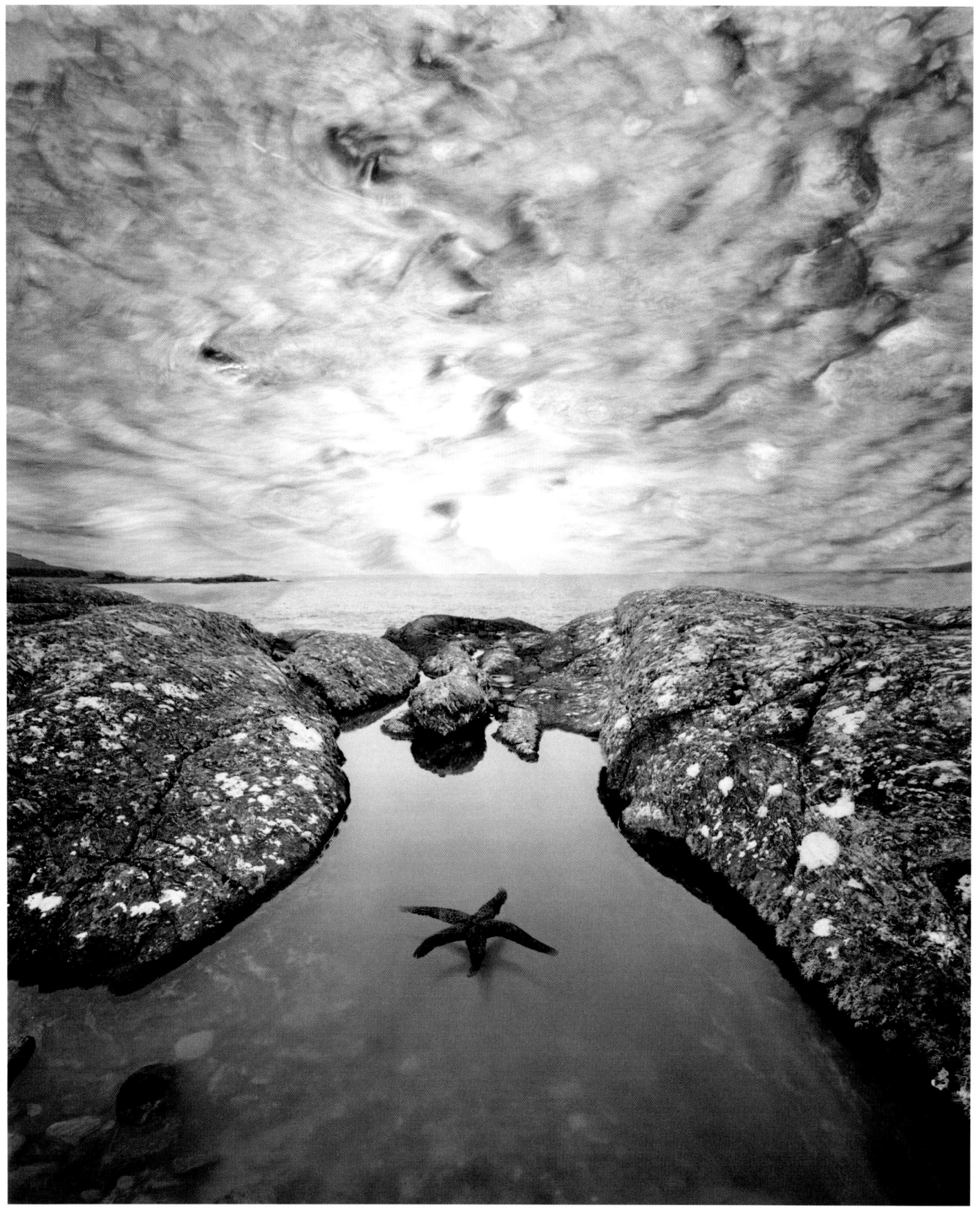

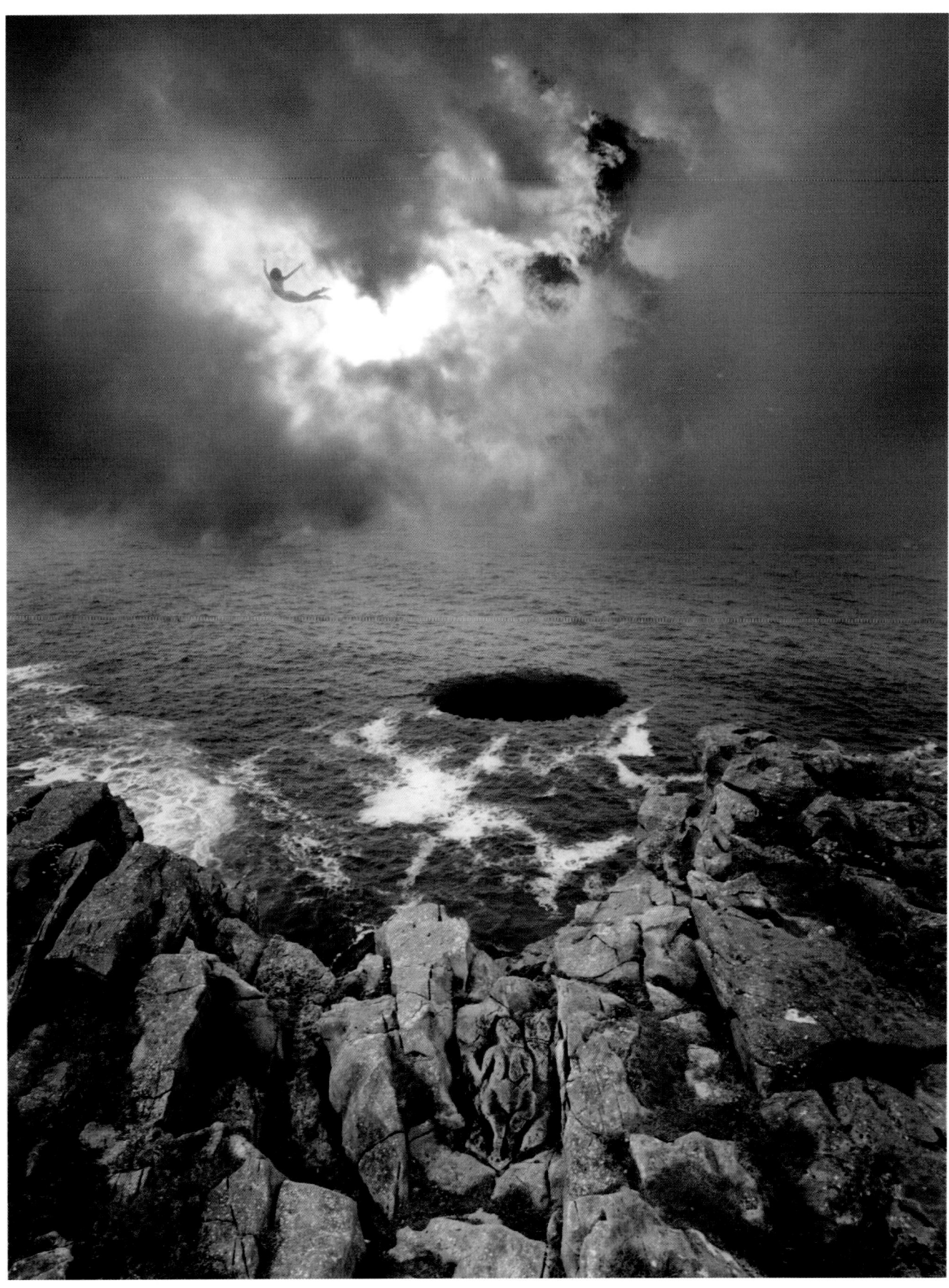

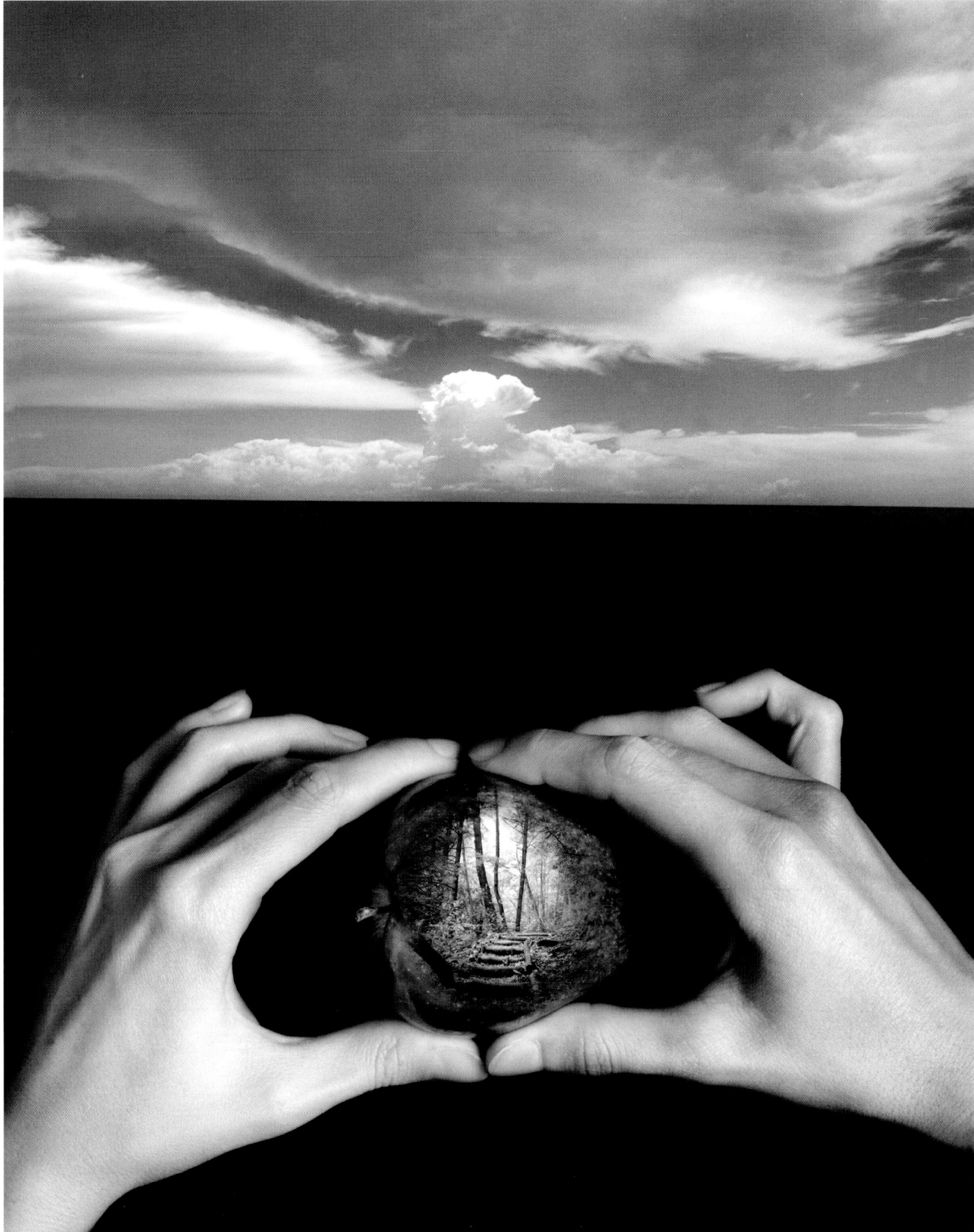

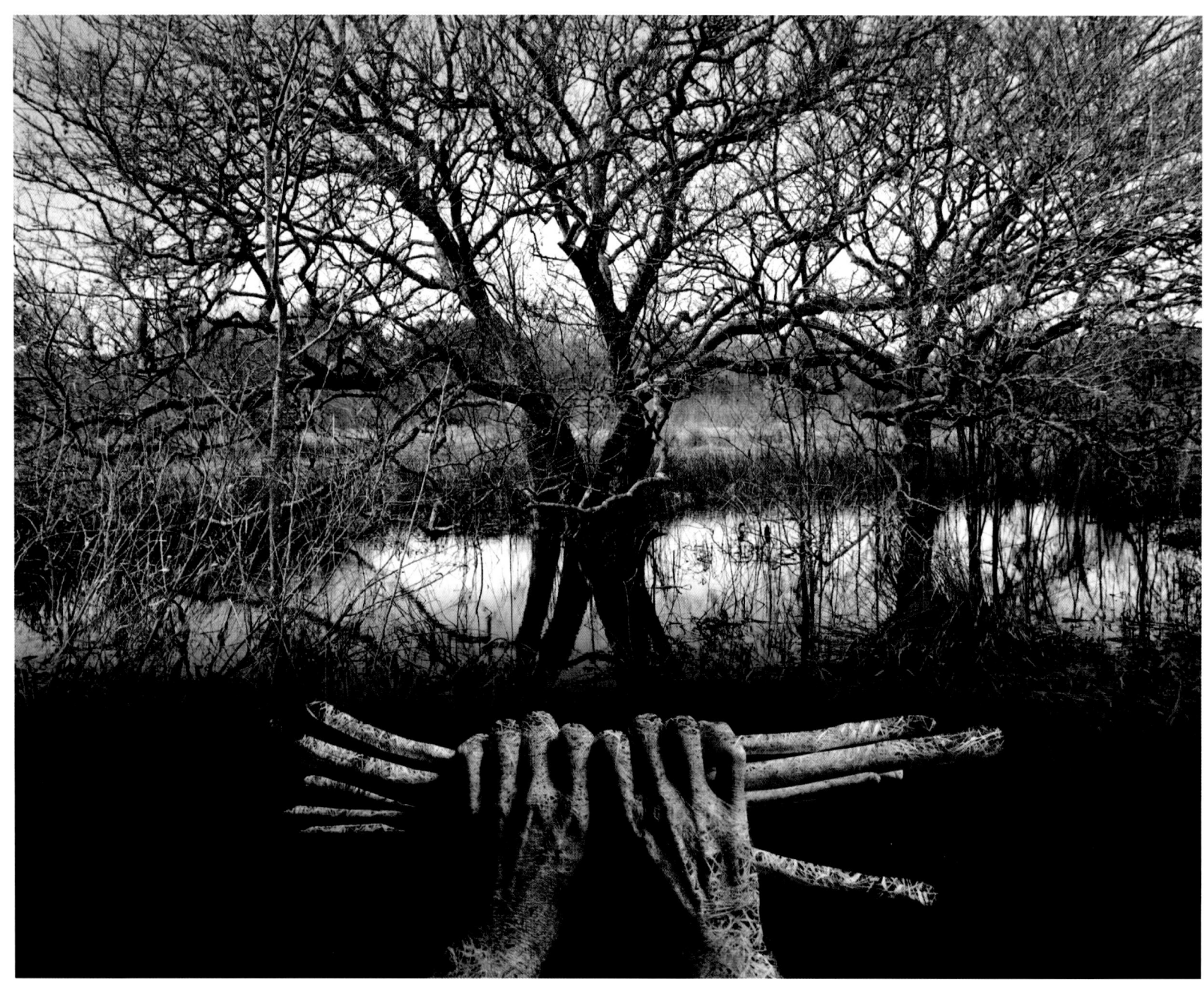

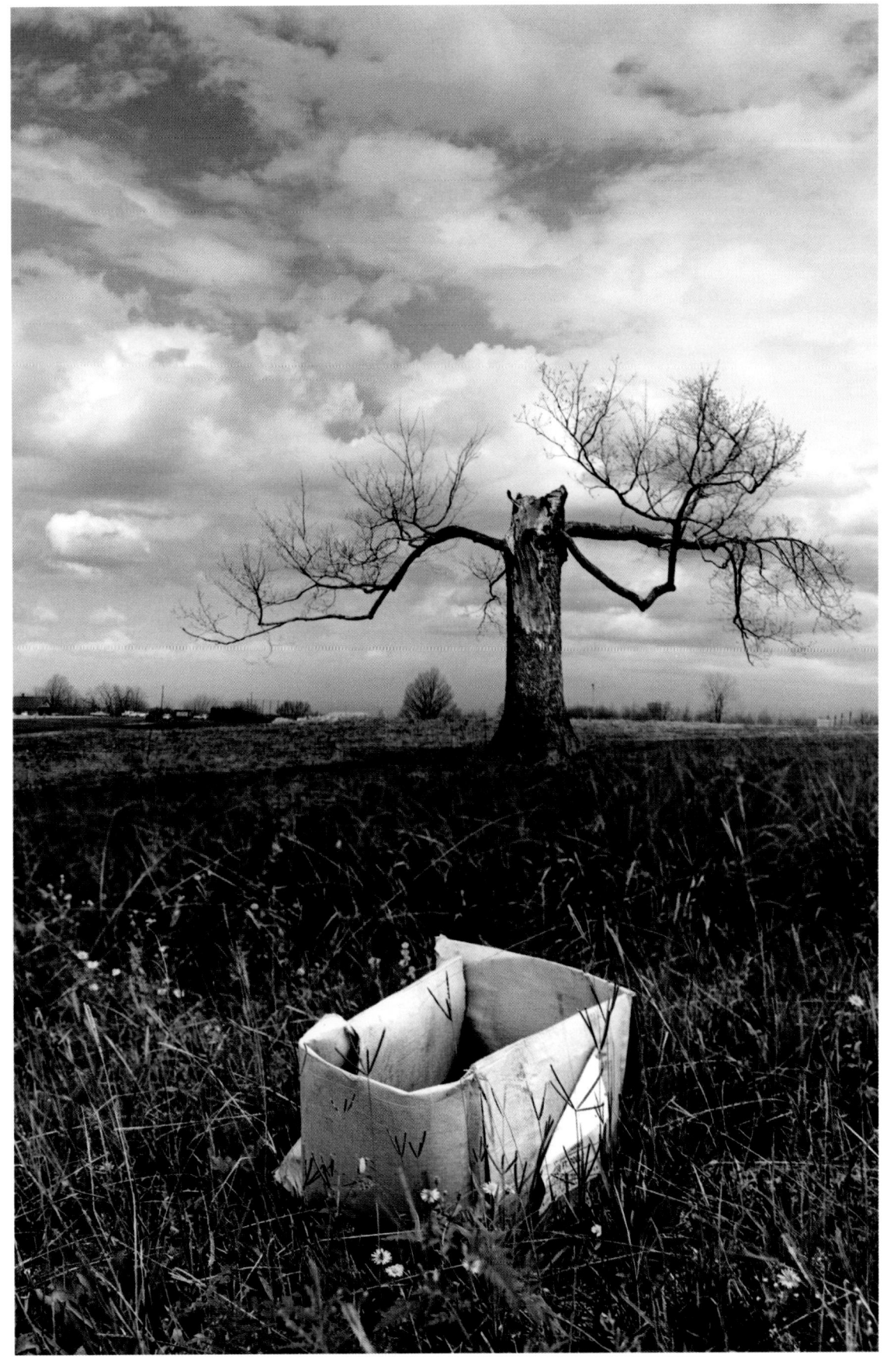

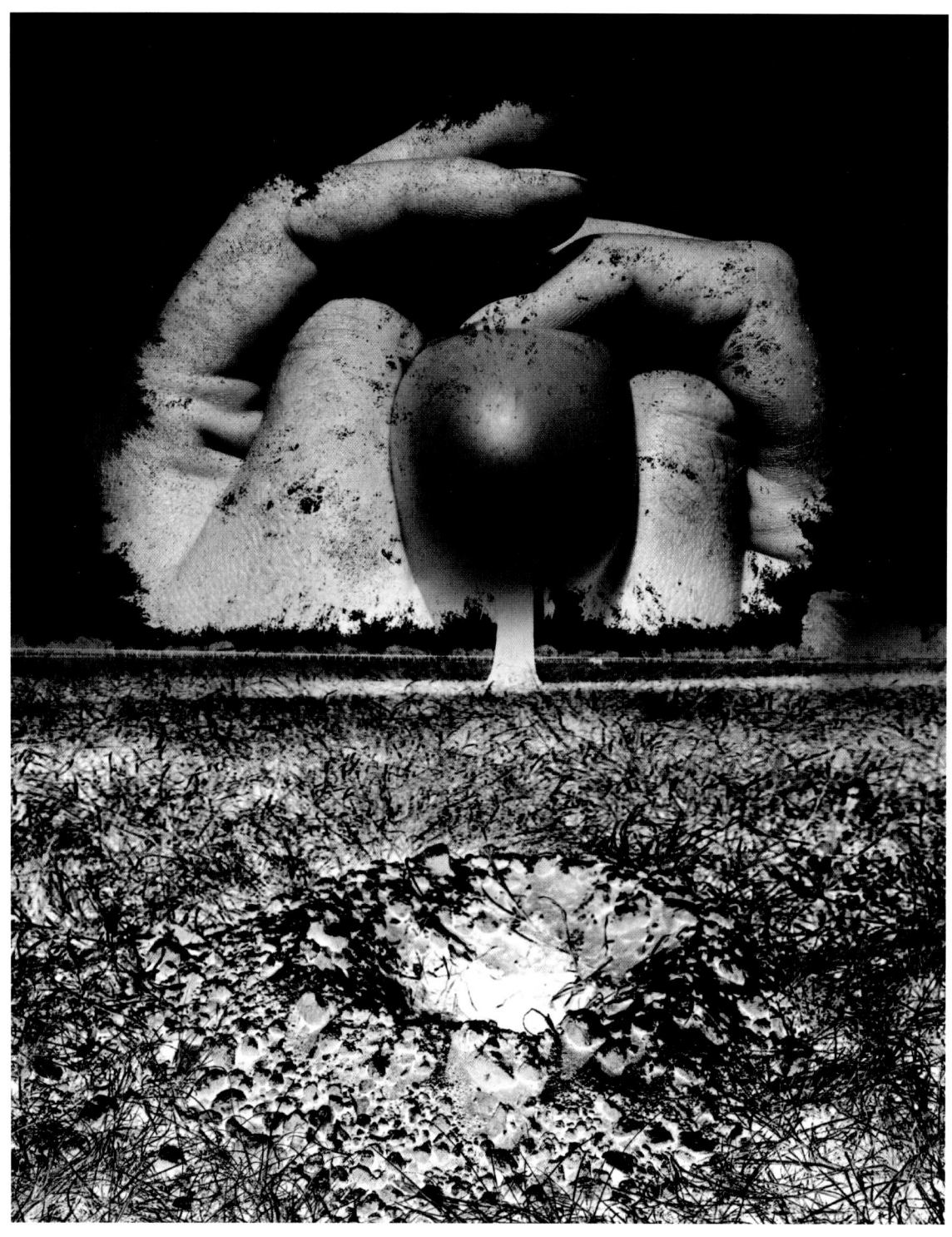

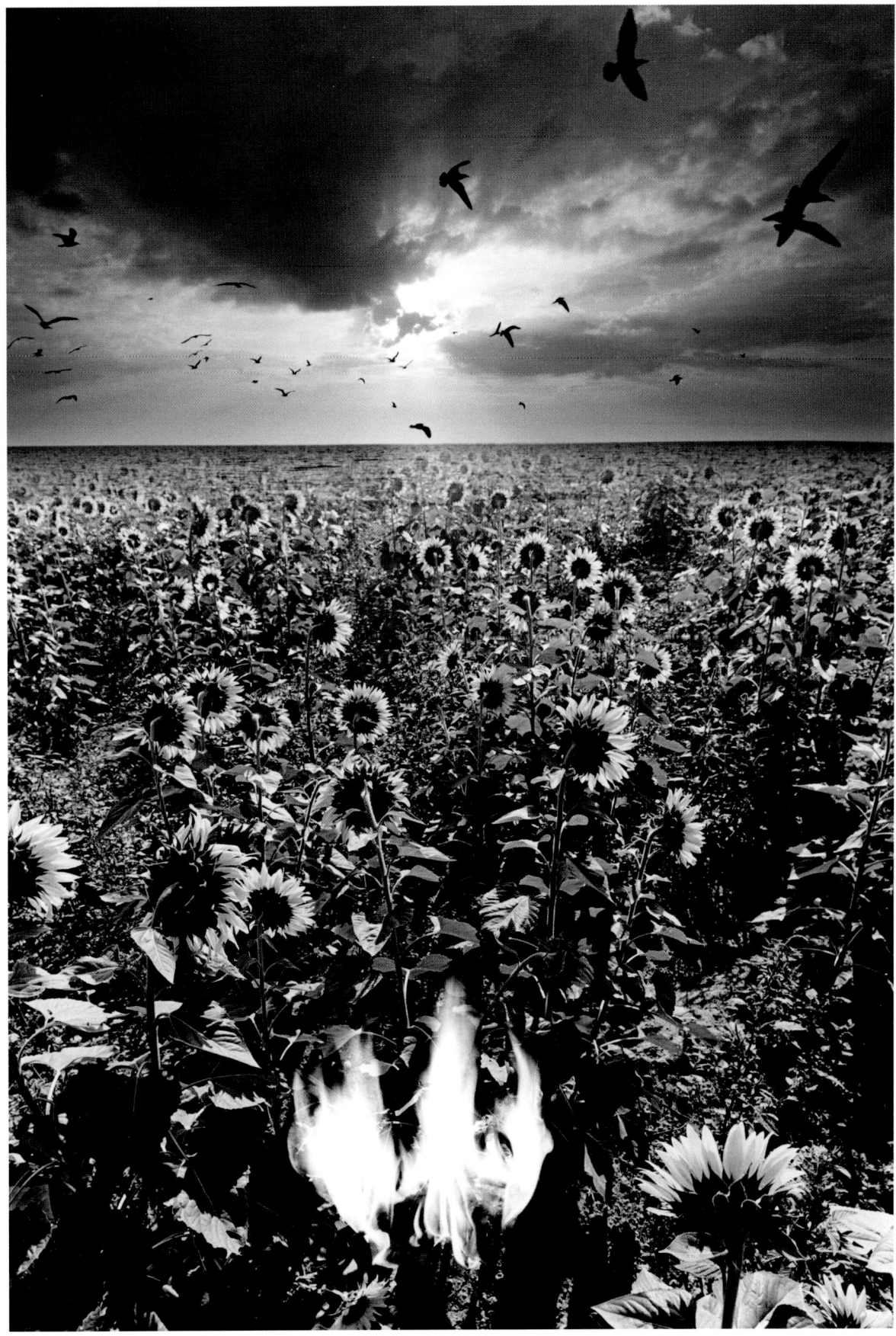

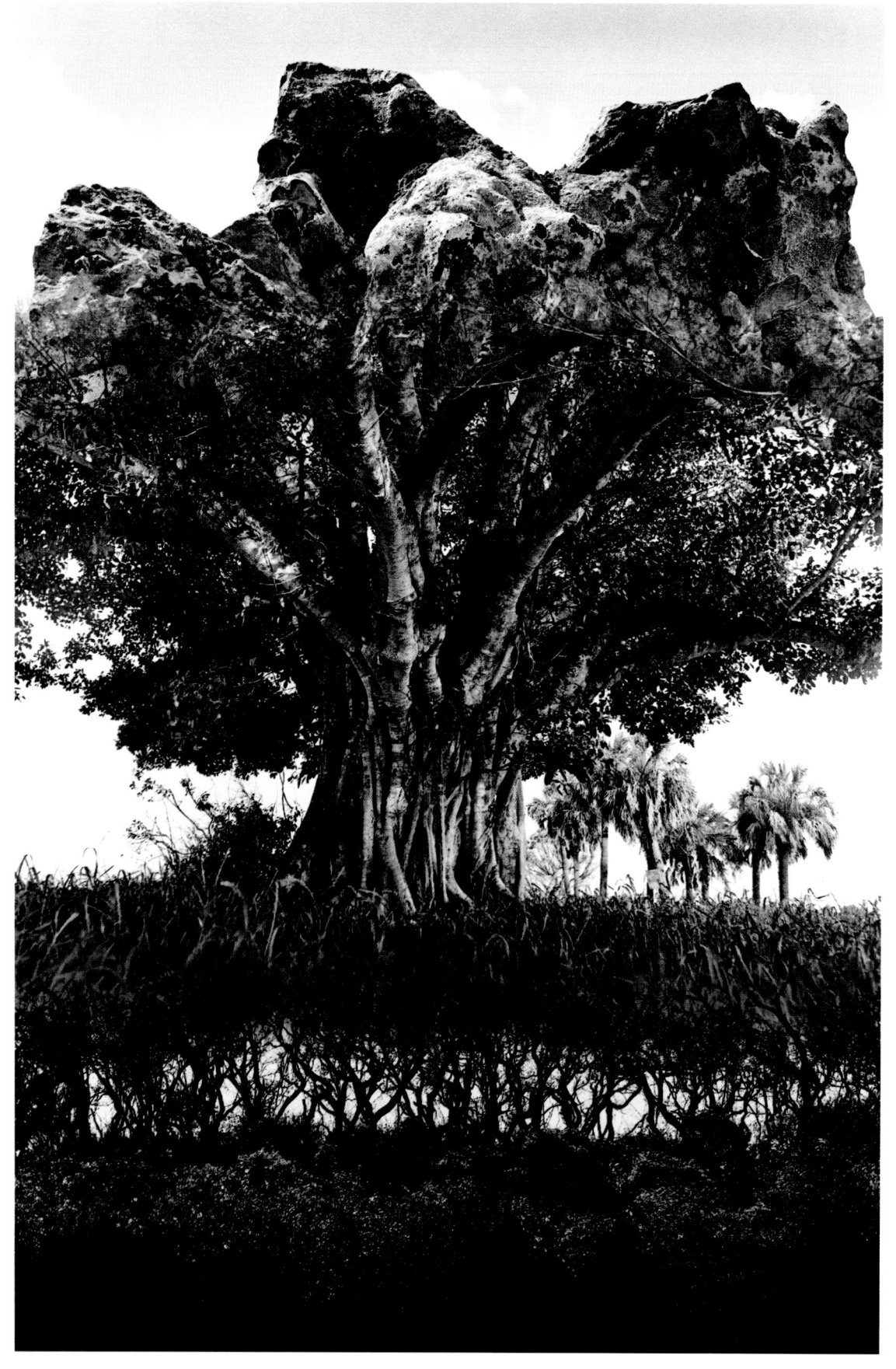

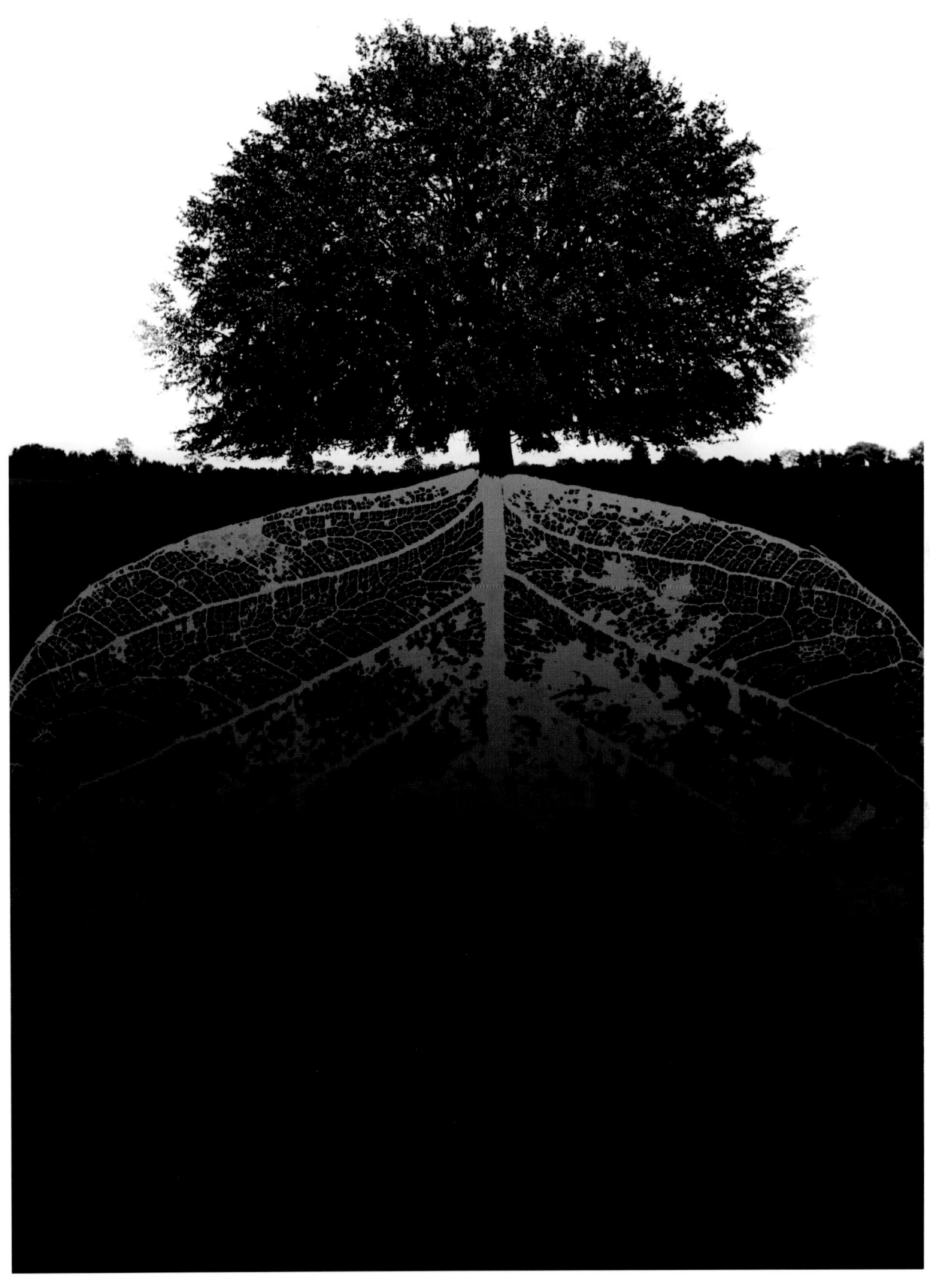

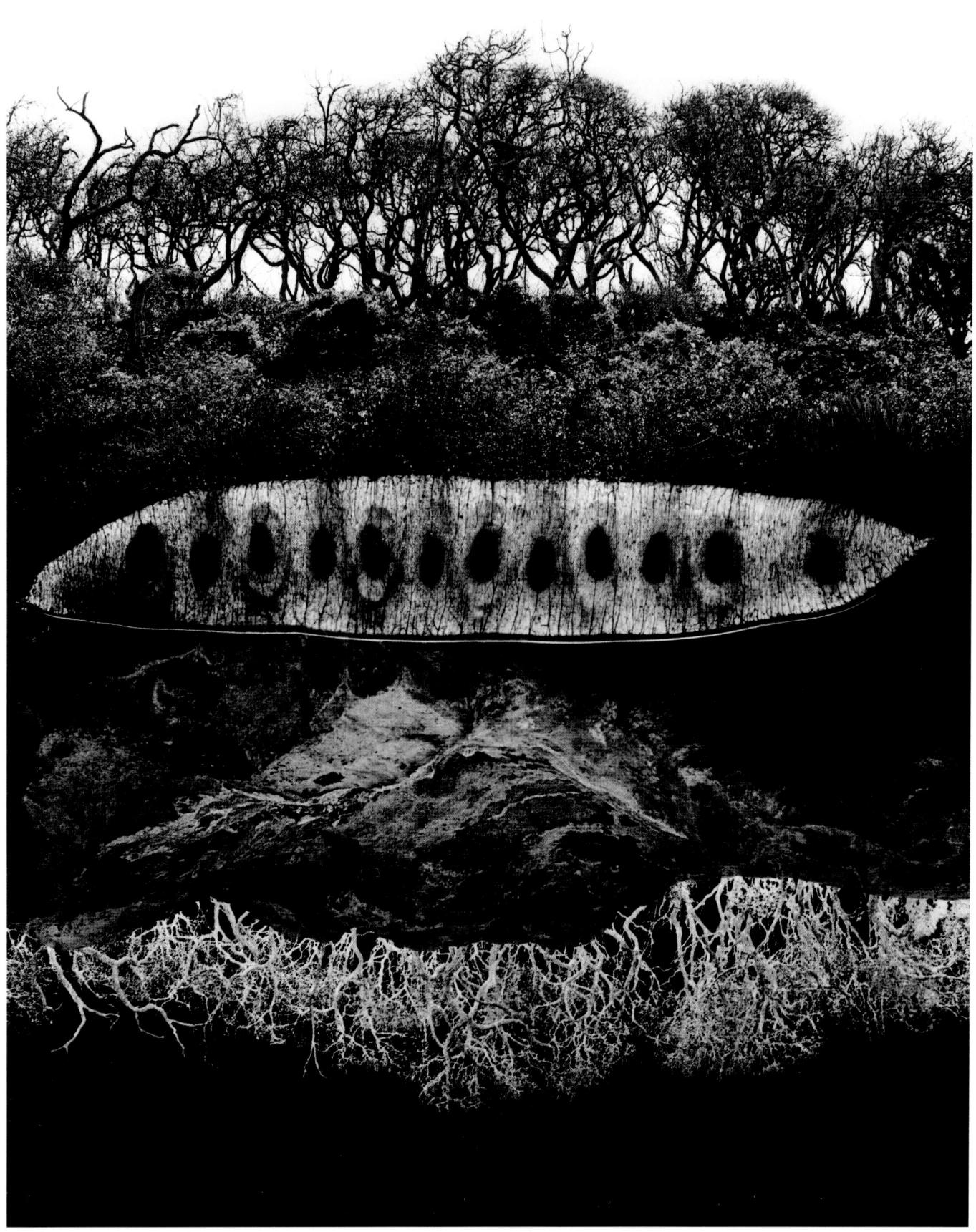

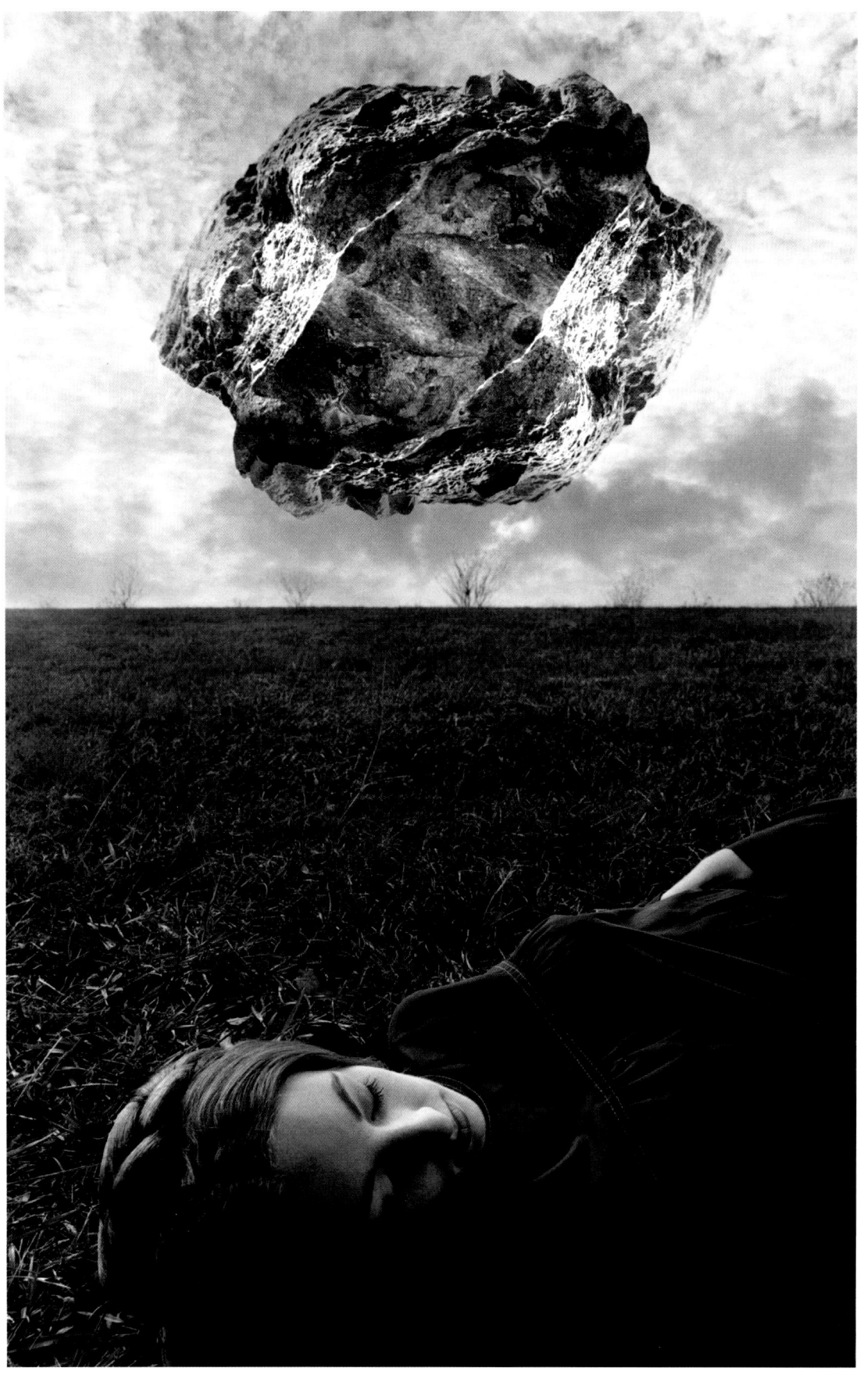

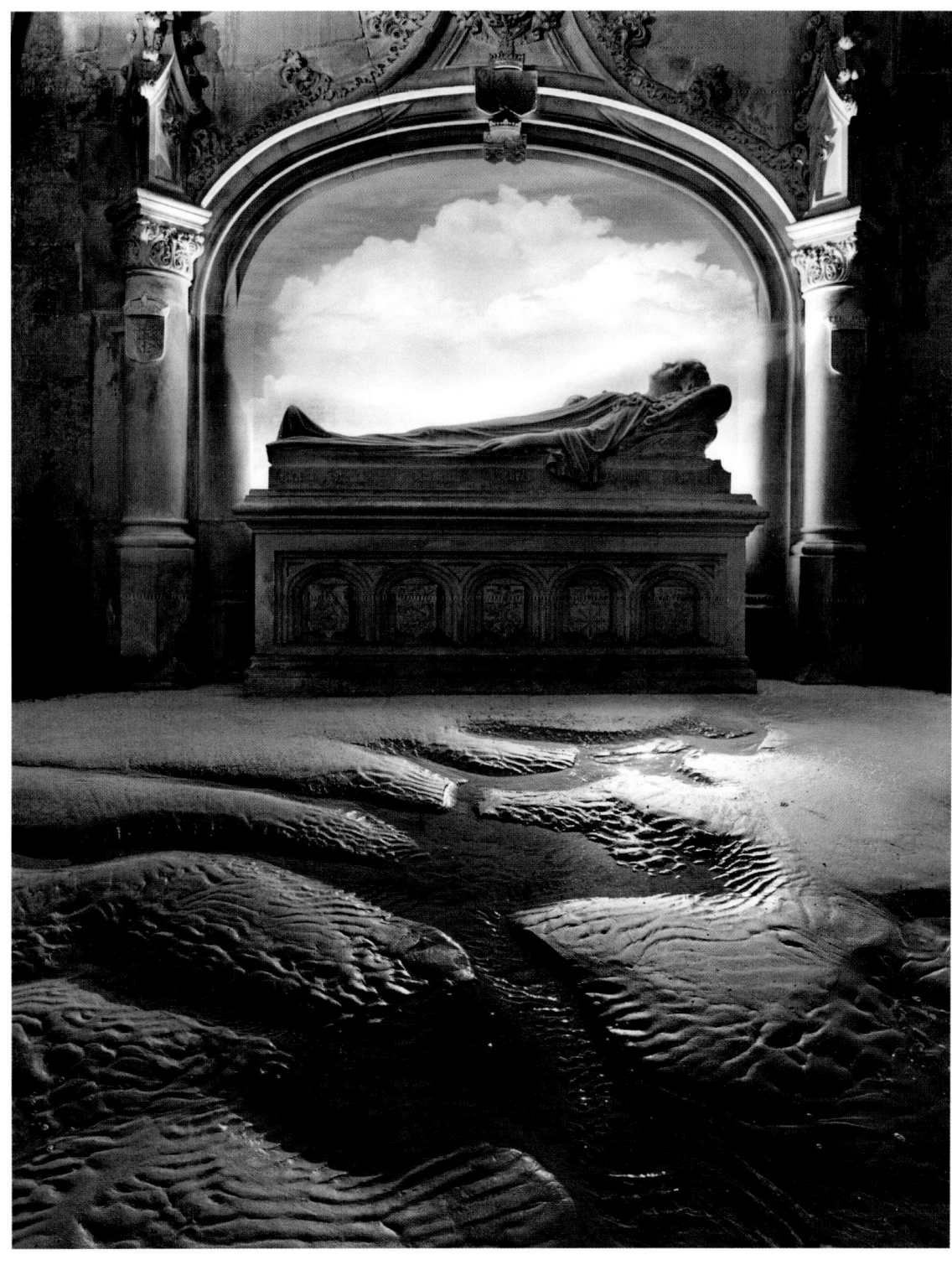

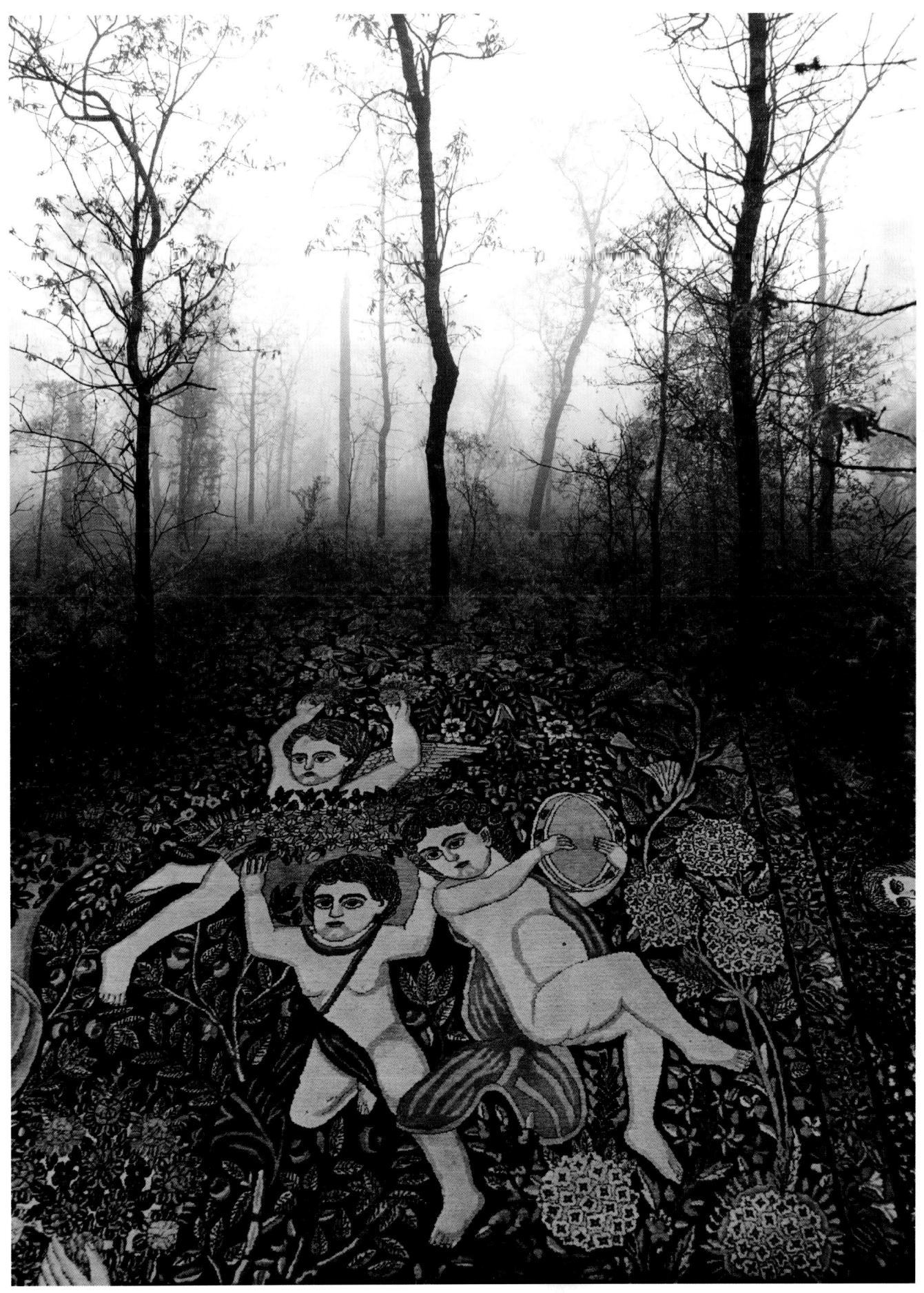

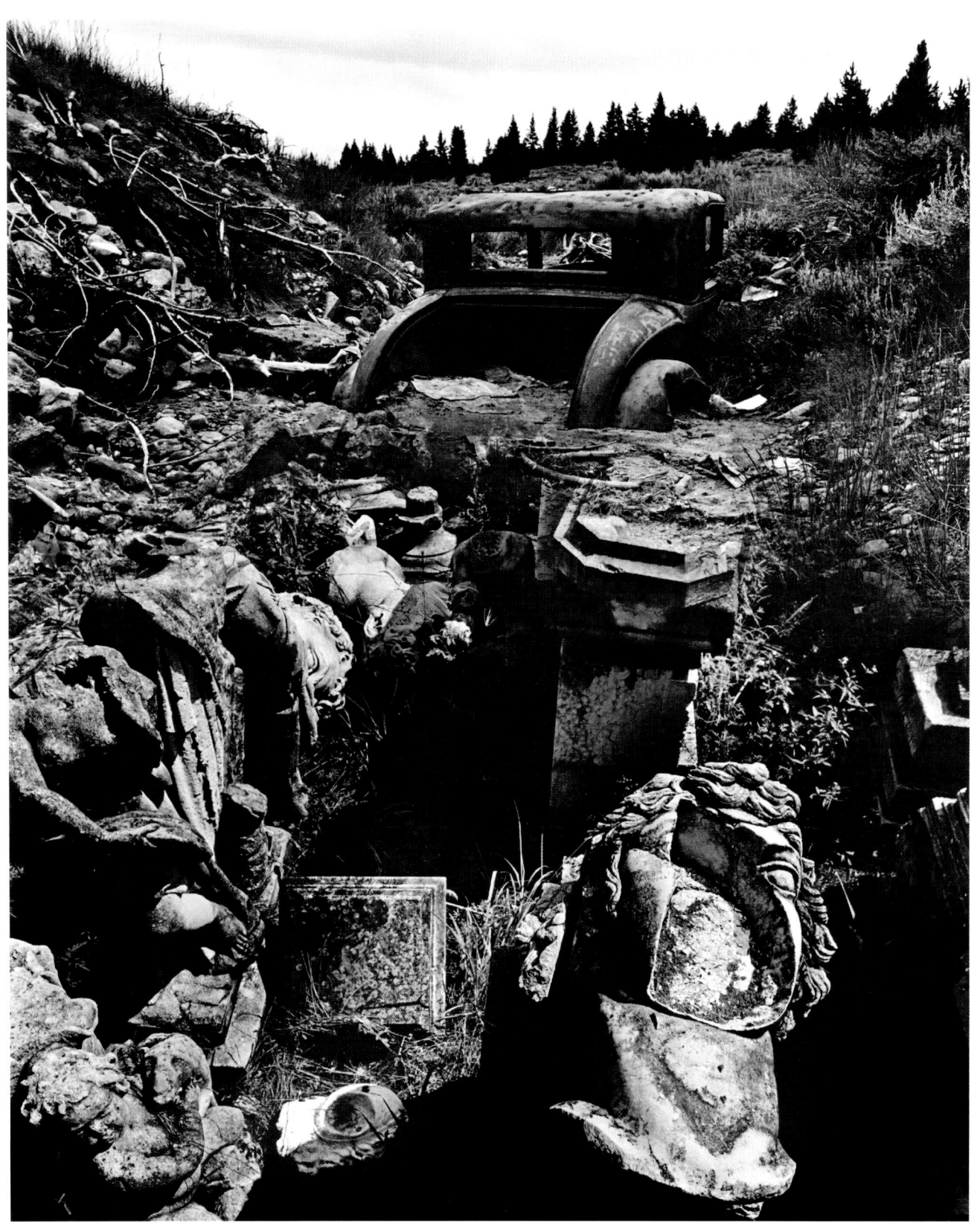

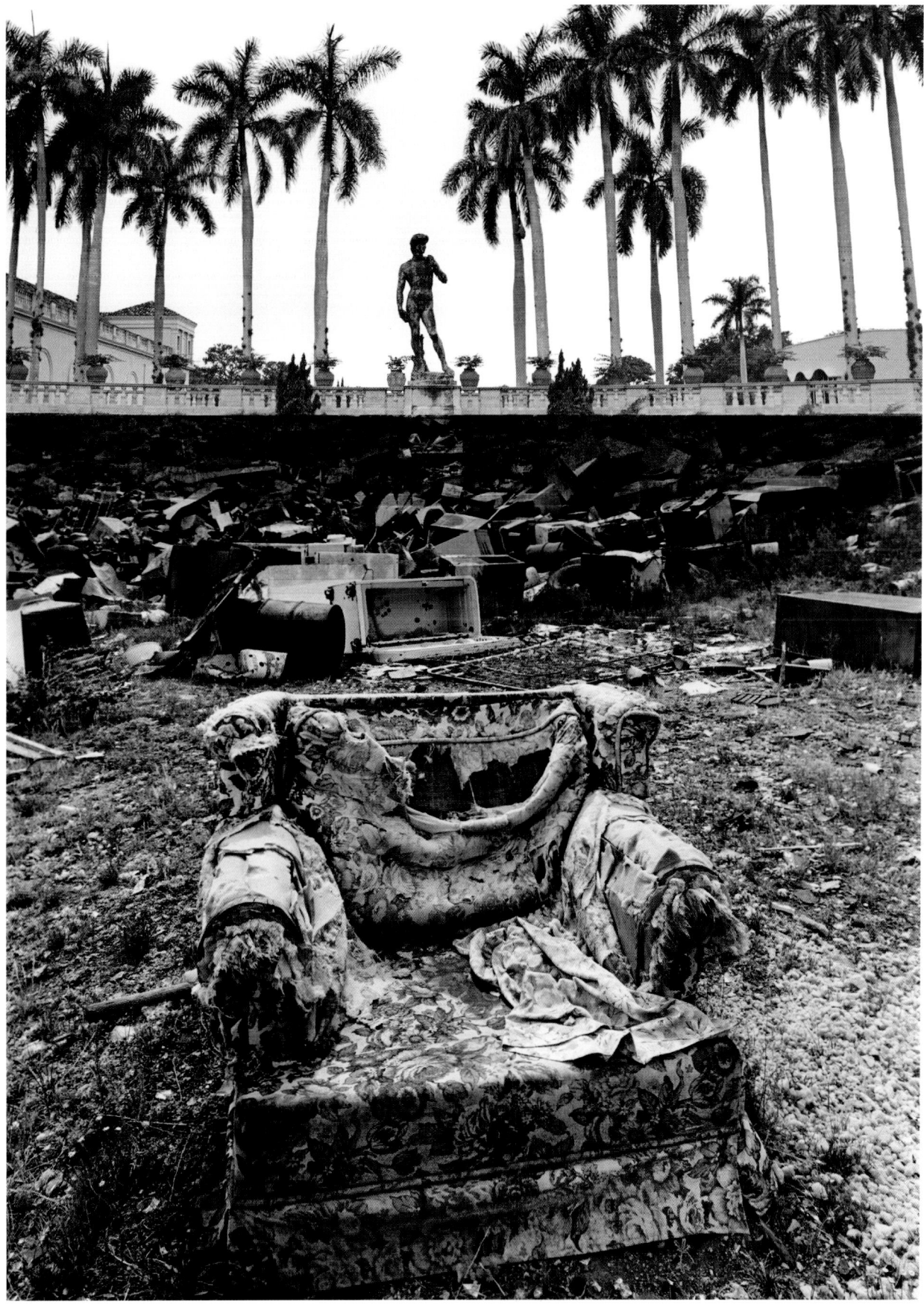

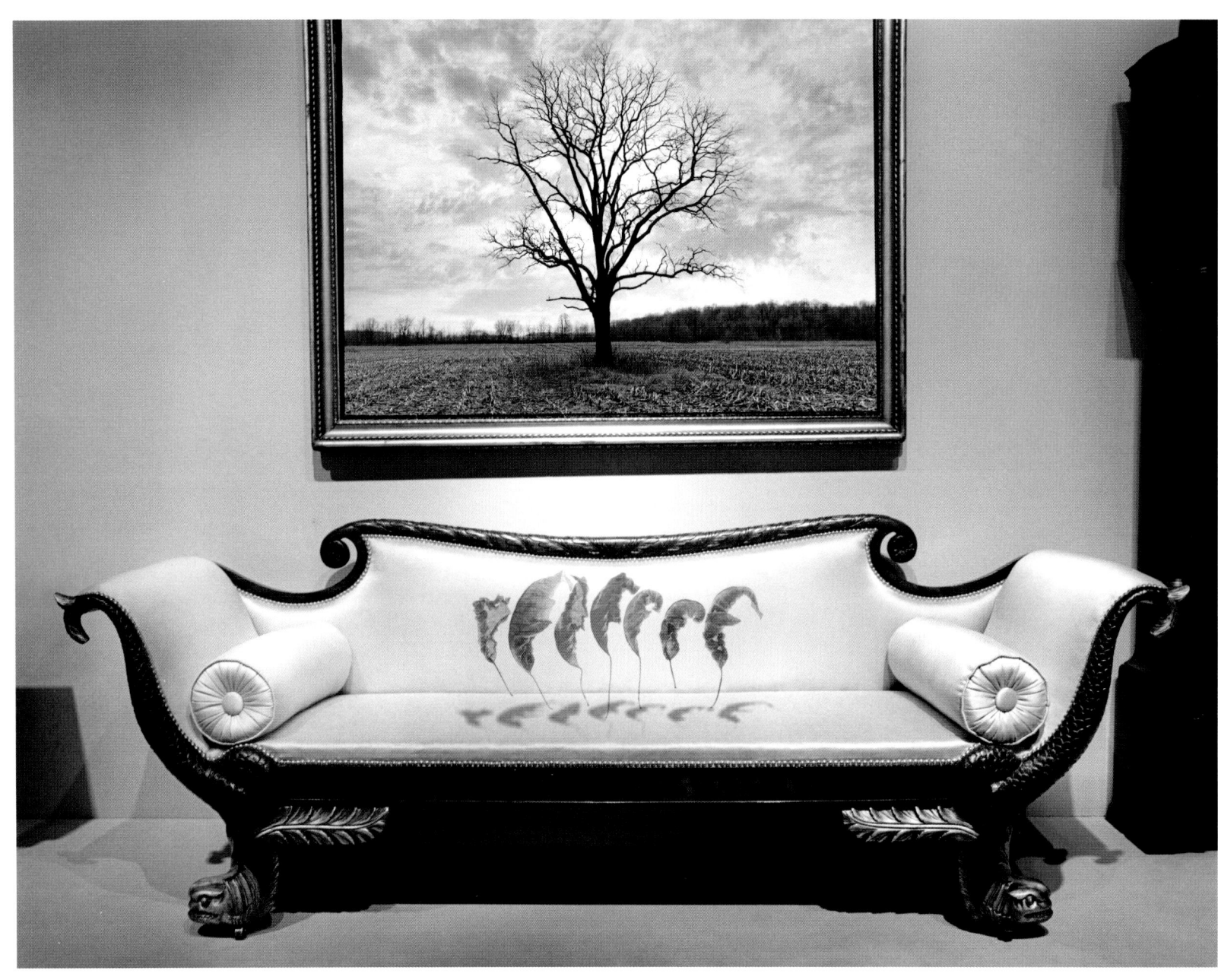

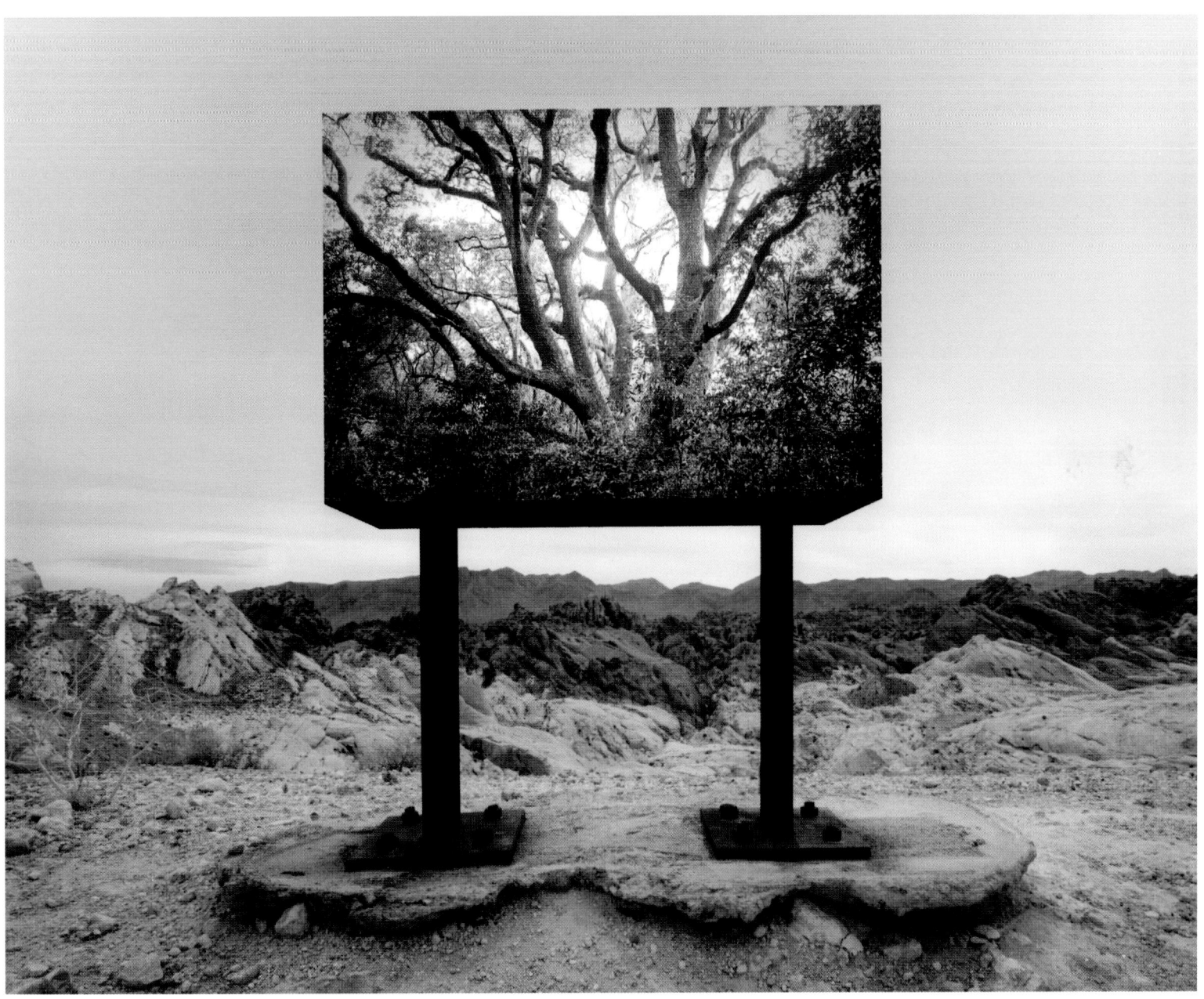

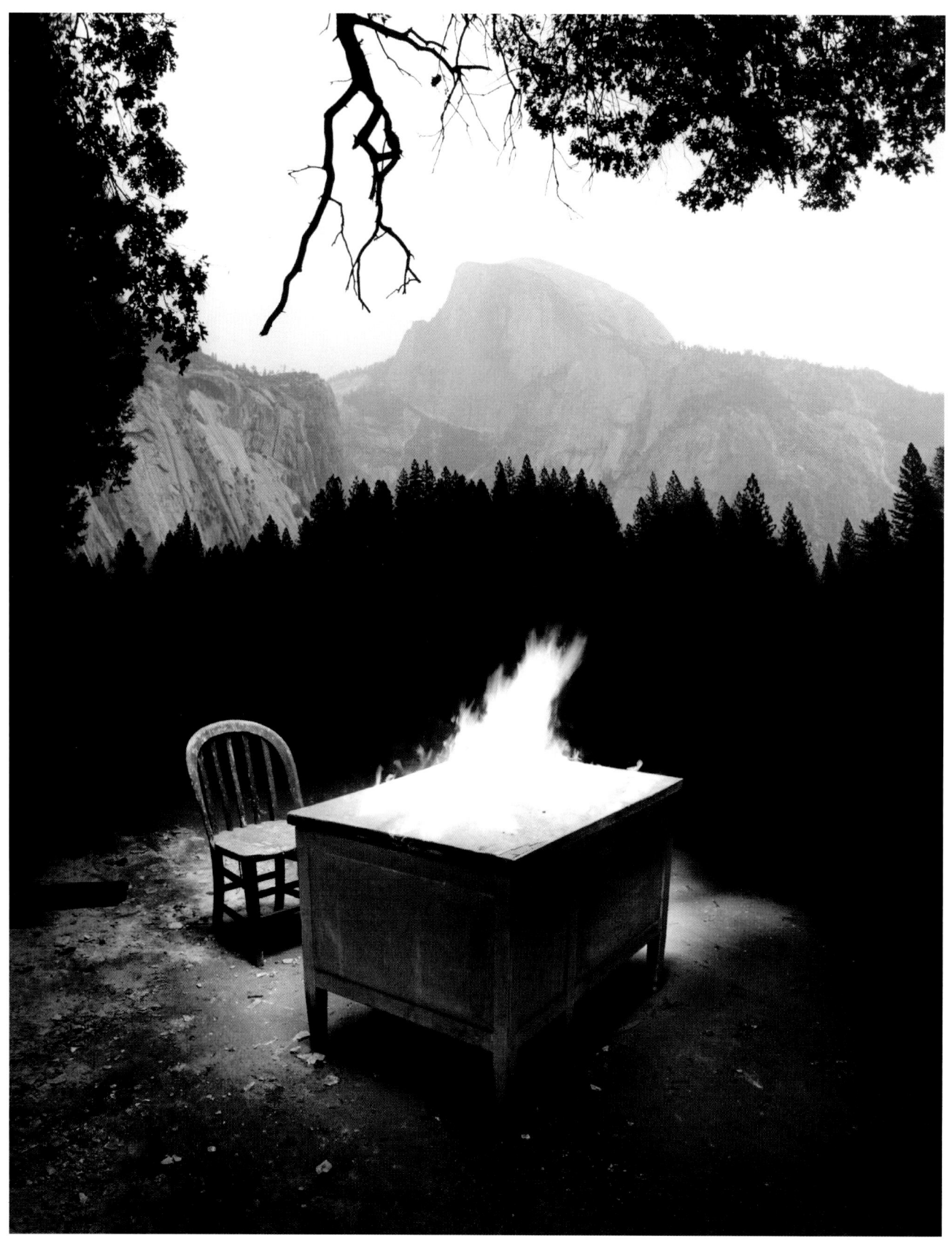

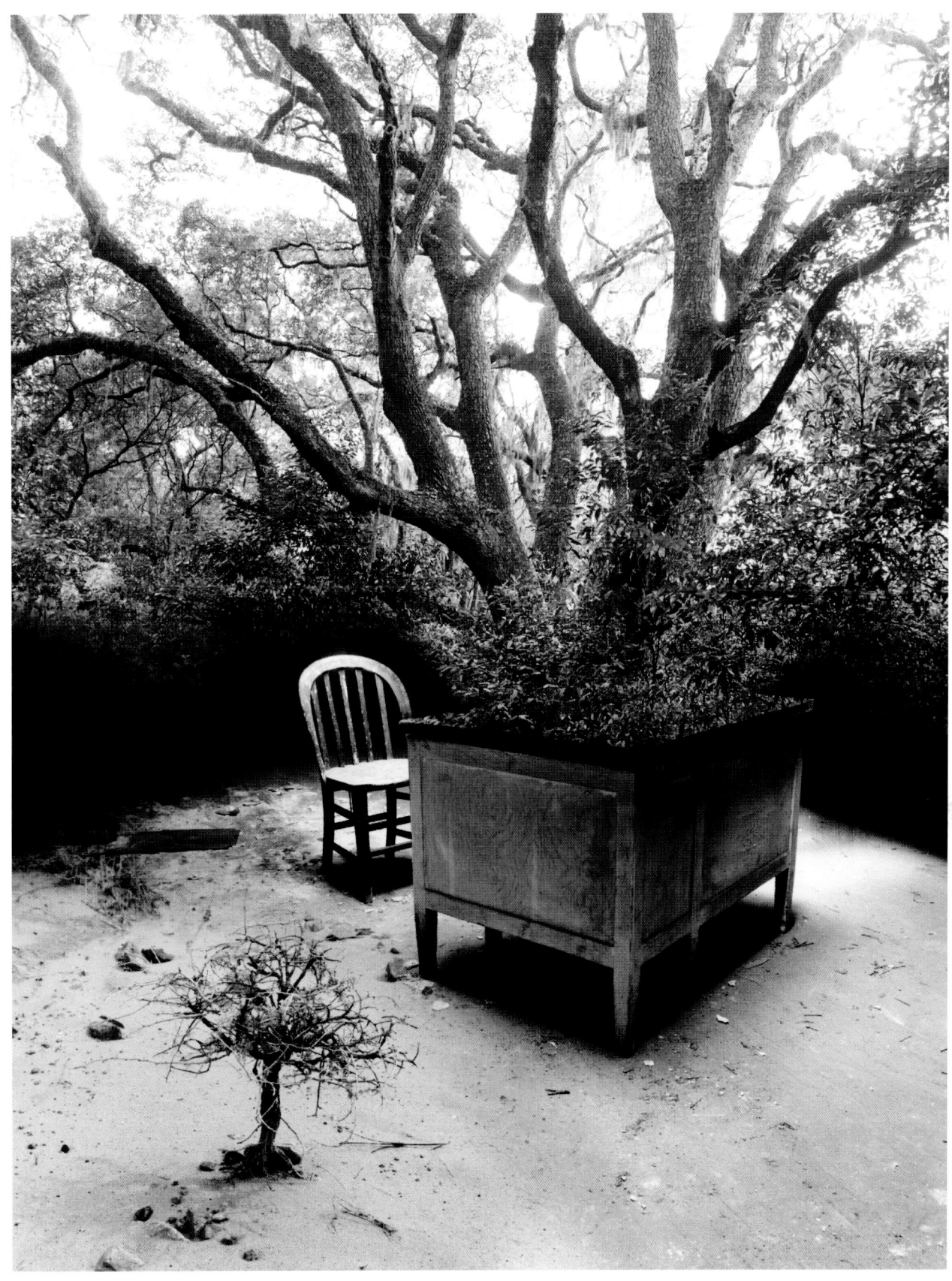

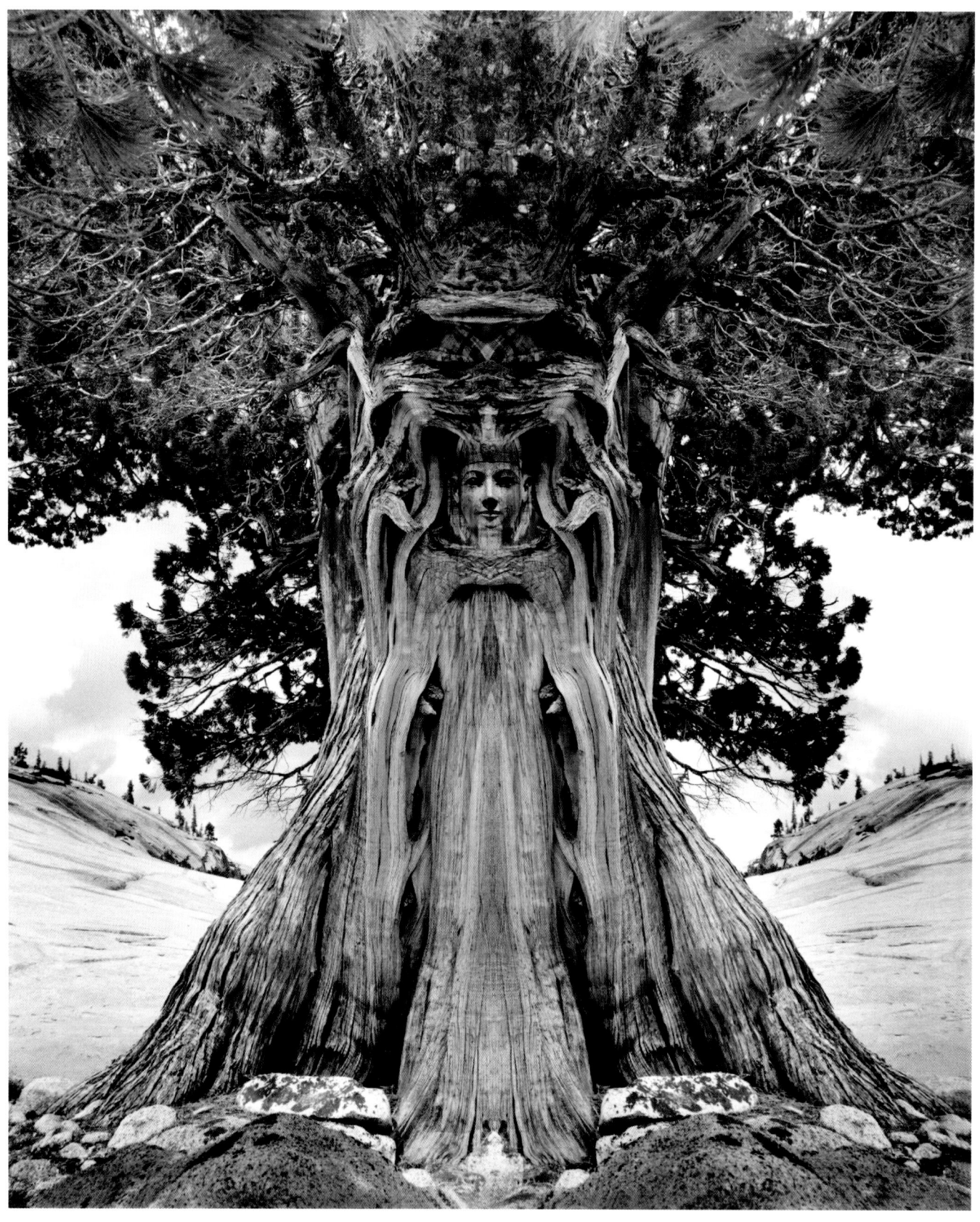

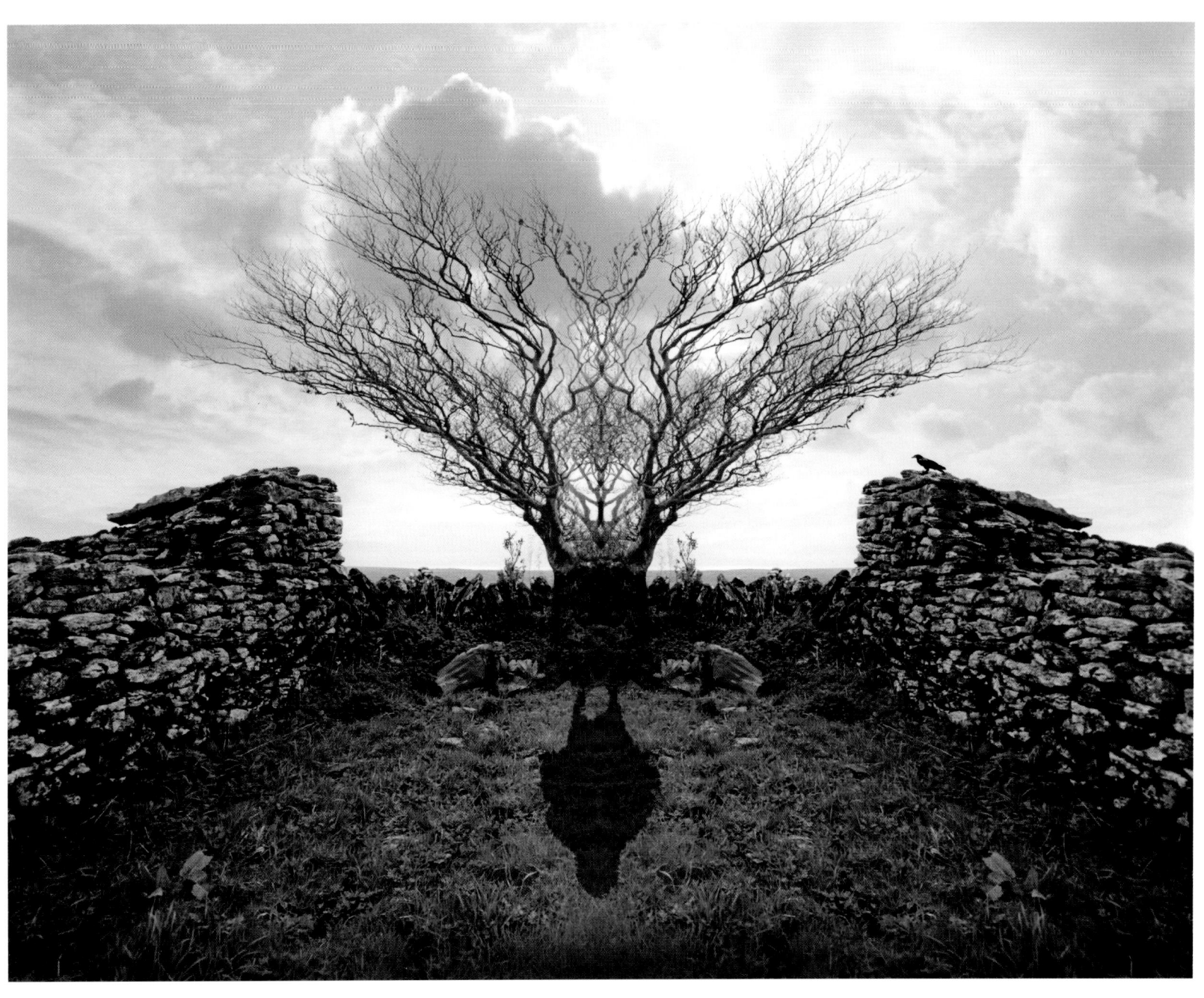

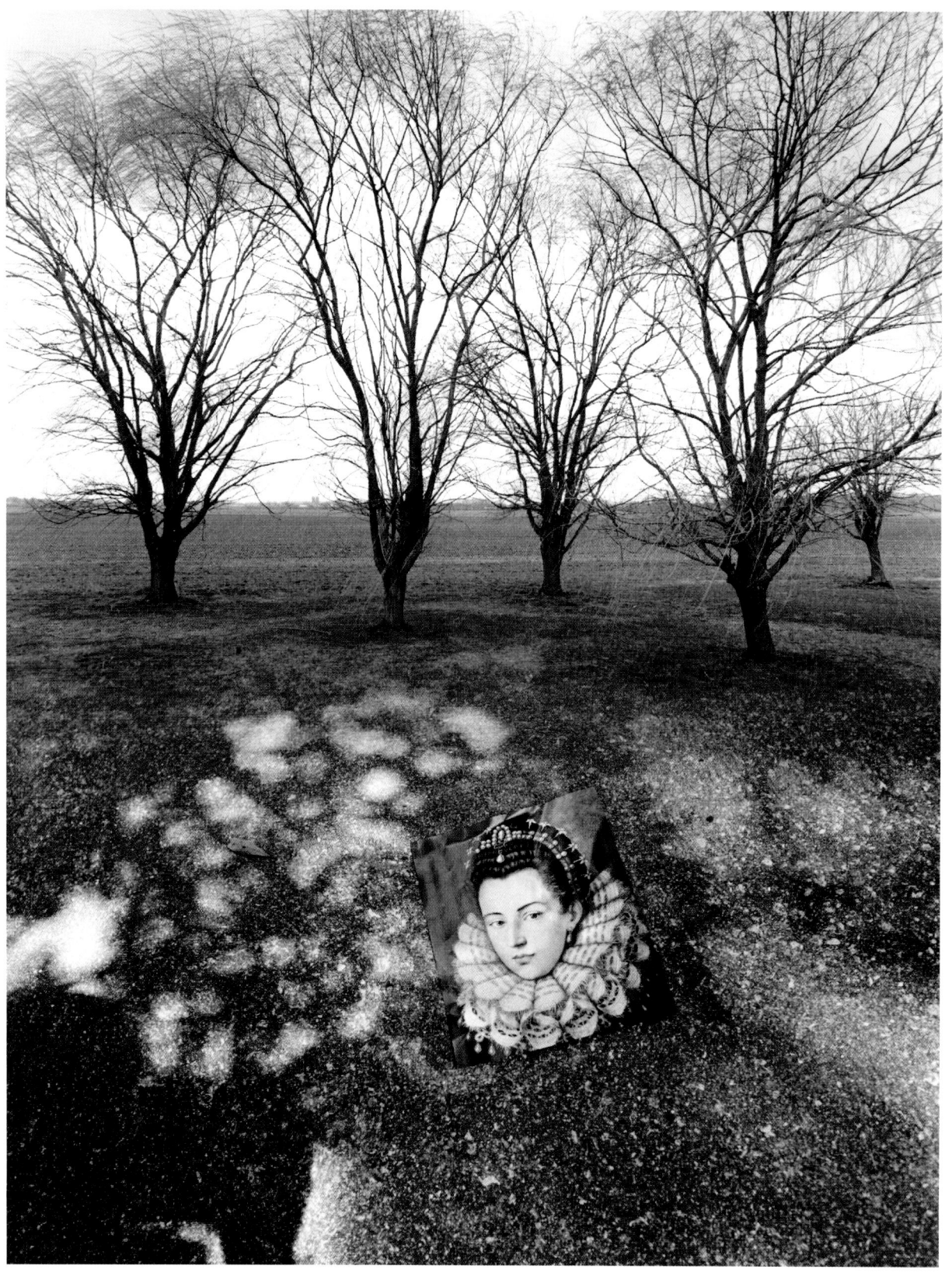

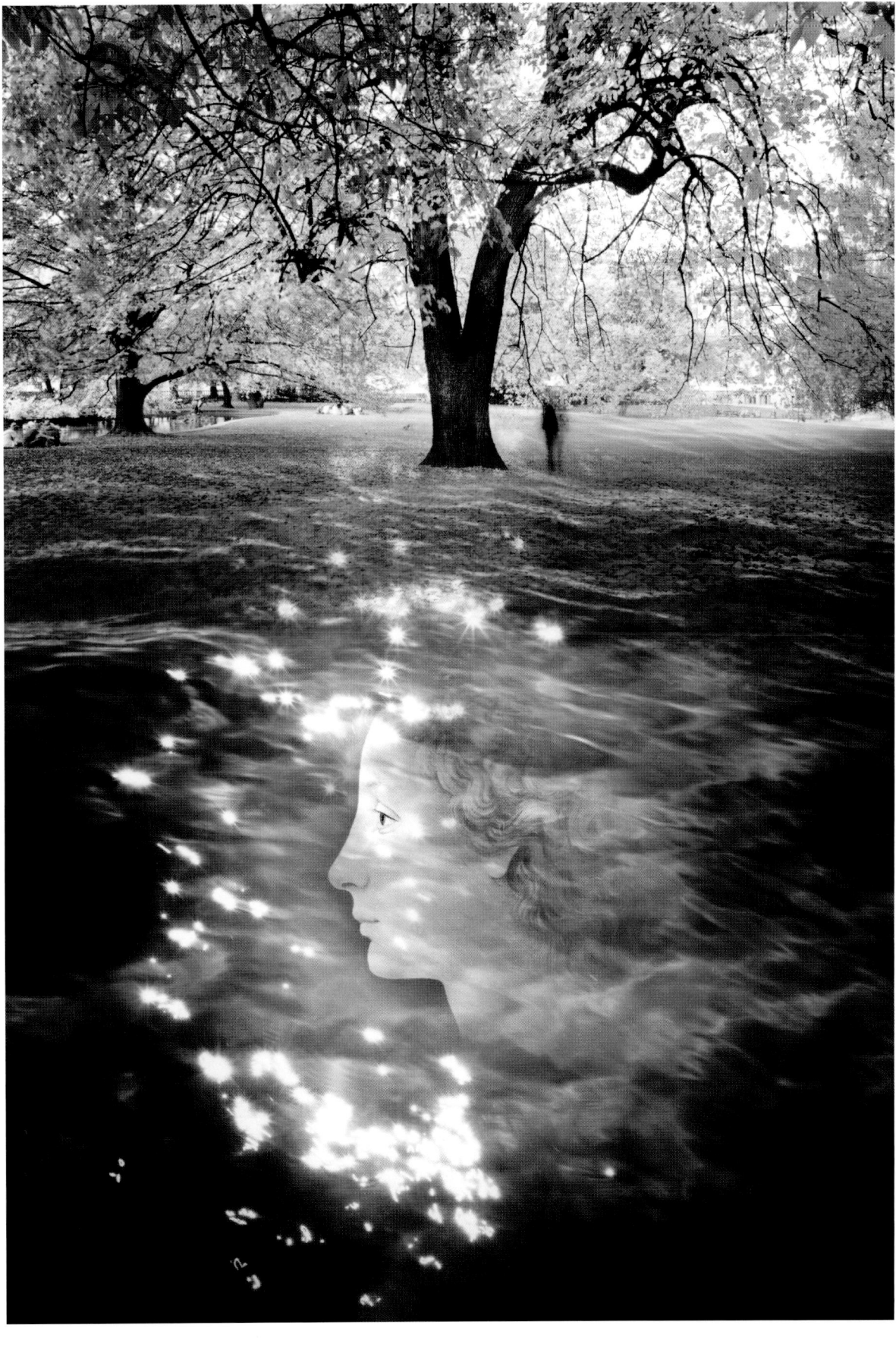

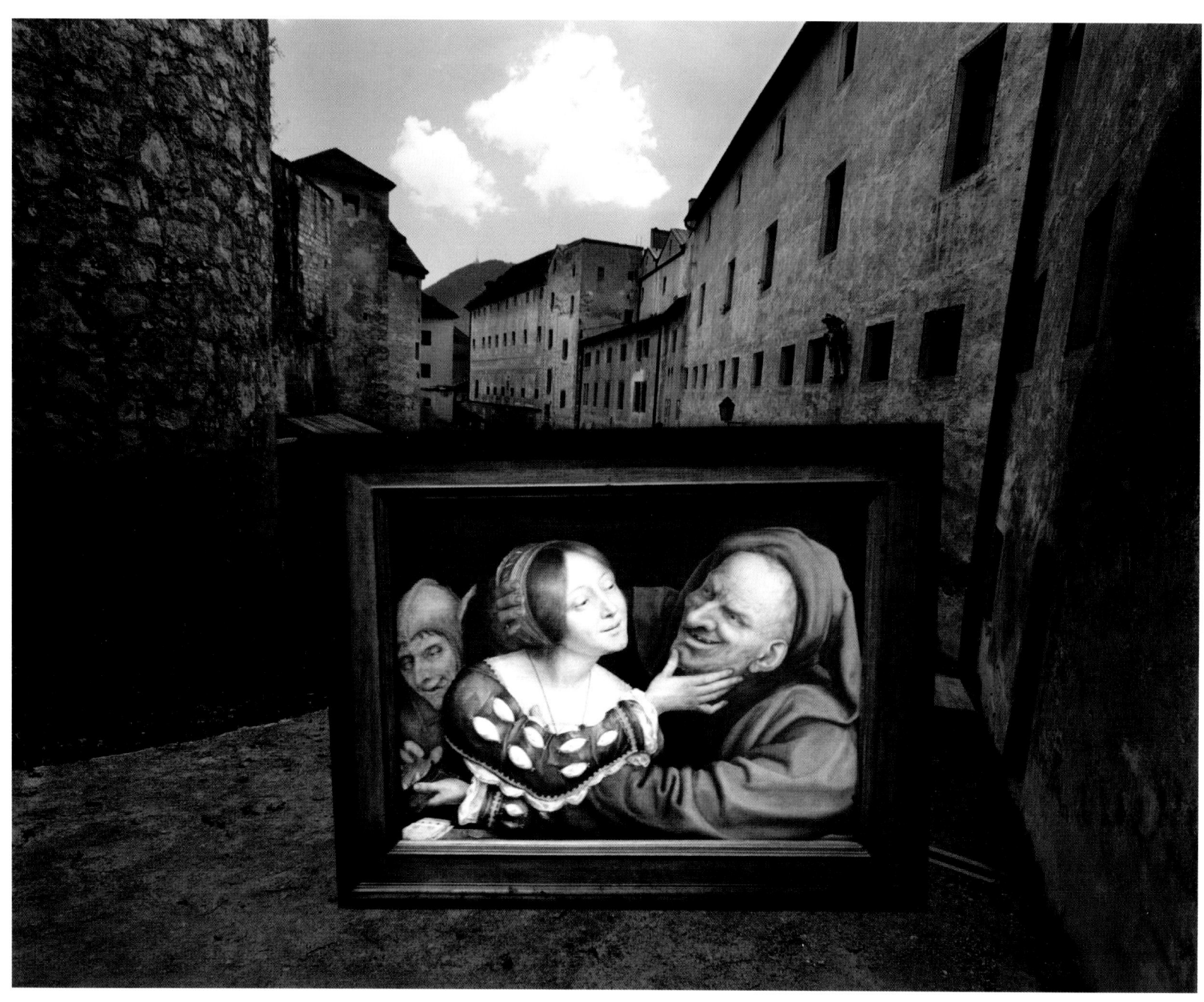

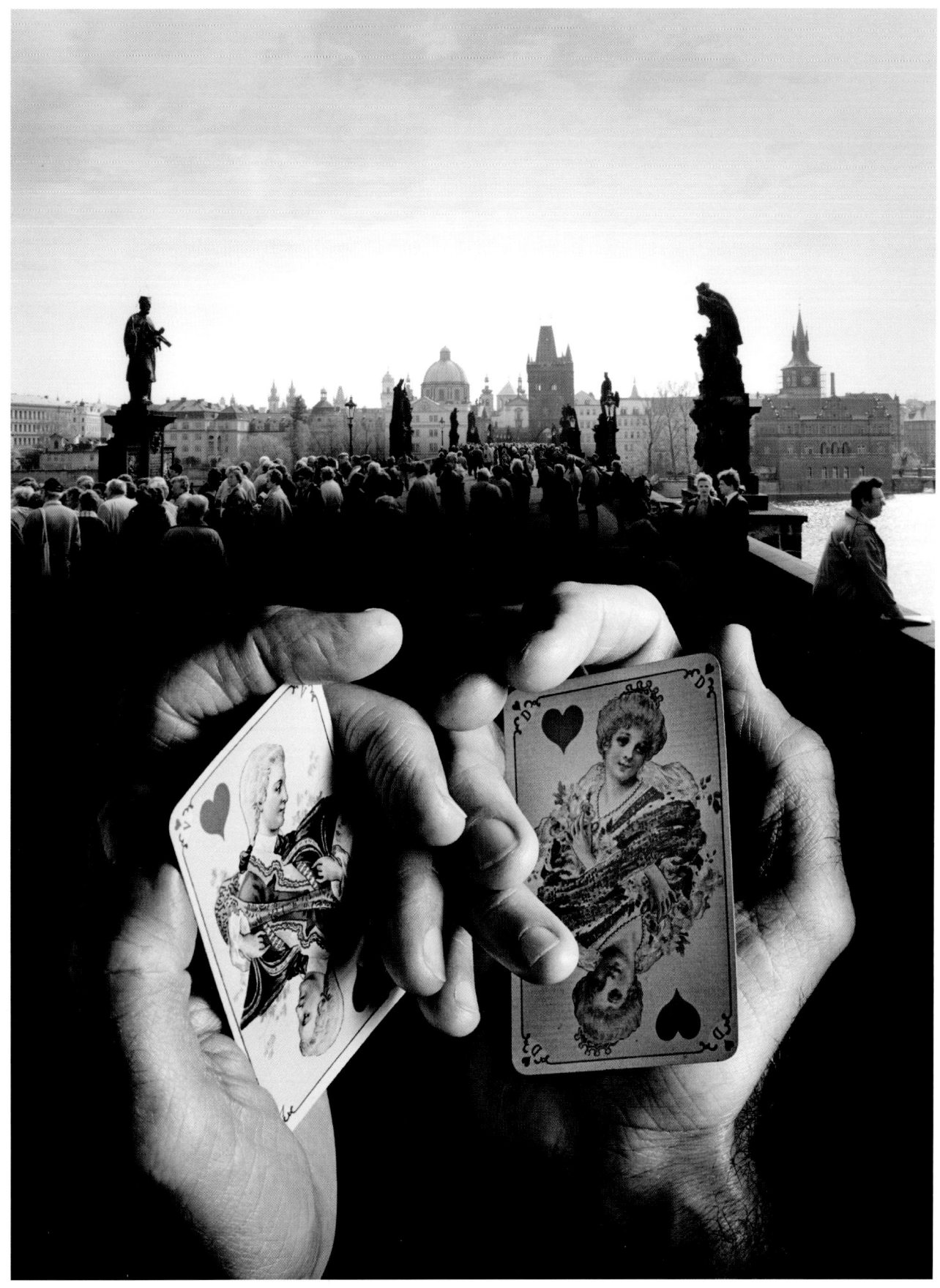

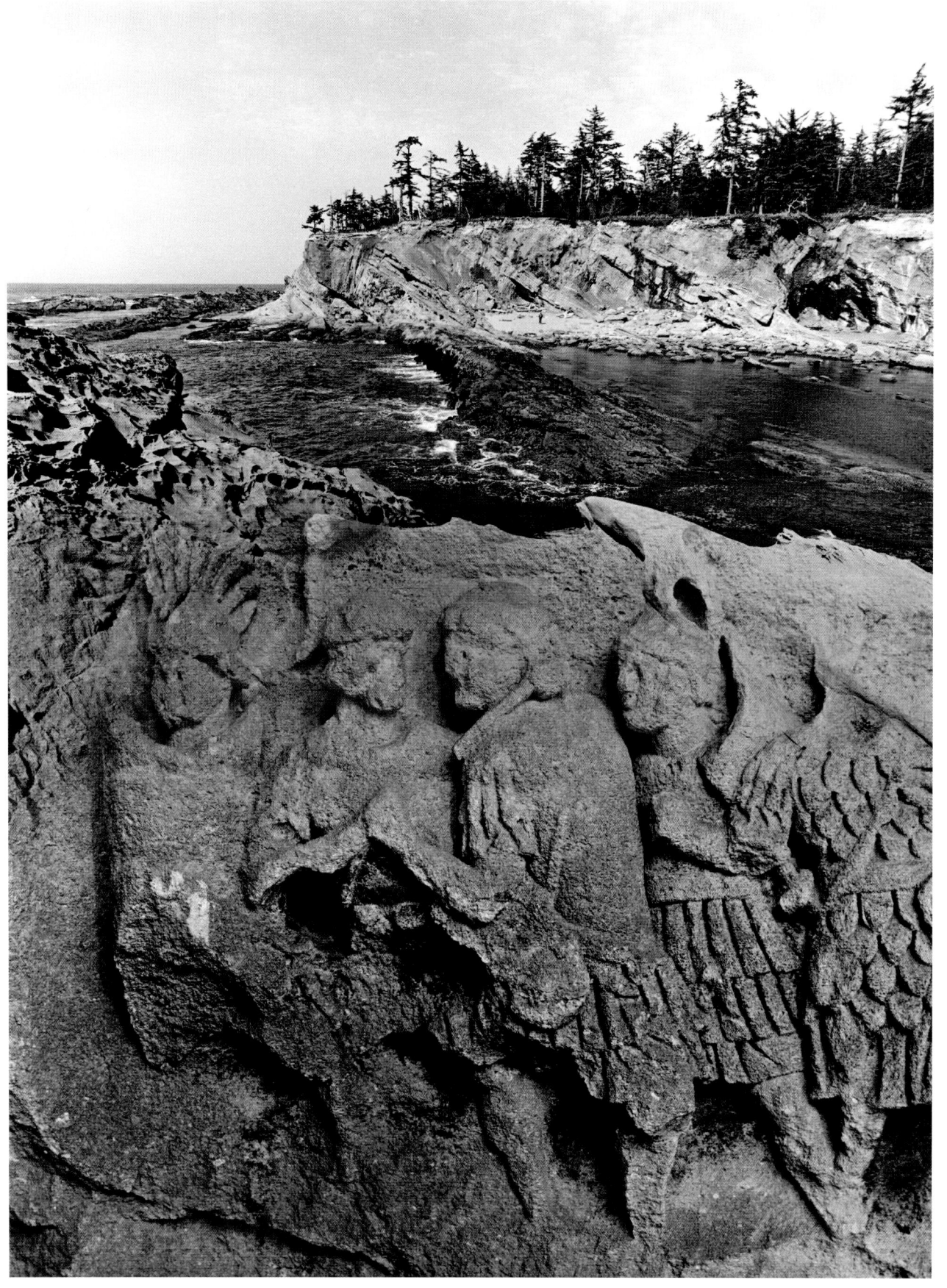

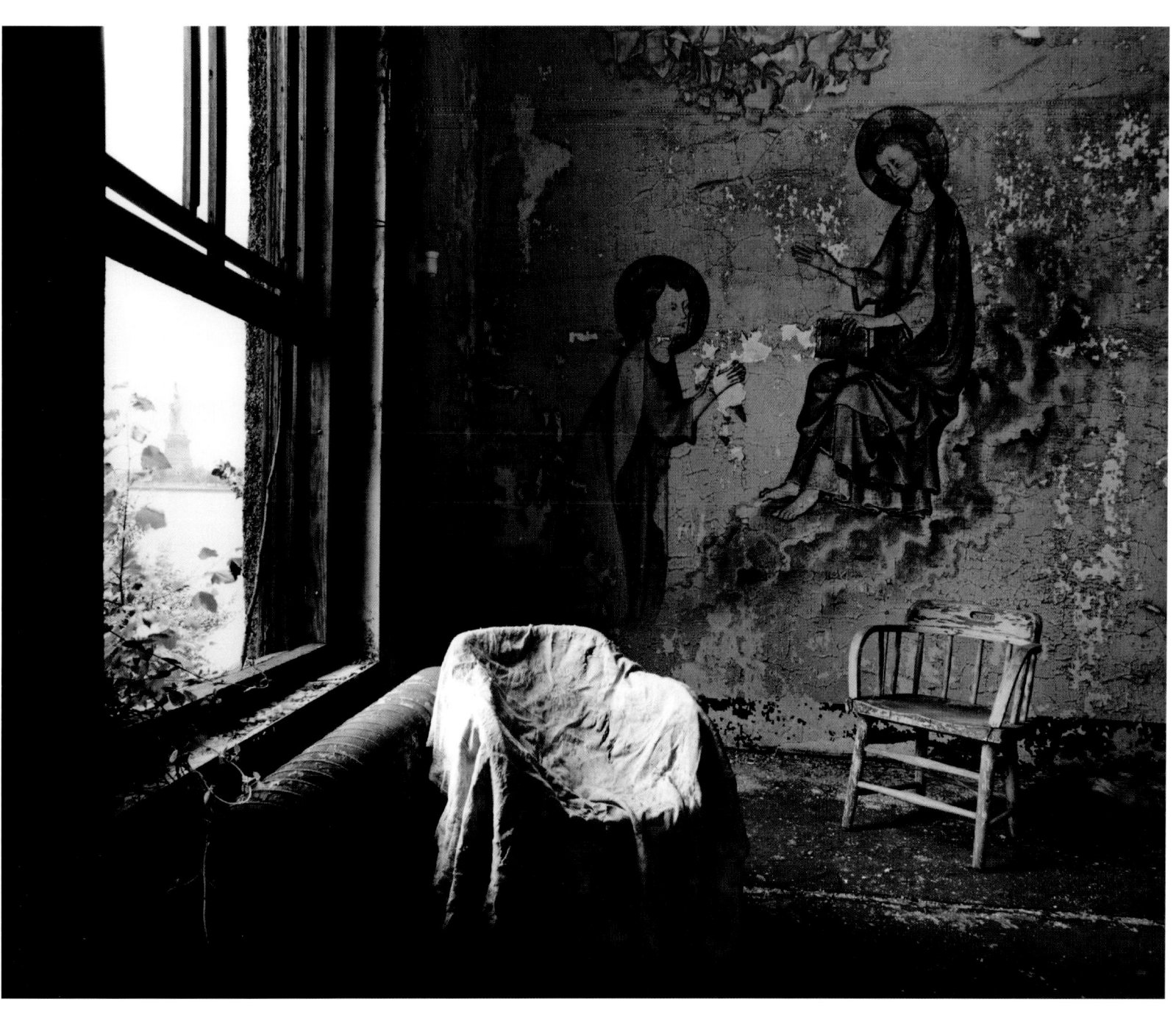

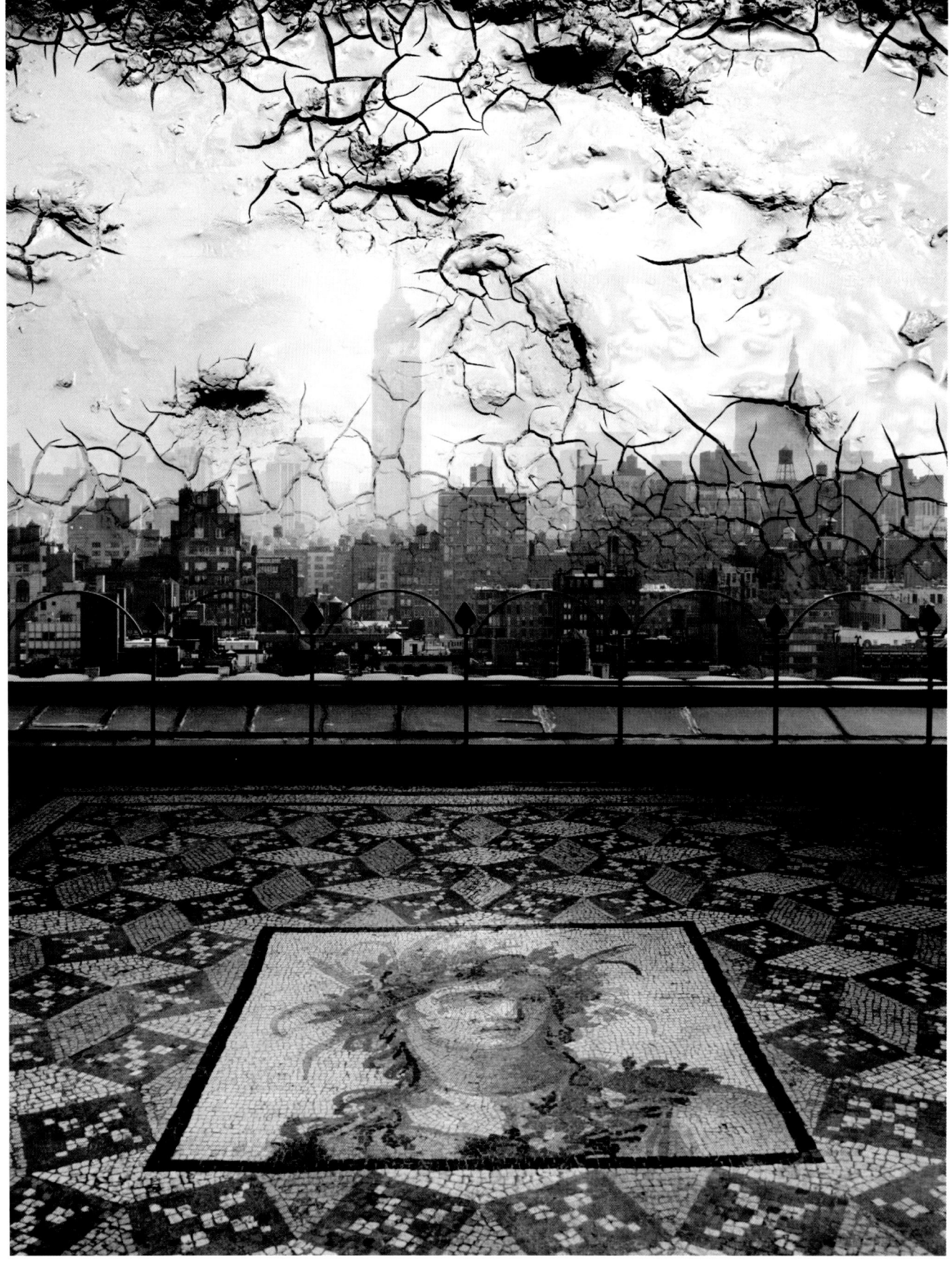

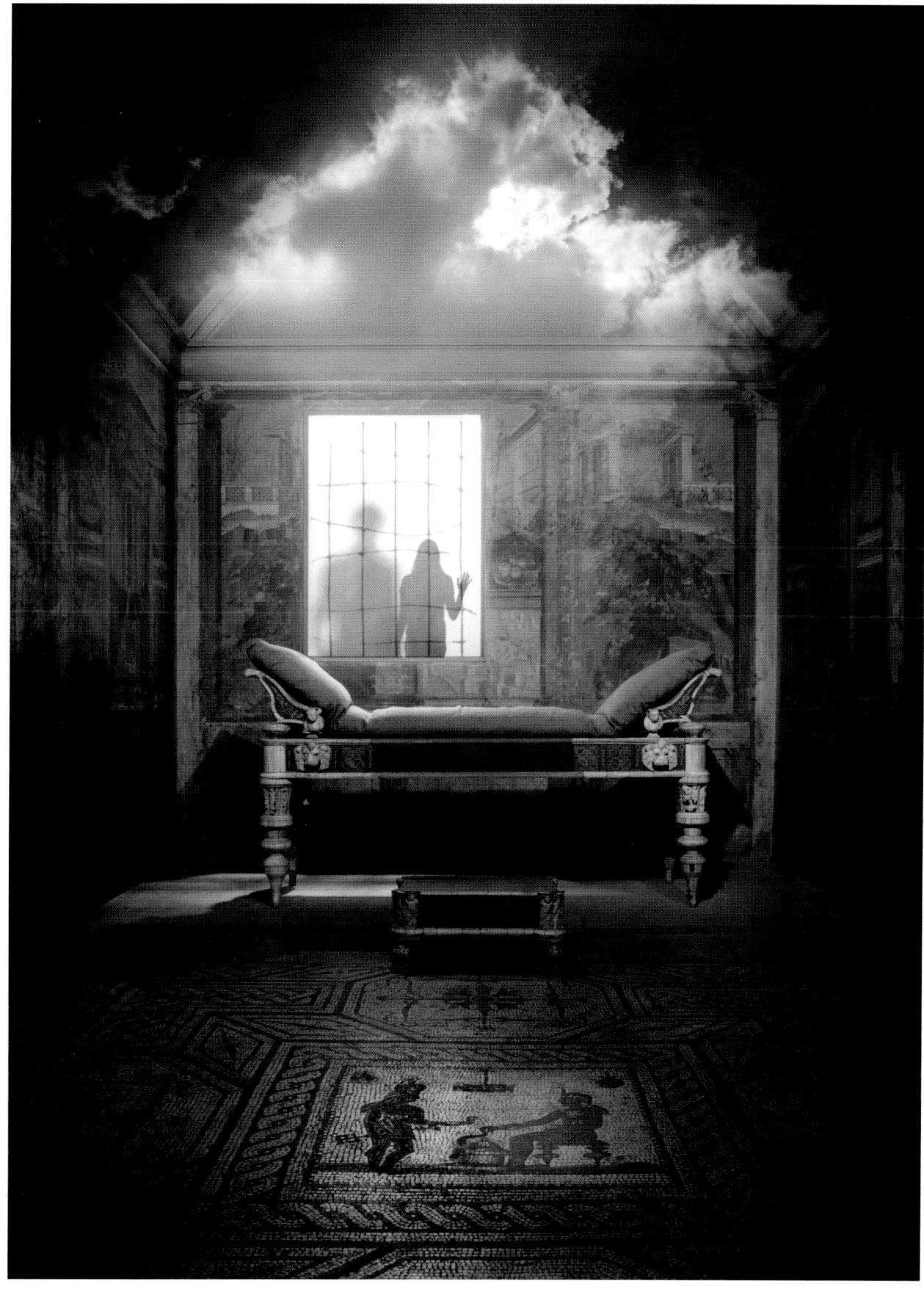

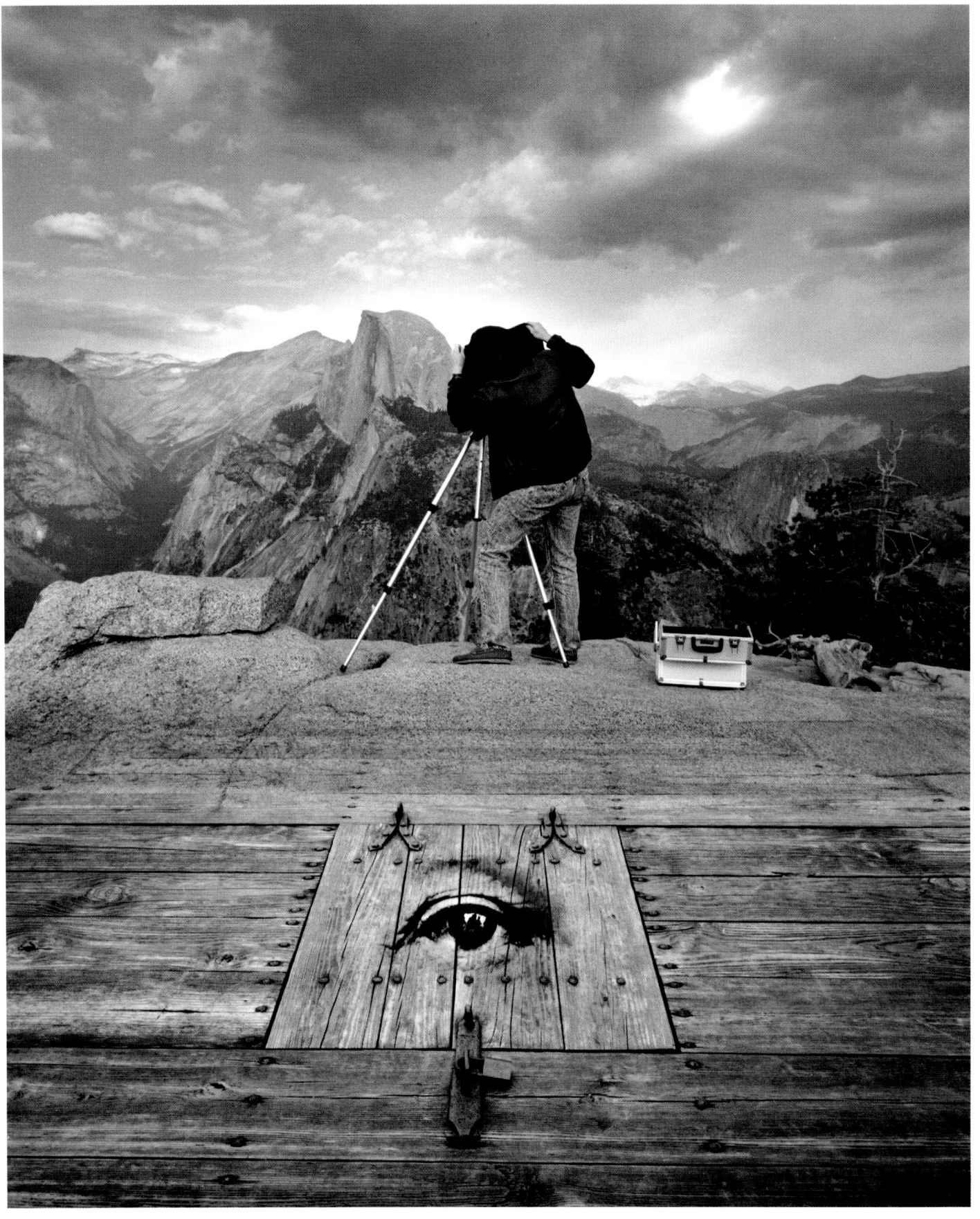

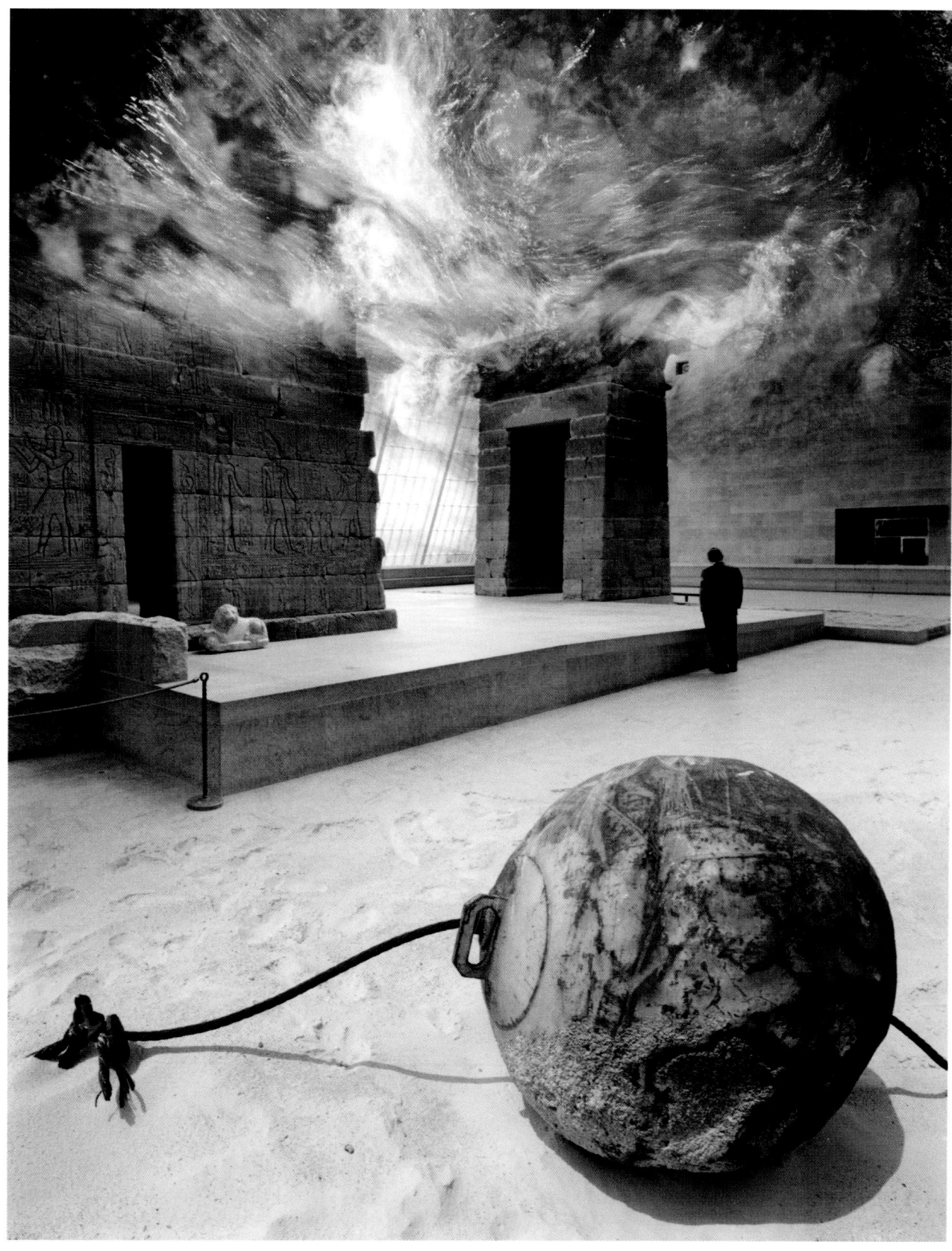

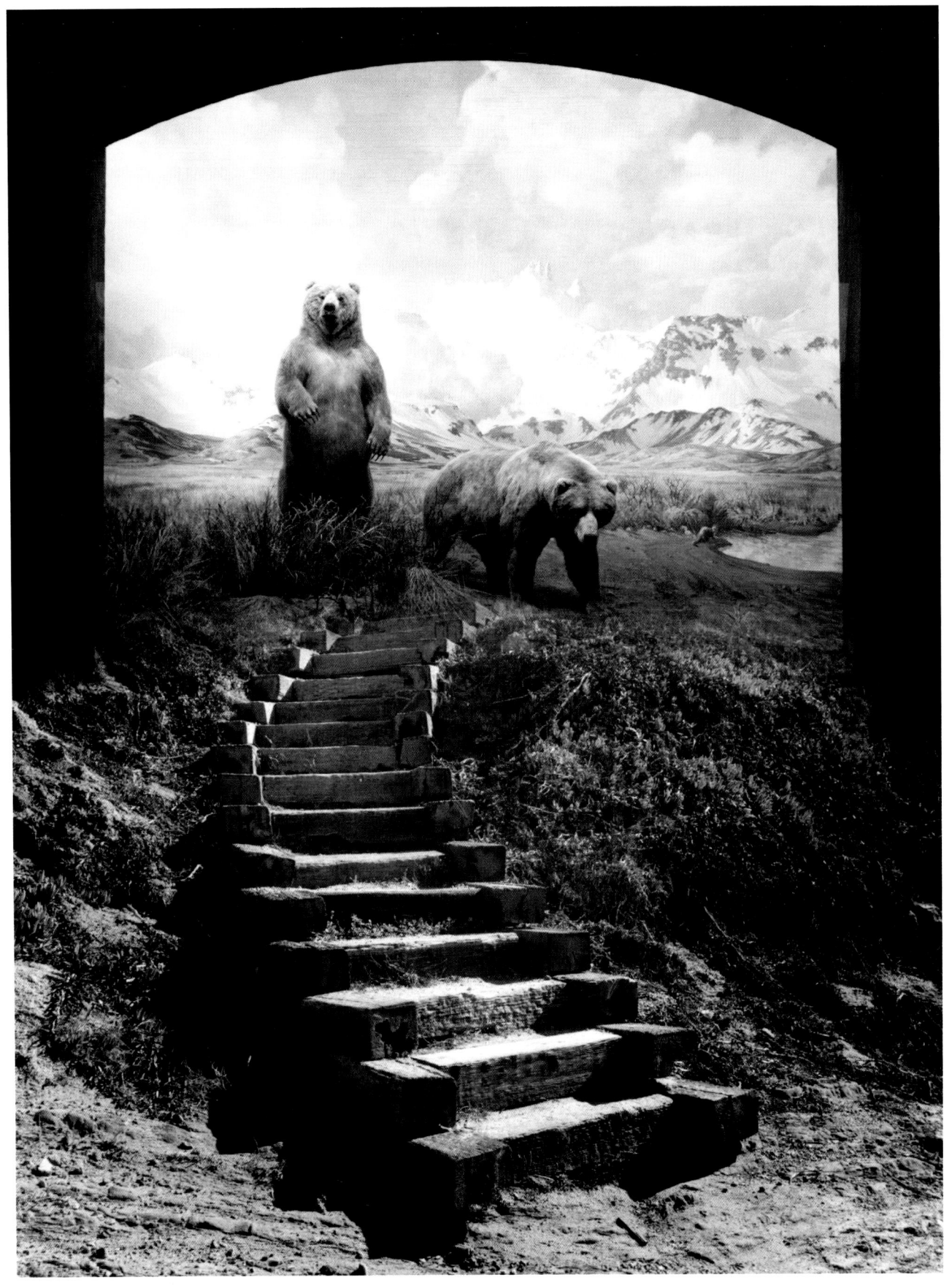

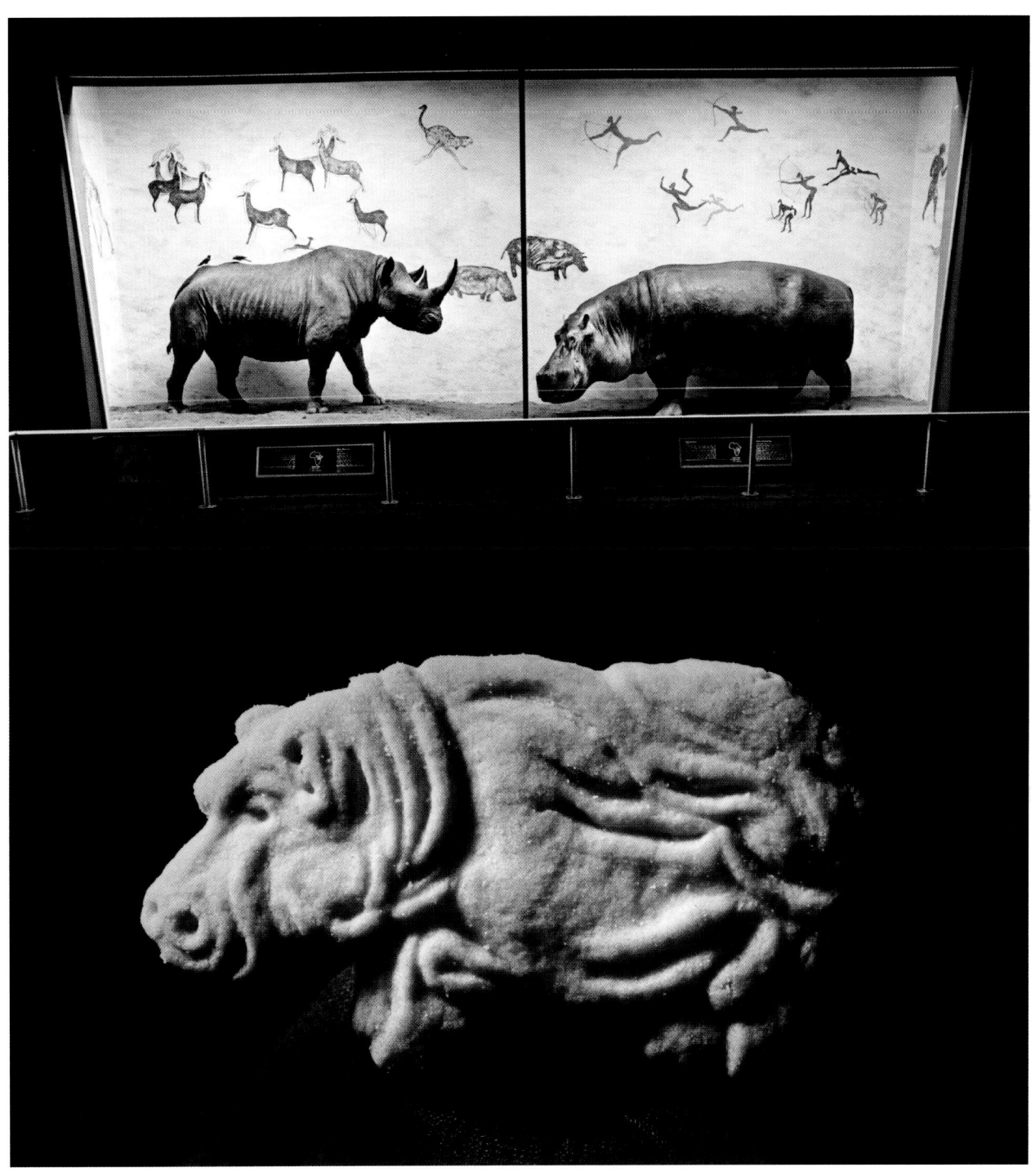

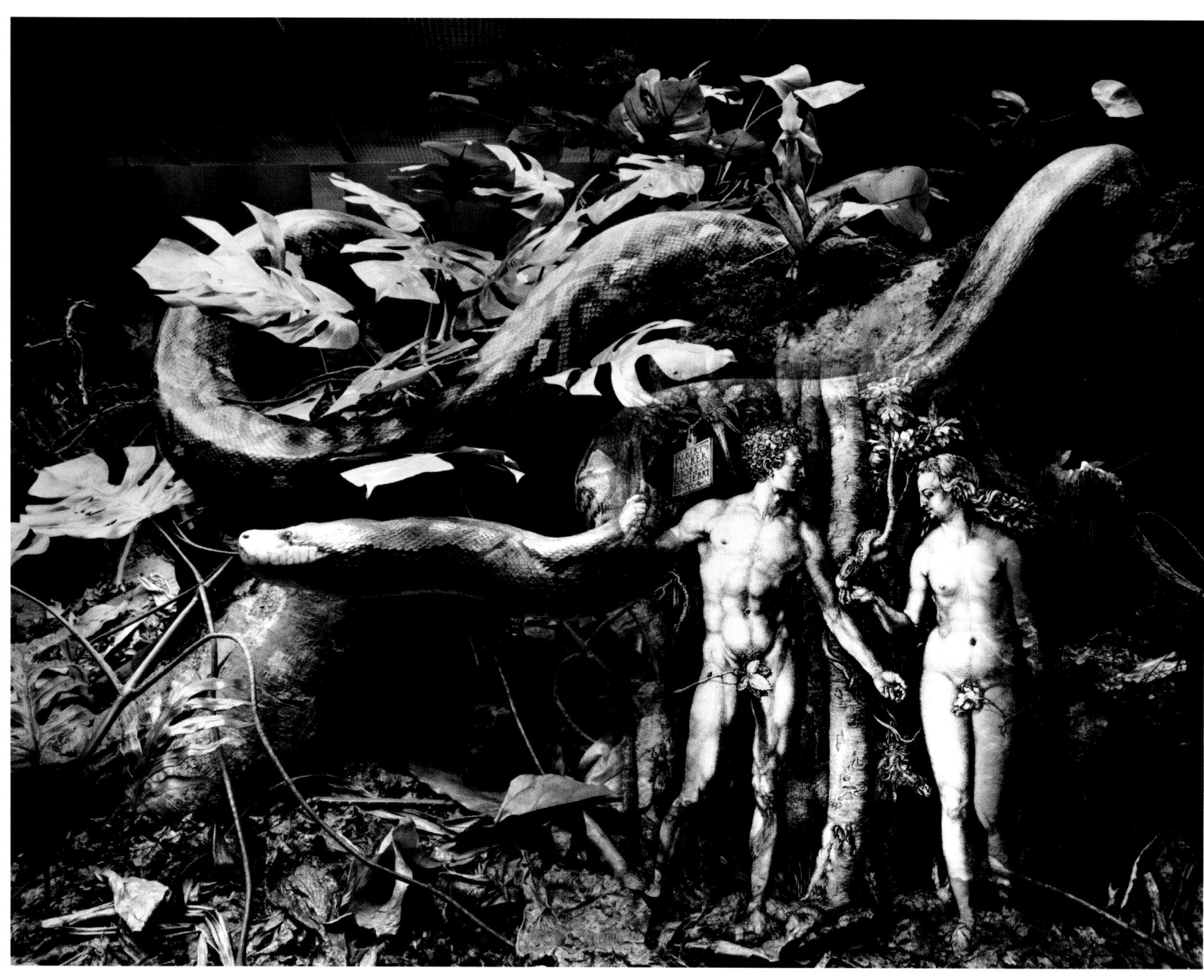

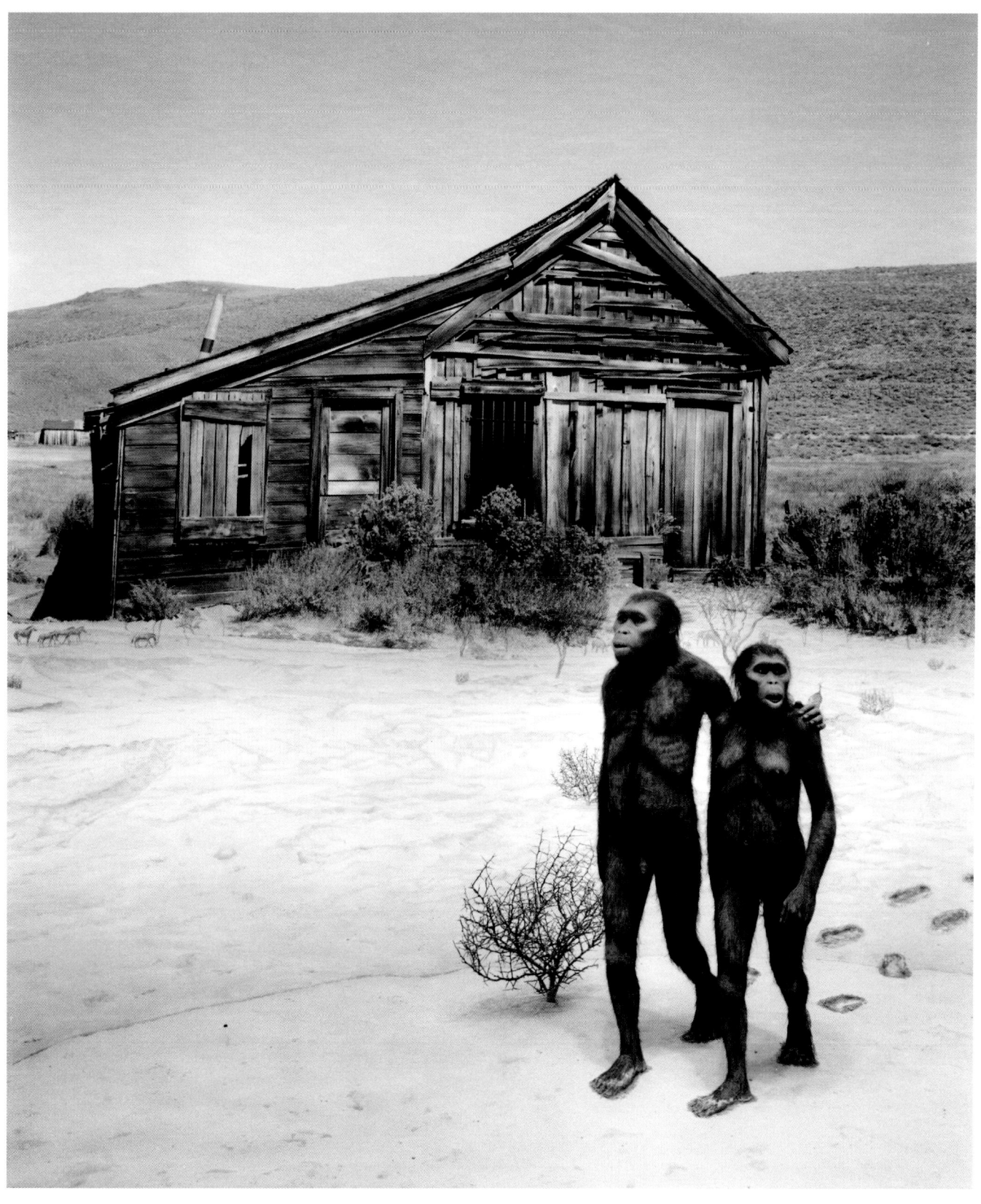

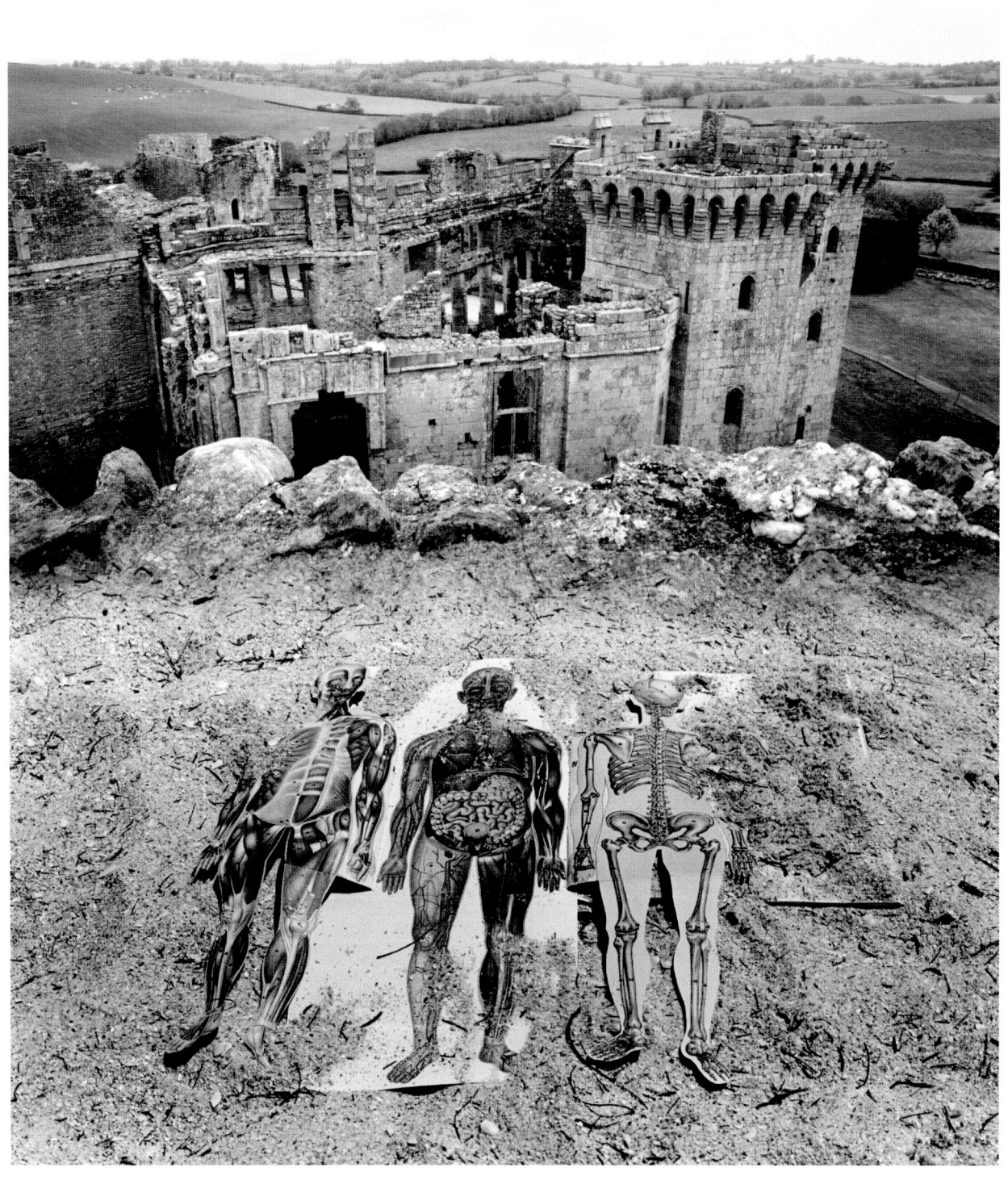

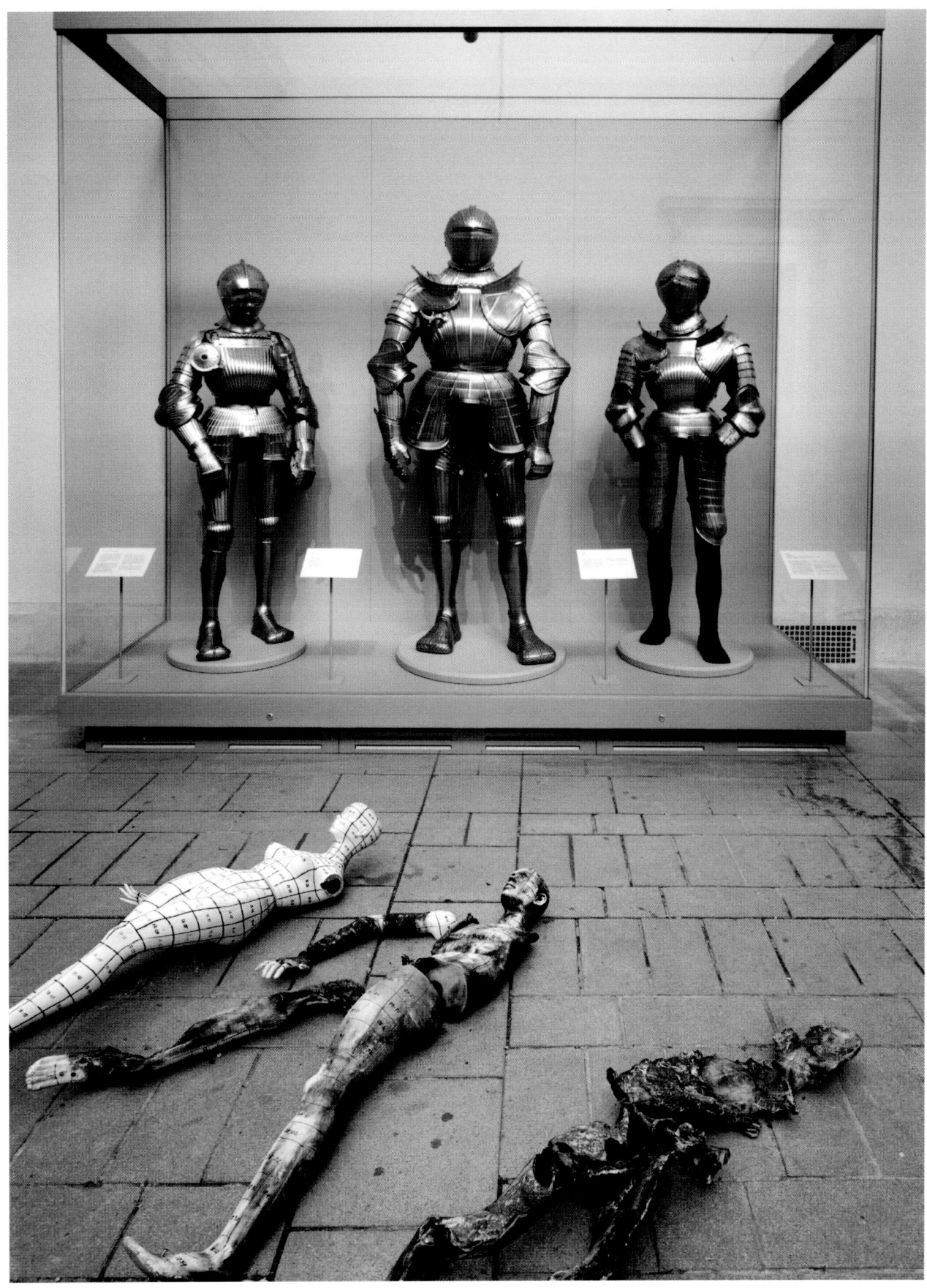

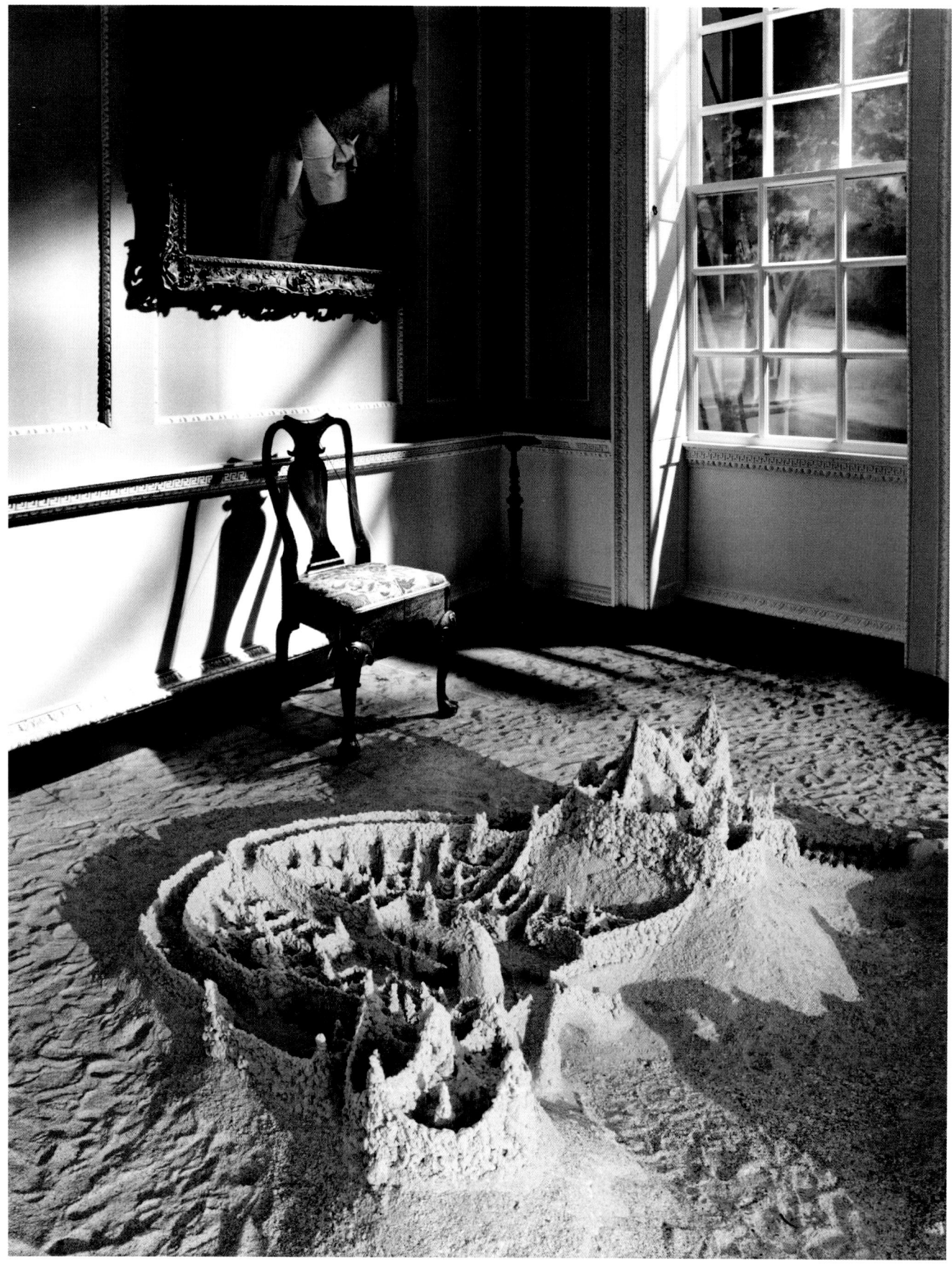

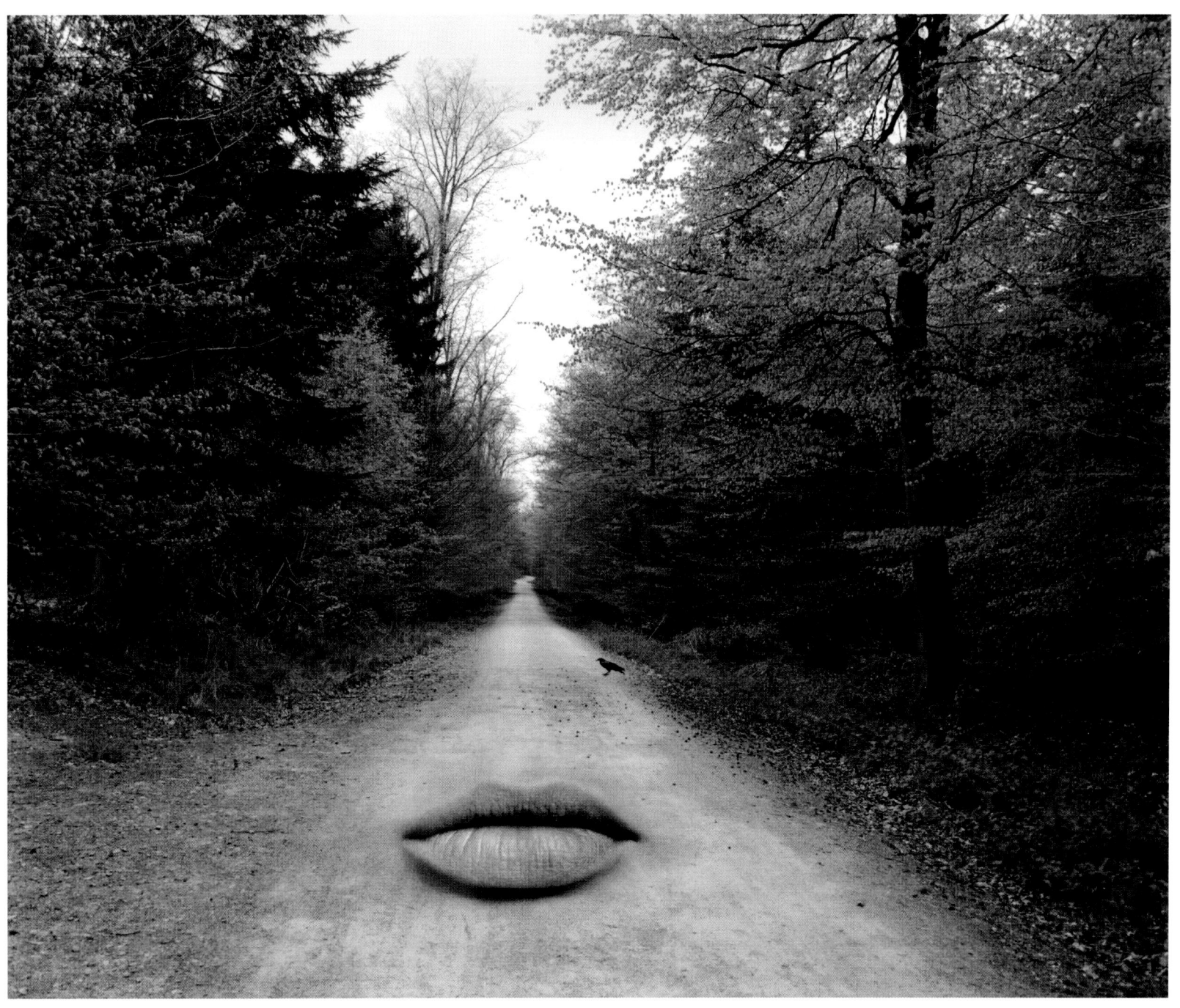

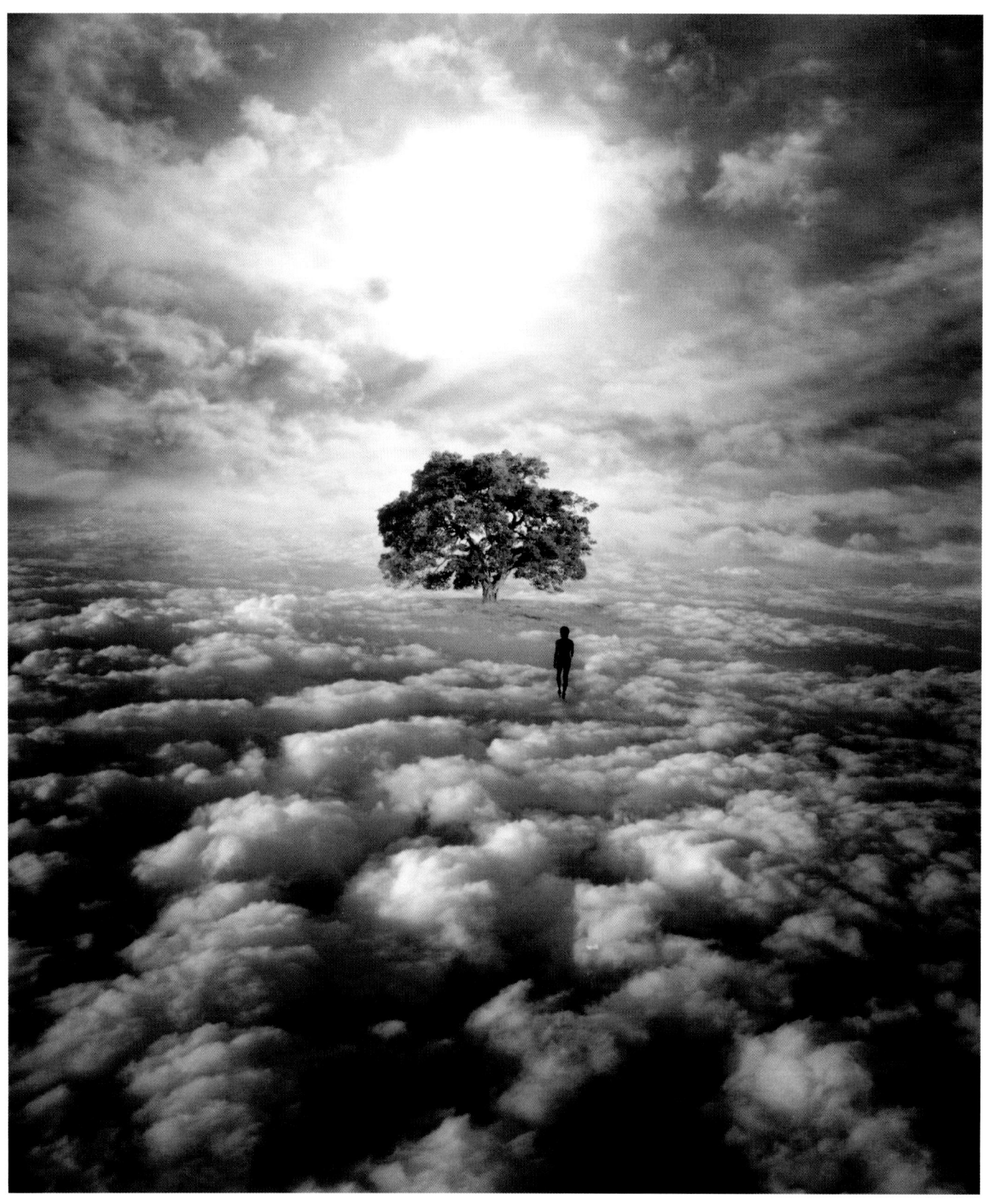

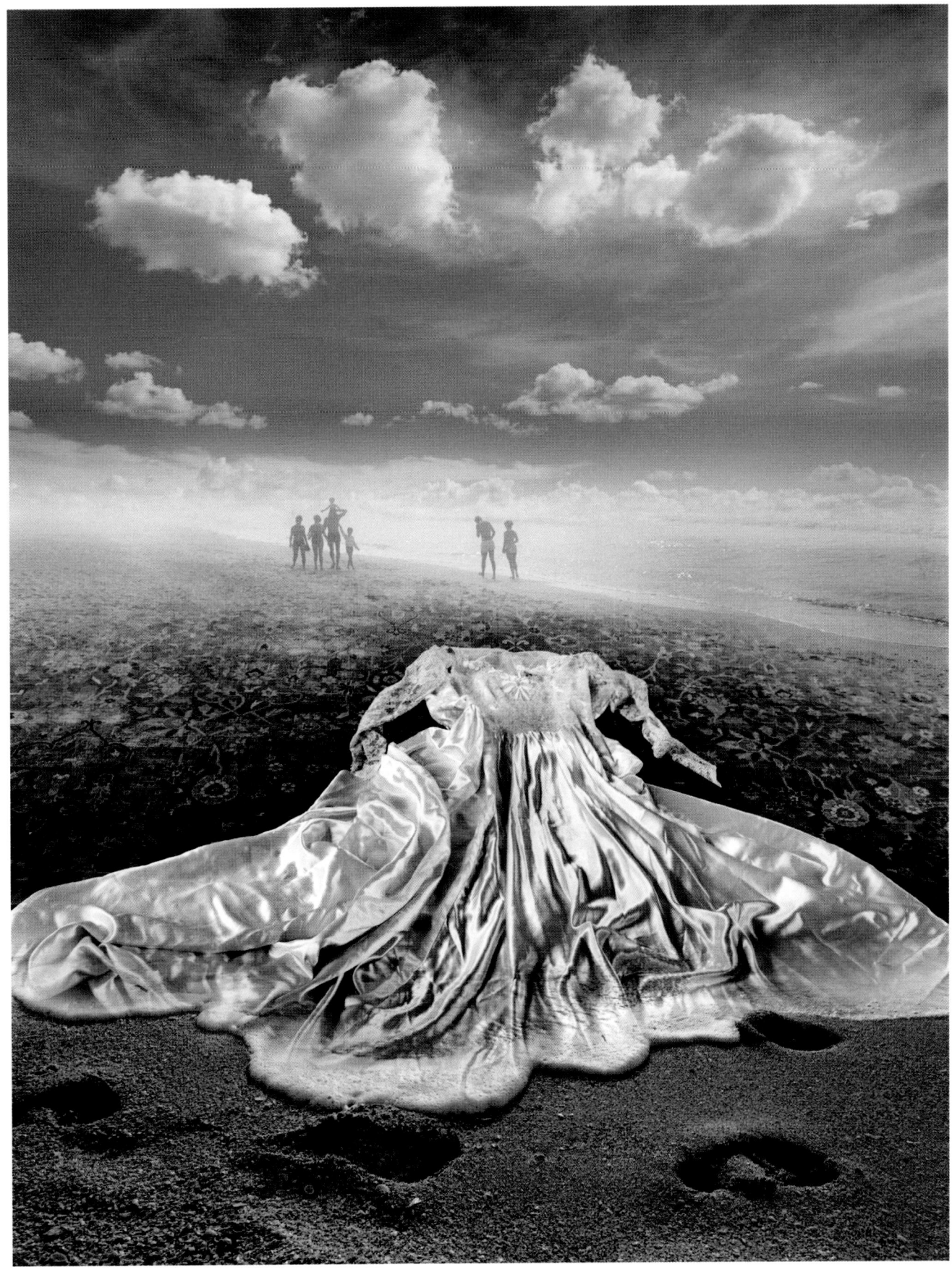

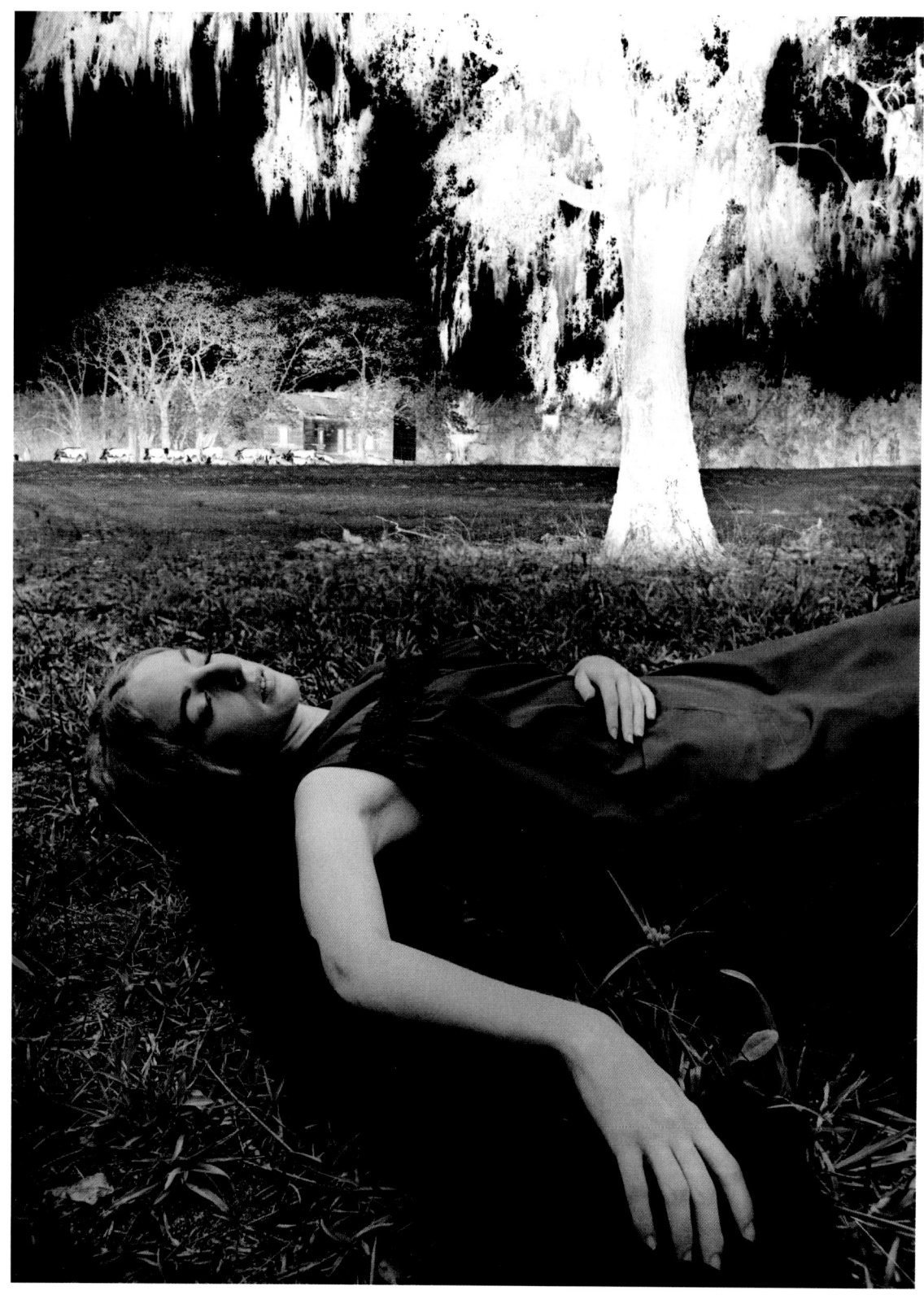

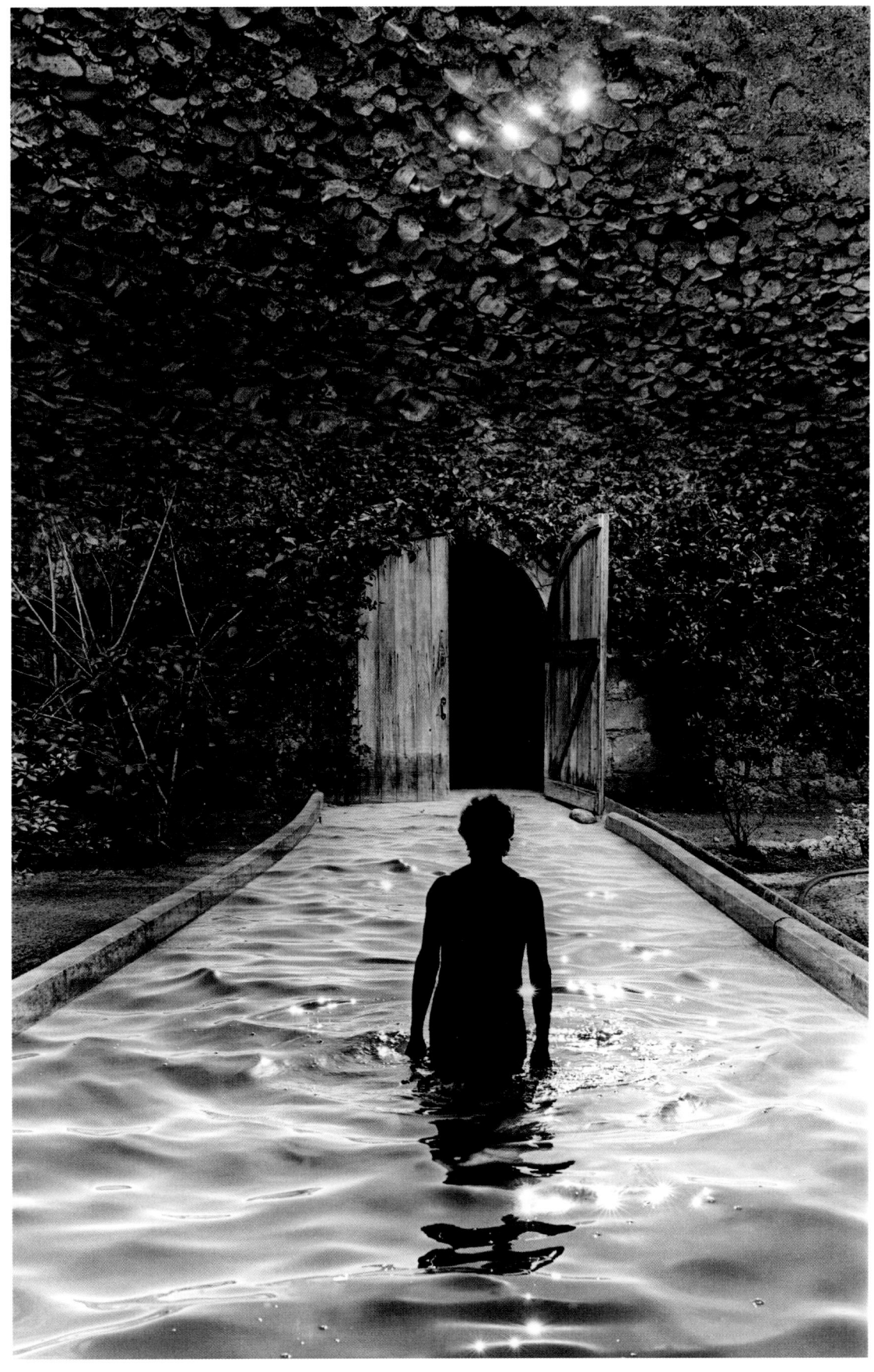

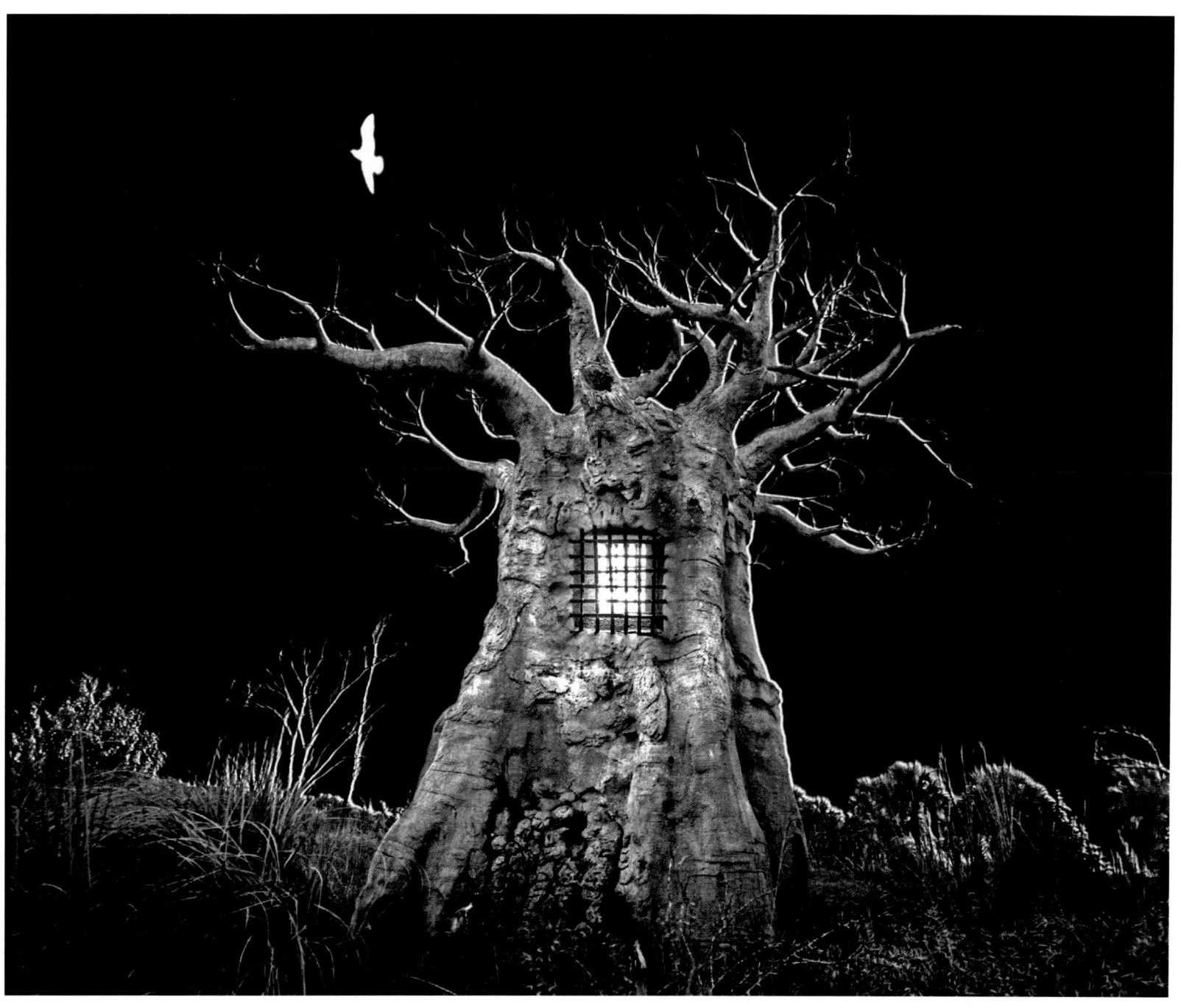

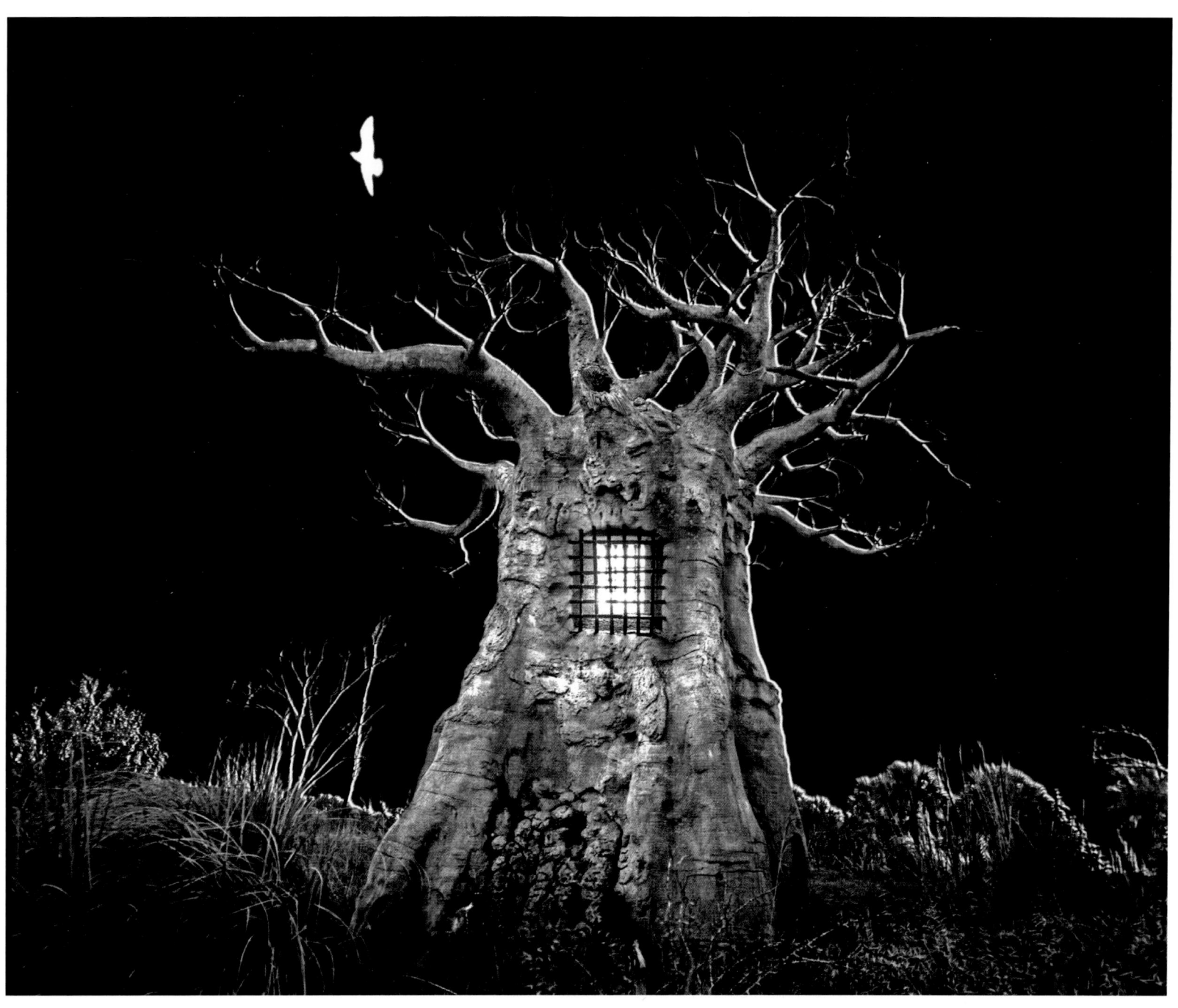

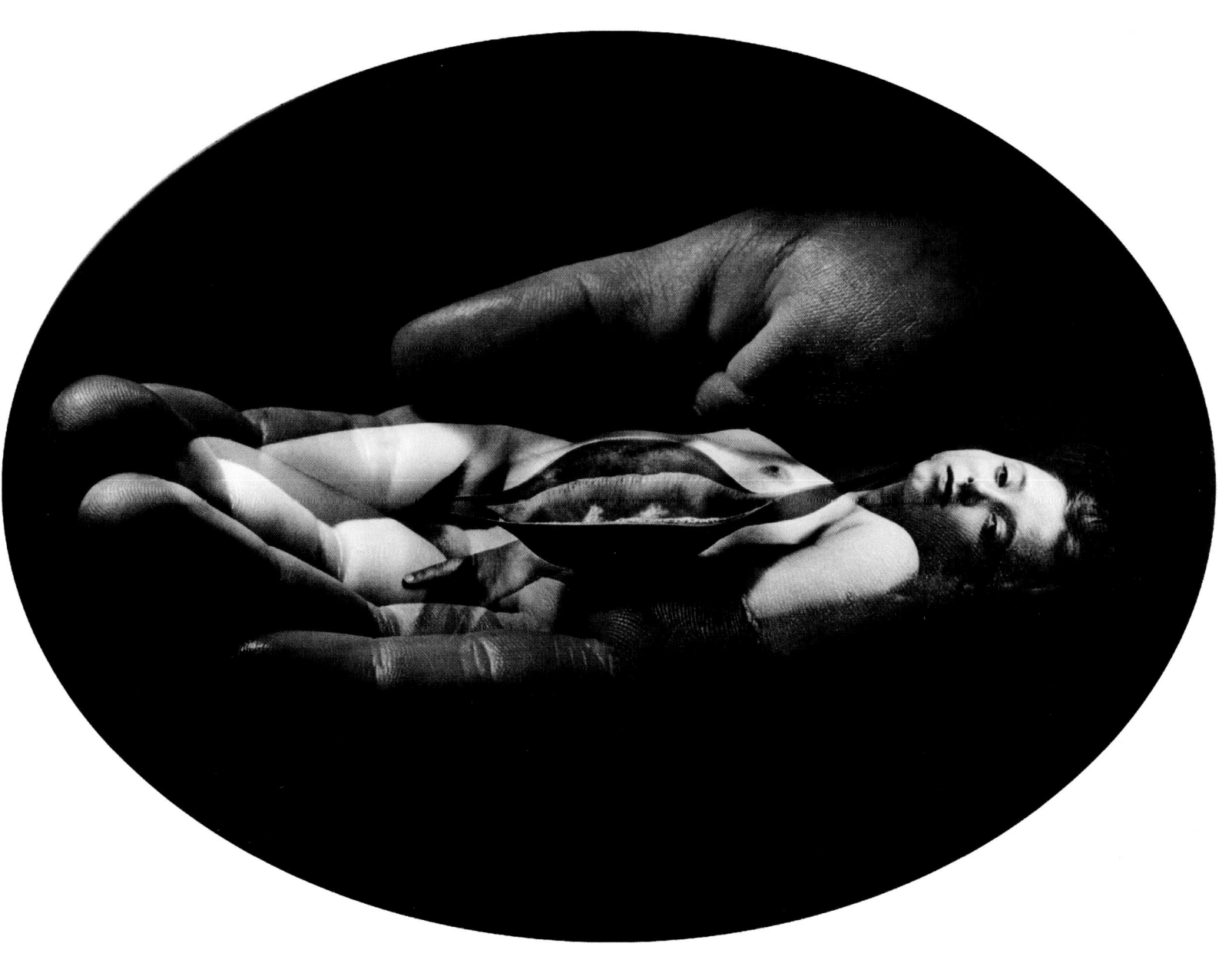

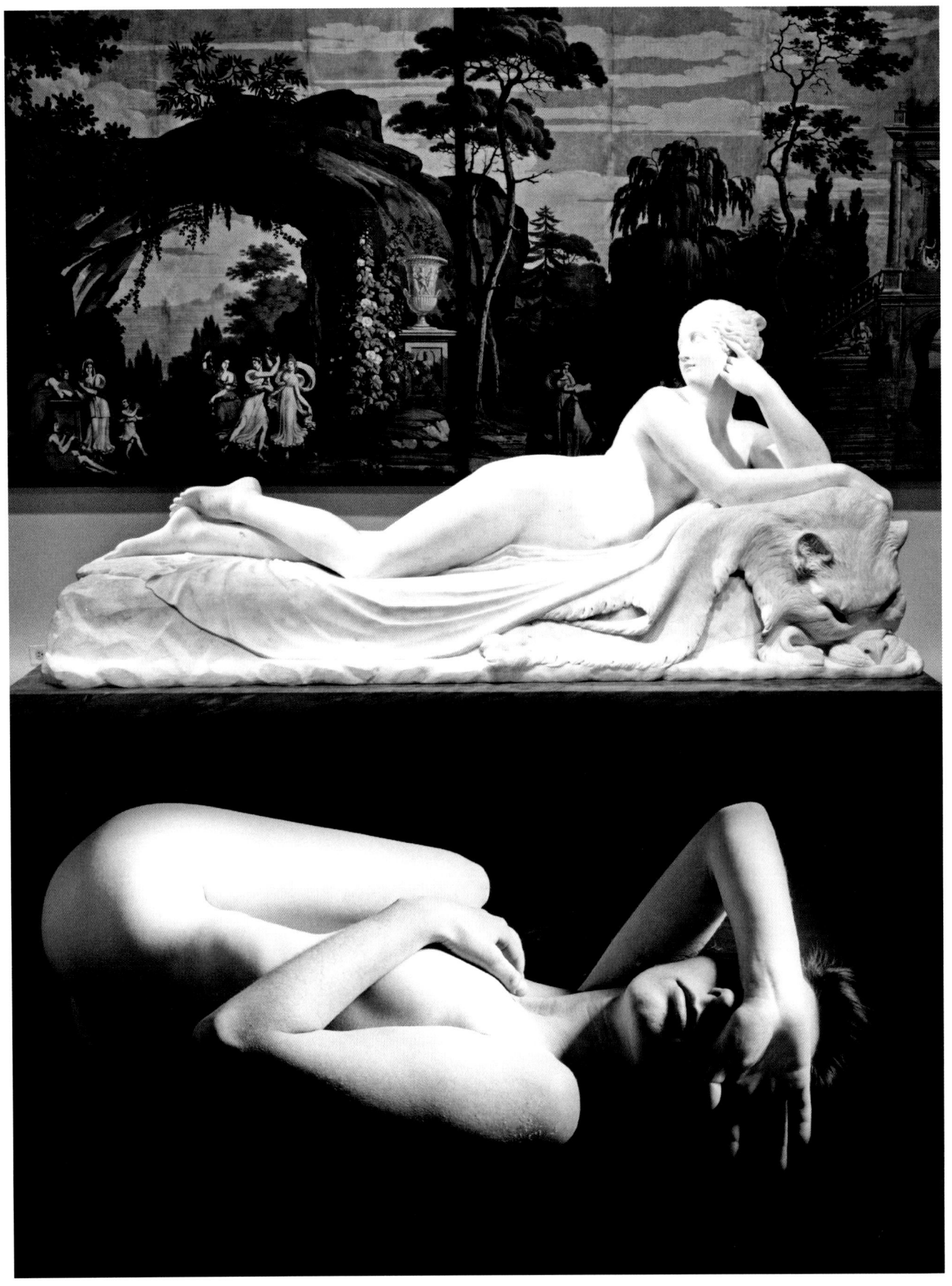

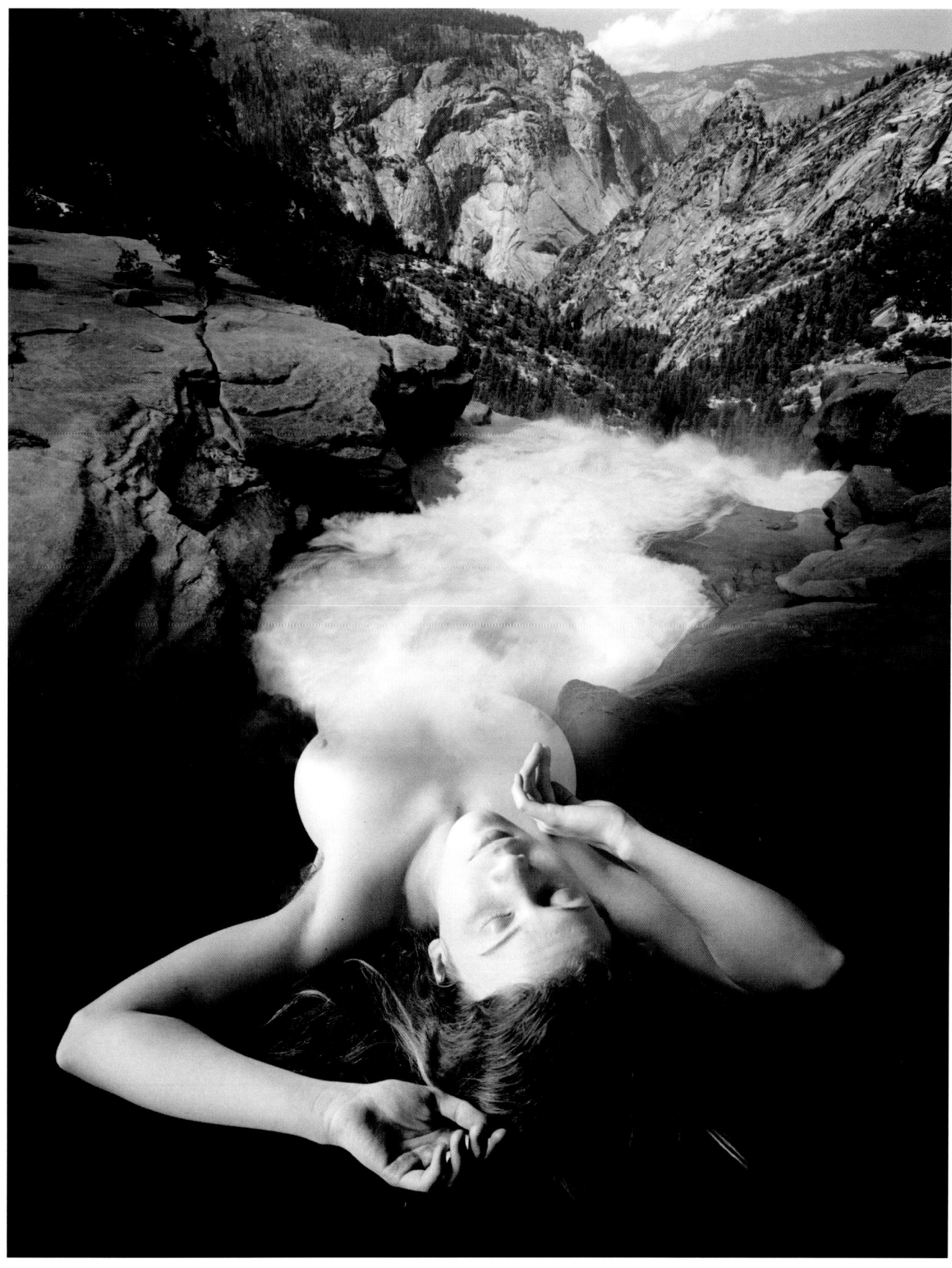

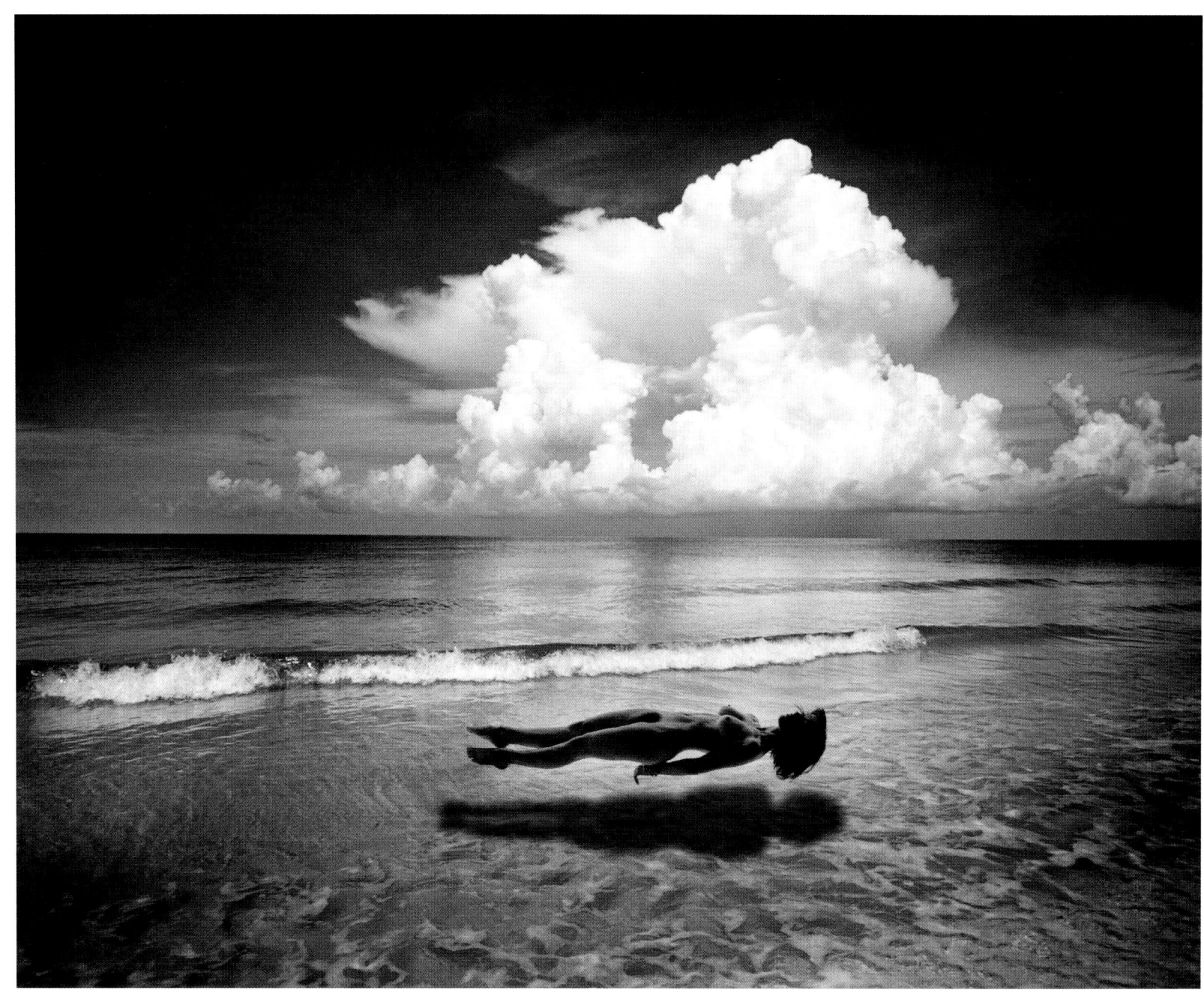

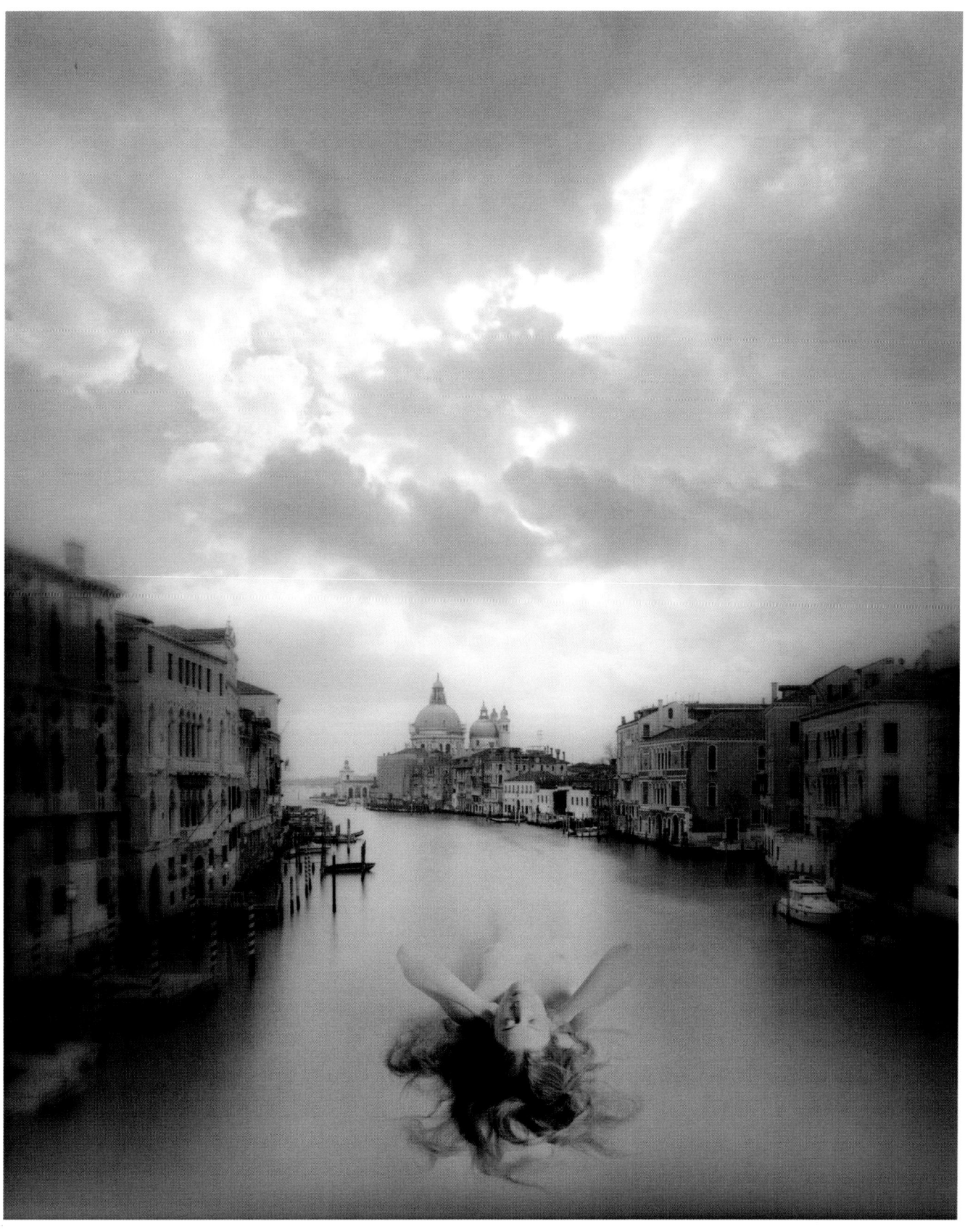

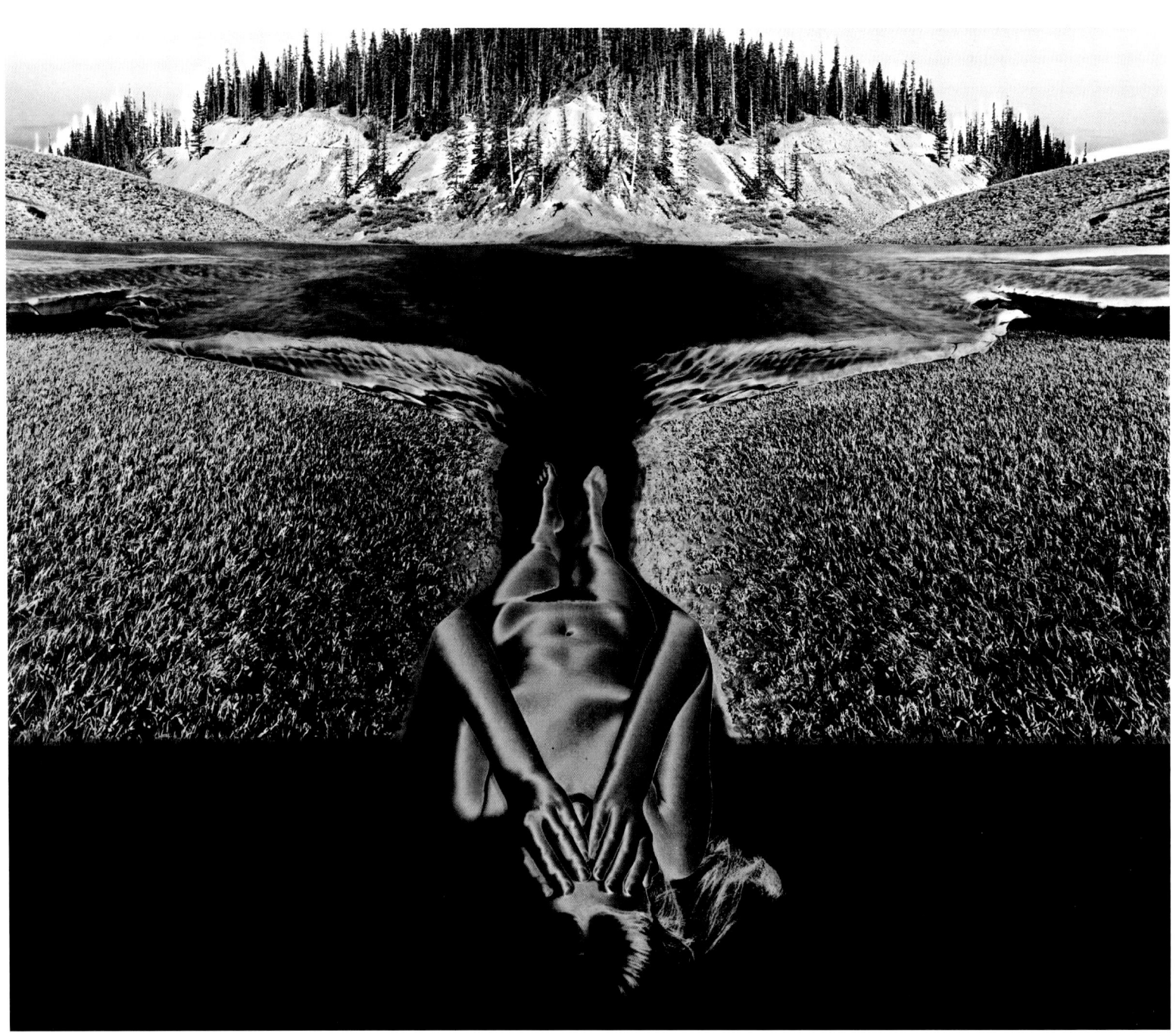

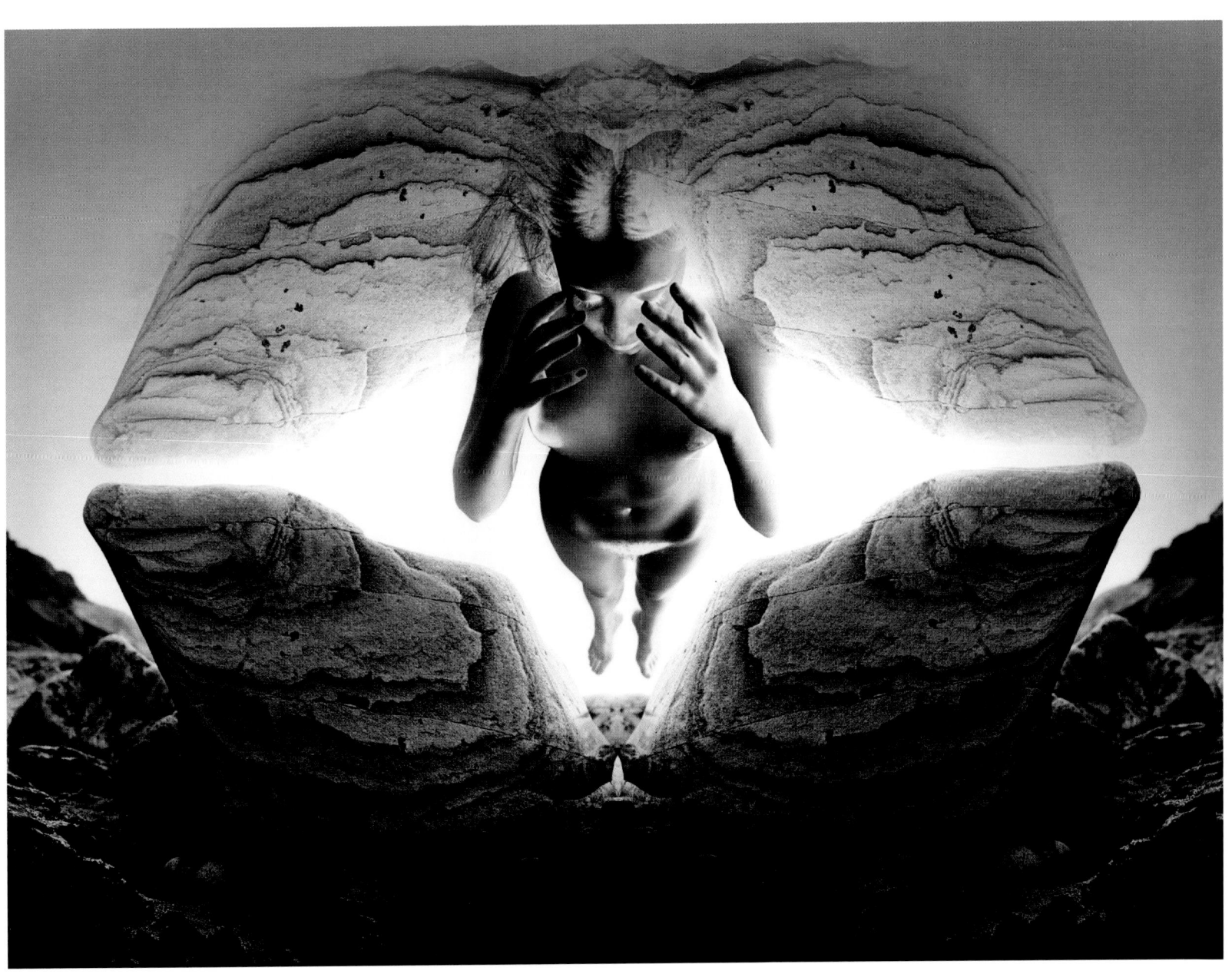

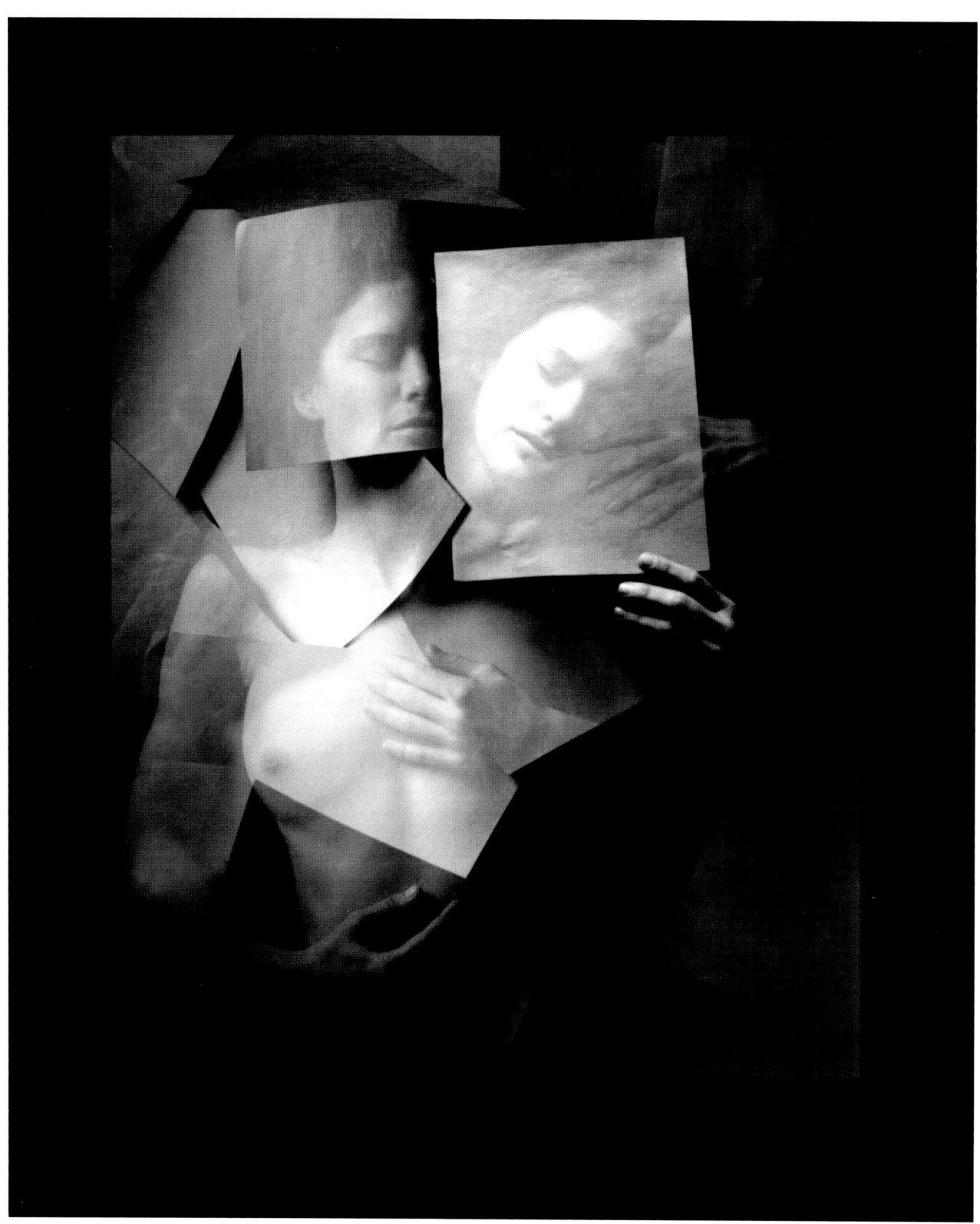

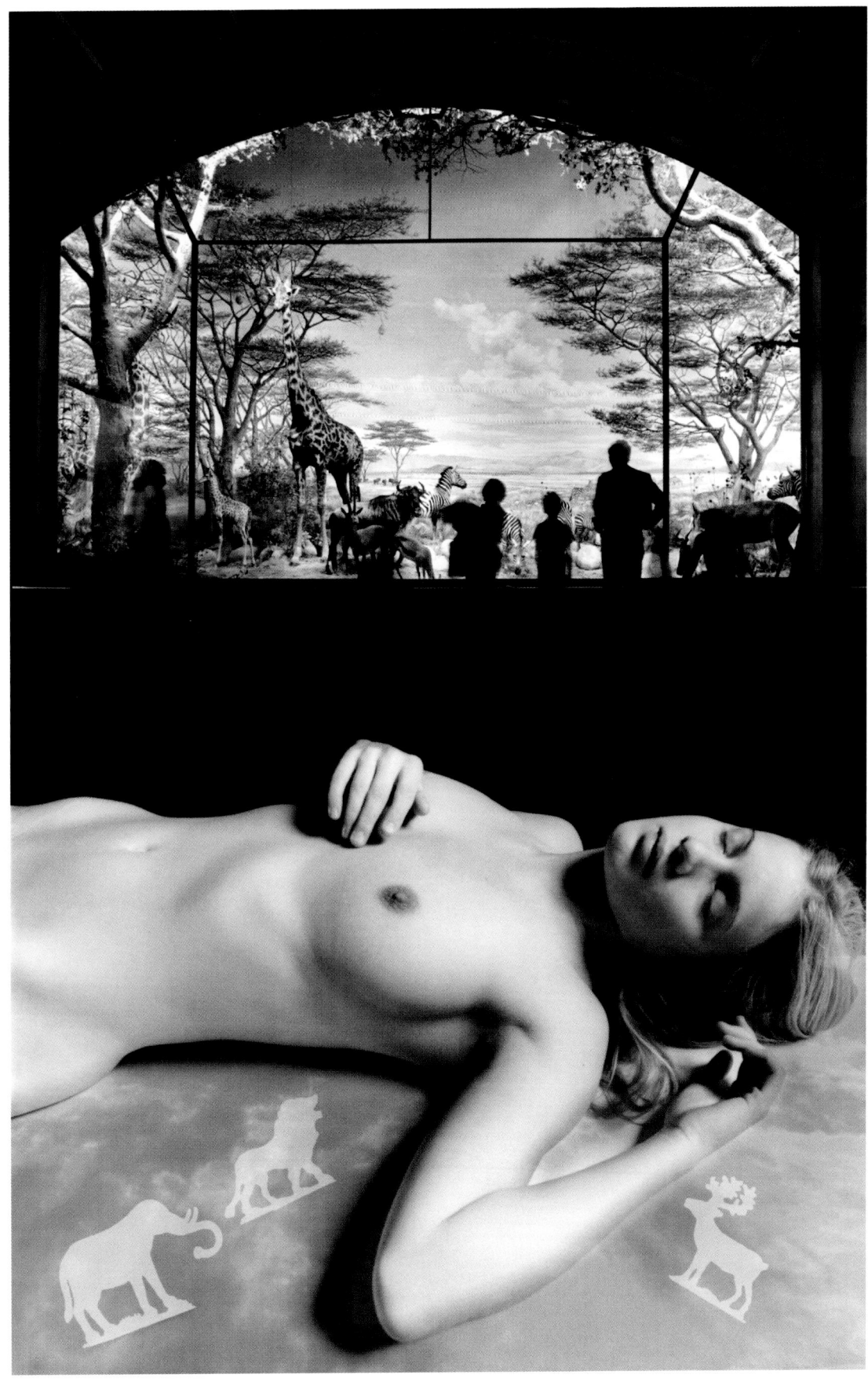

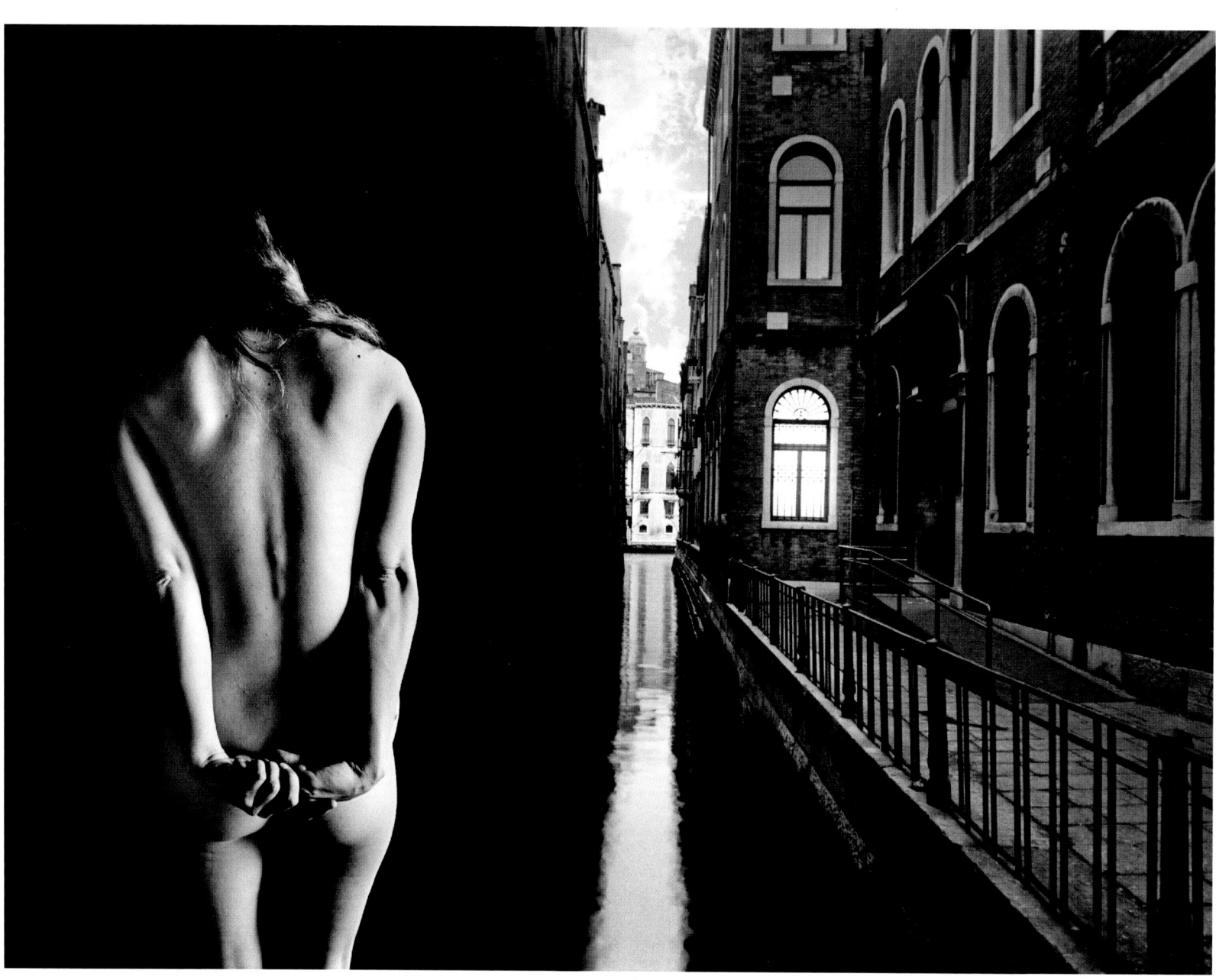

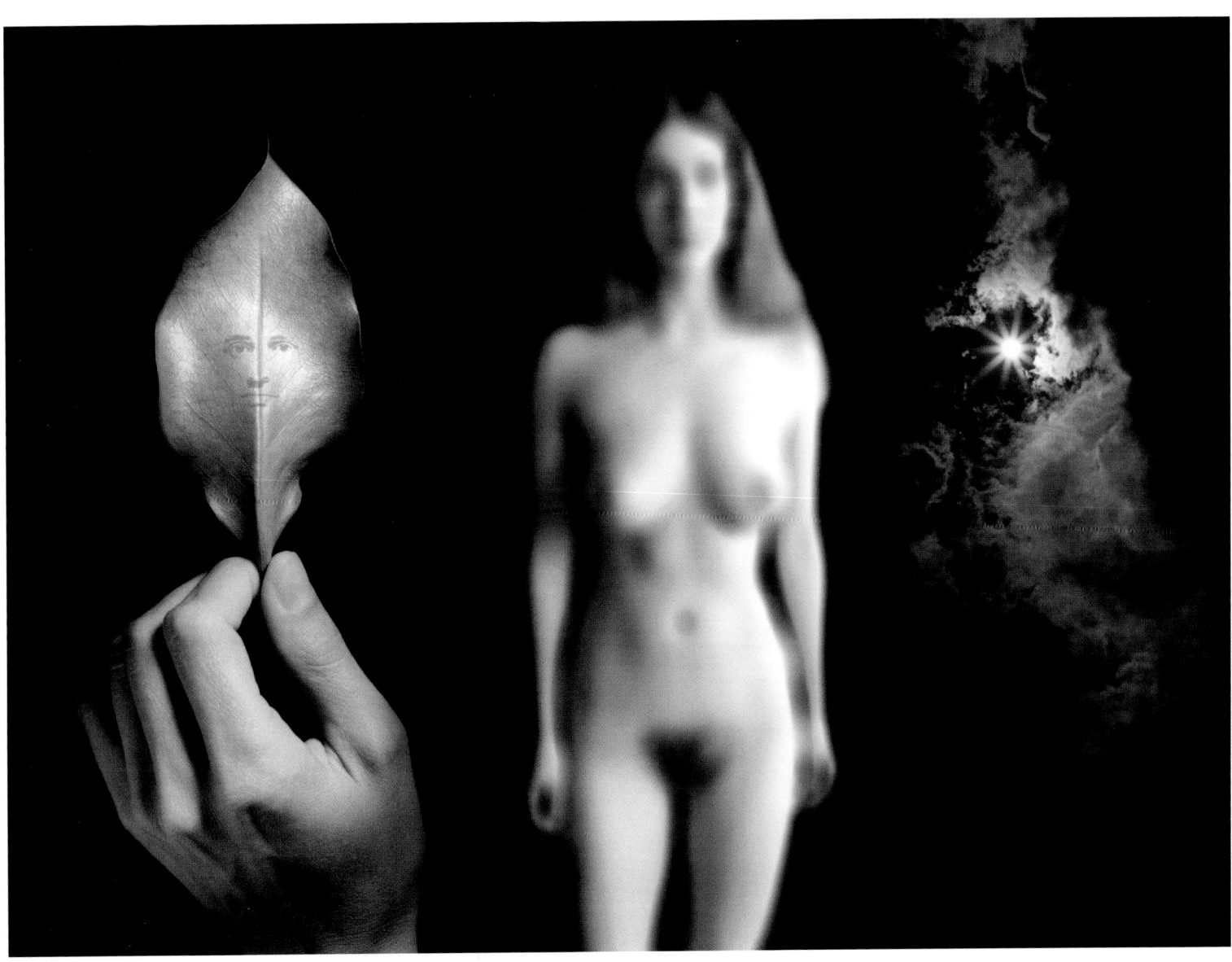

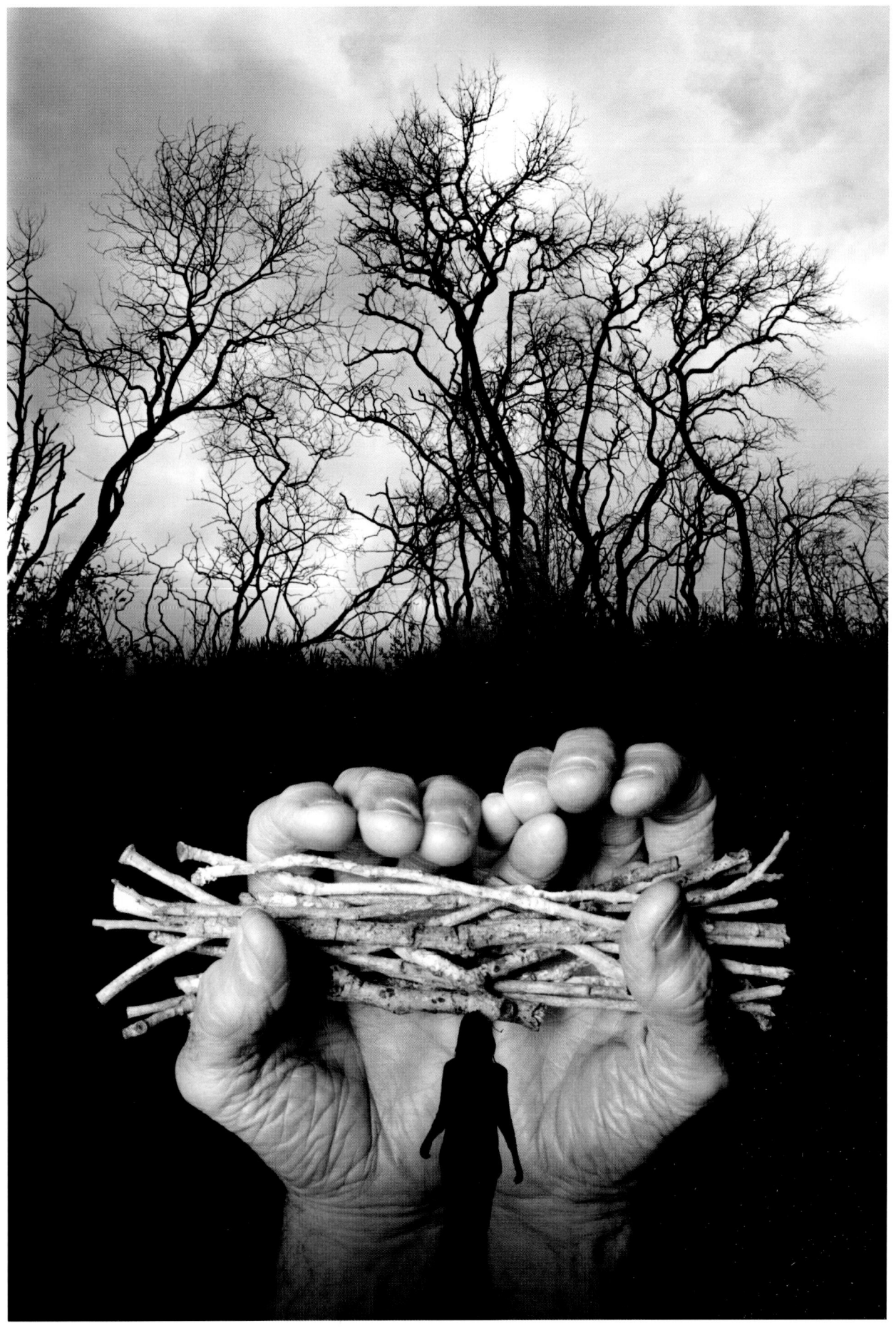

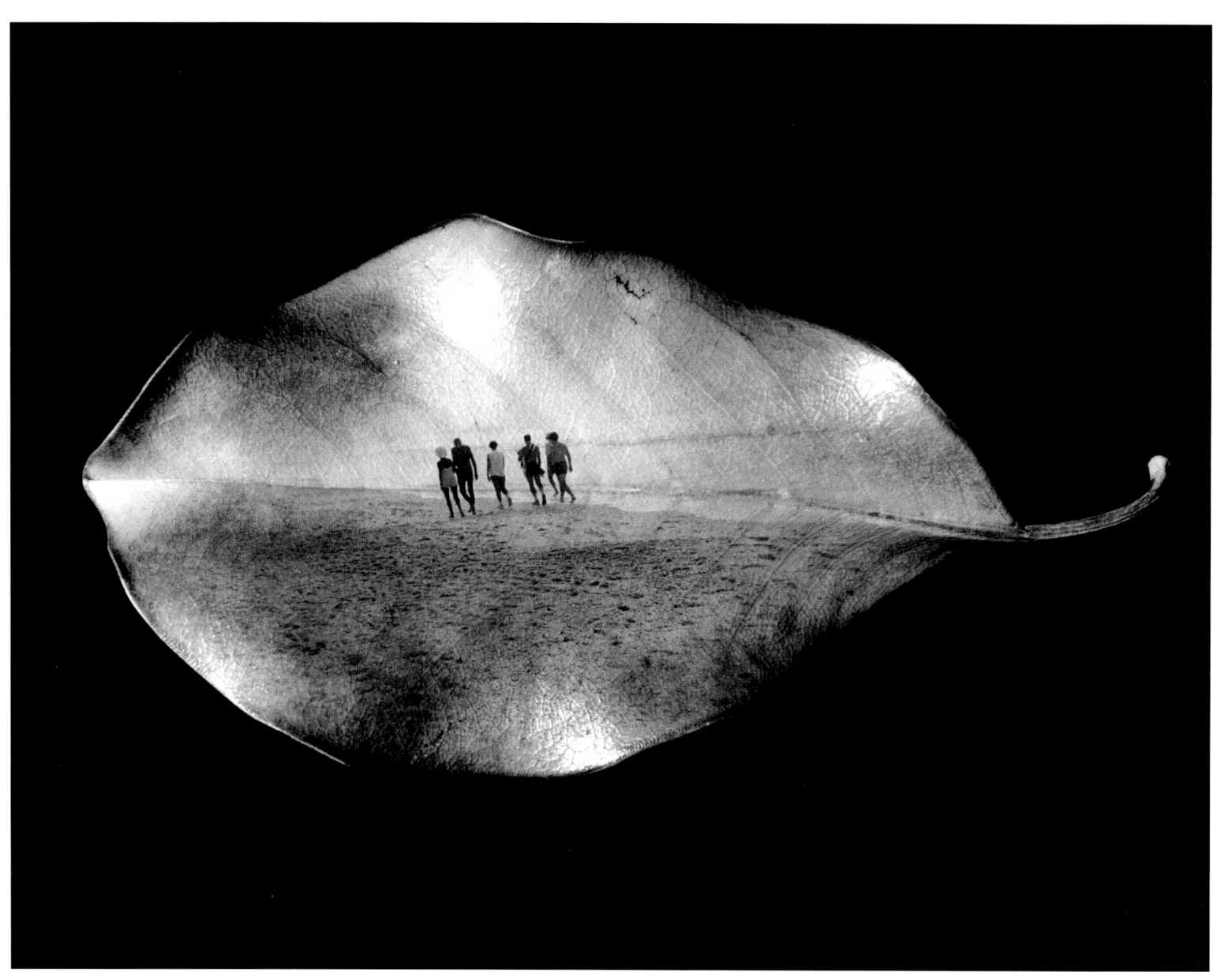

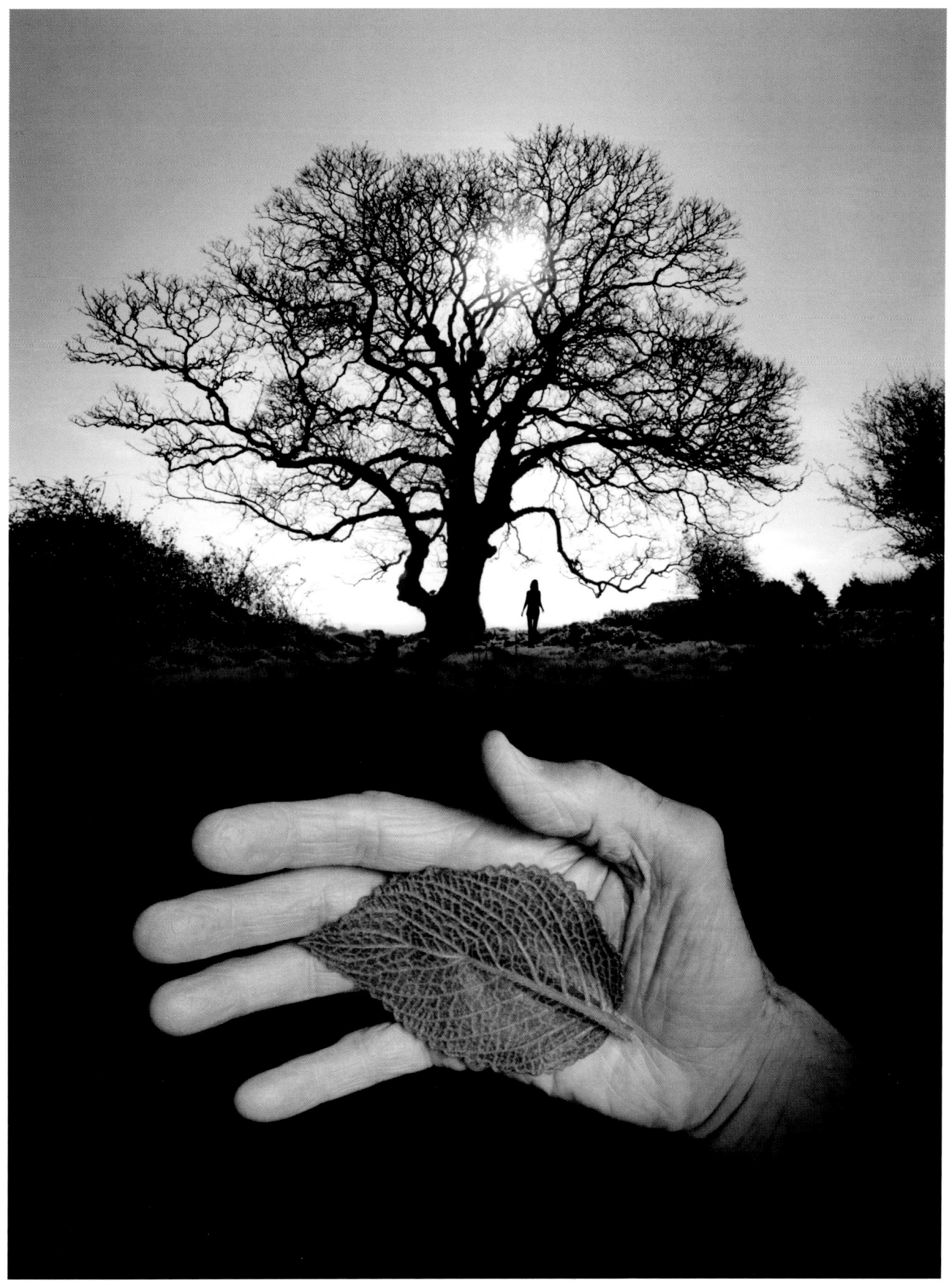

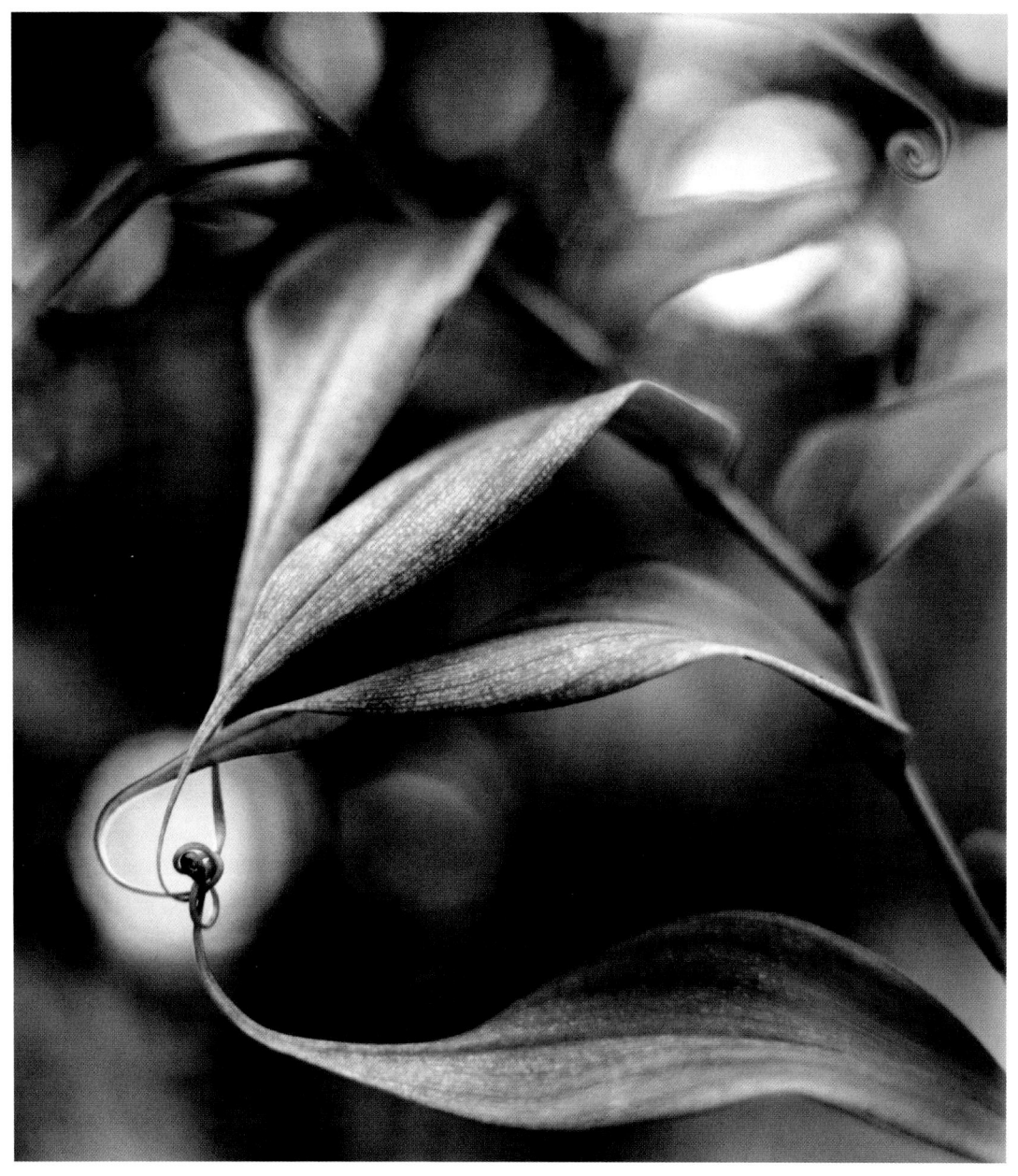

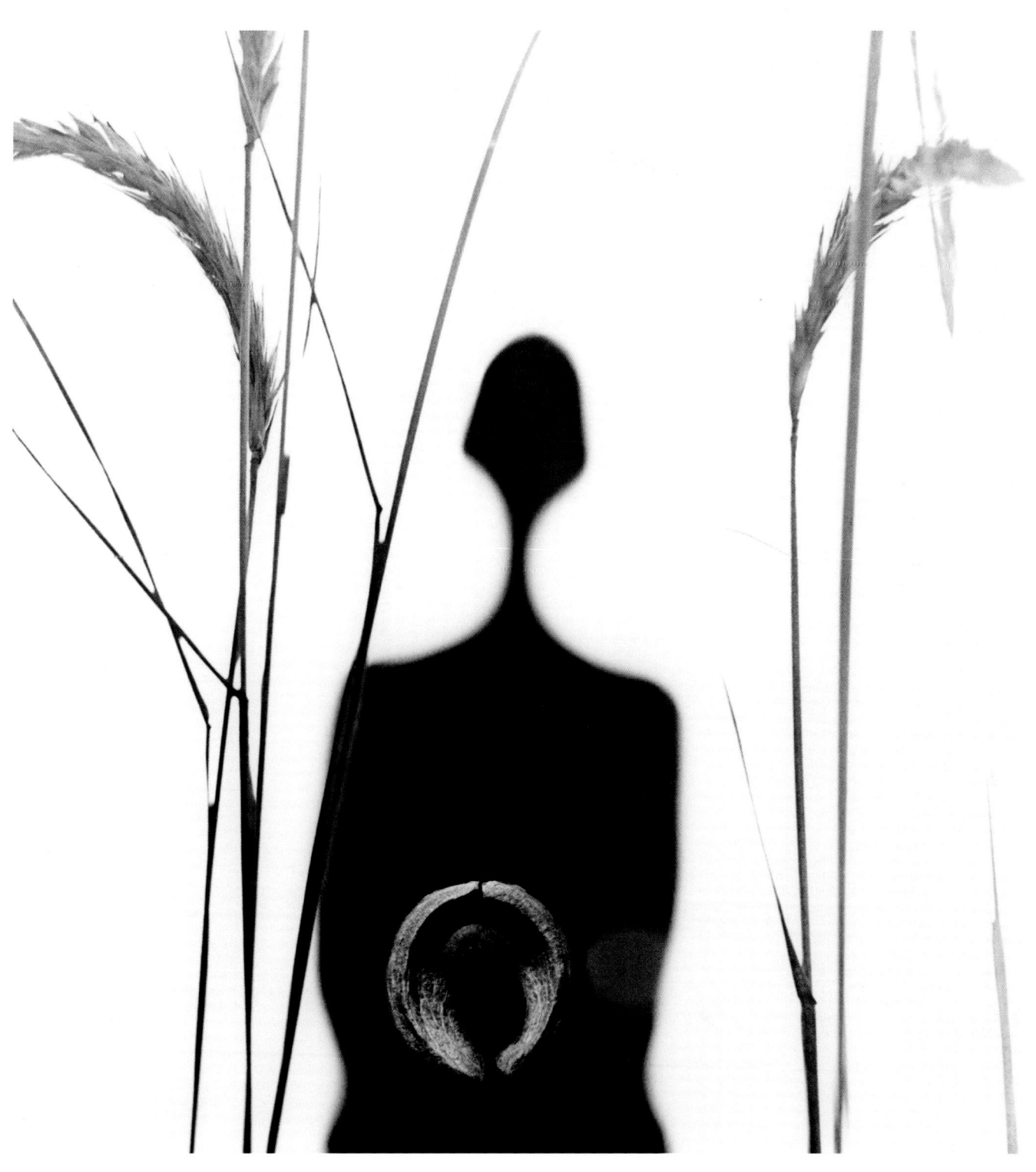

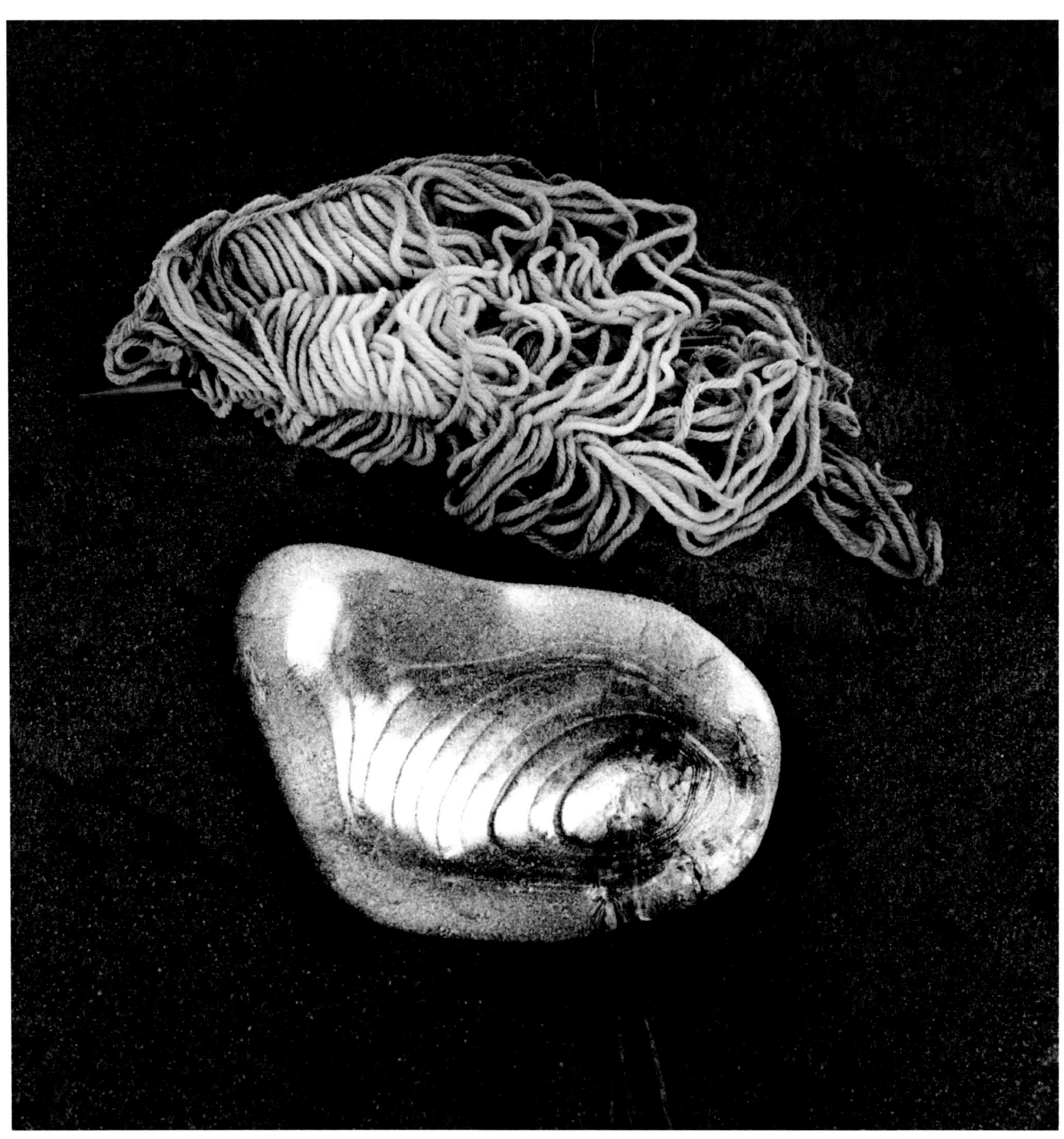

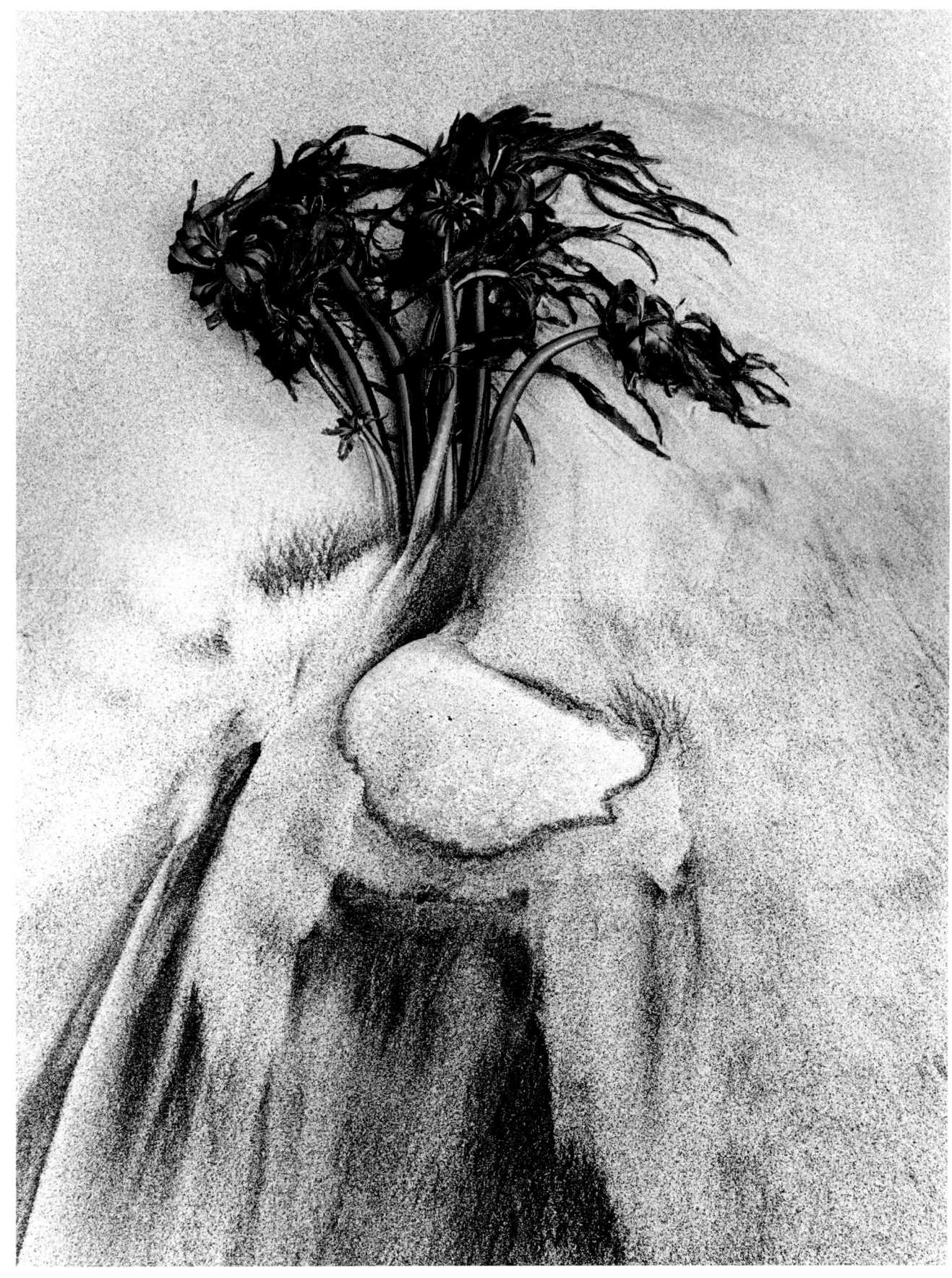

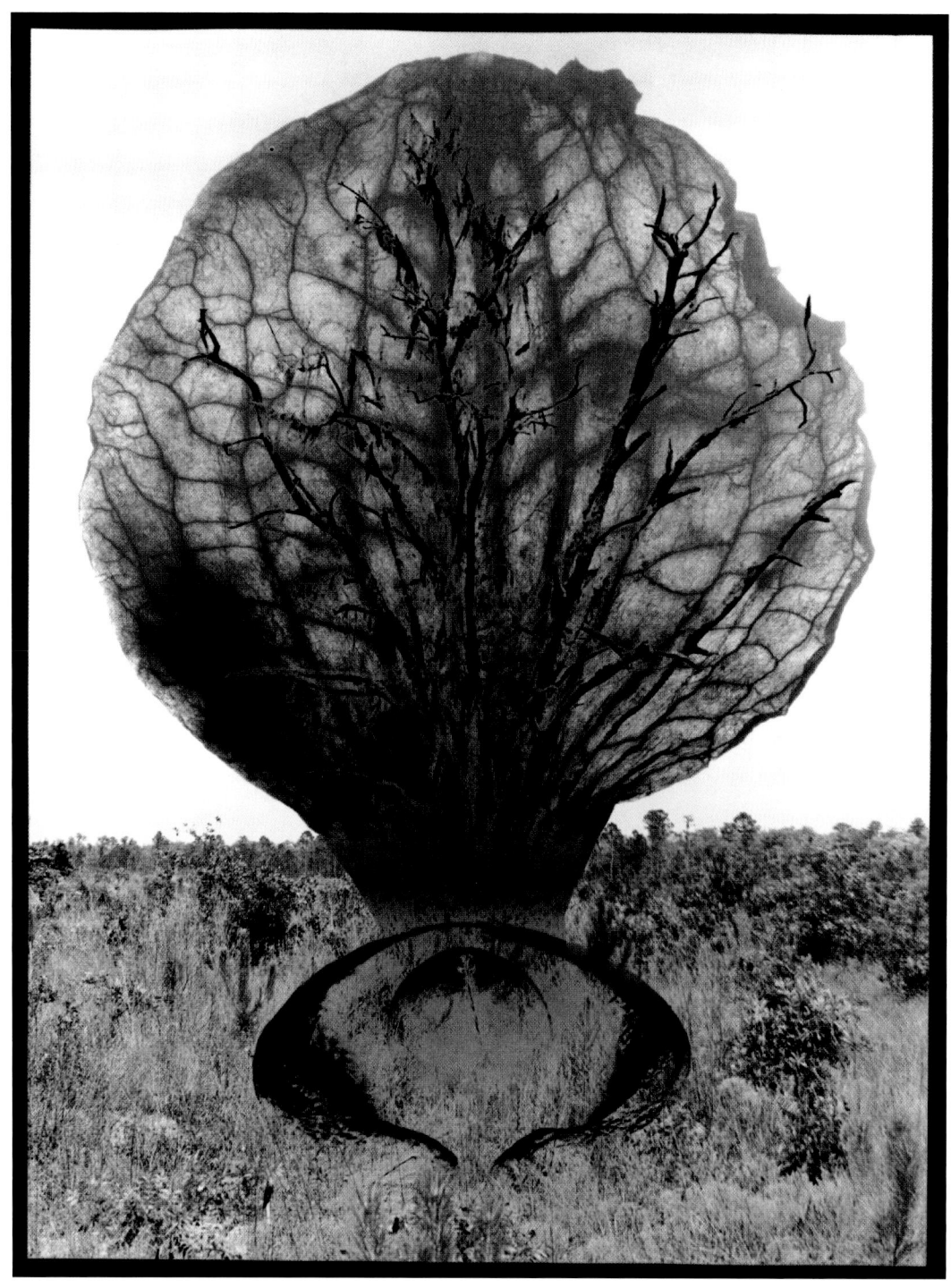

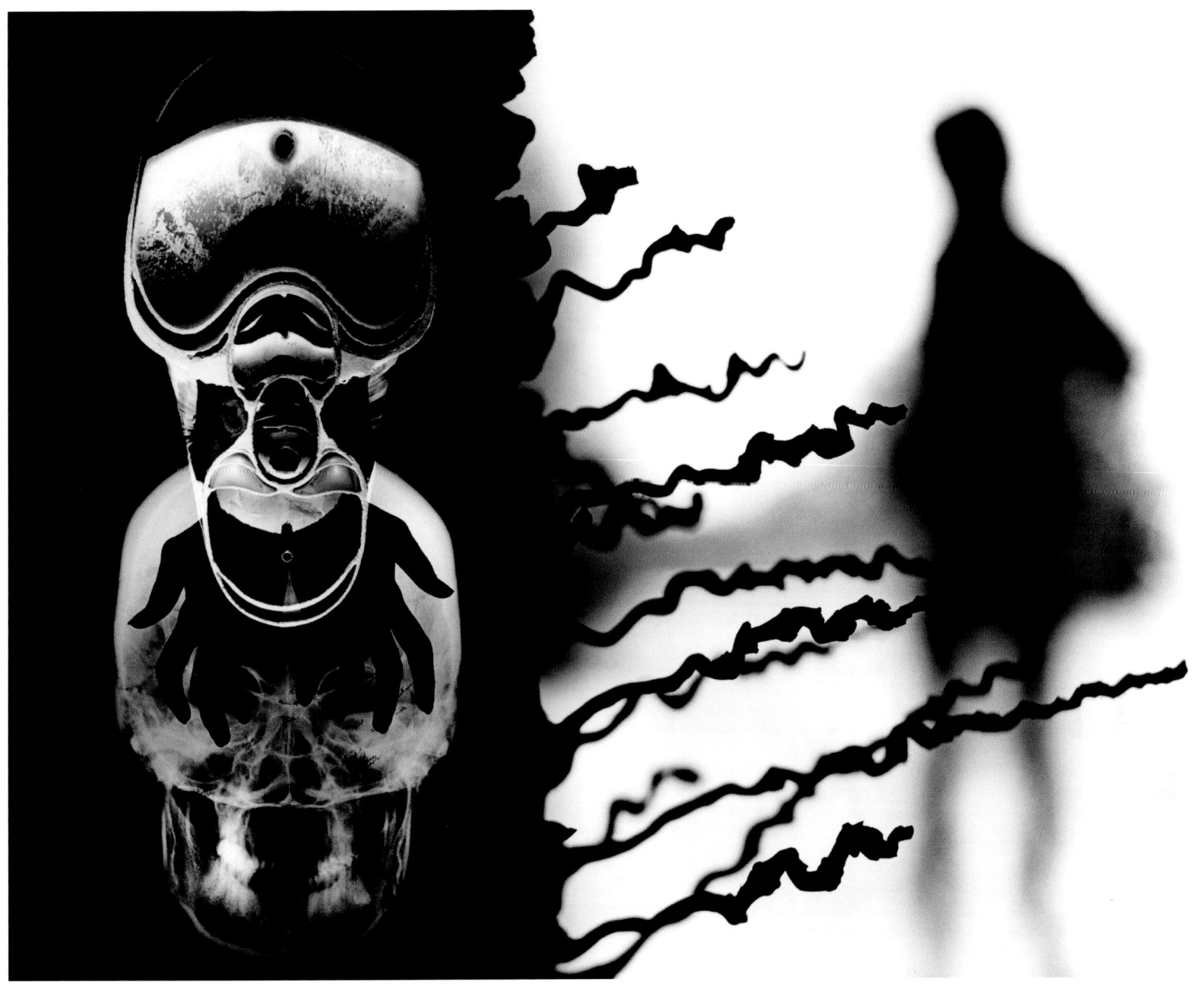

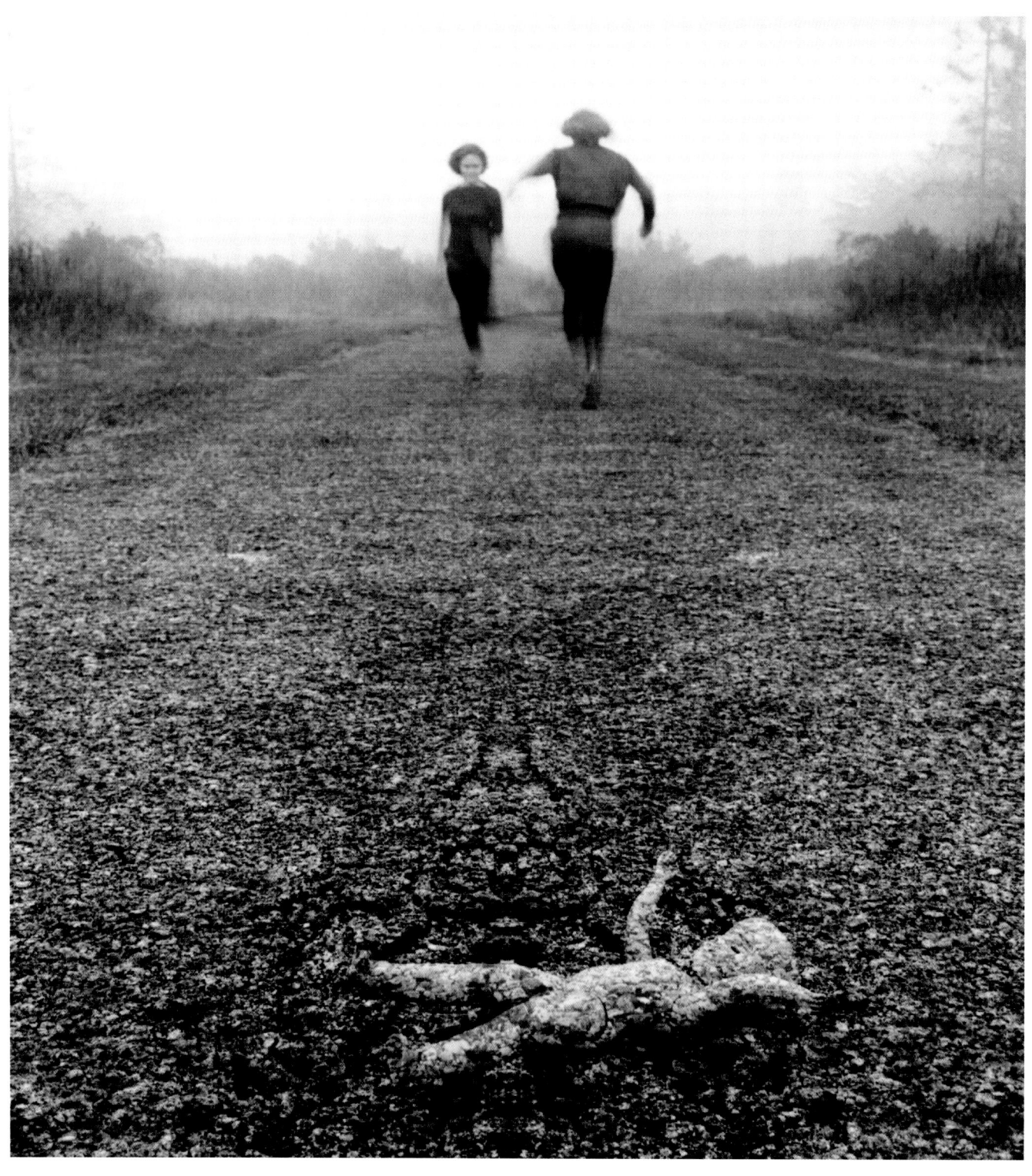

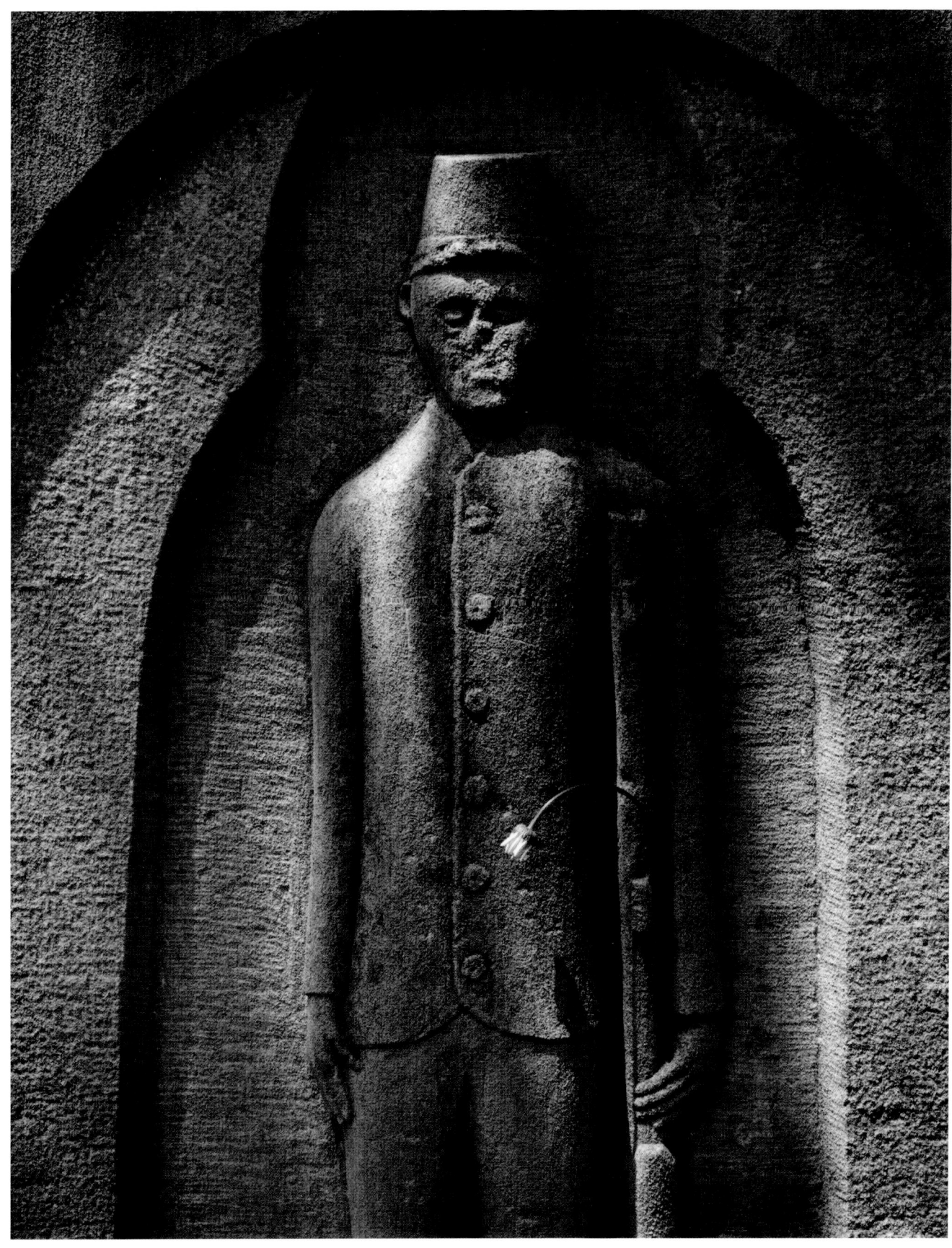

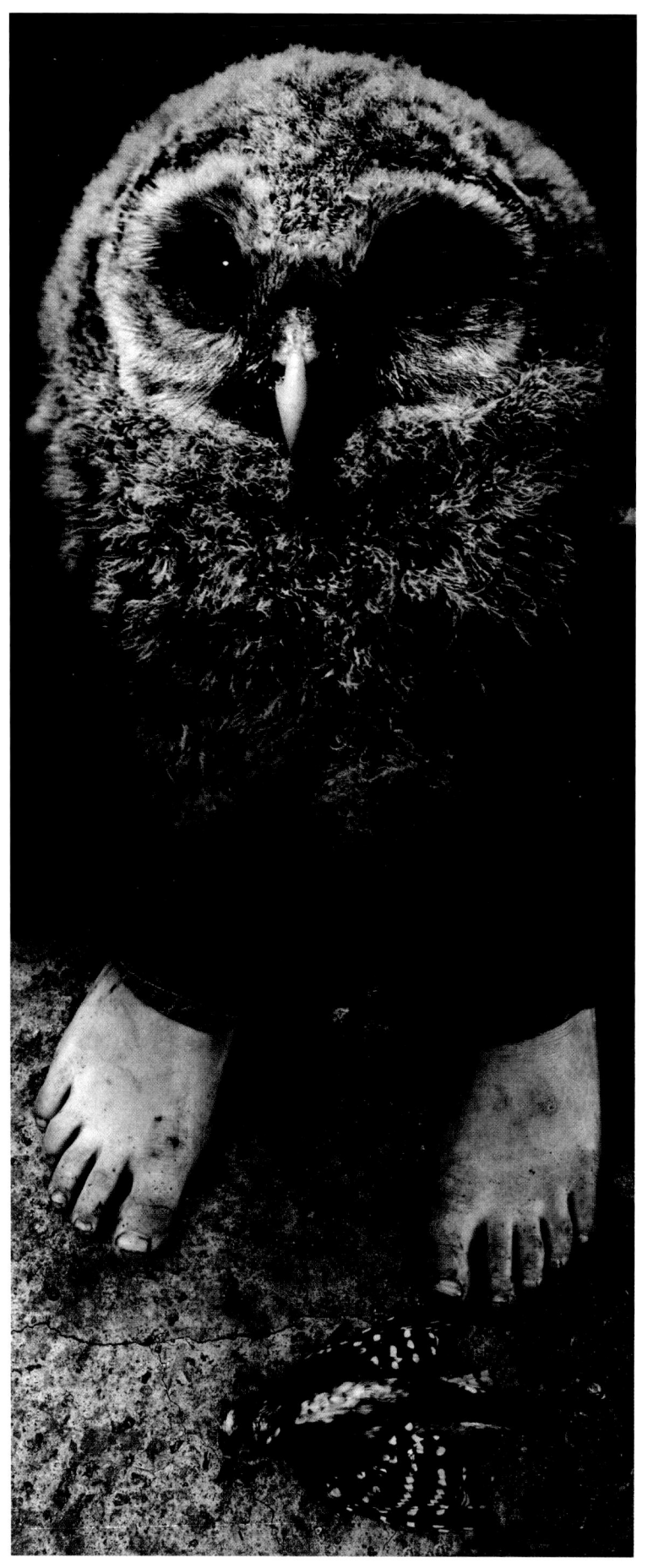

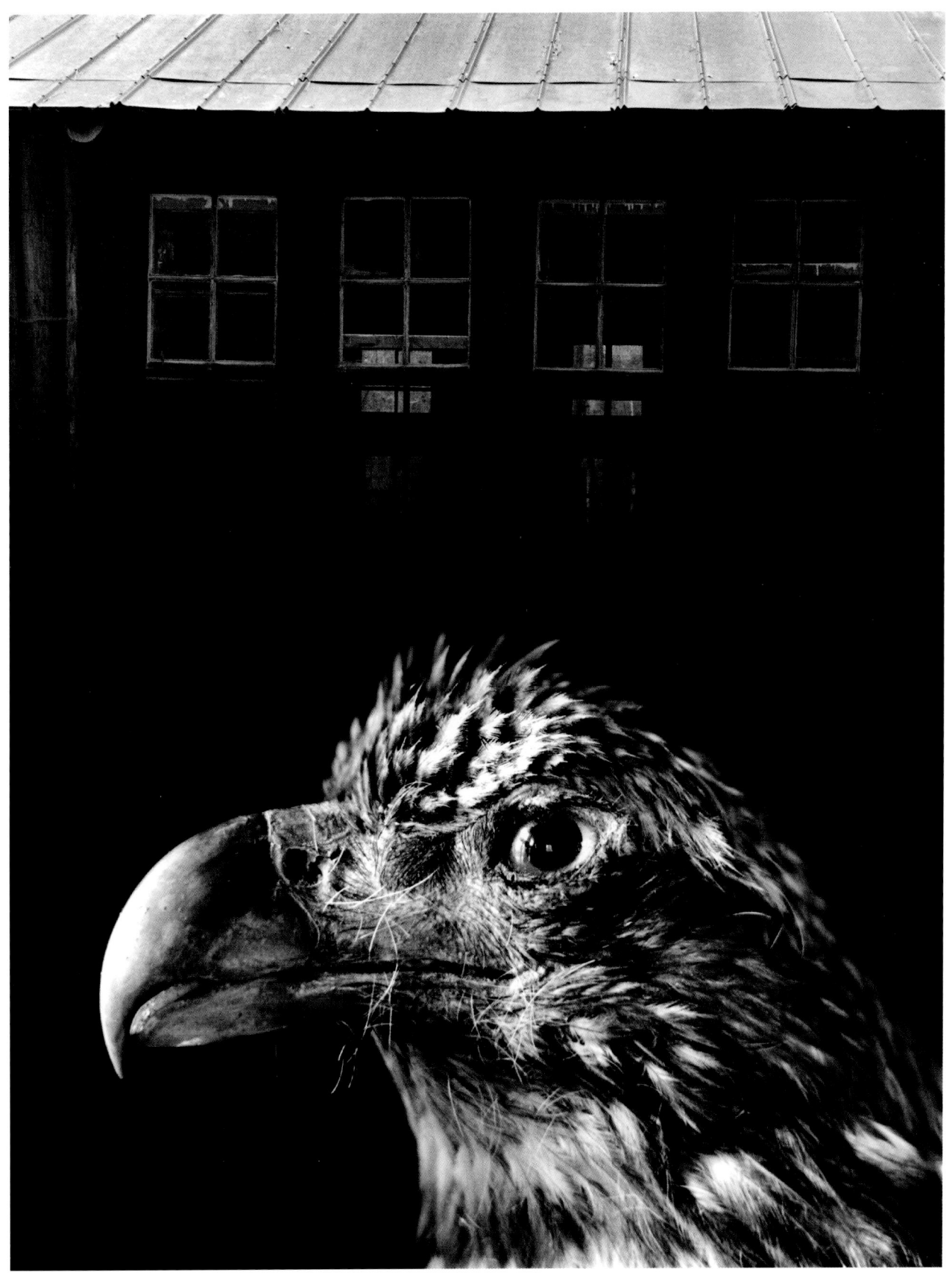

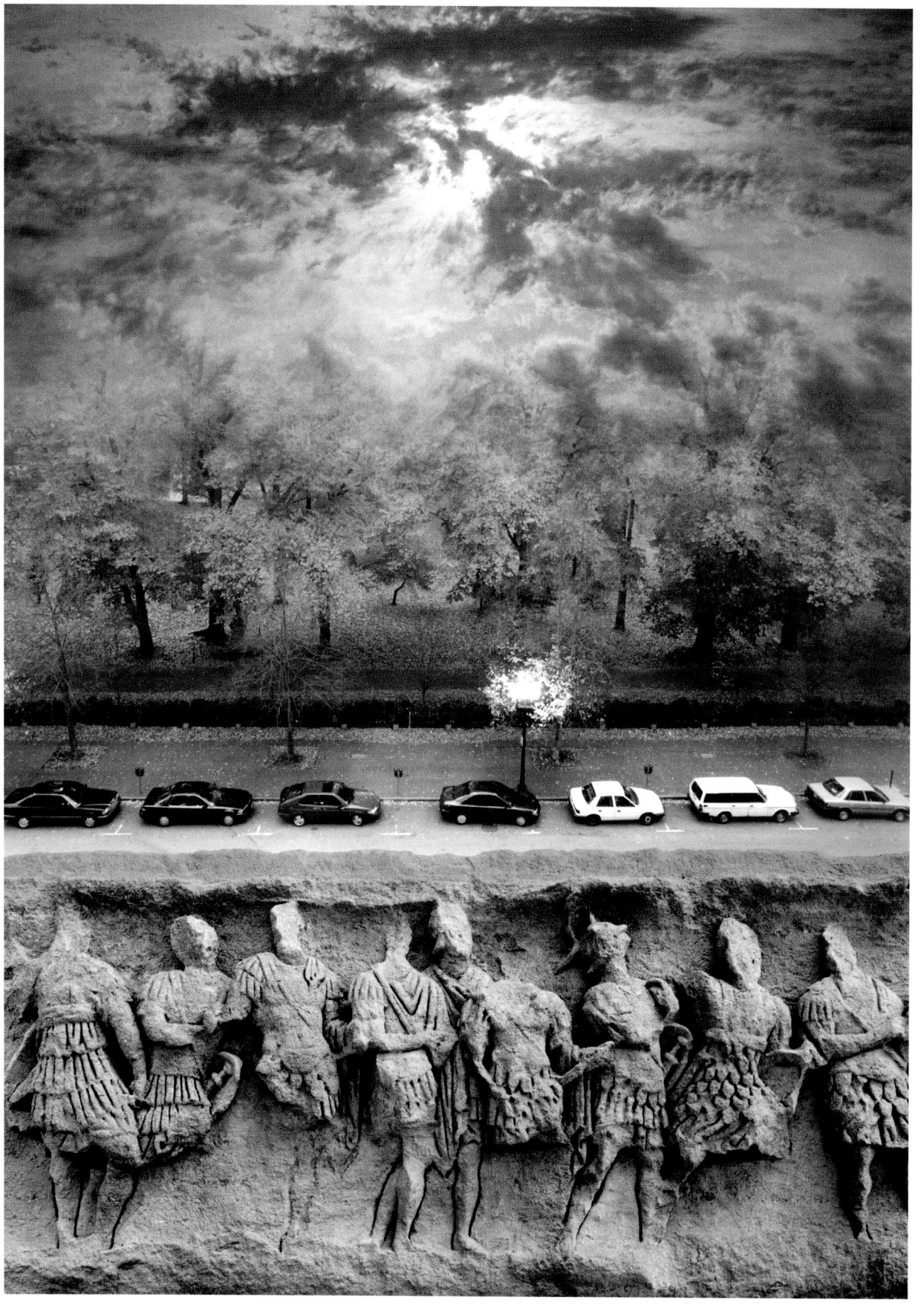

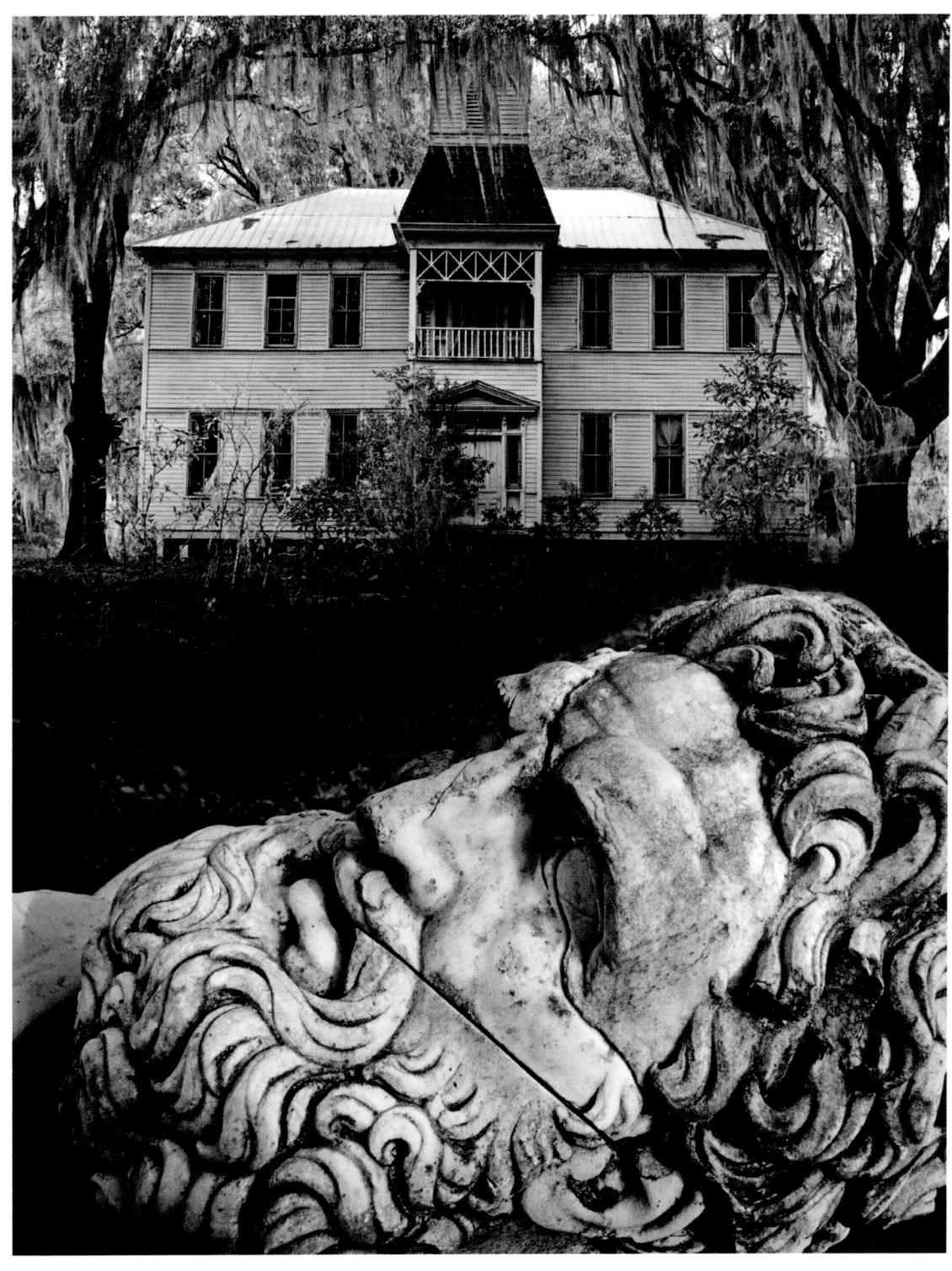

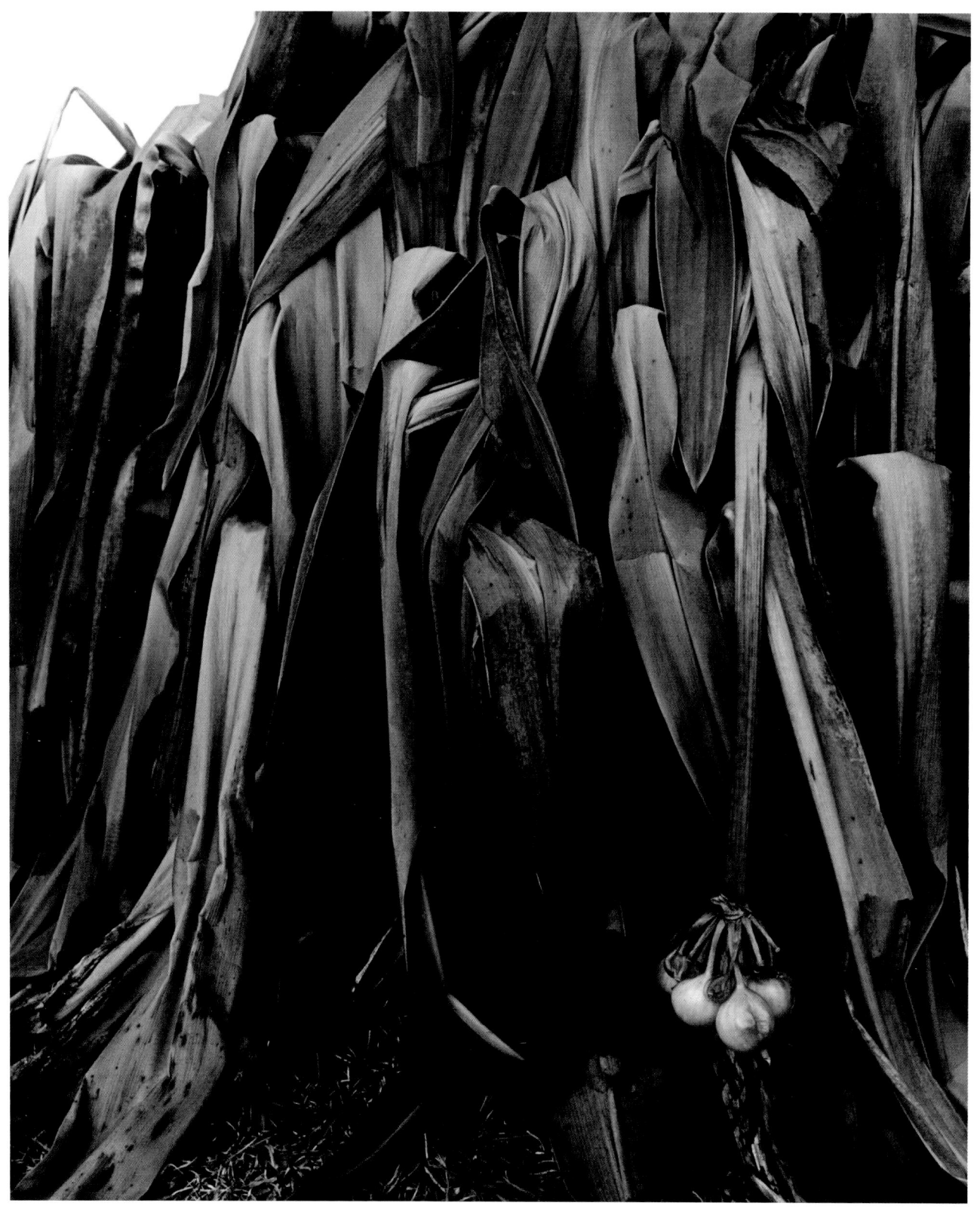

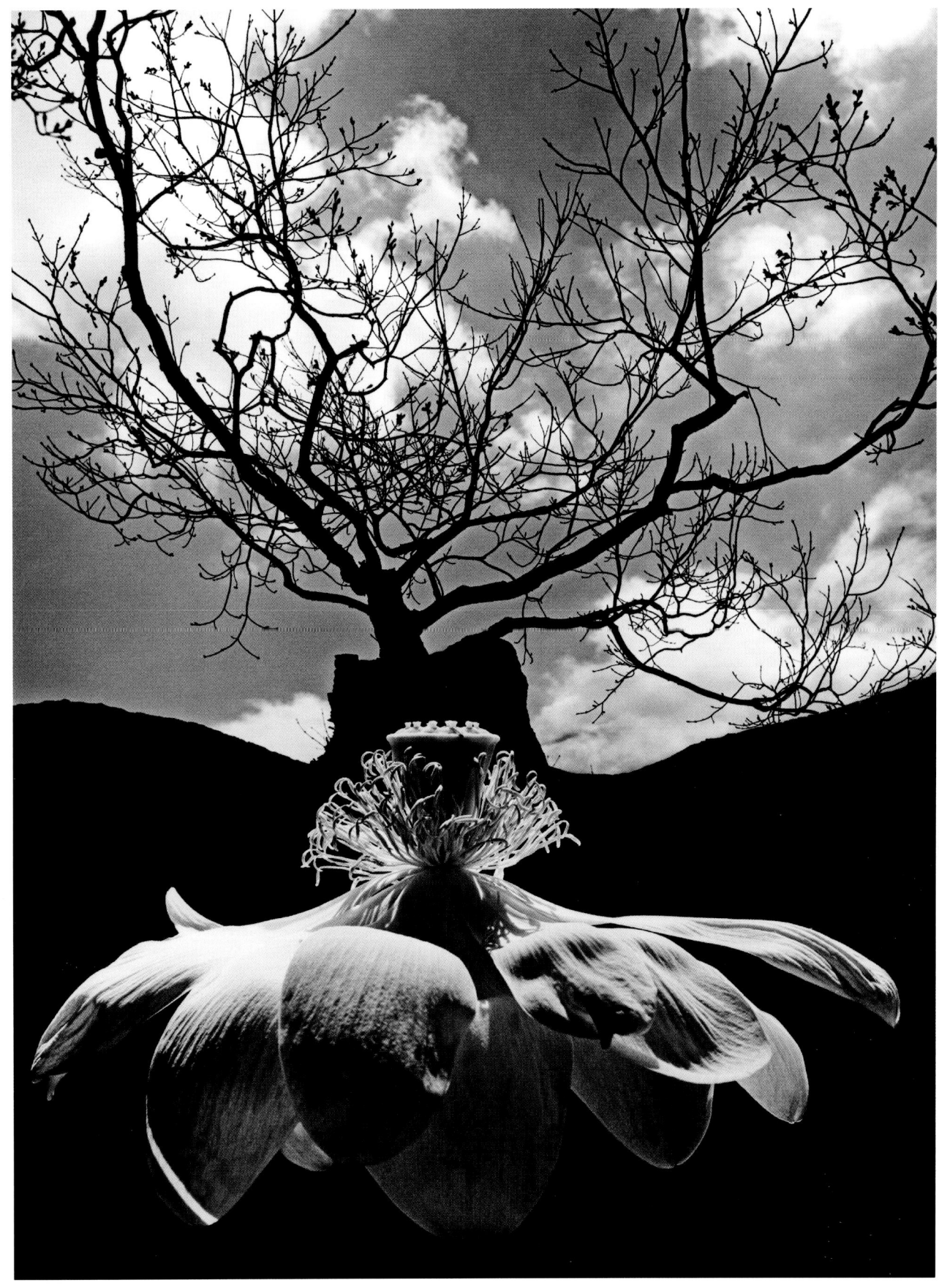

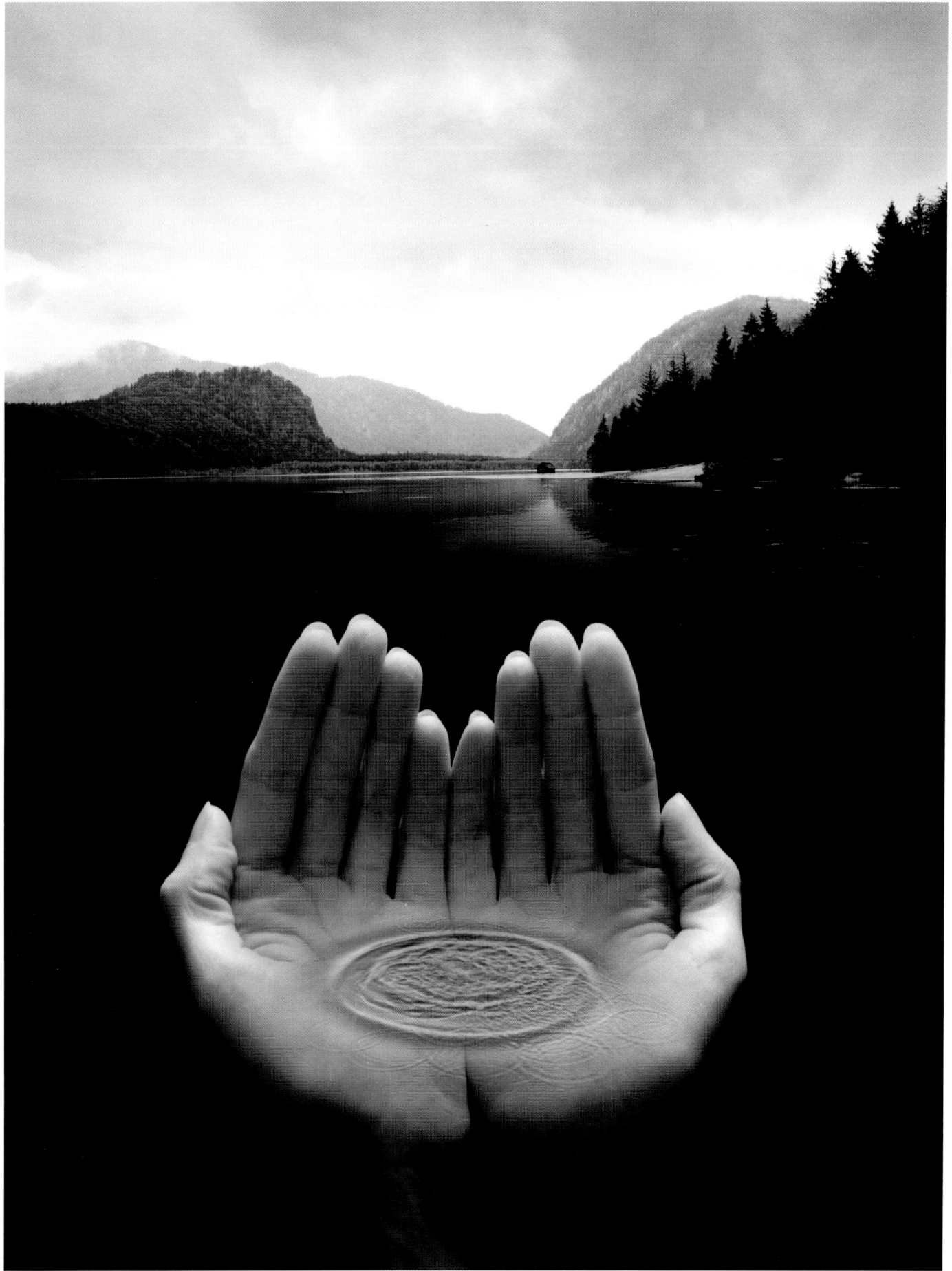

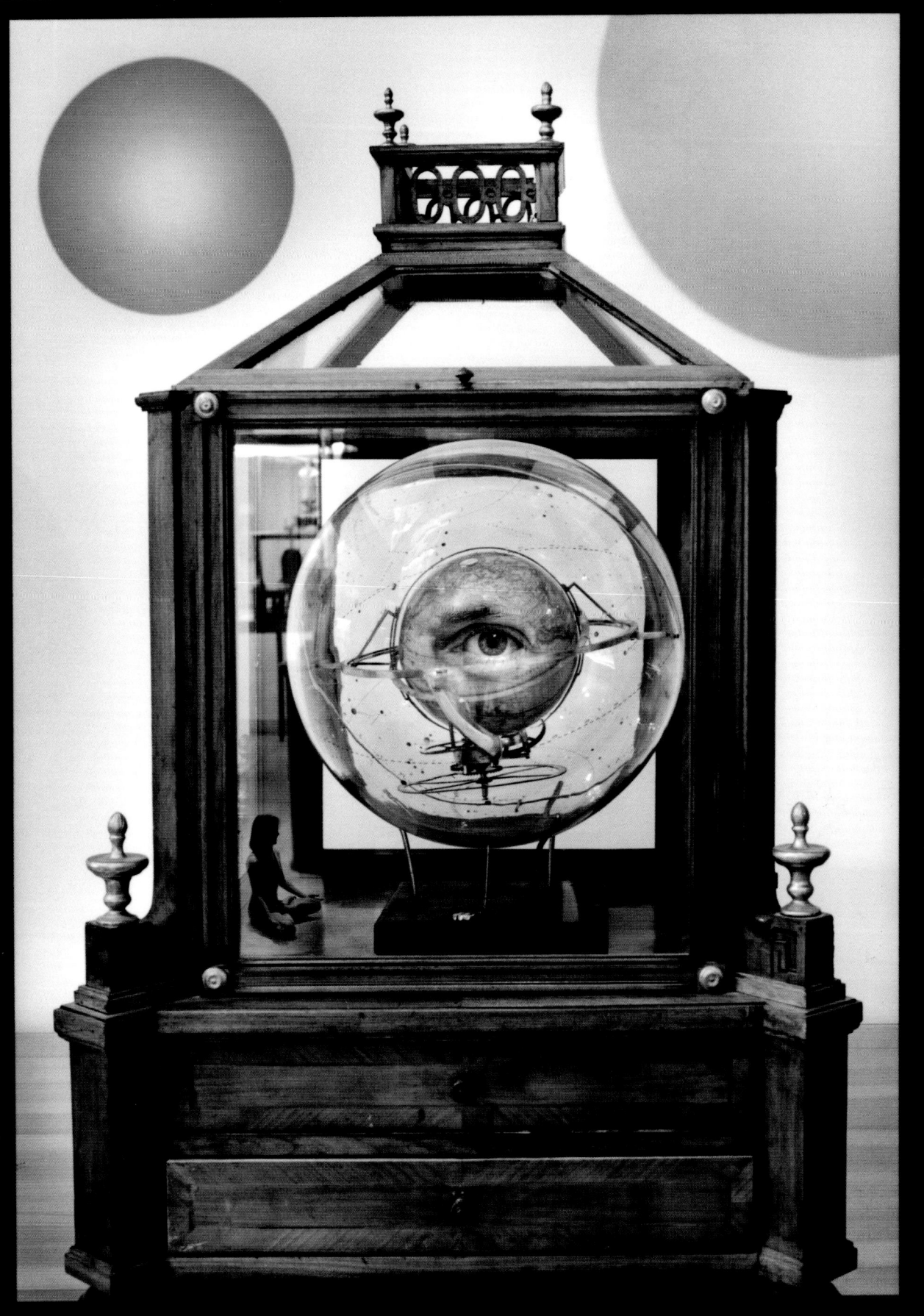

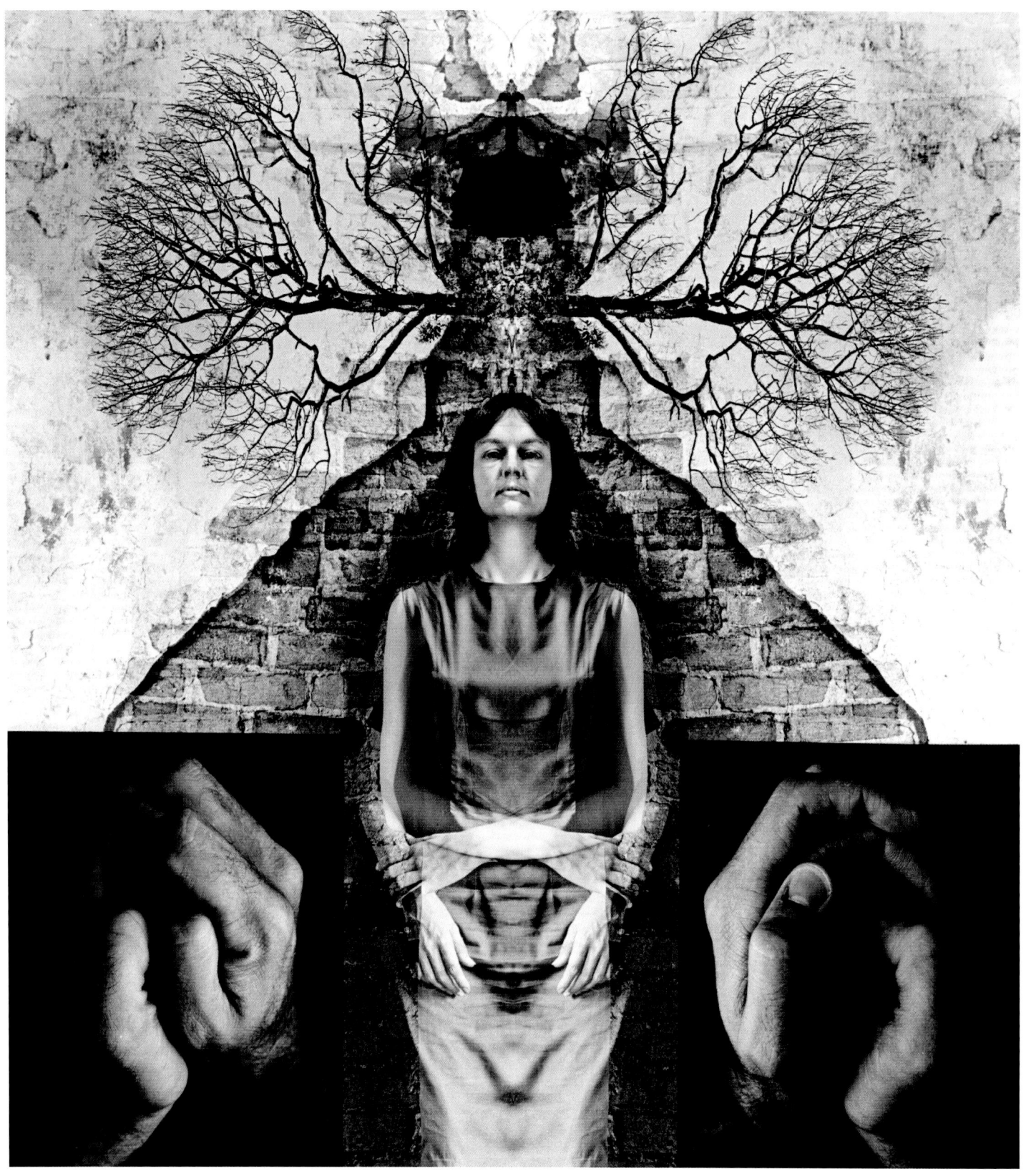

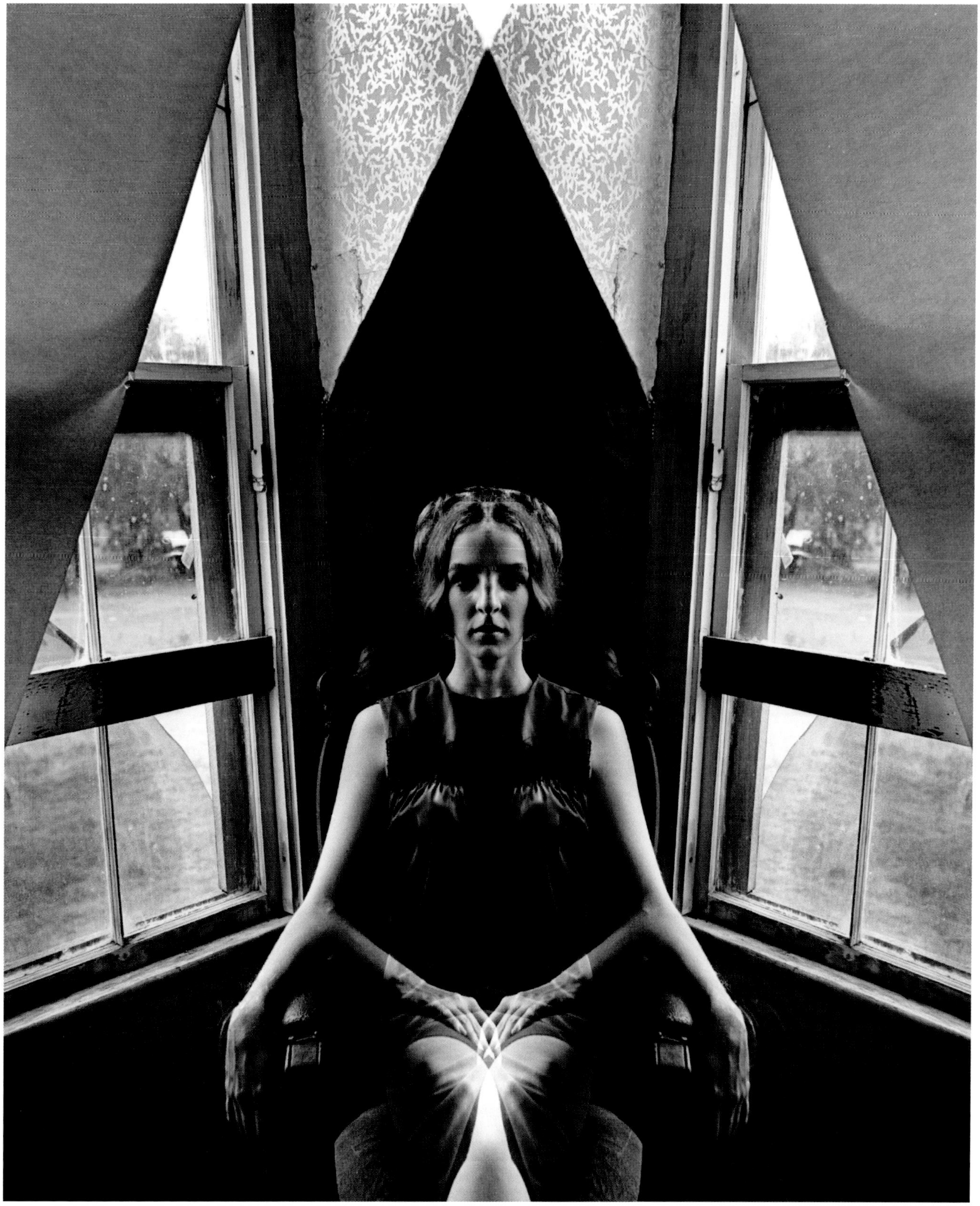

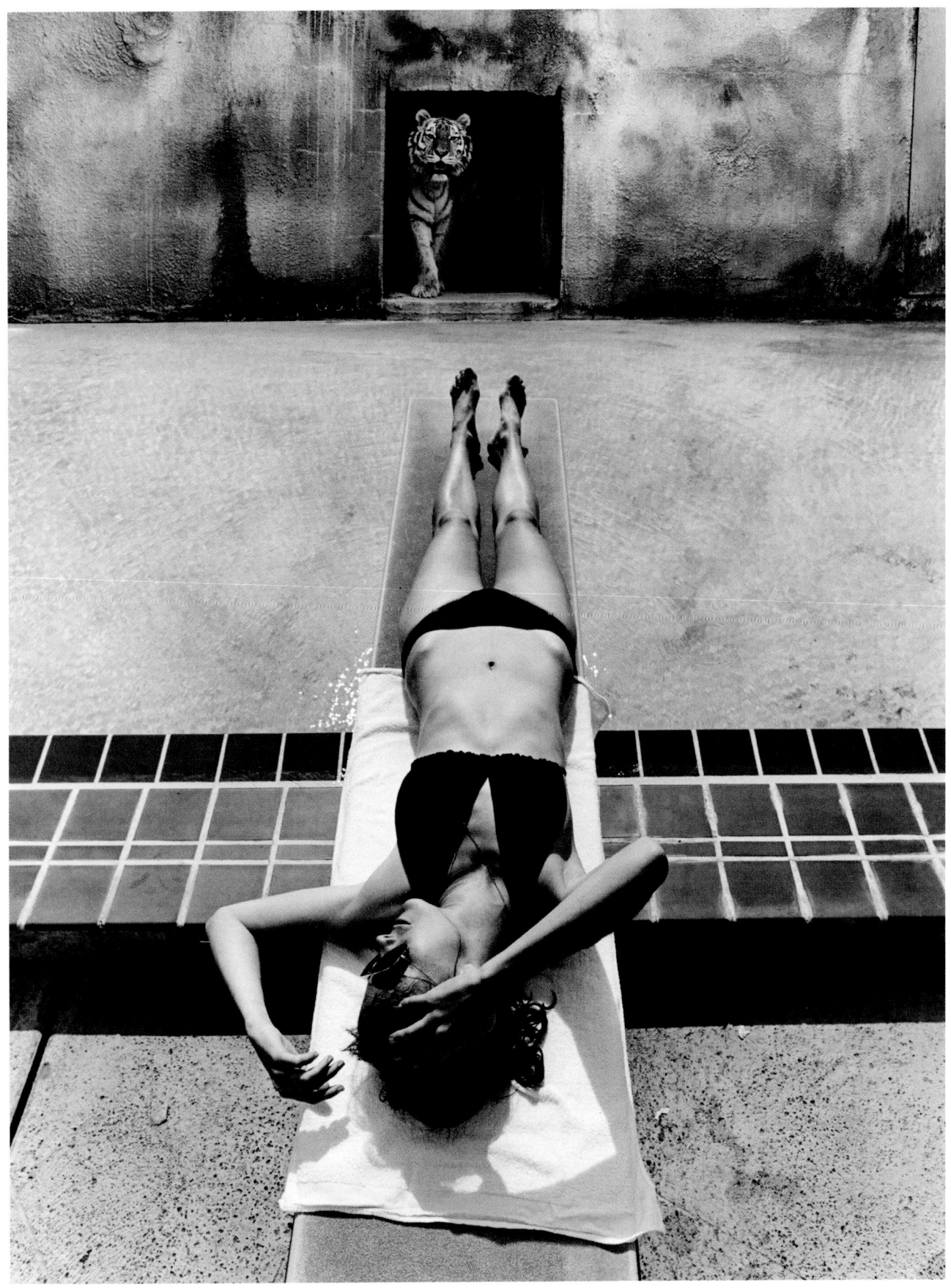

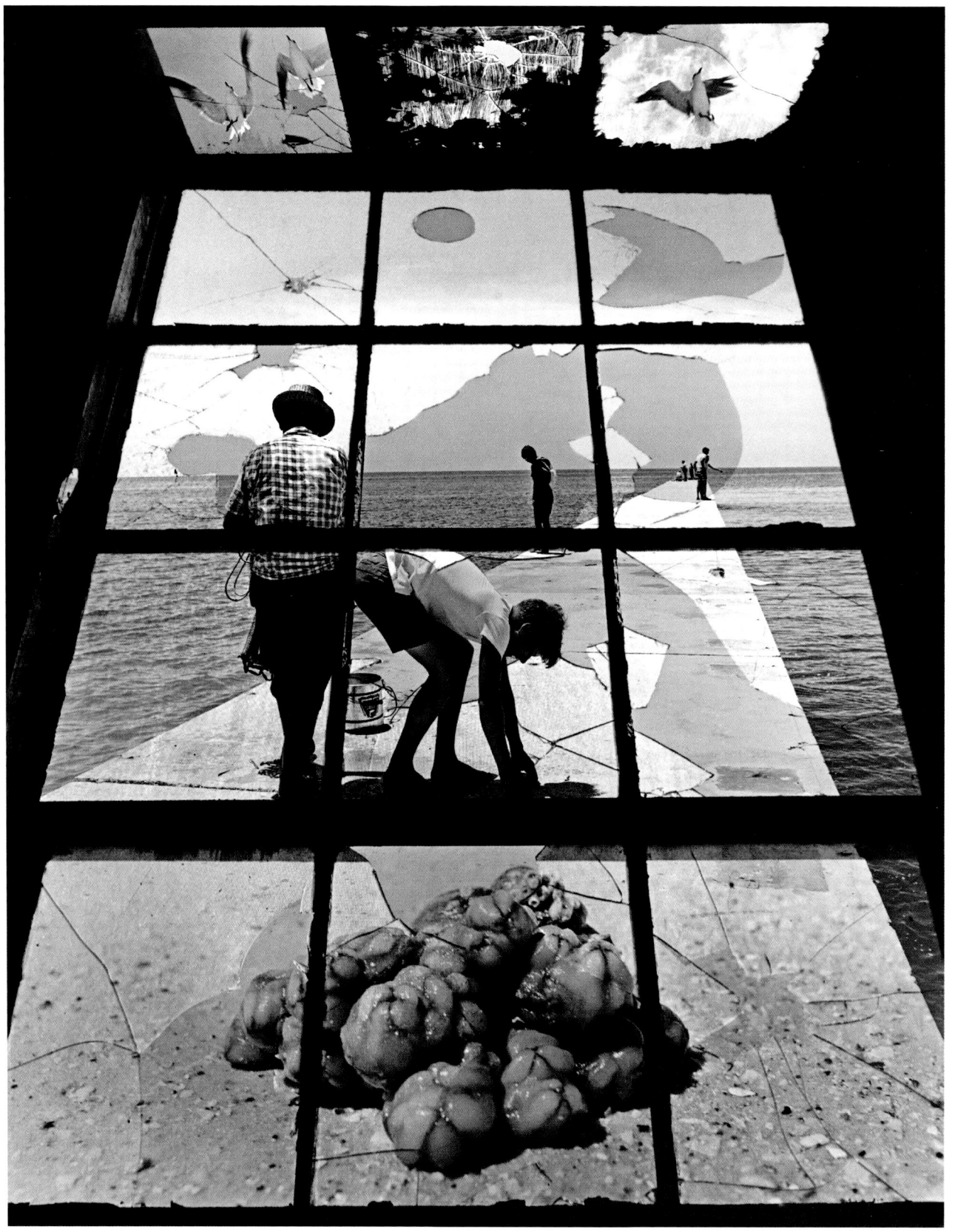

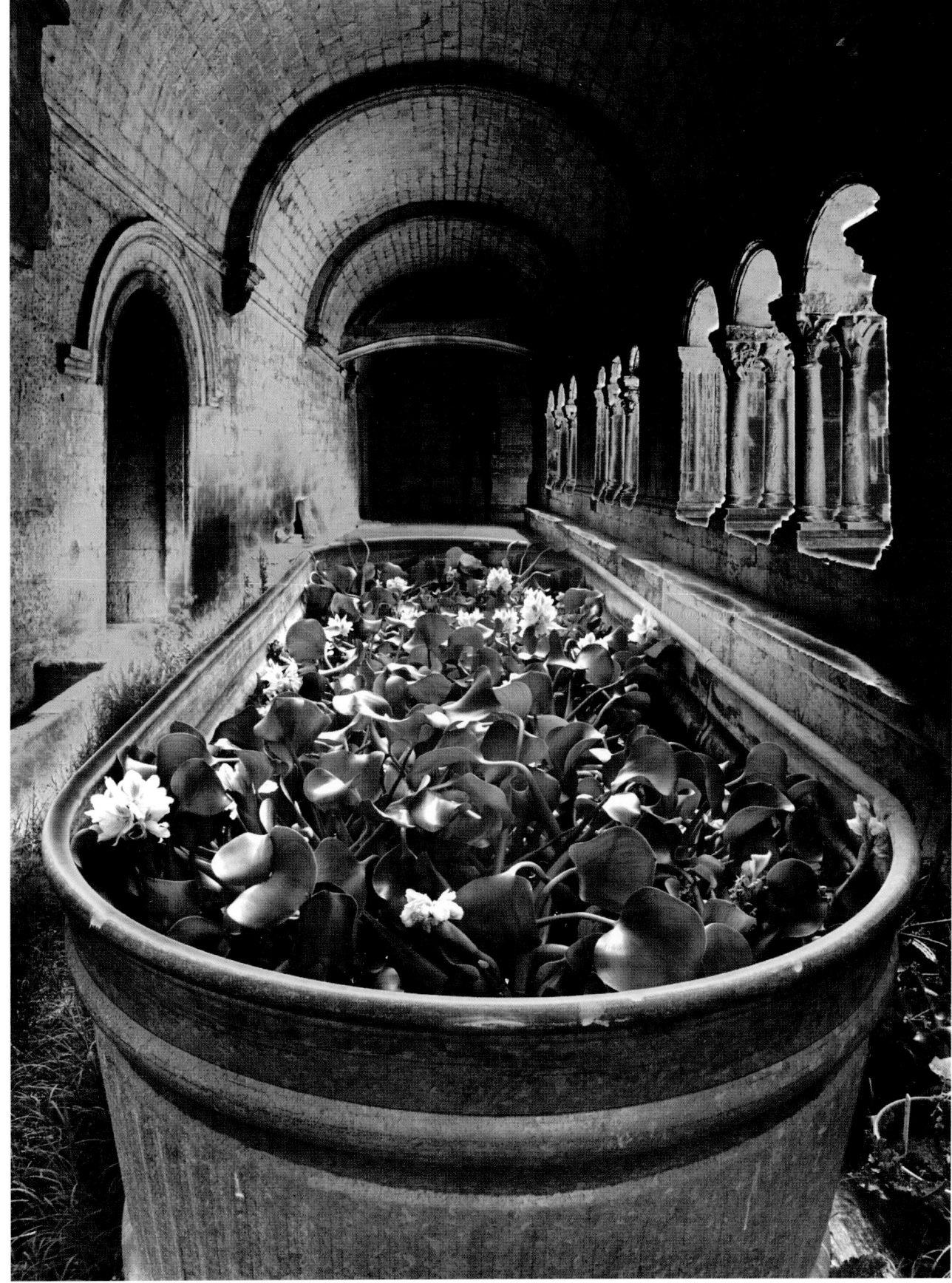

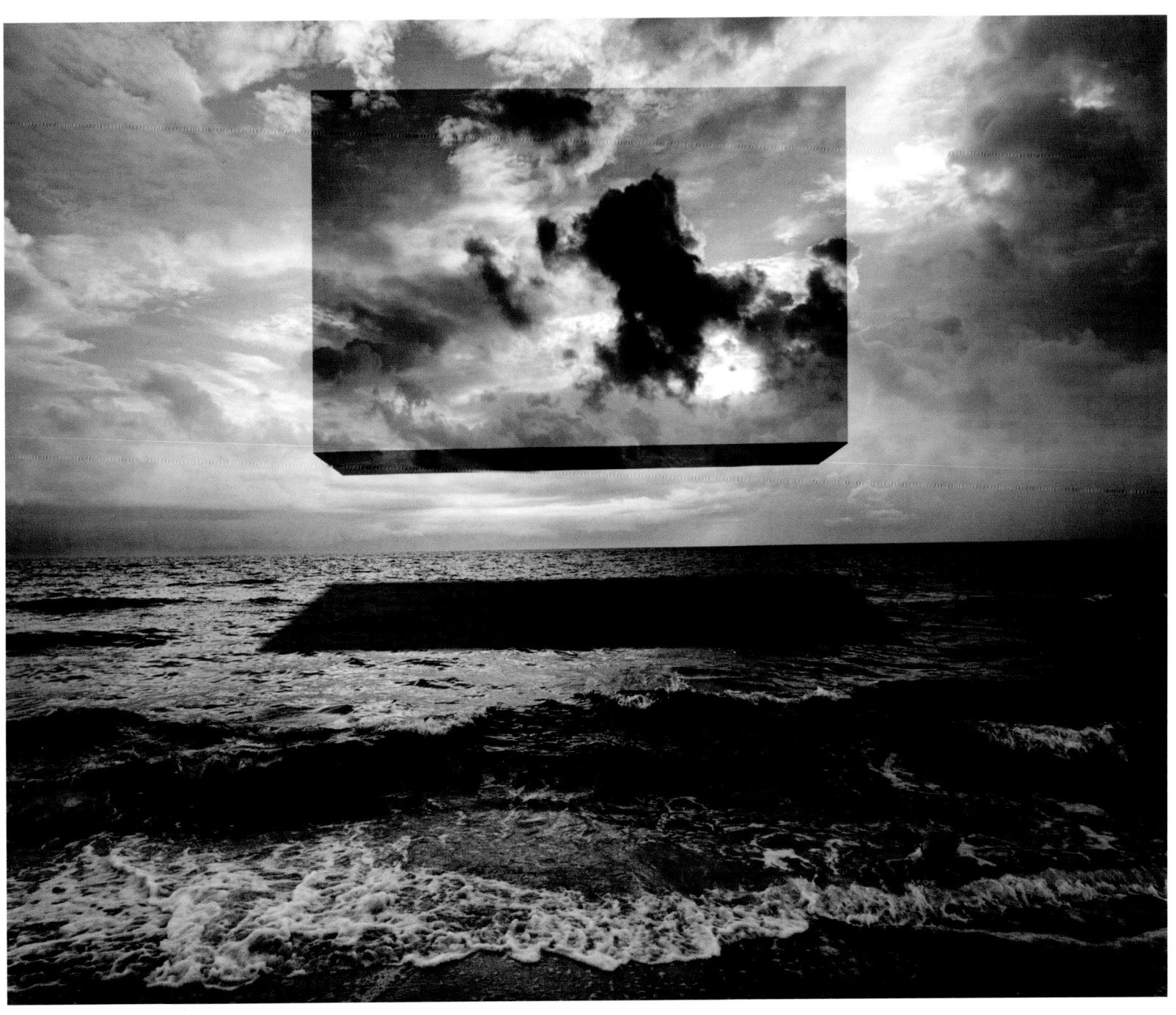

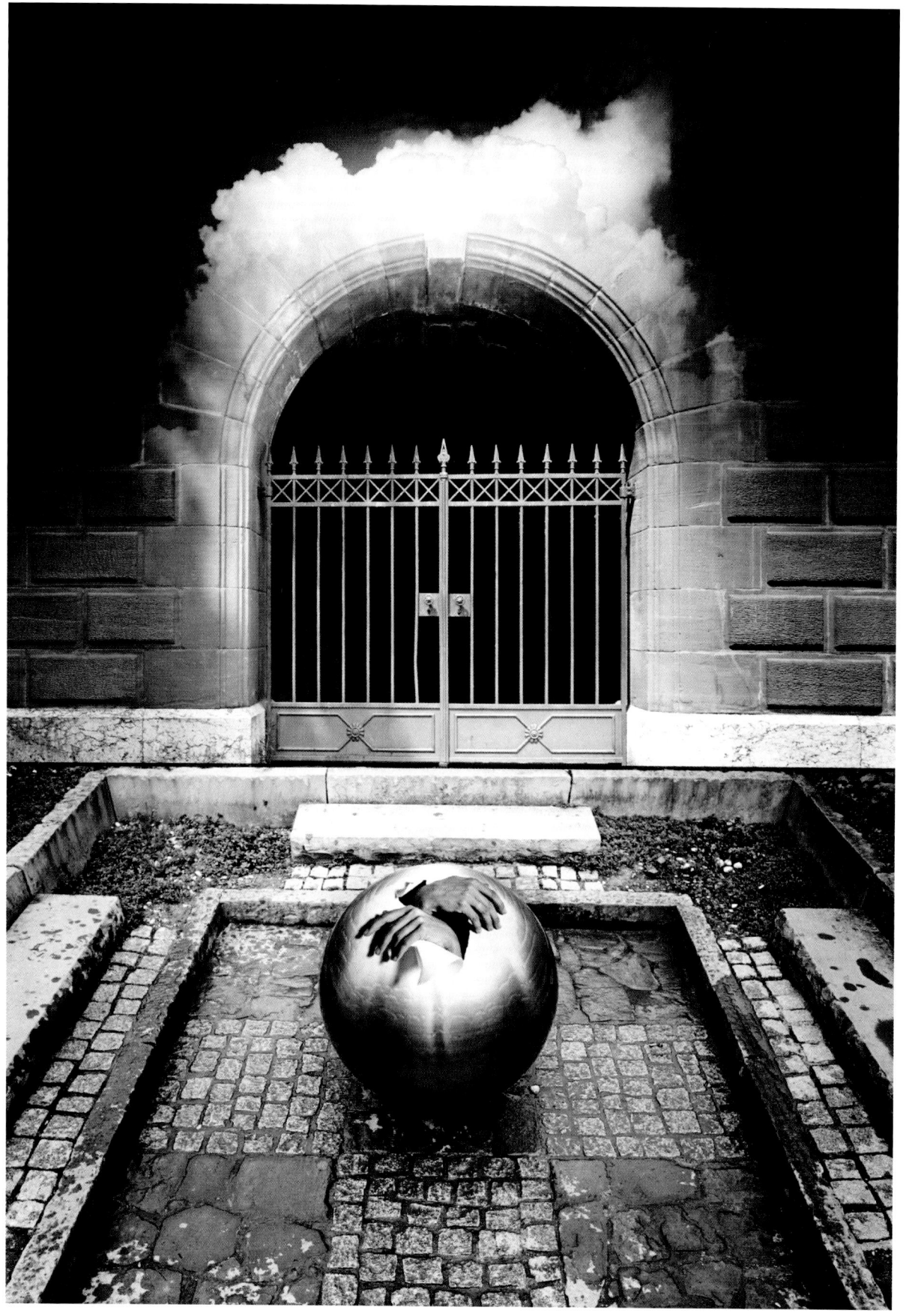

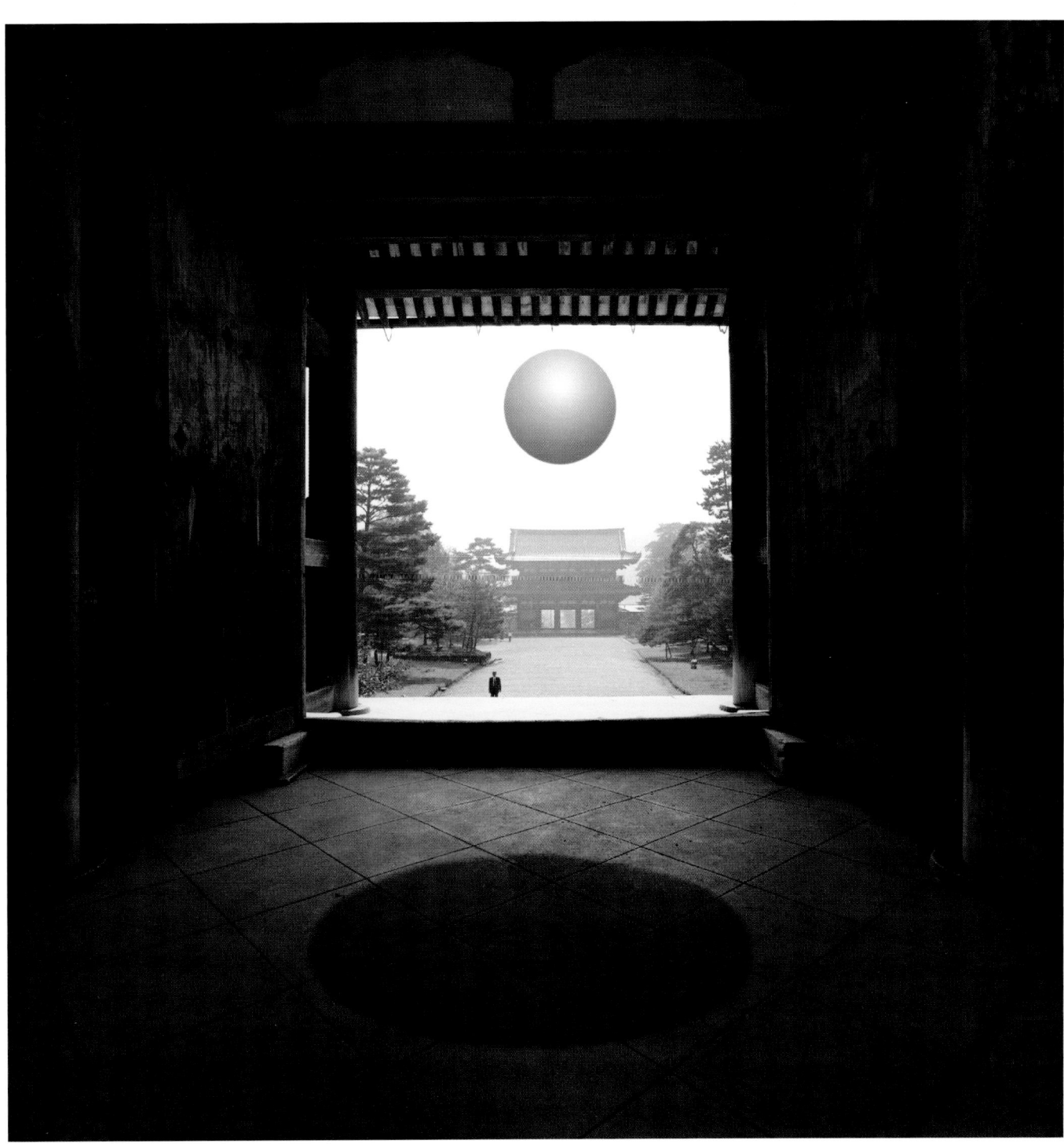

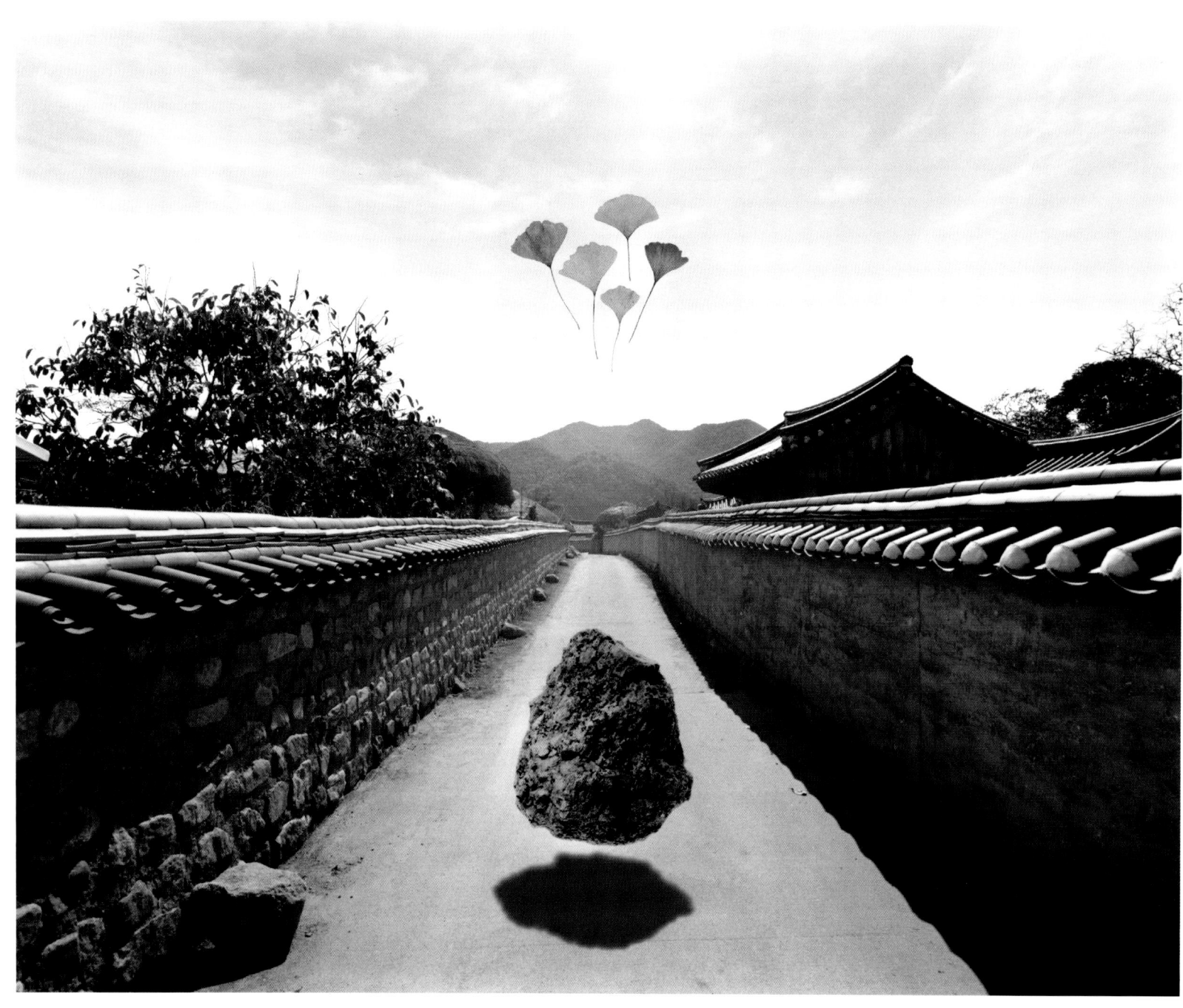

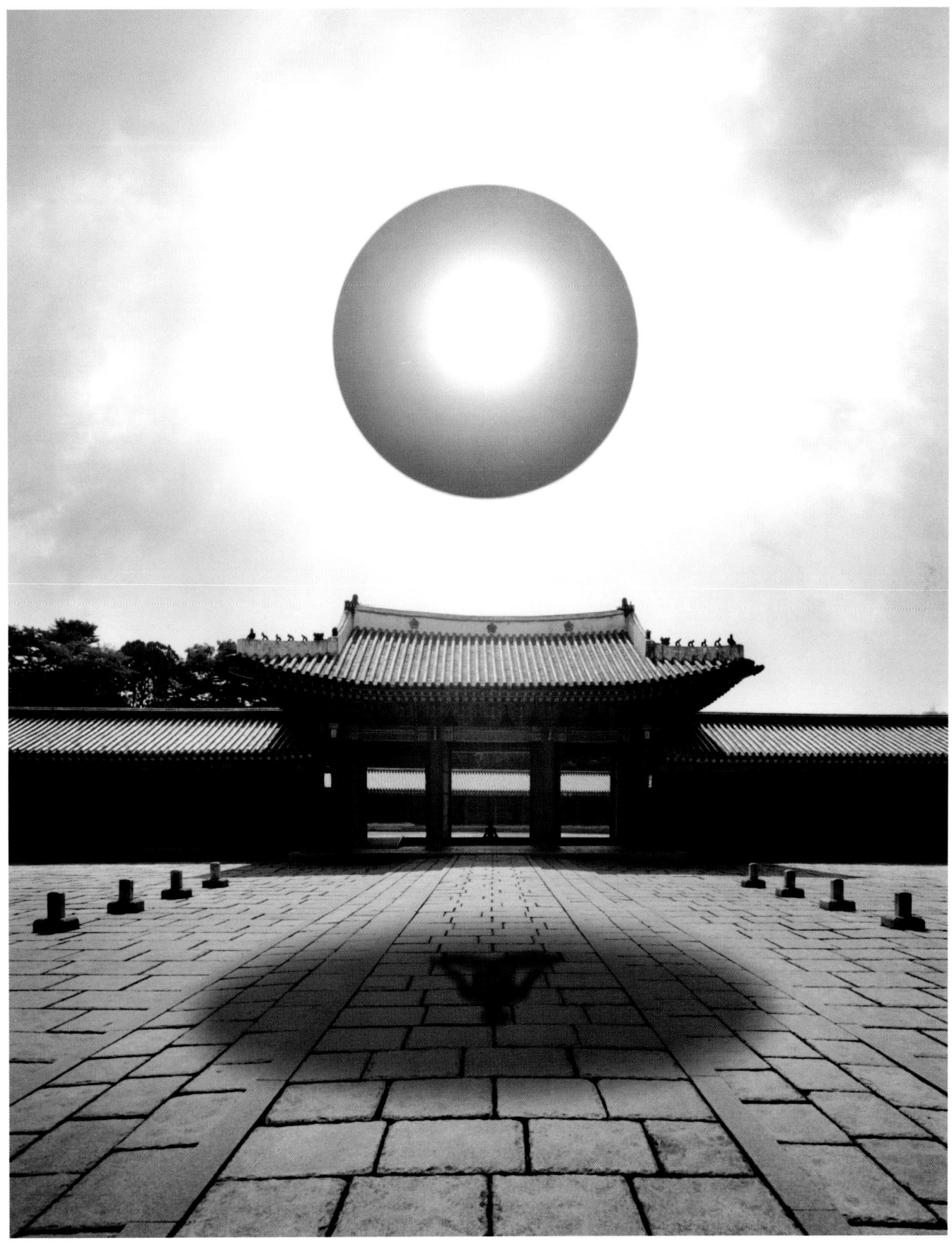

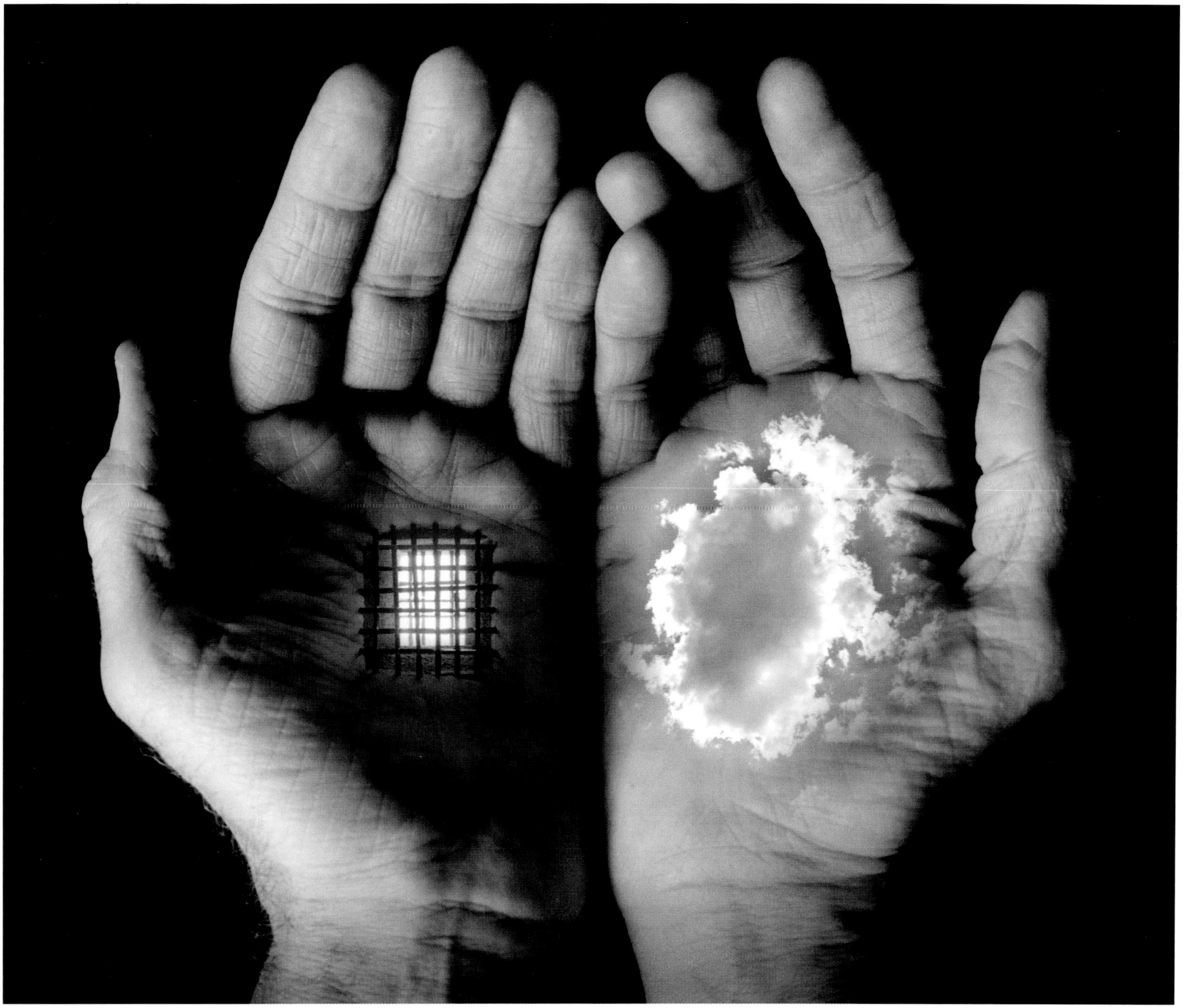

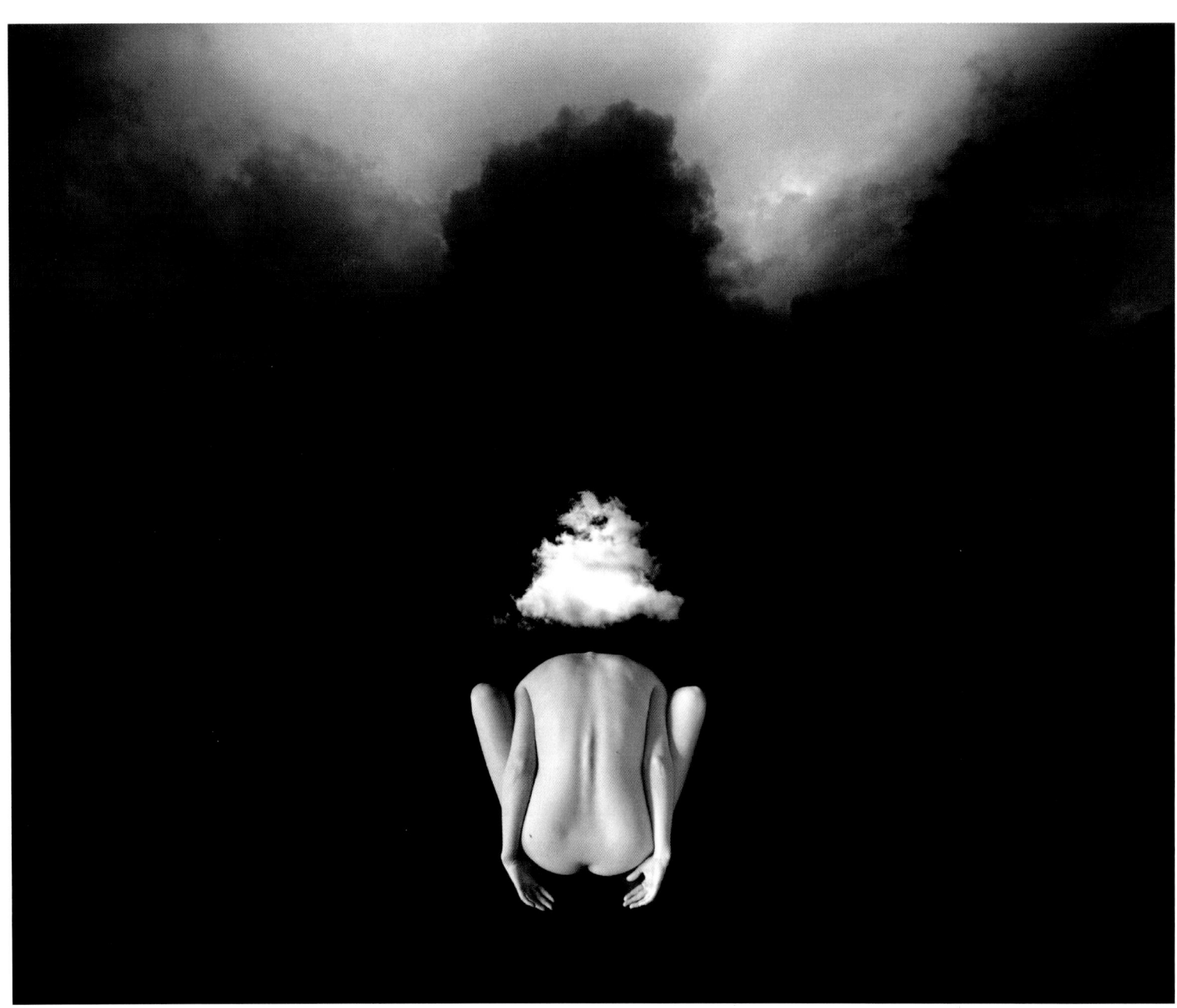

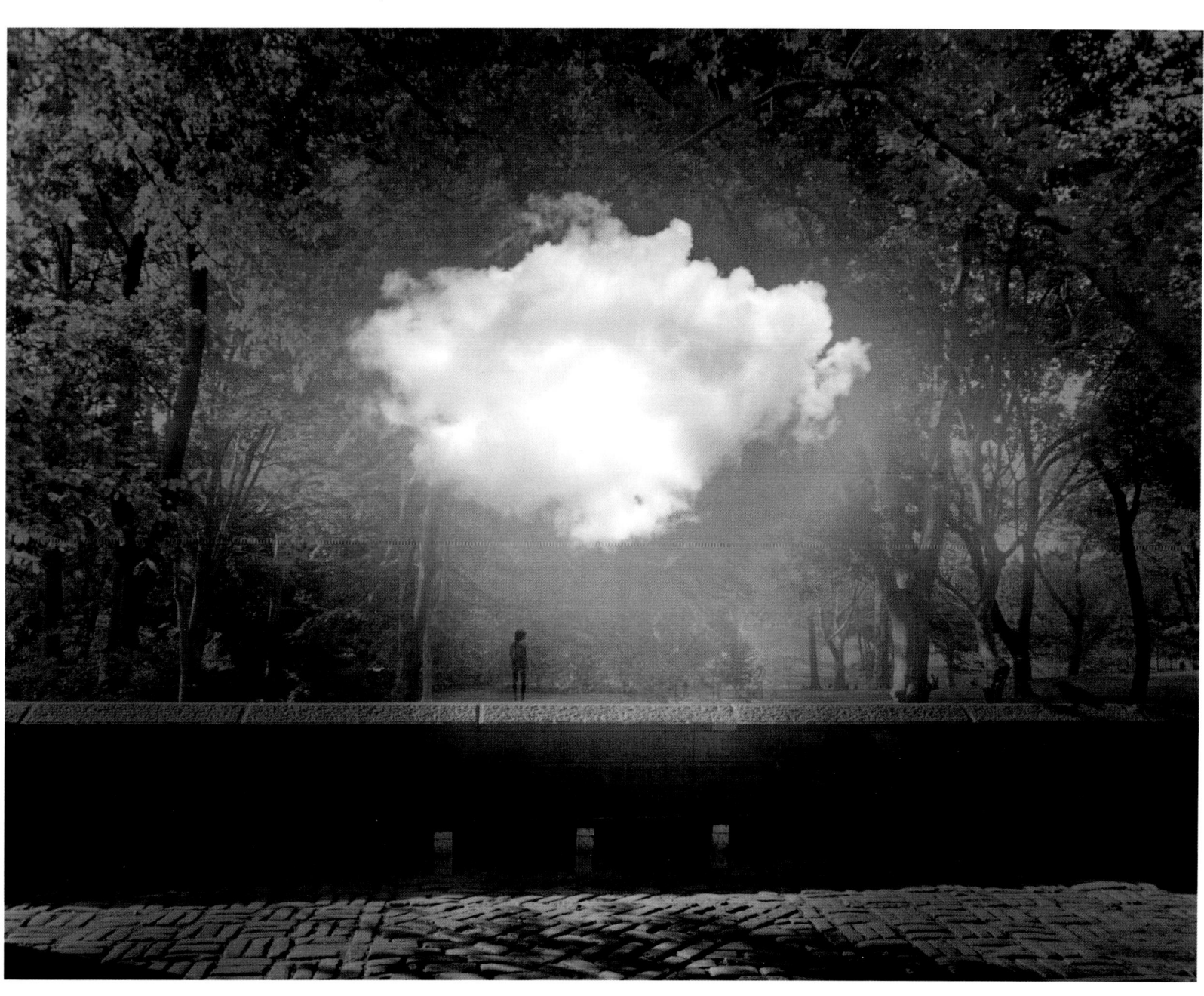

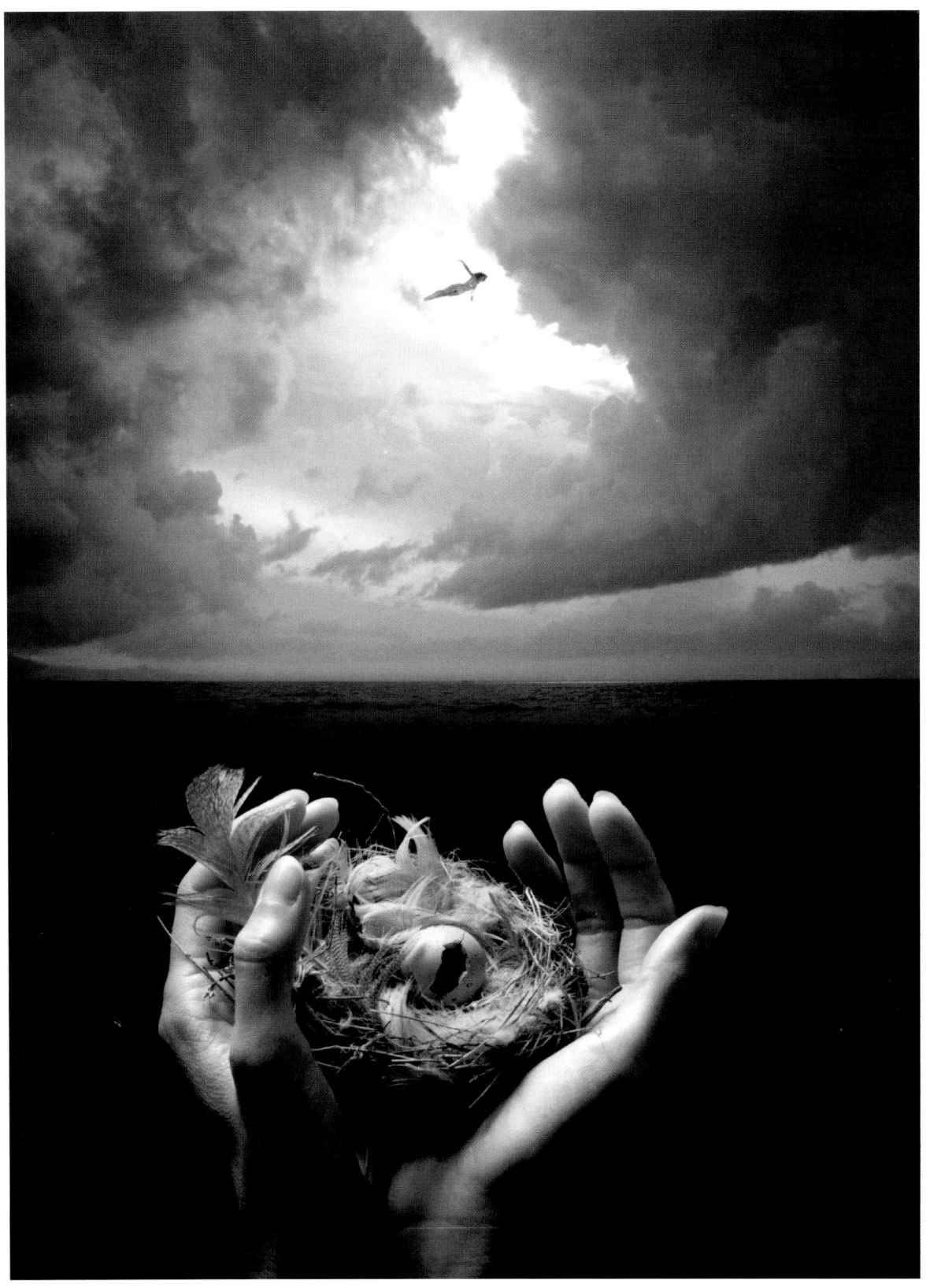

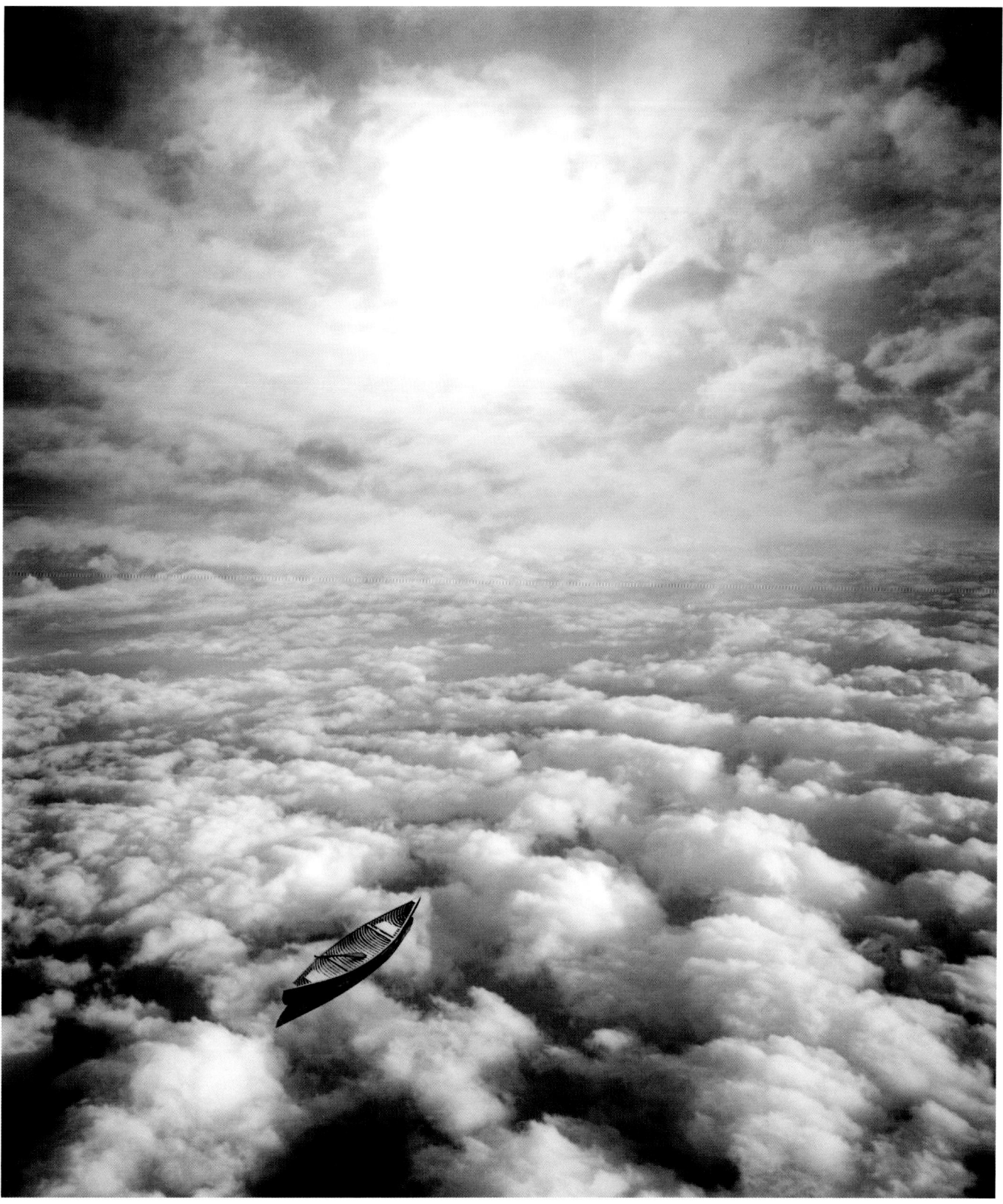

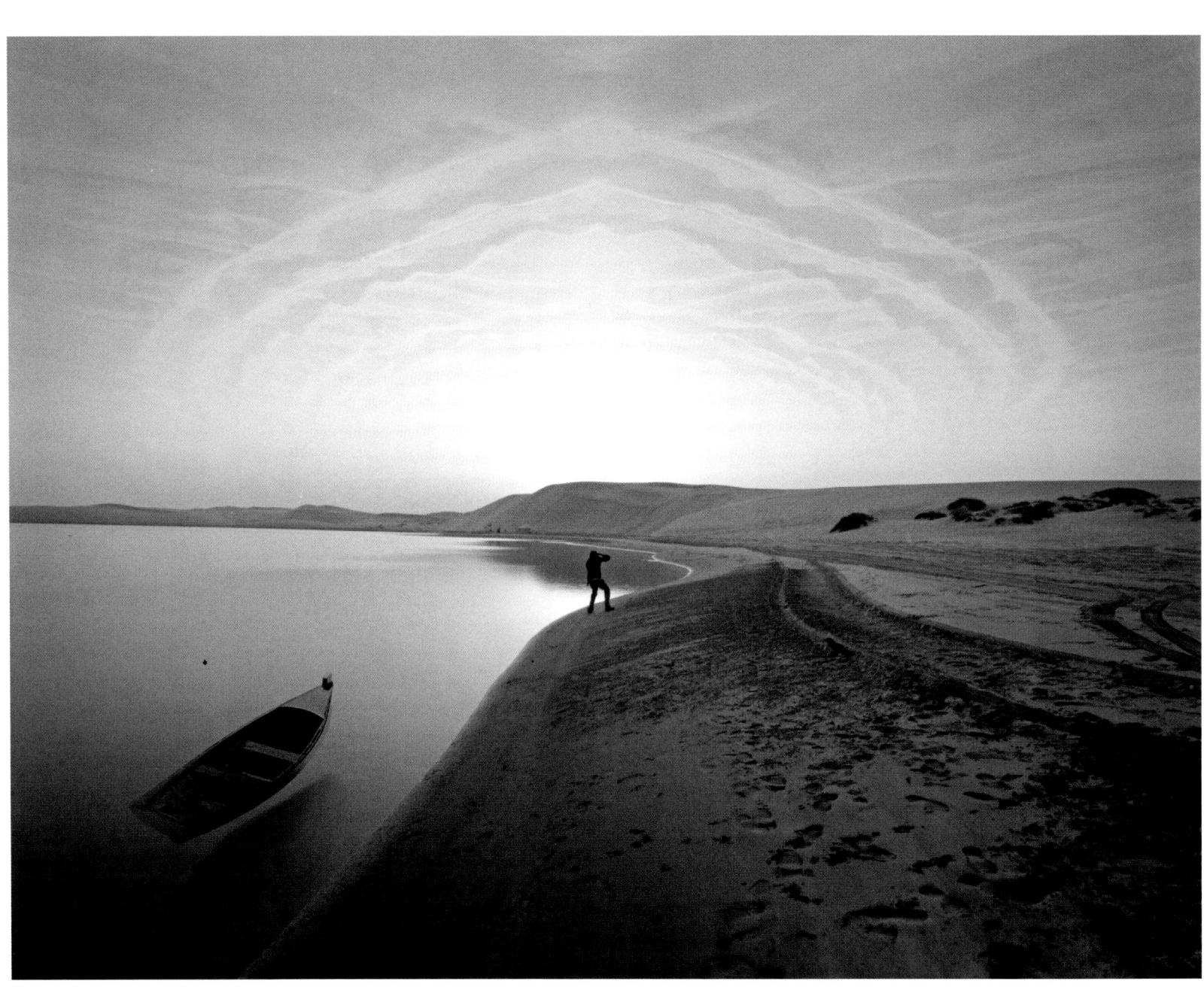

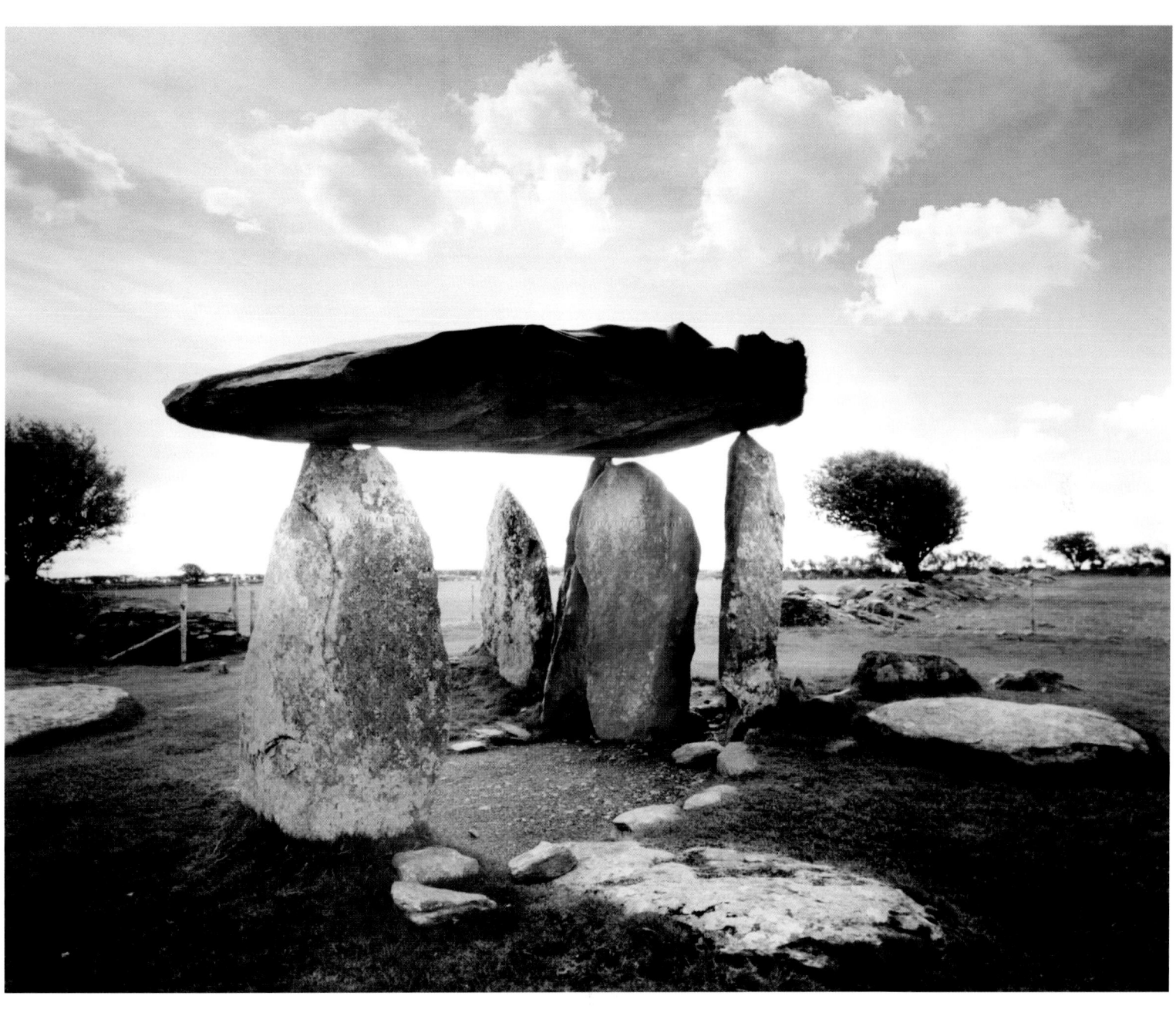

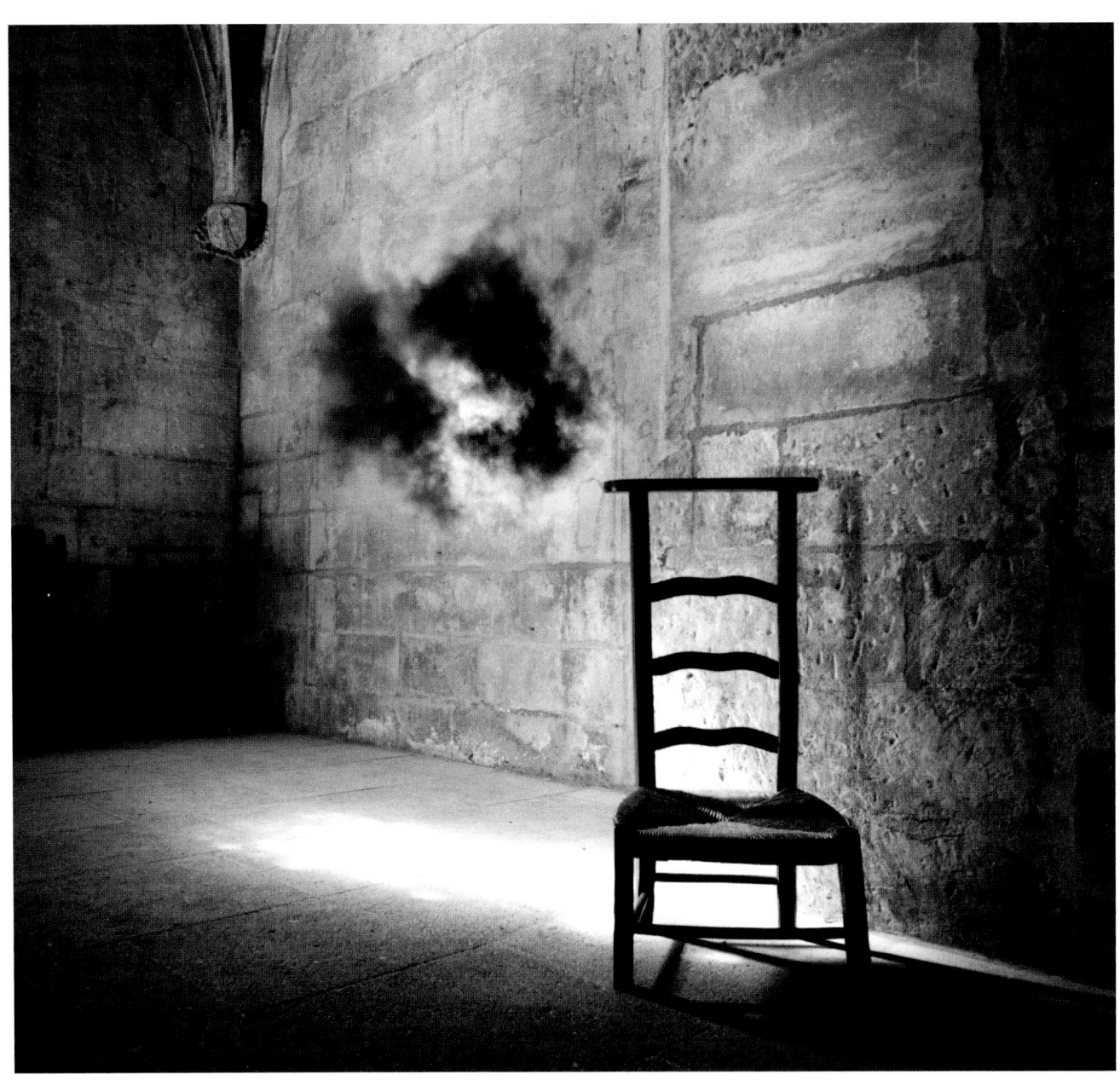

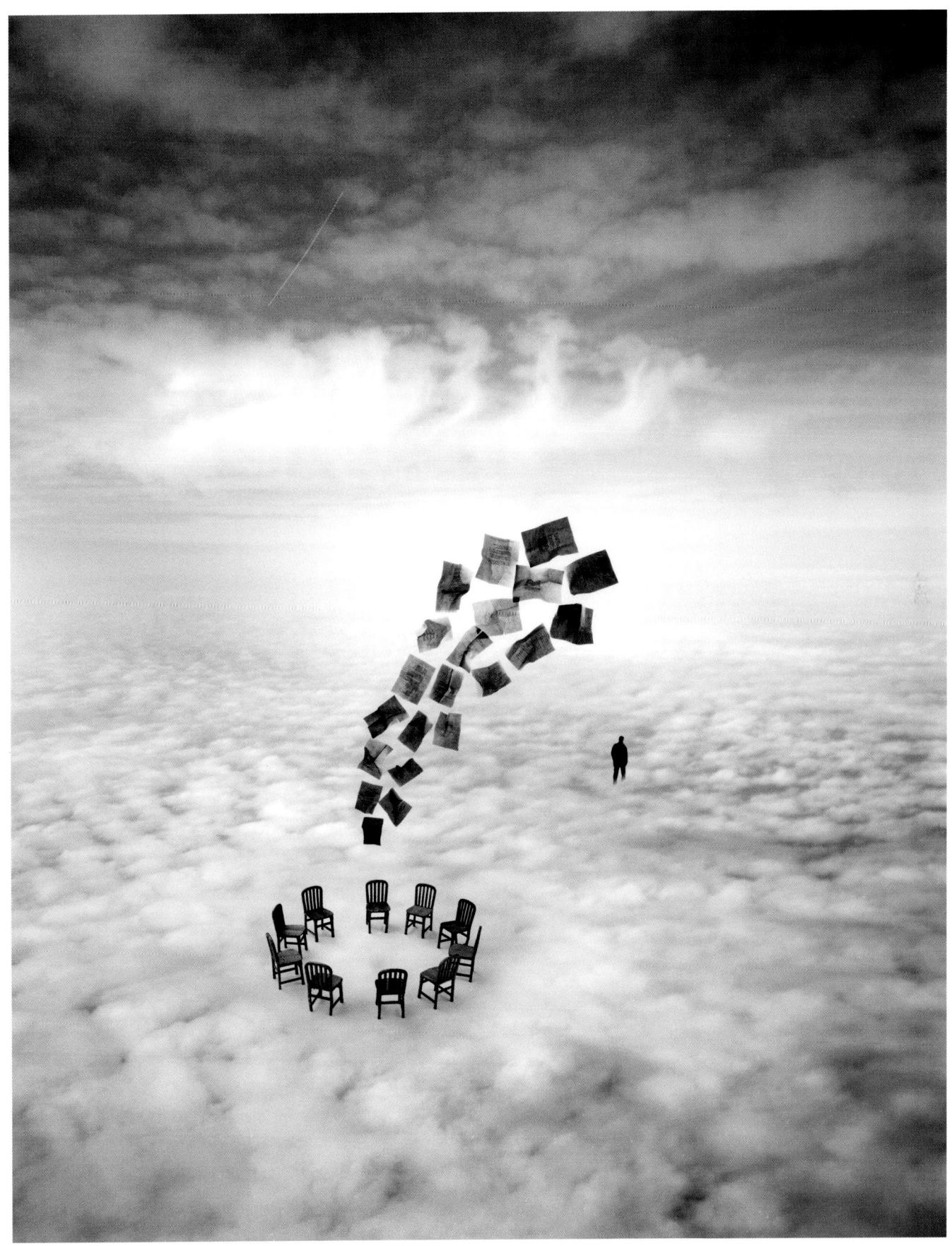

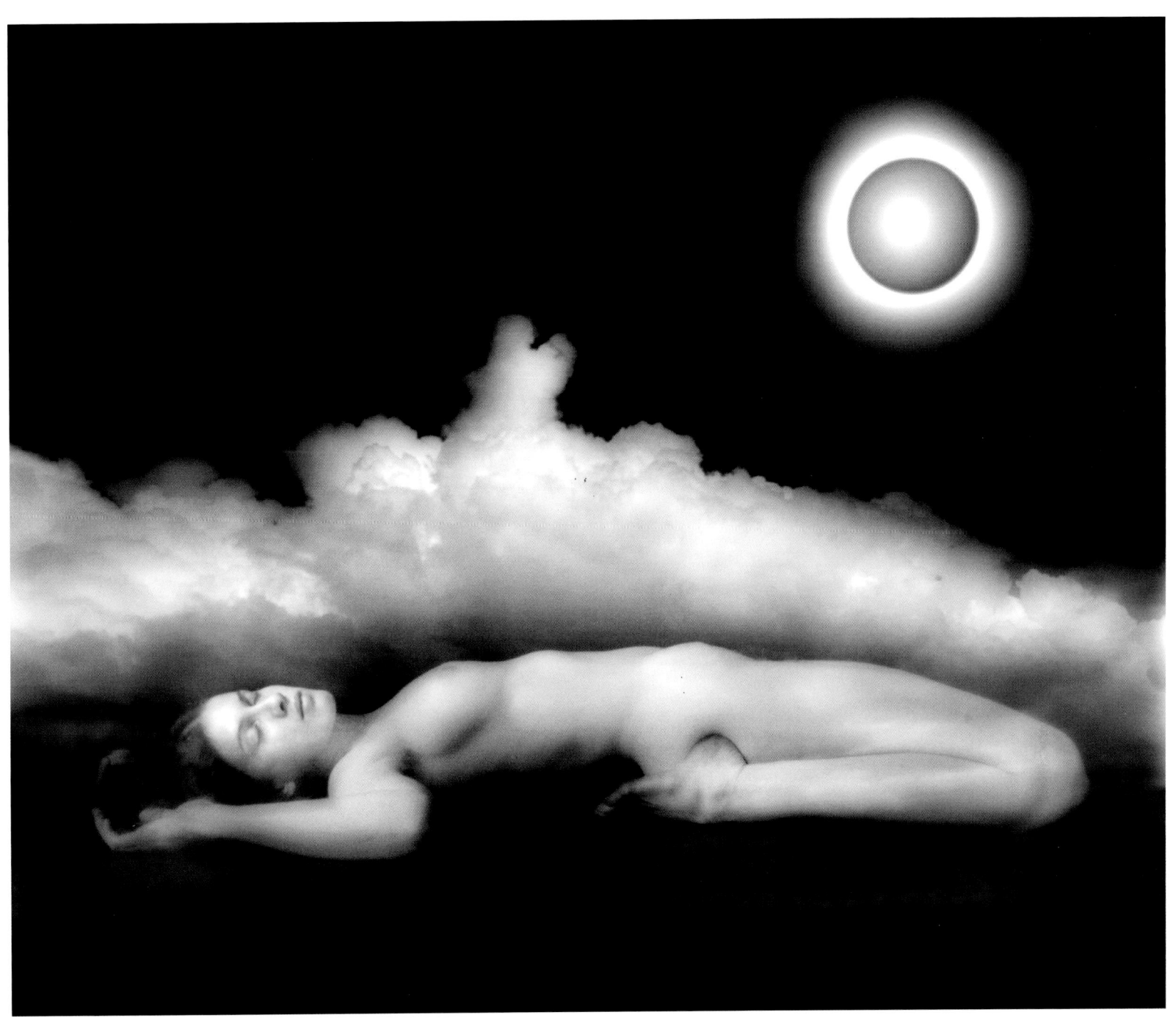

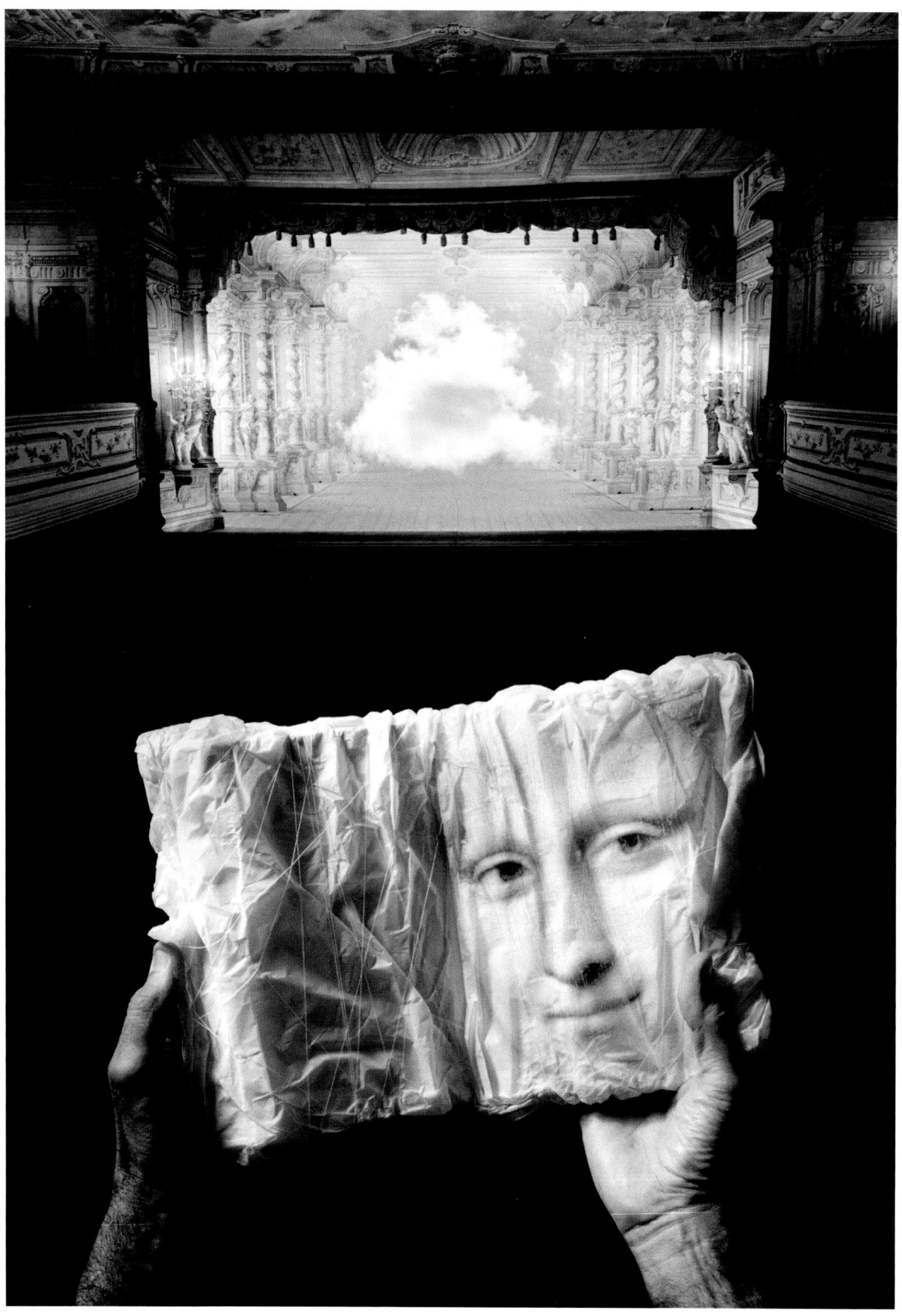

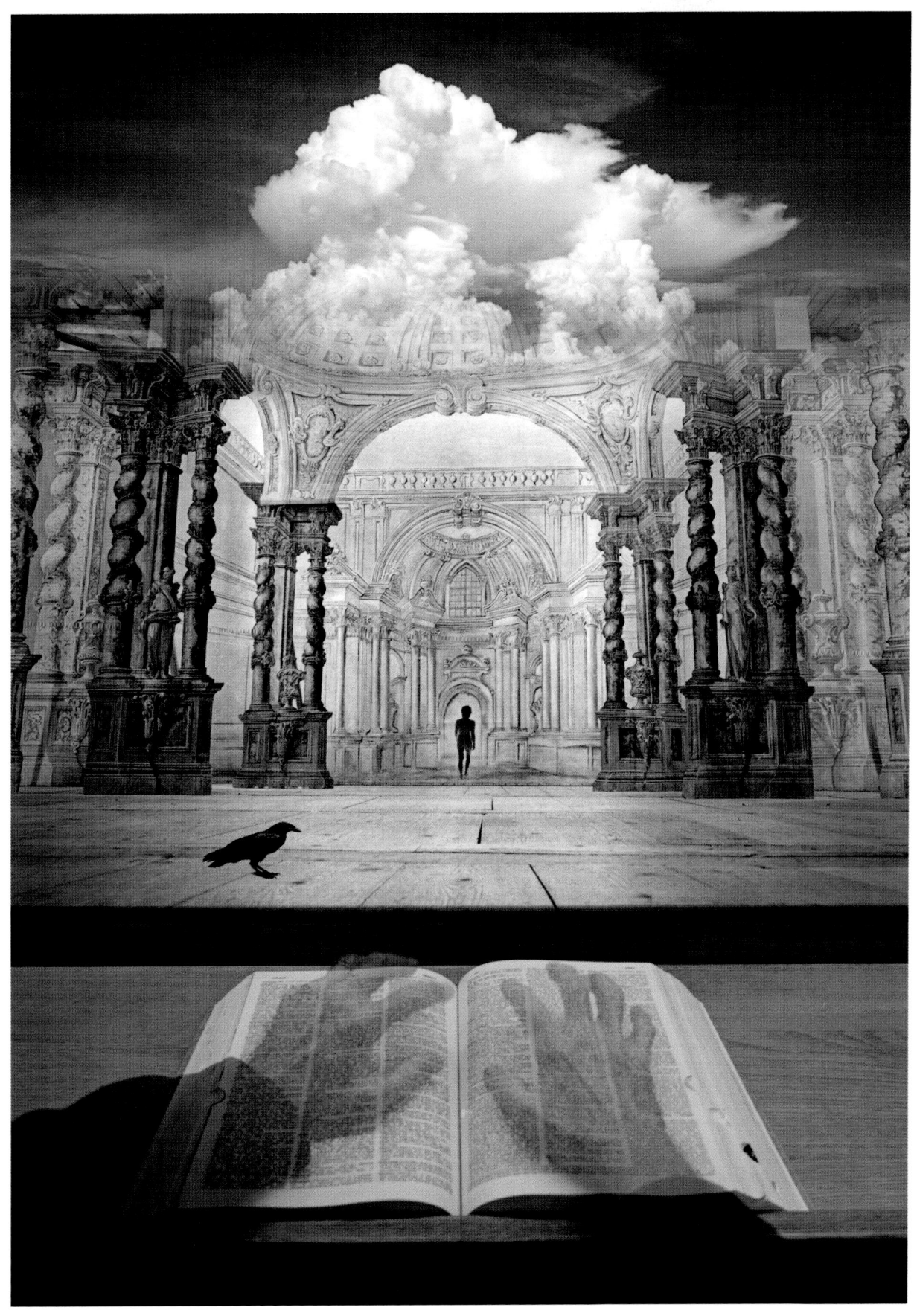

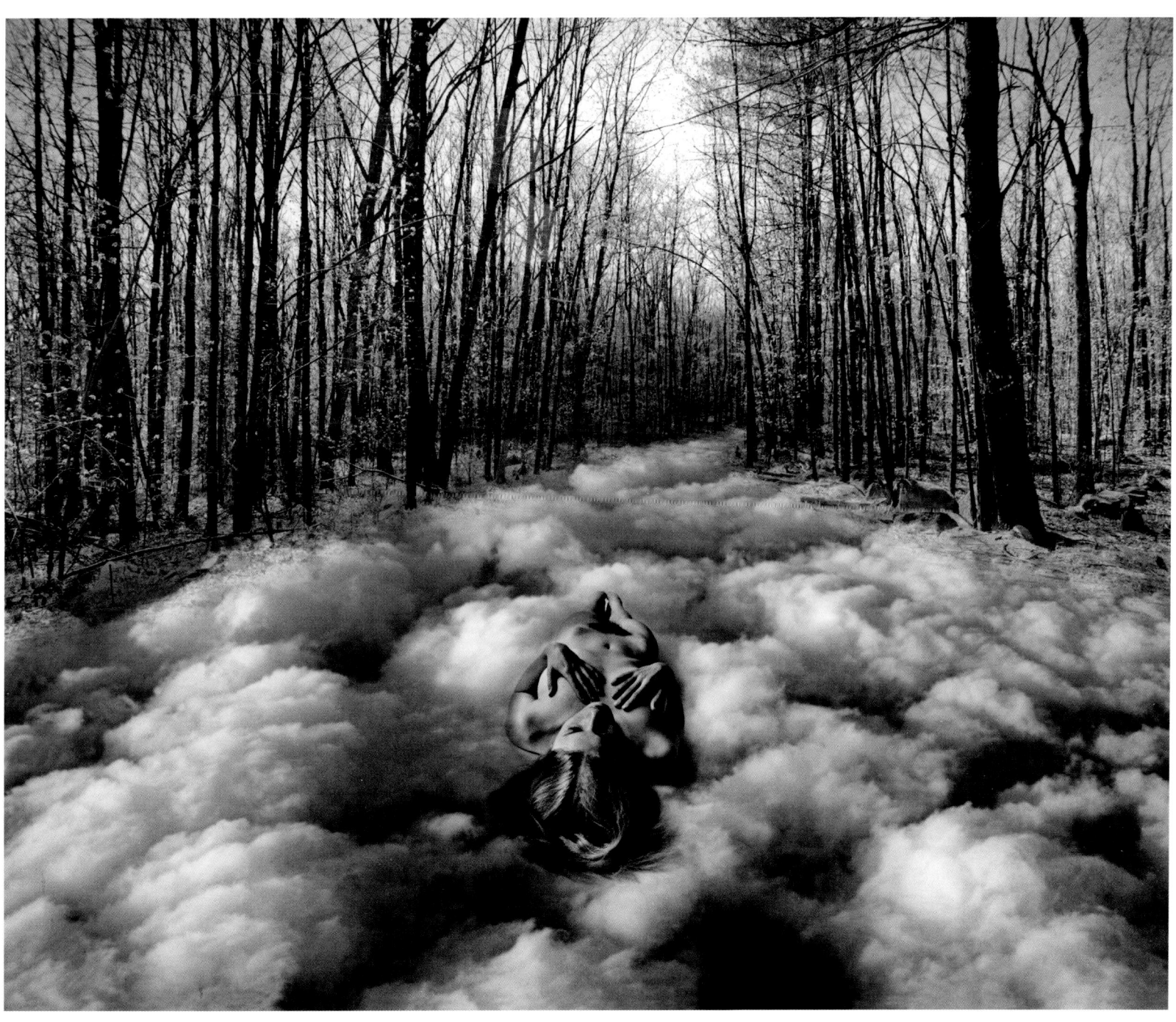

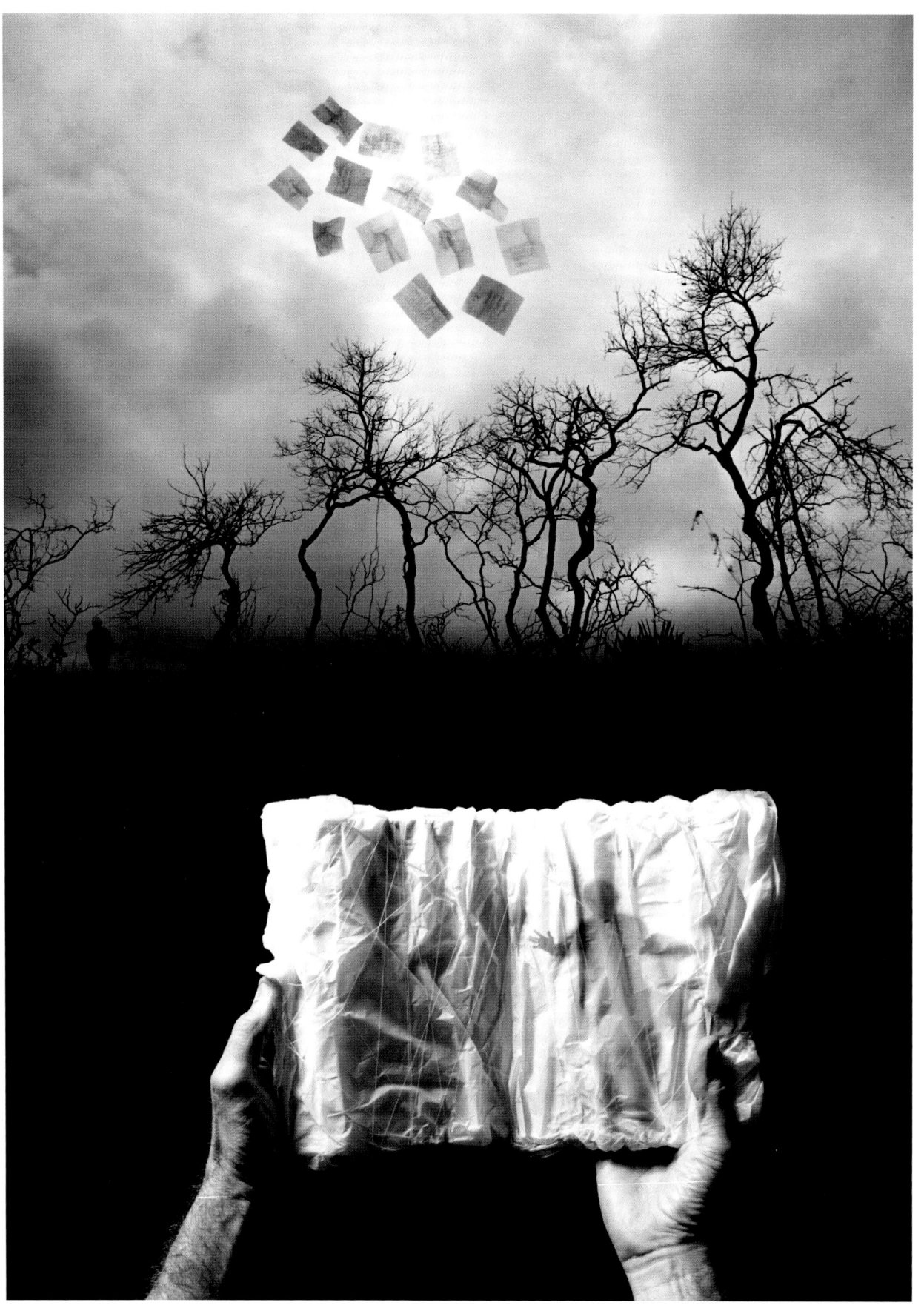

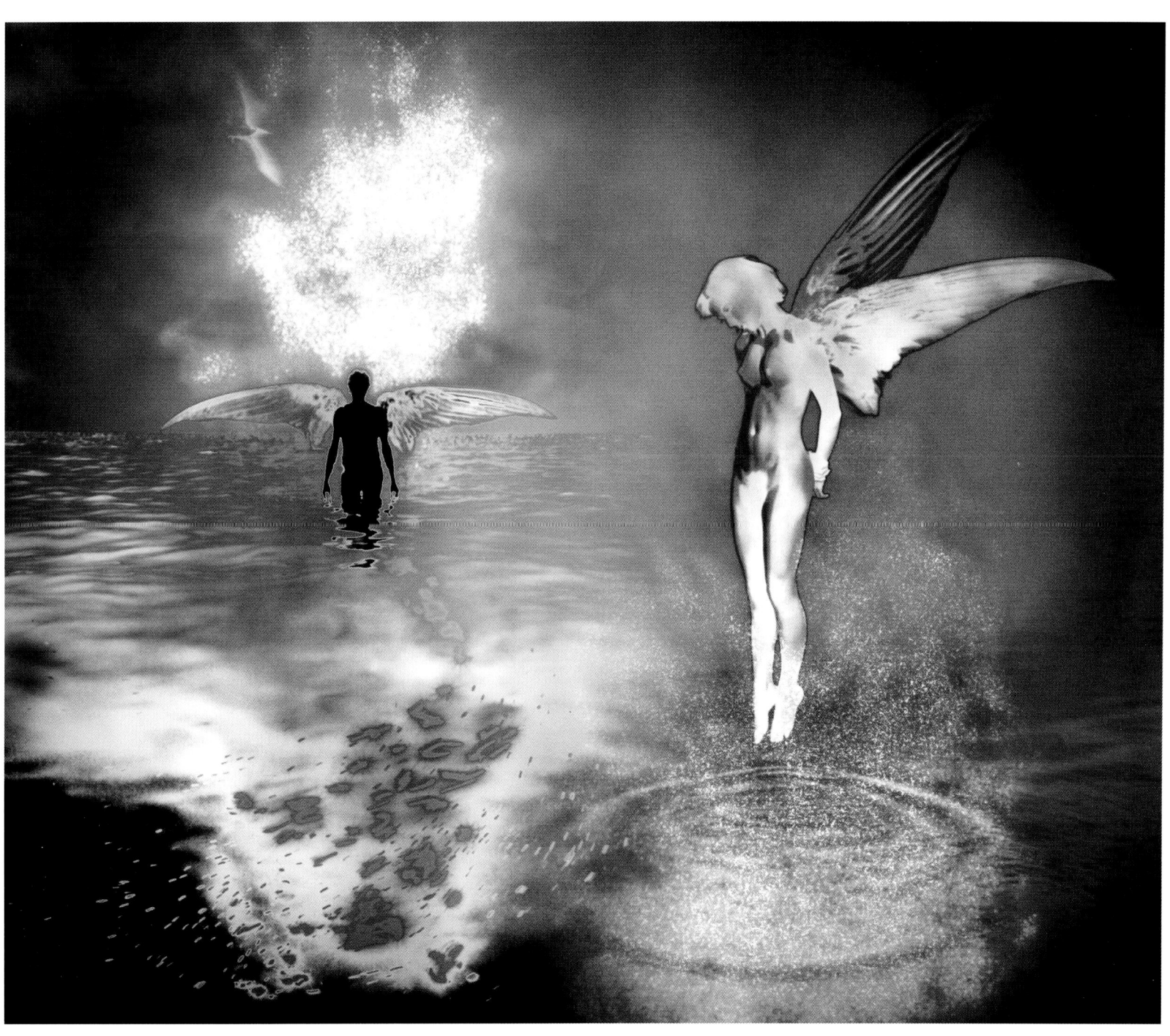

187 | Homage to Man Ray 1997

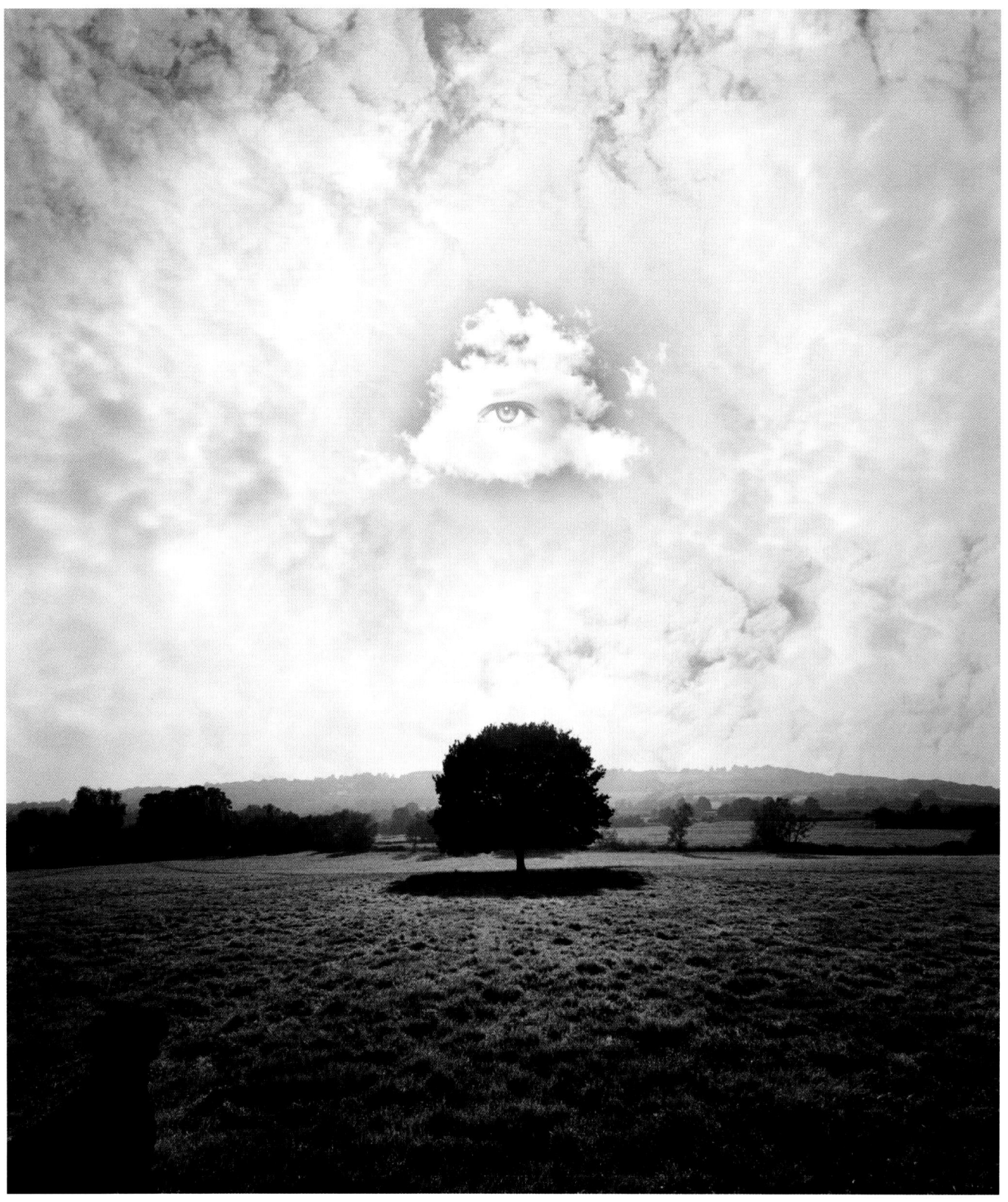

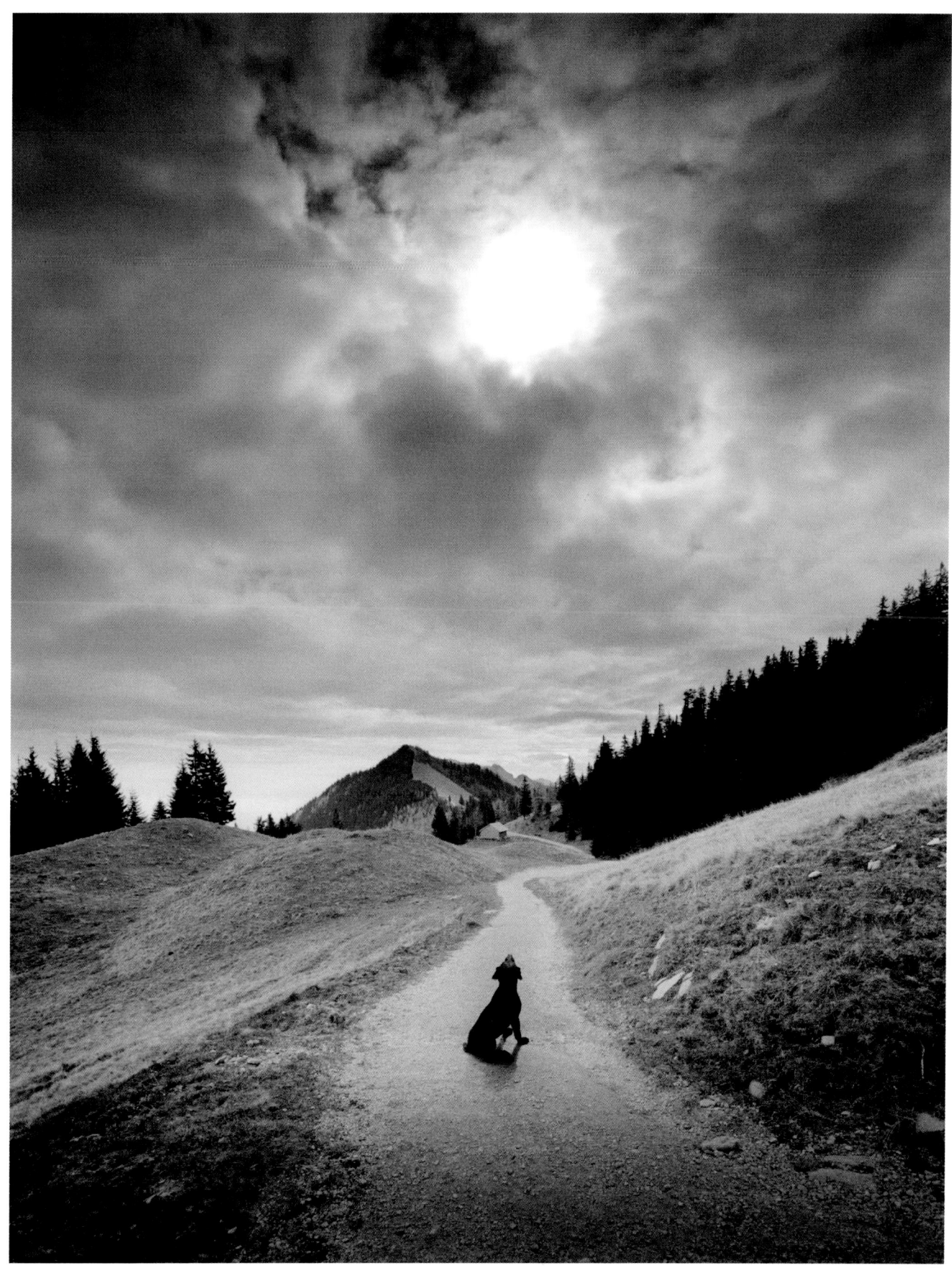

189 | (For All the Dogs That Have Blessed My Life) 2002

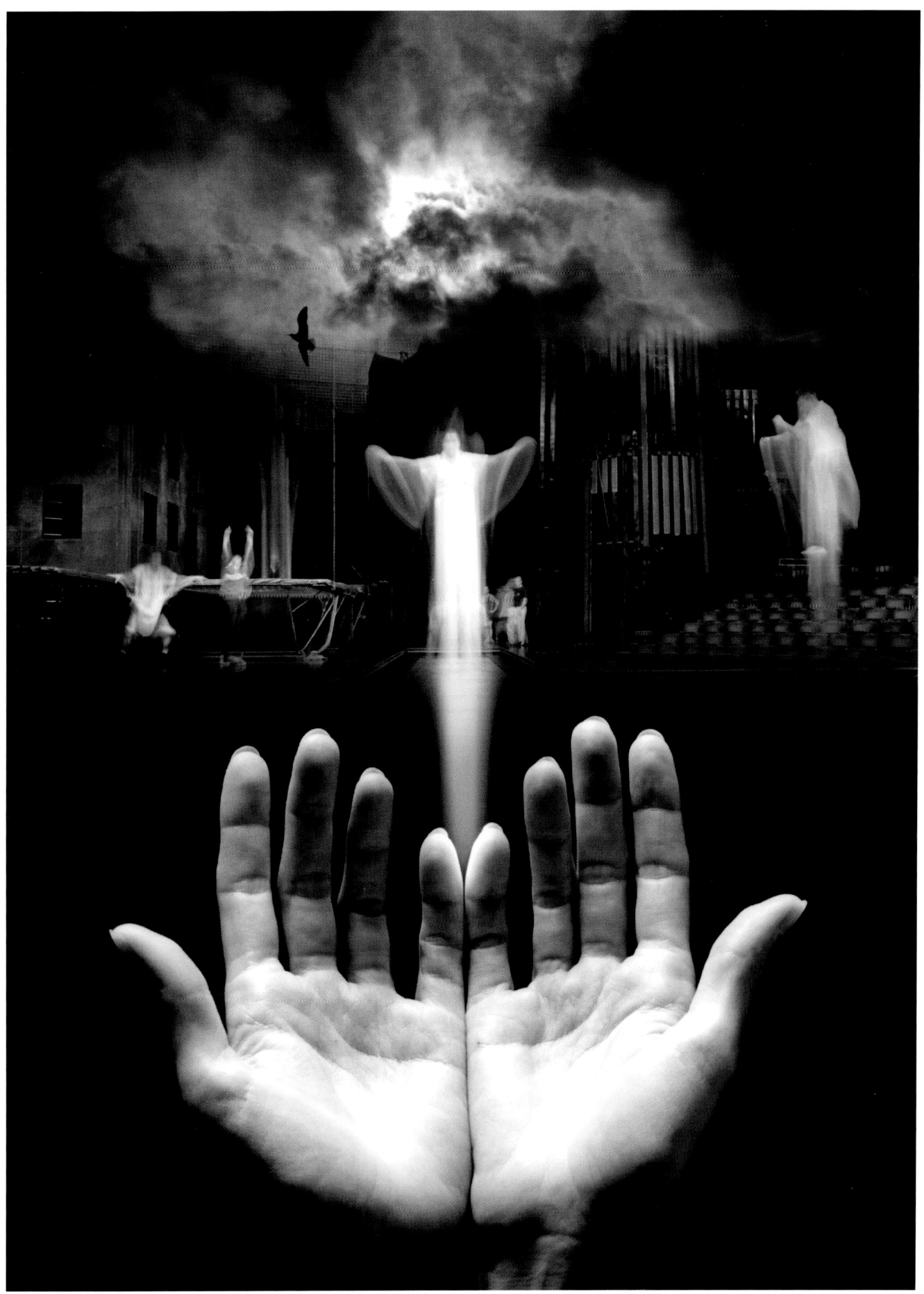

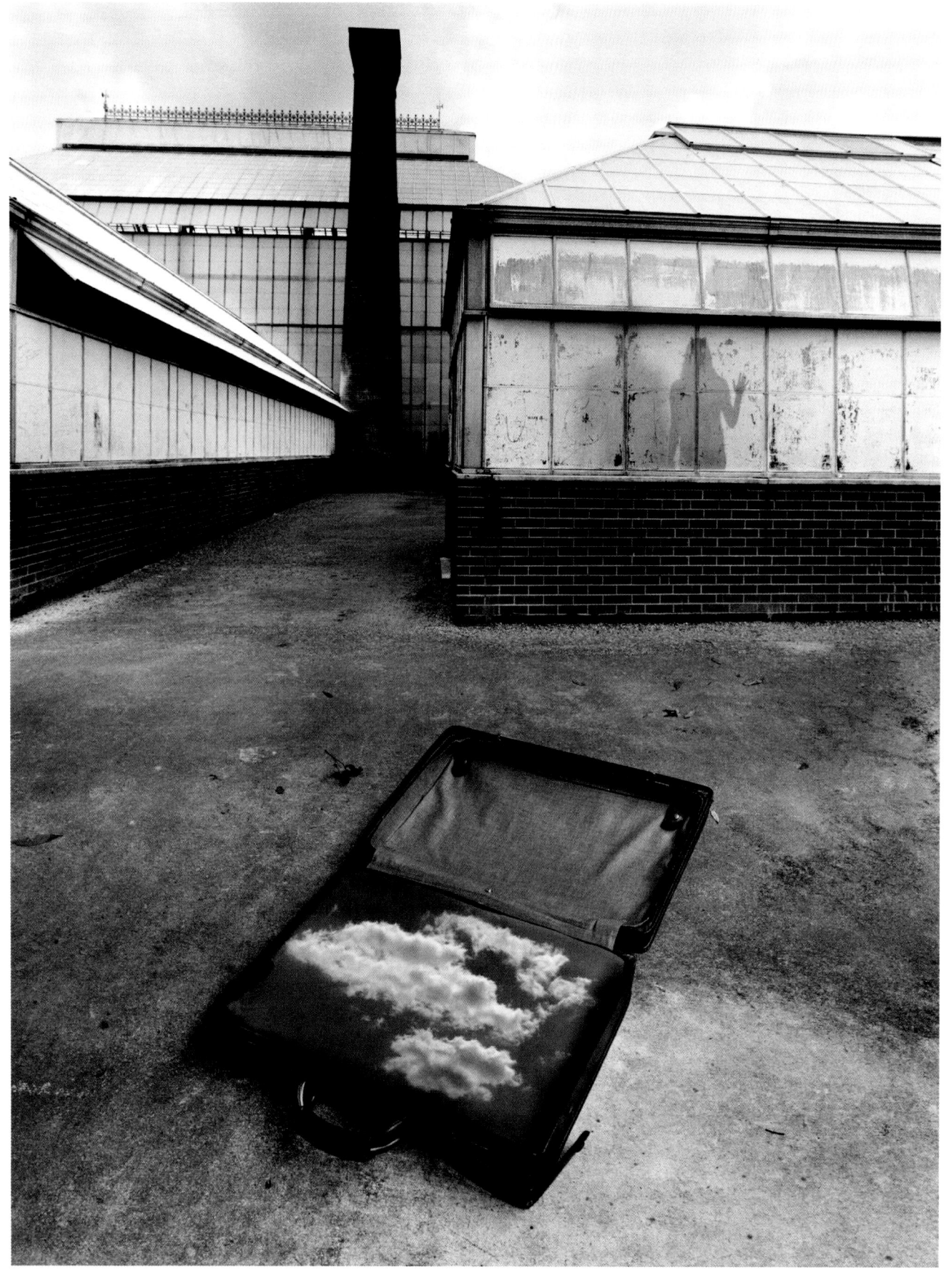

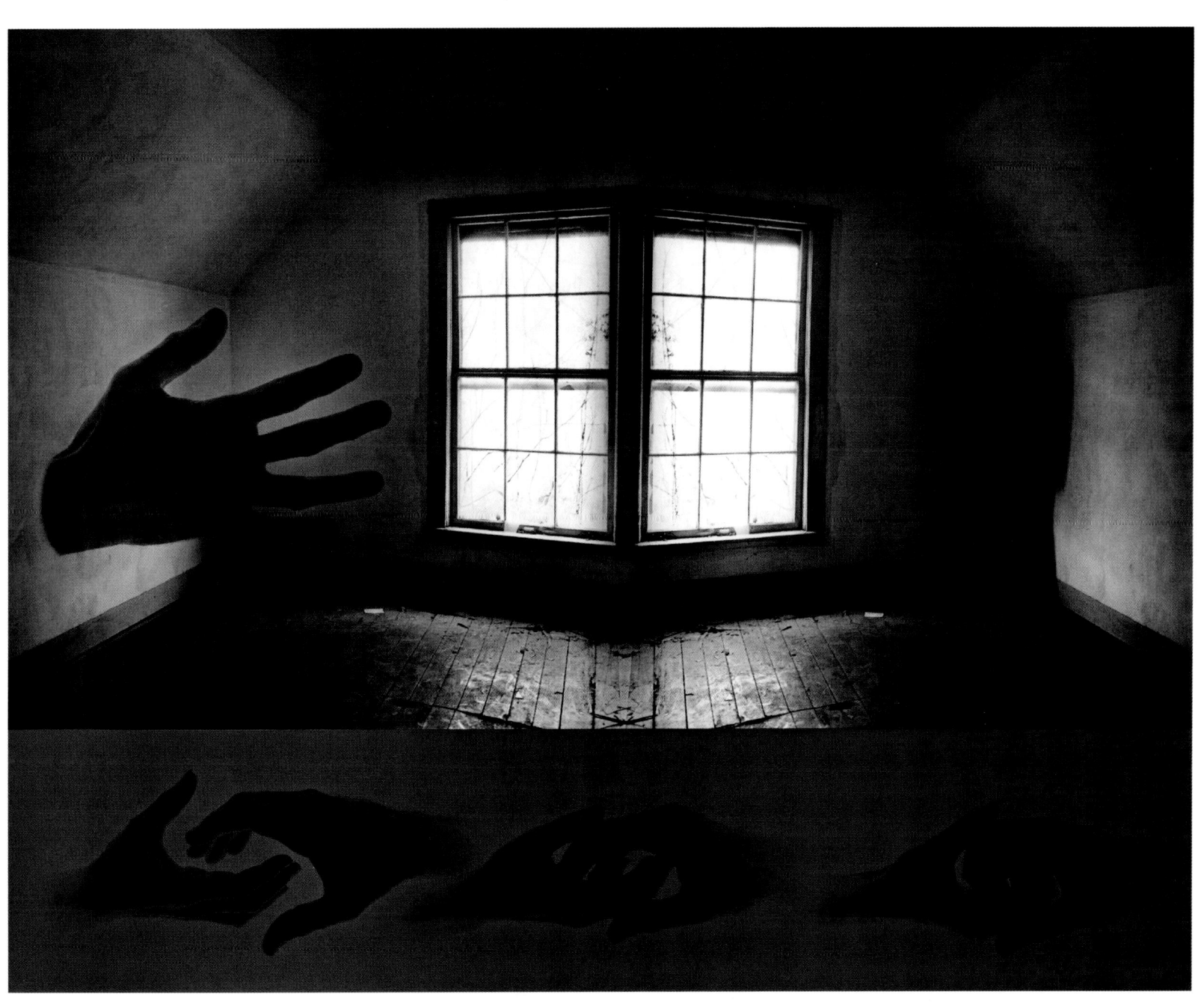

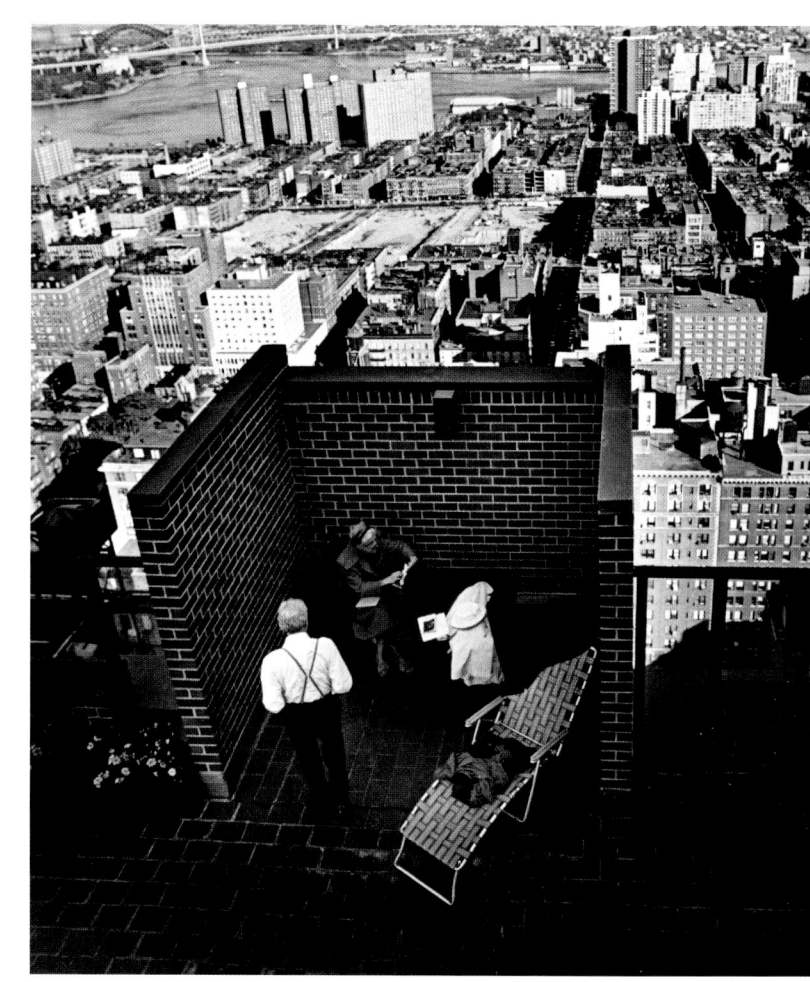

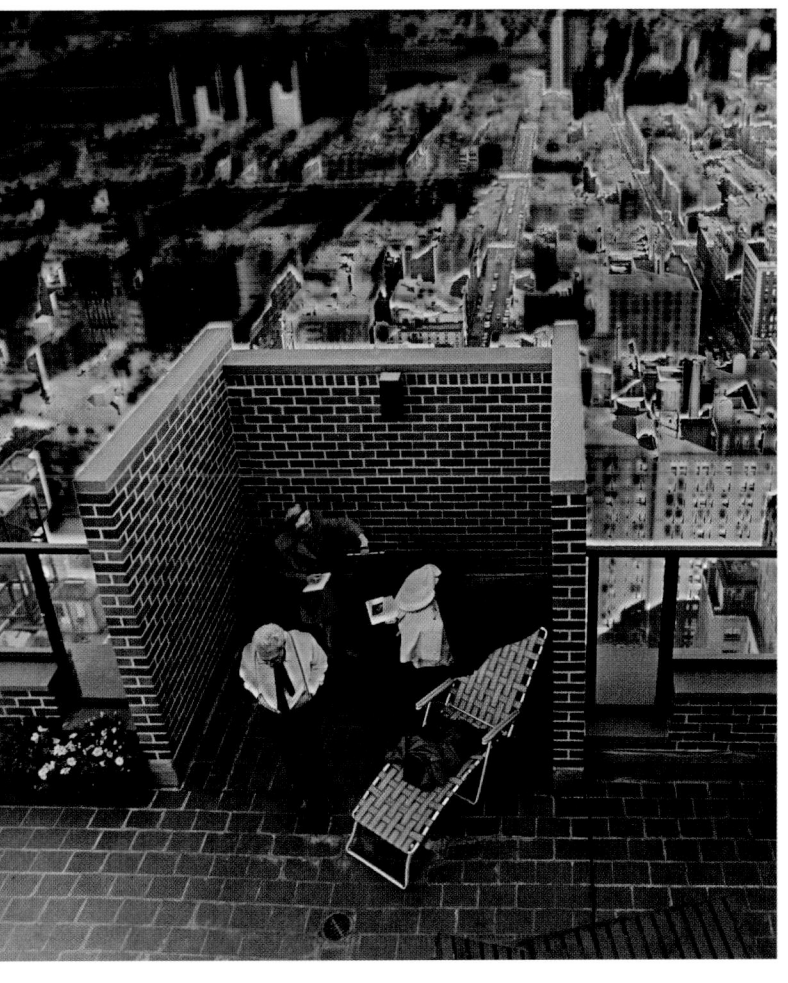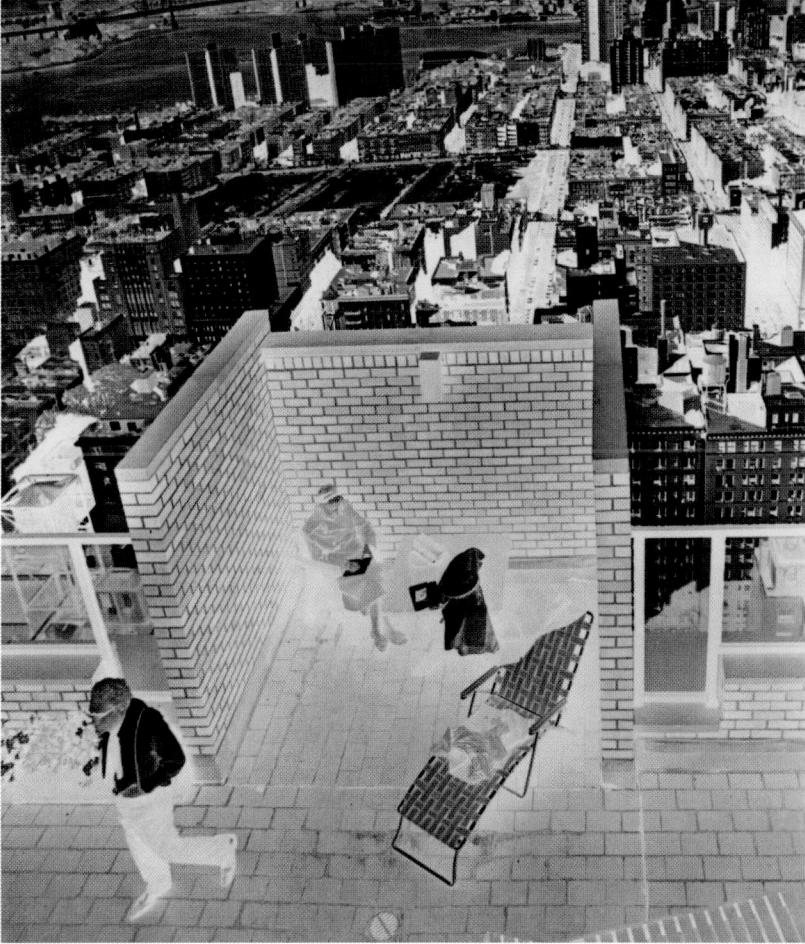

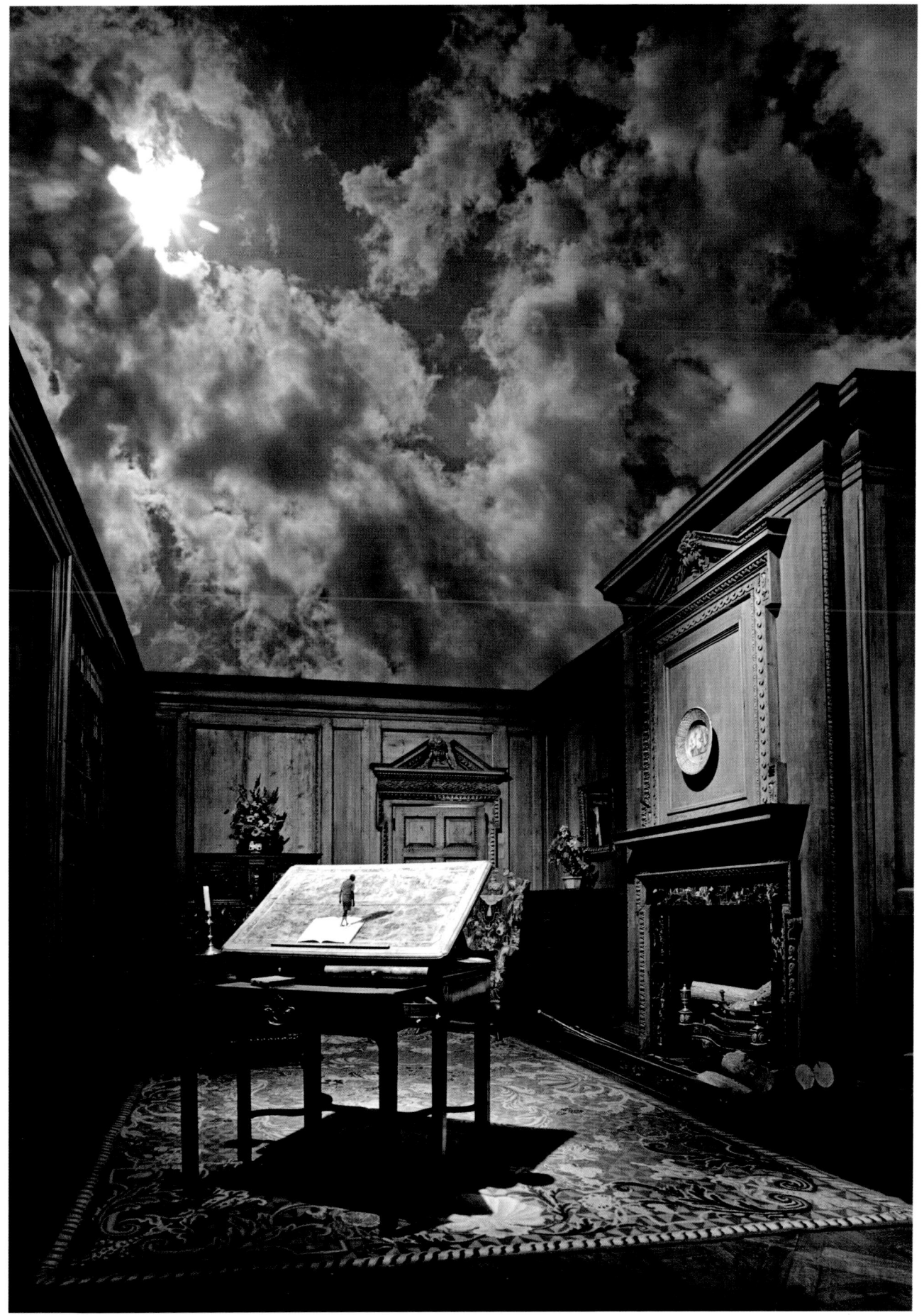

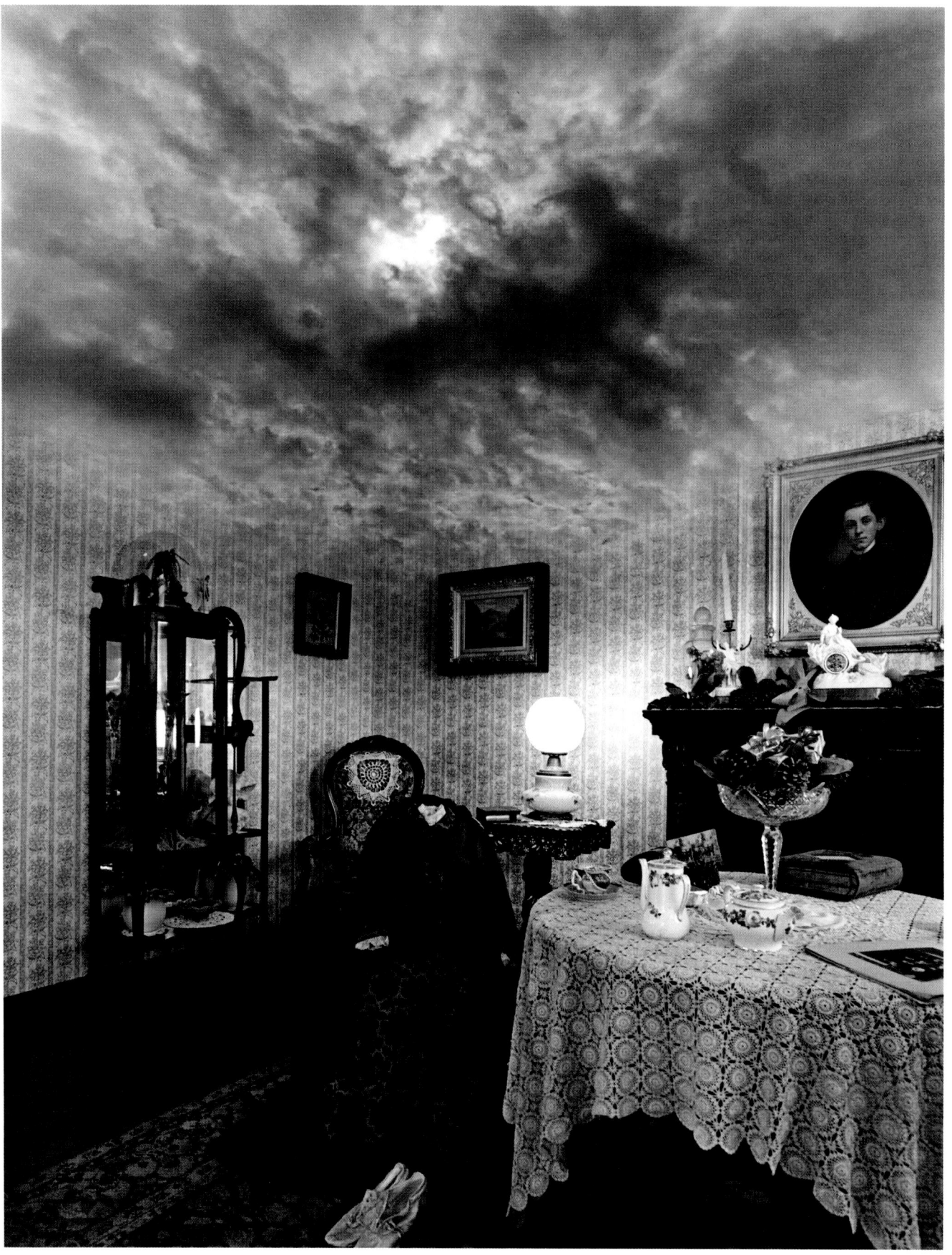

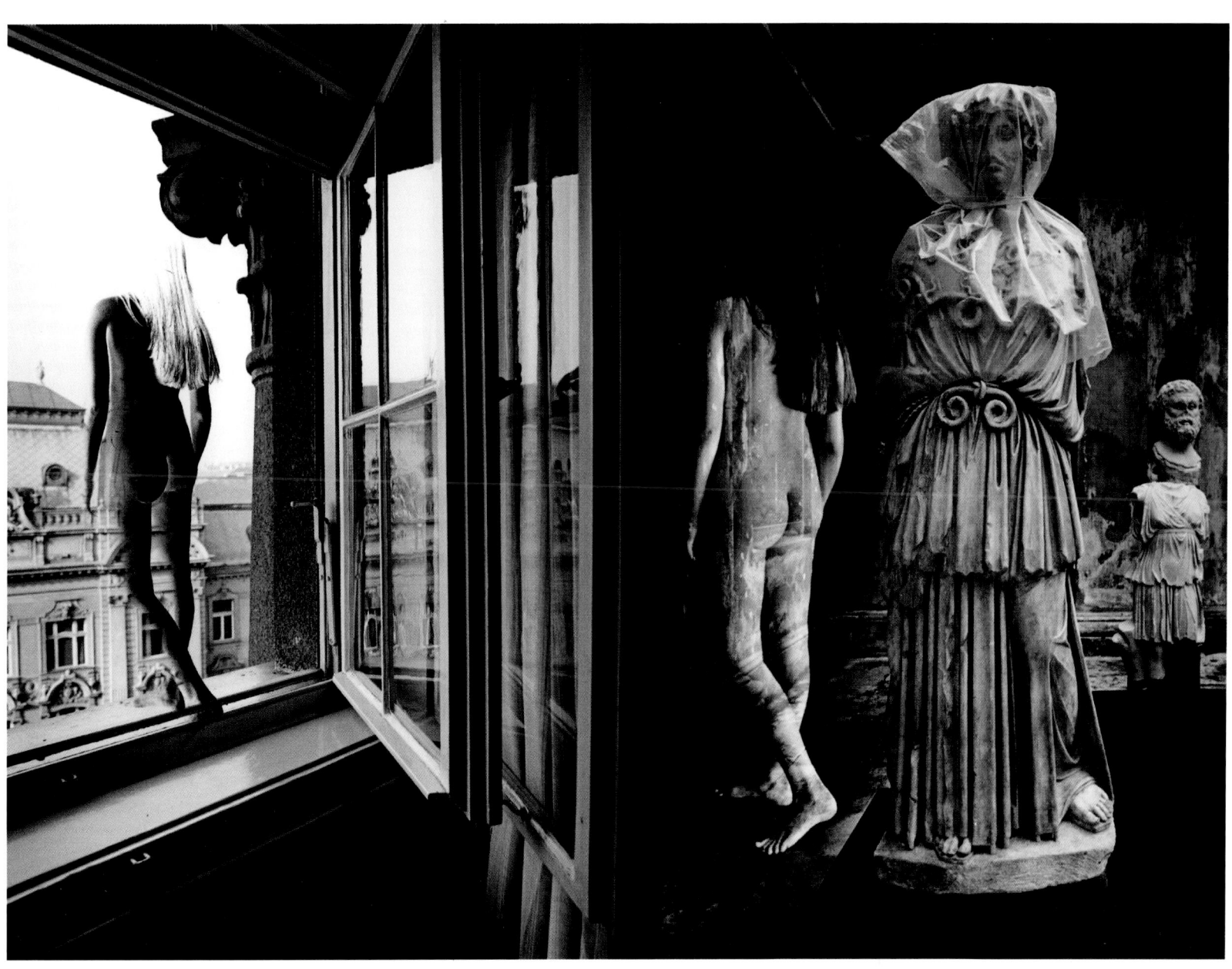

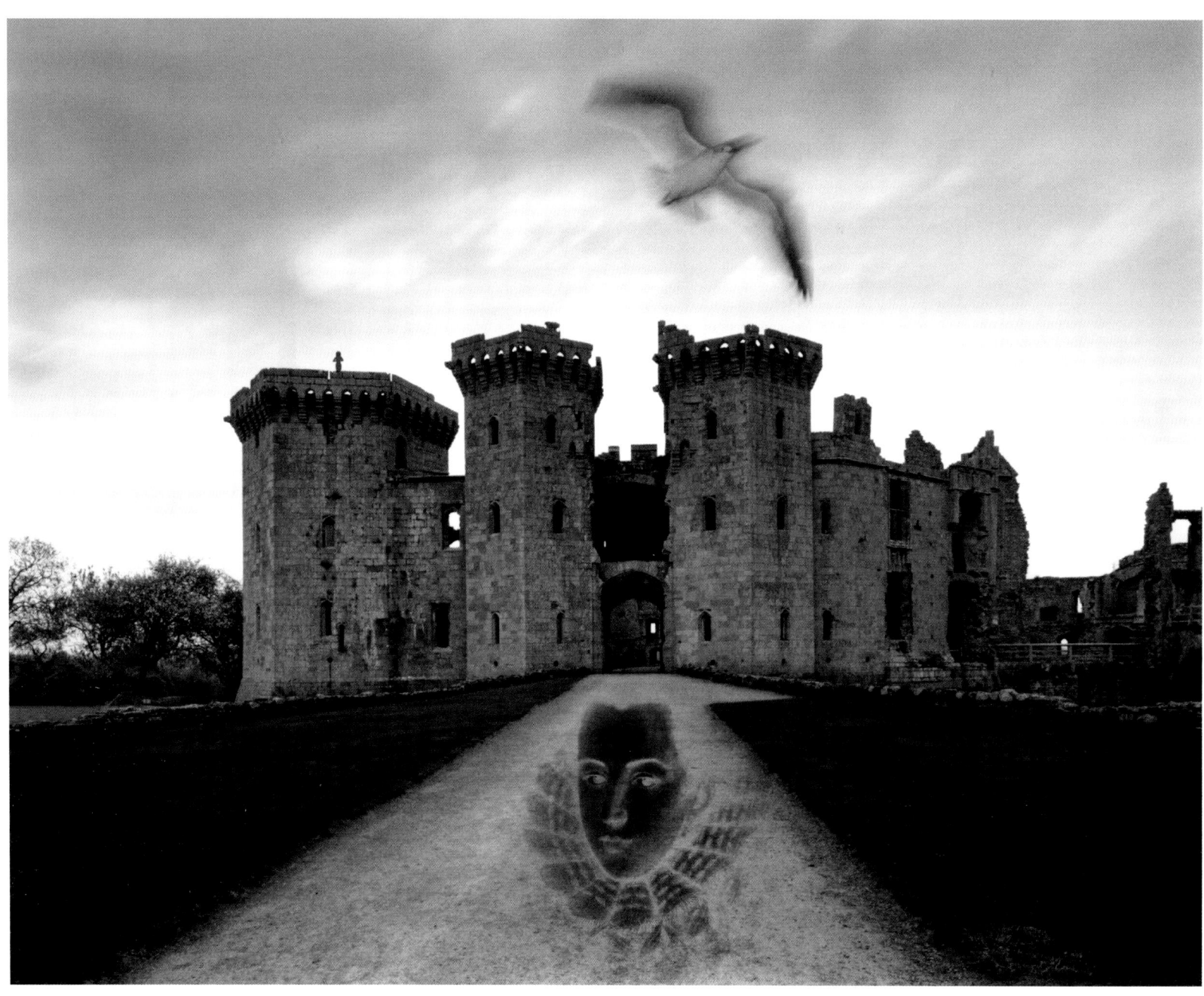

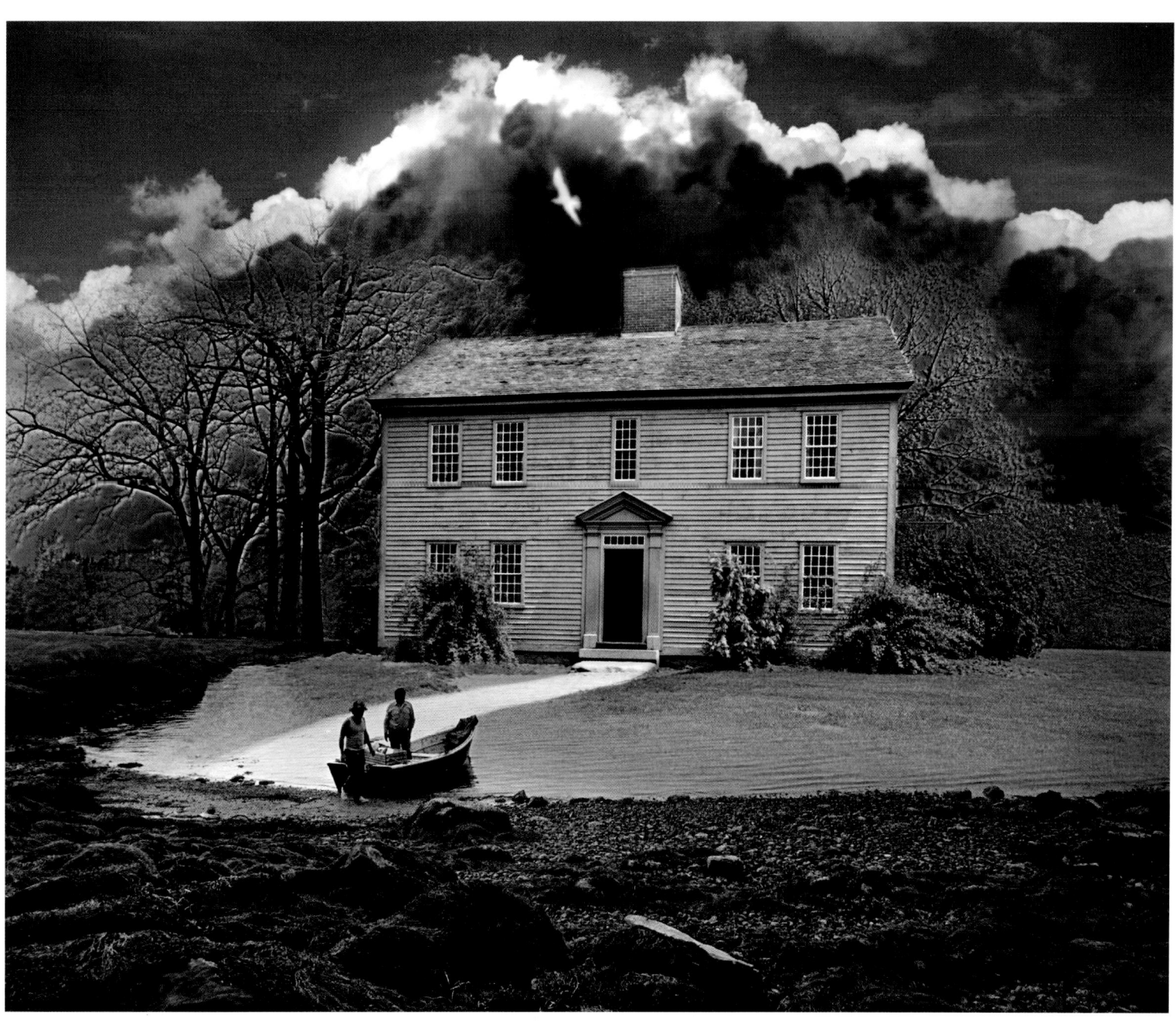

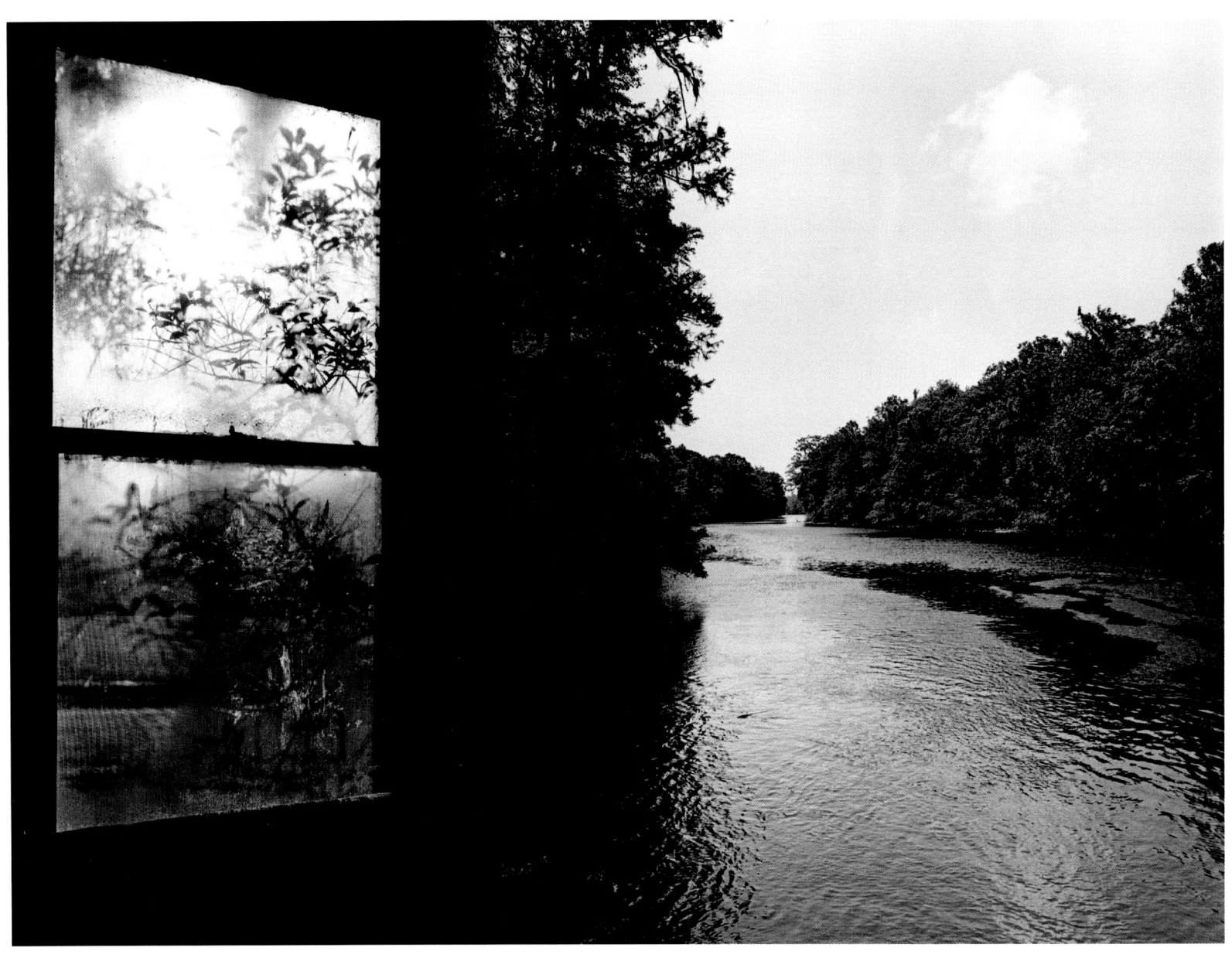

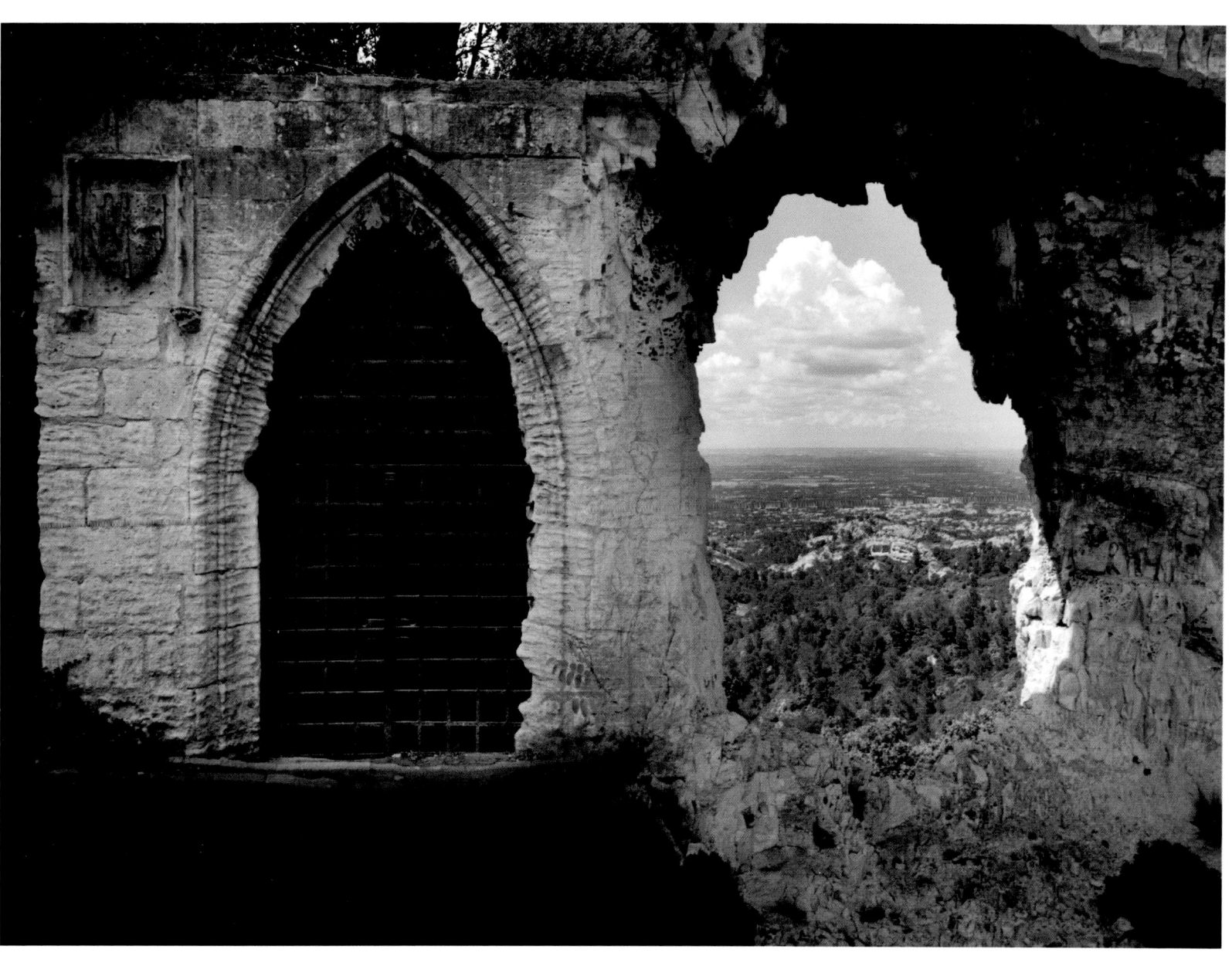

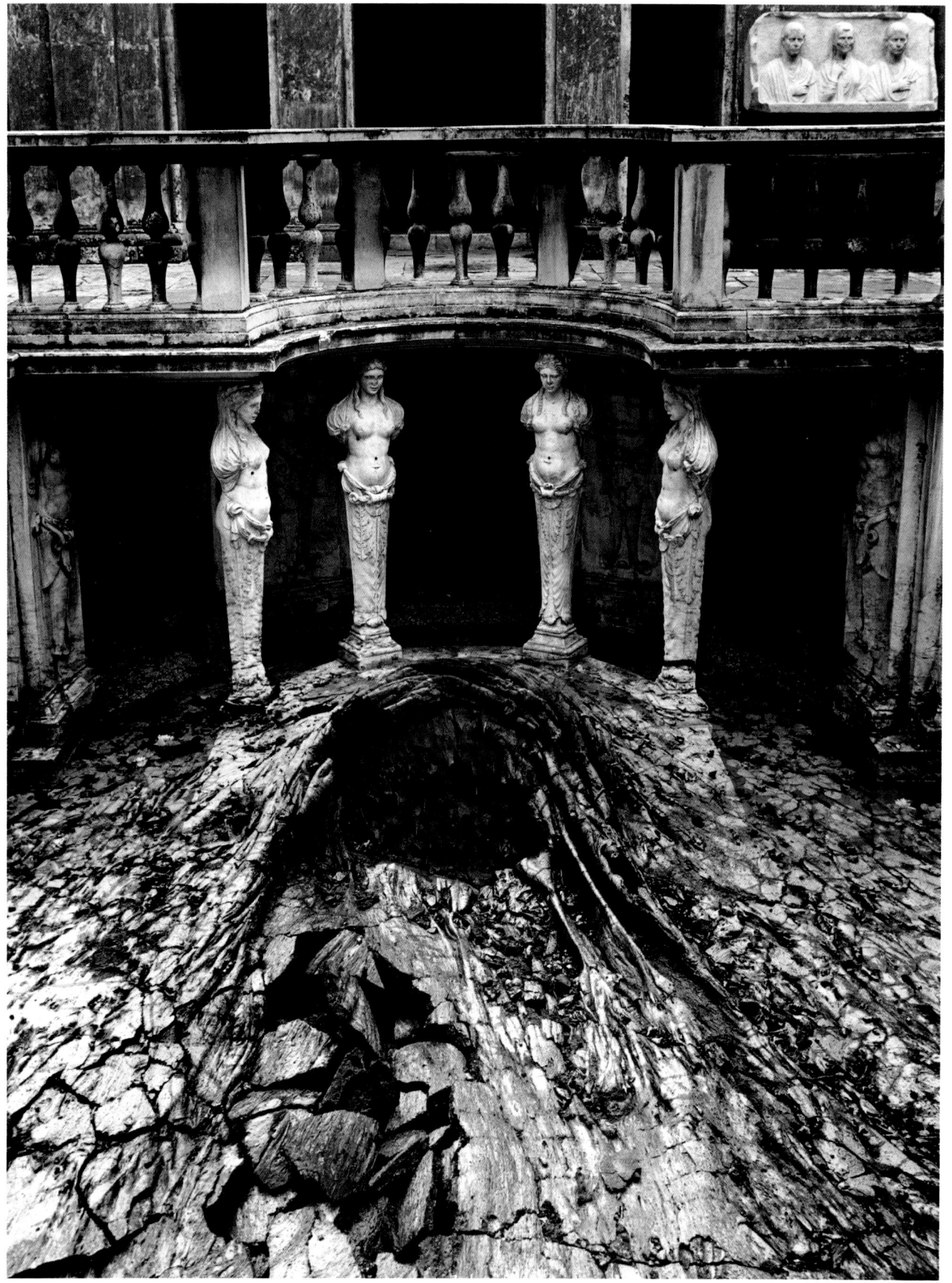

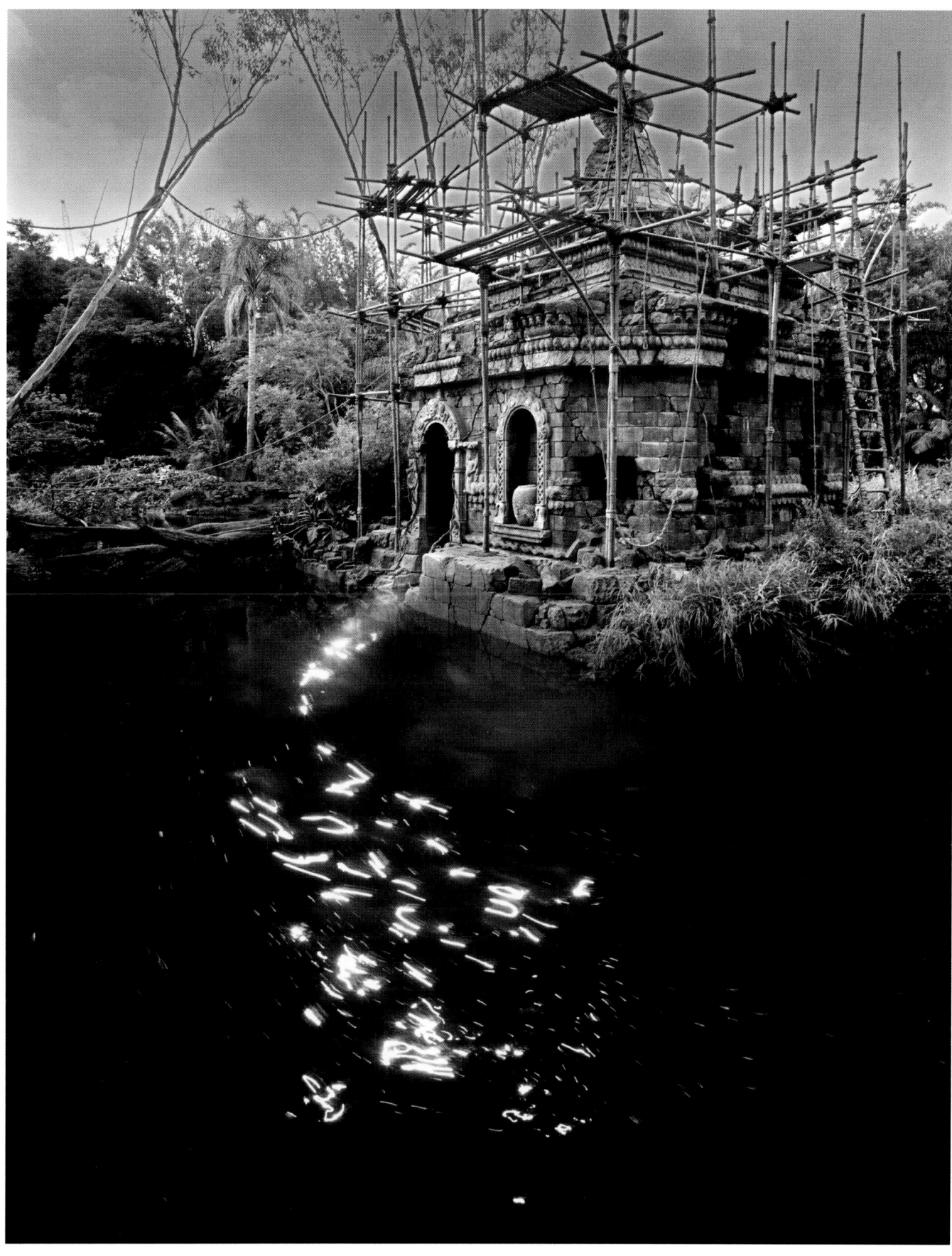

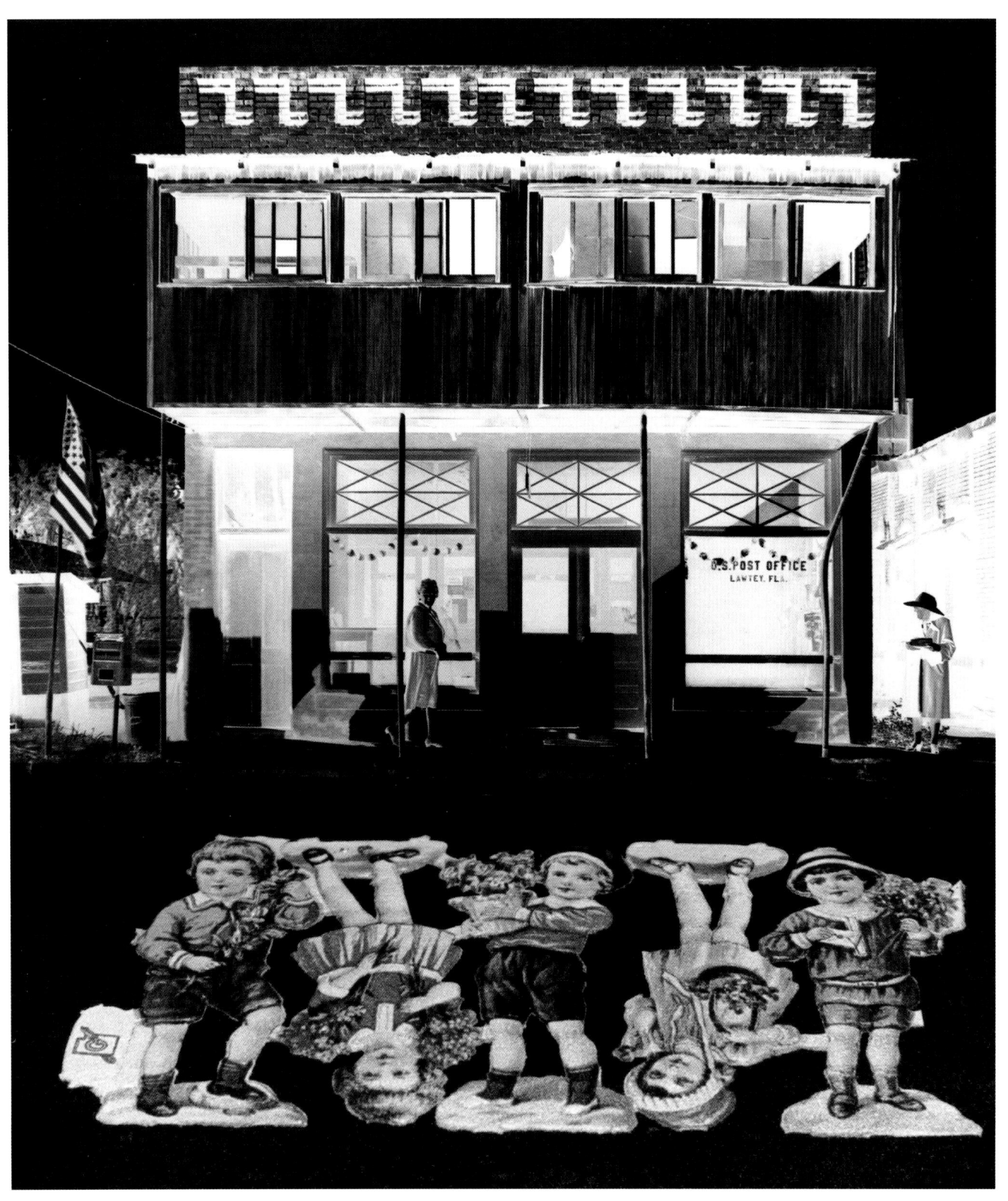

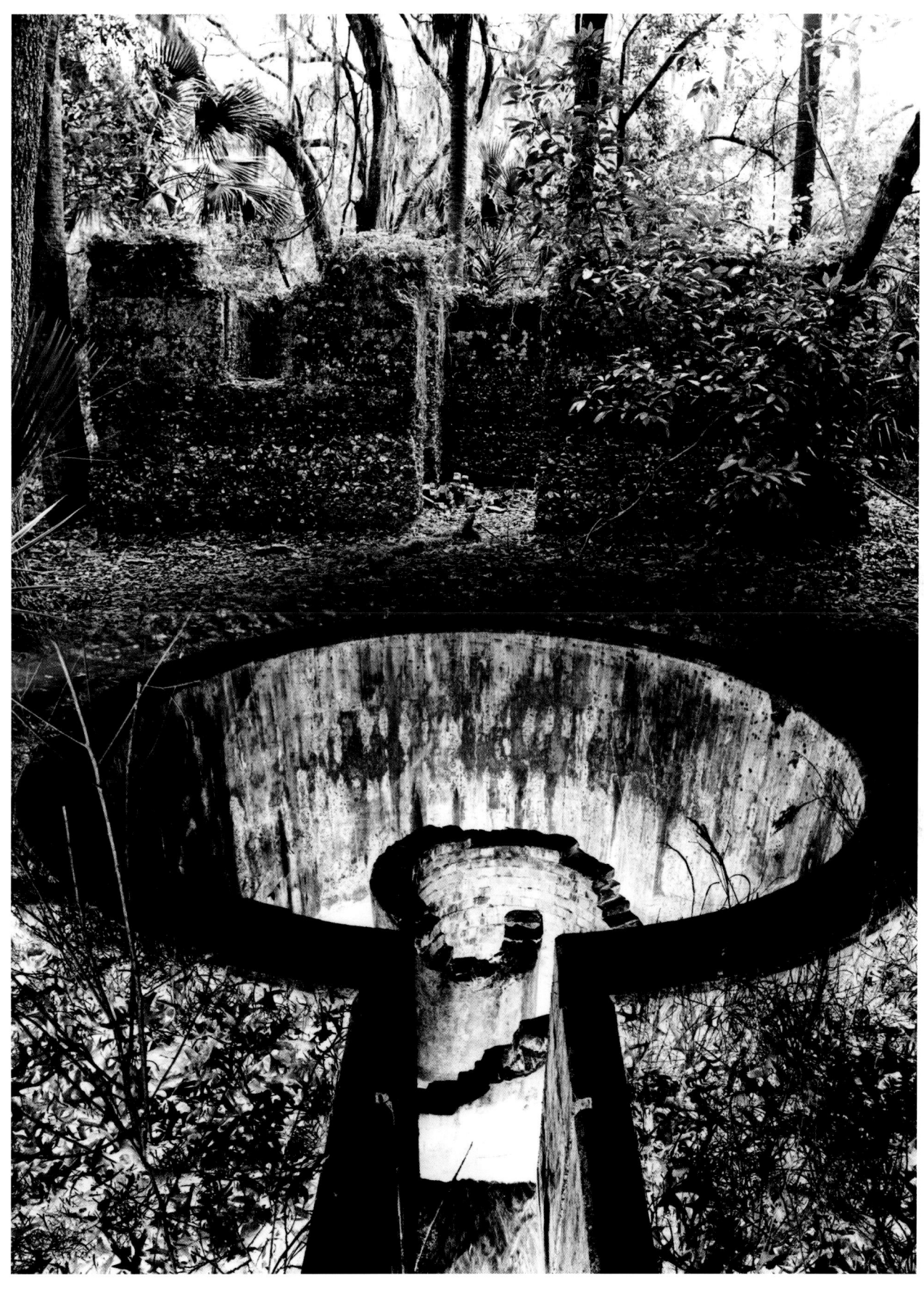

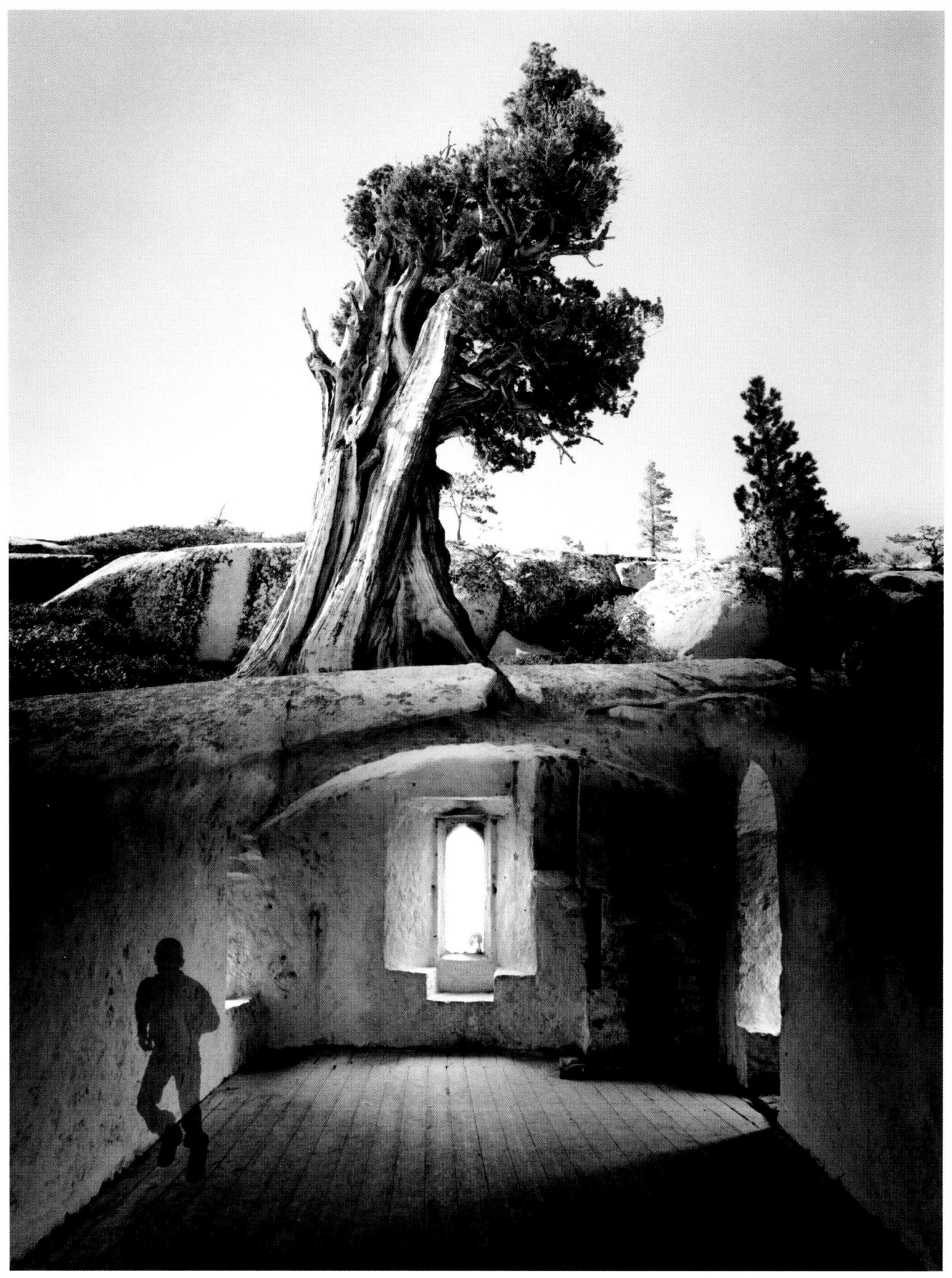

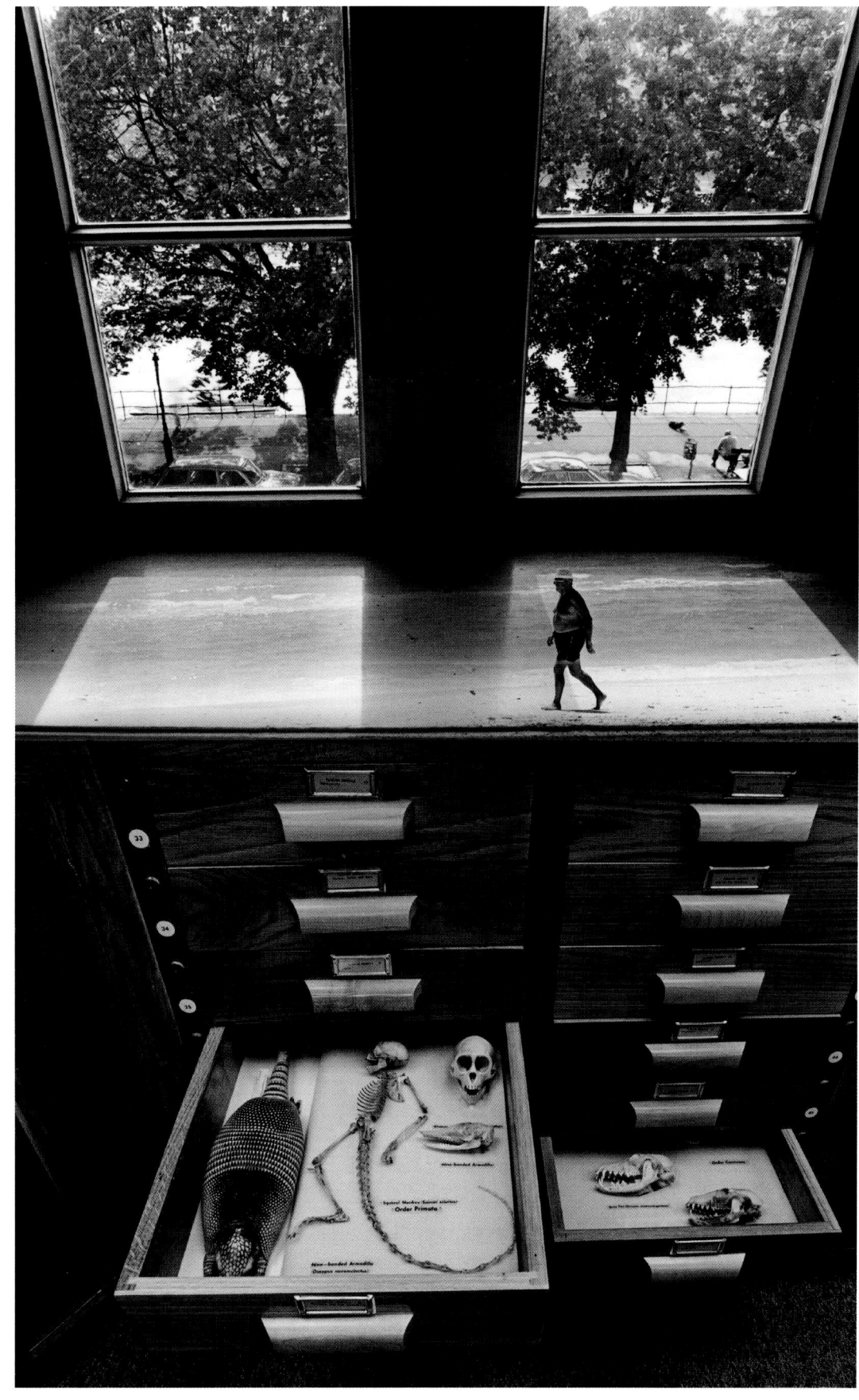

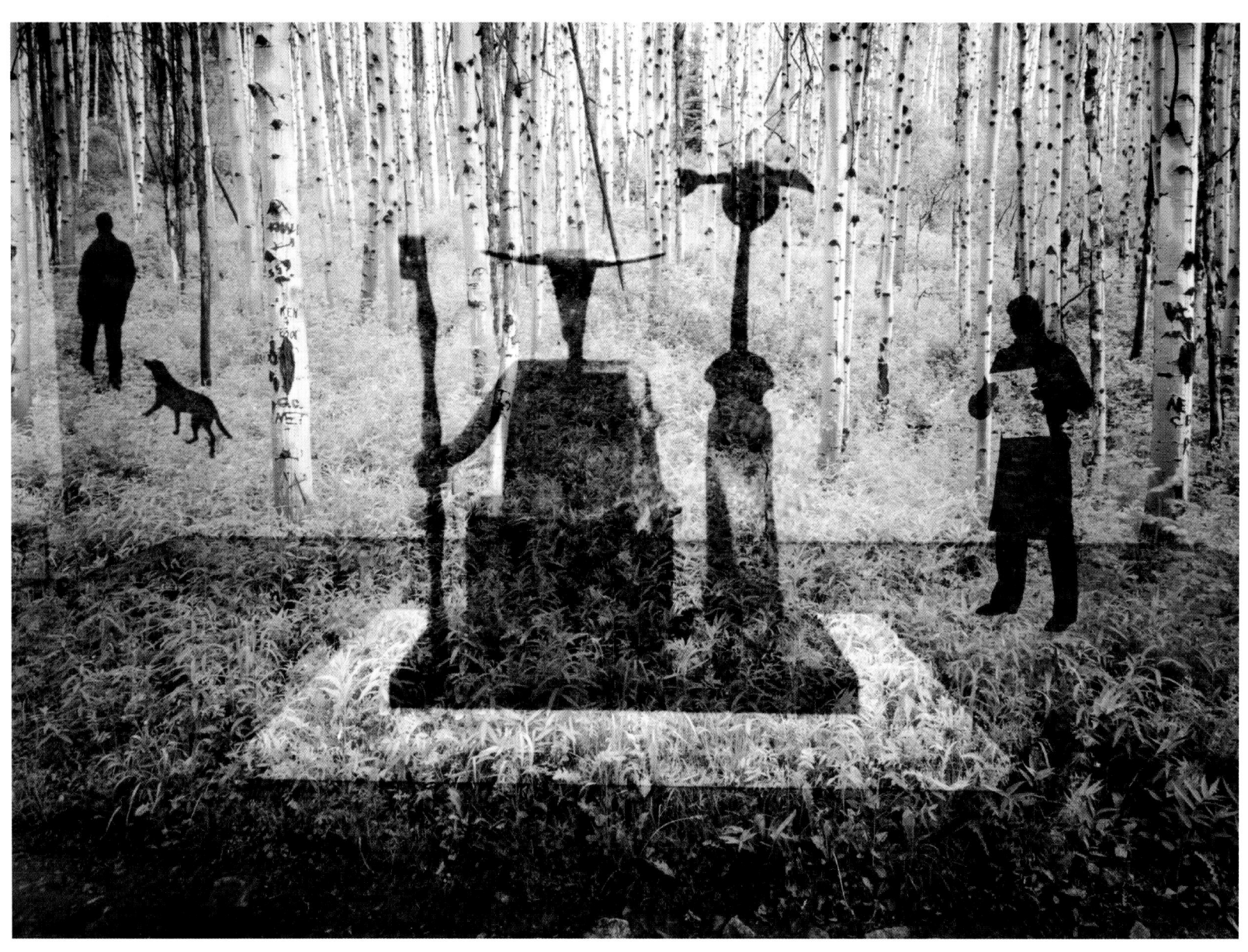

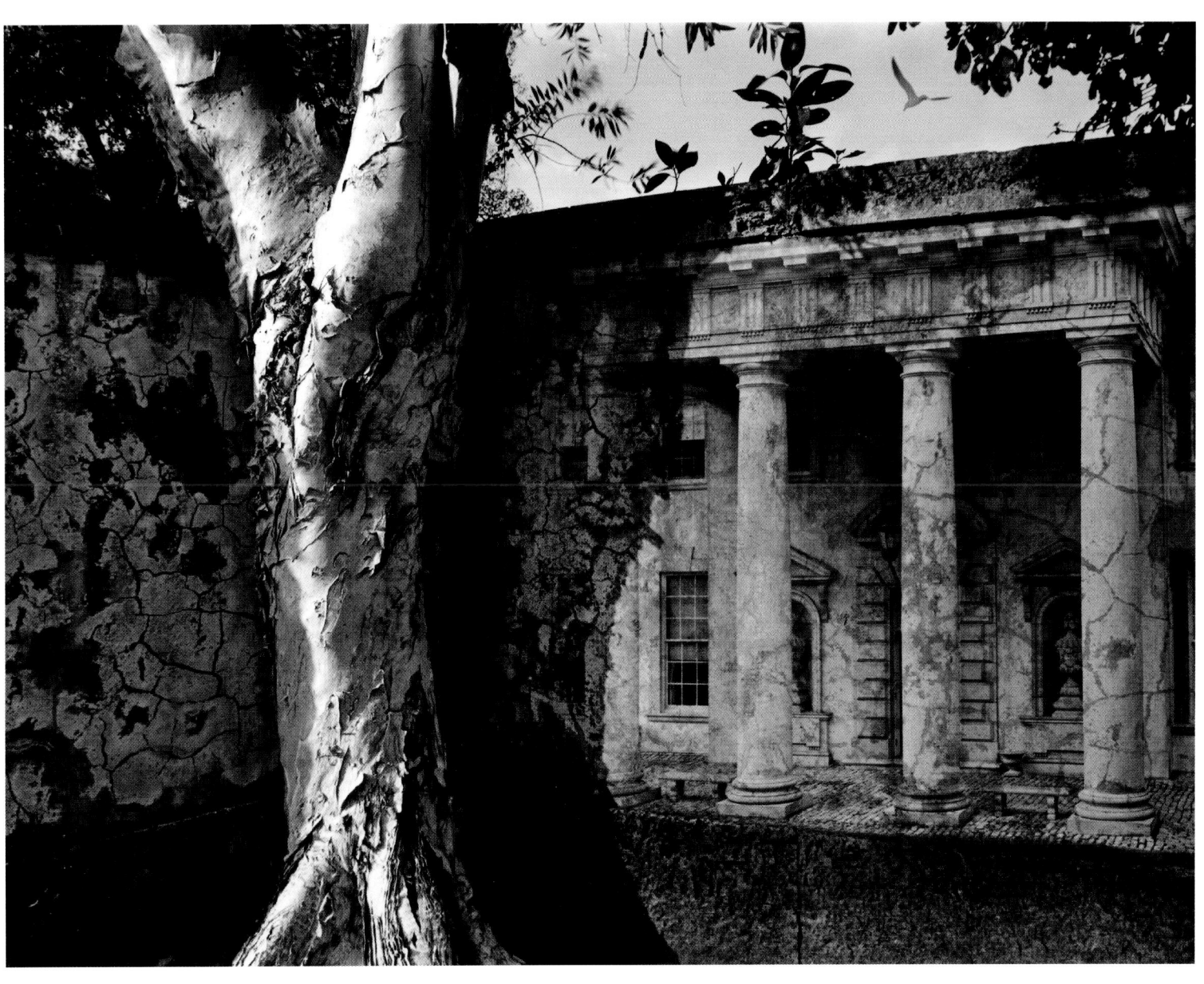

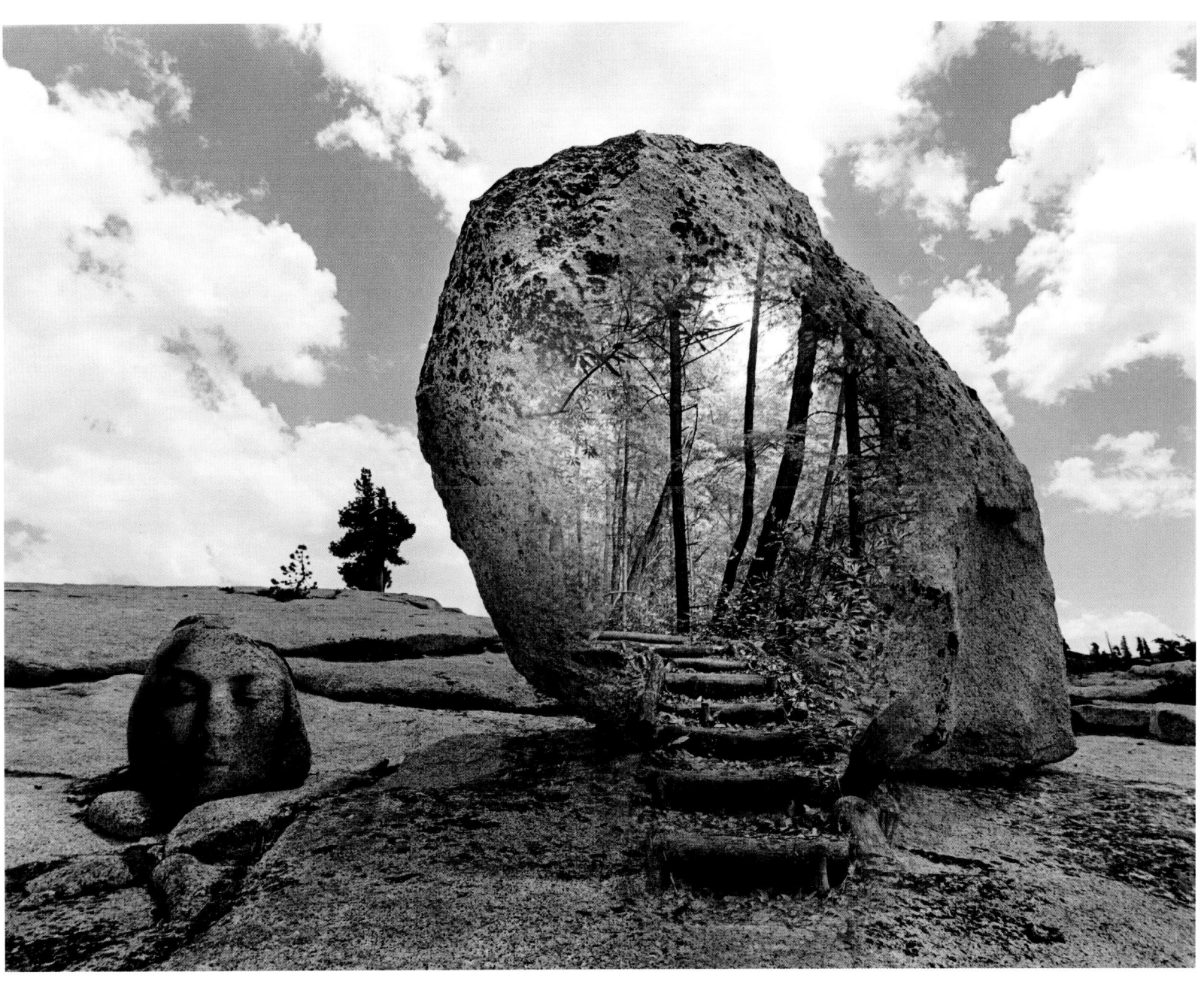

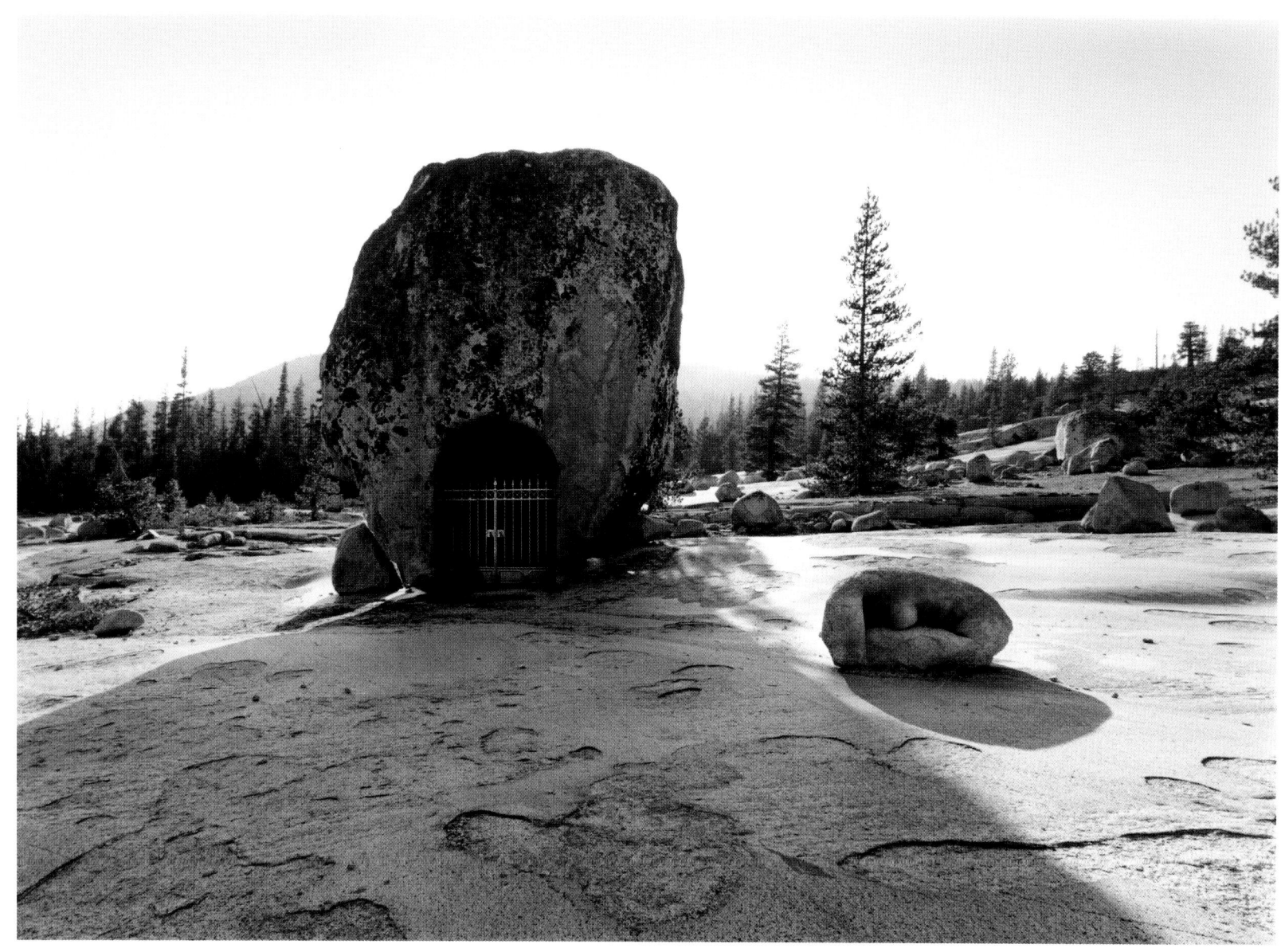

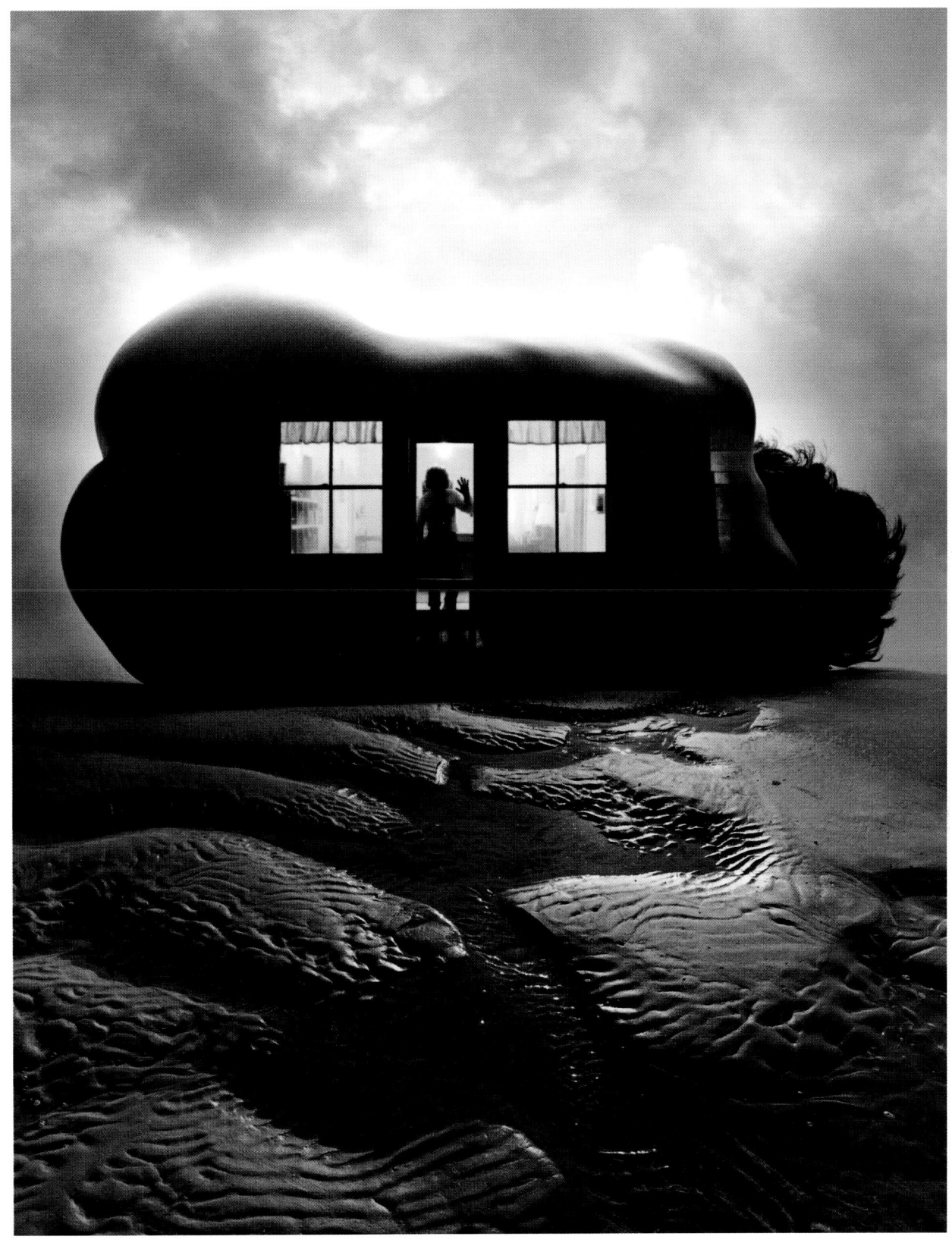

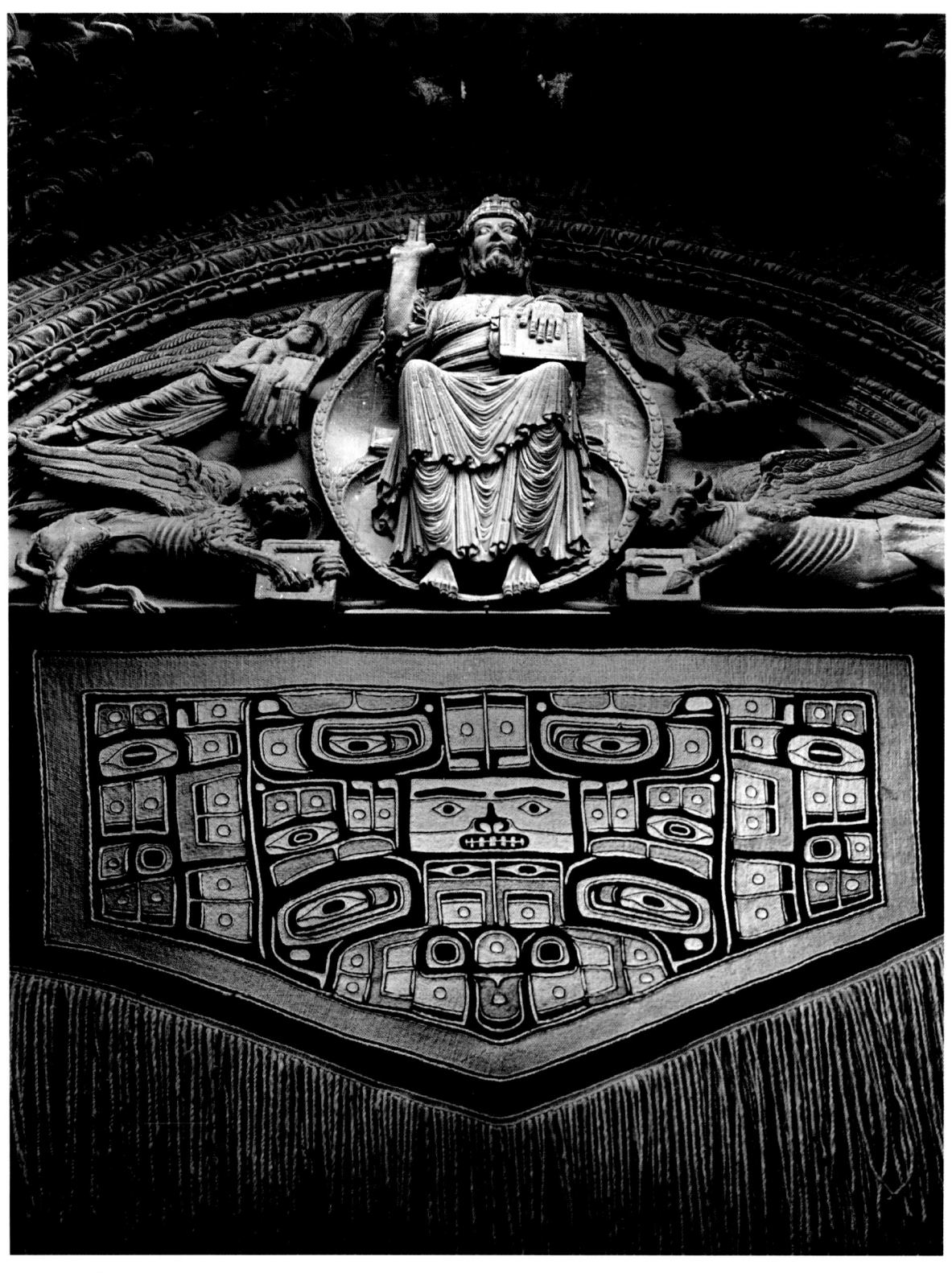

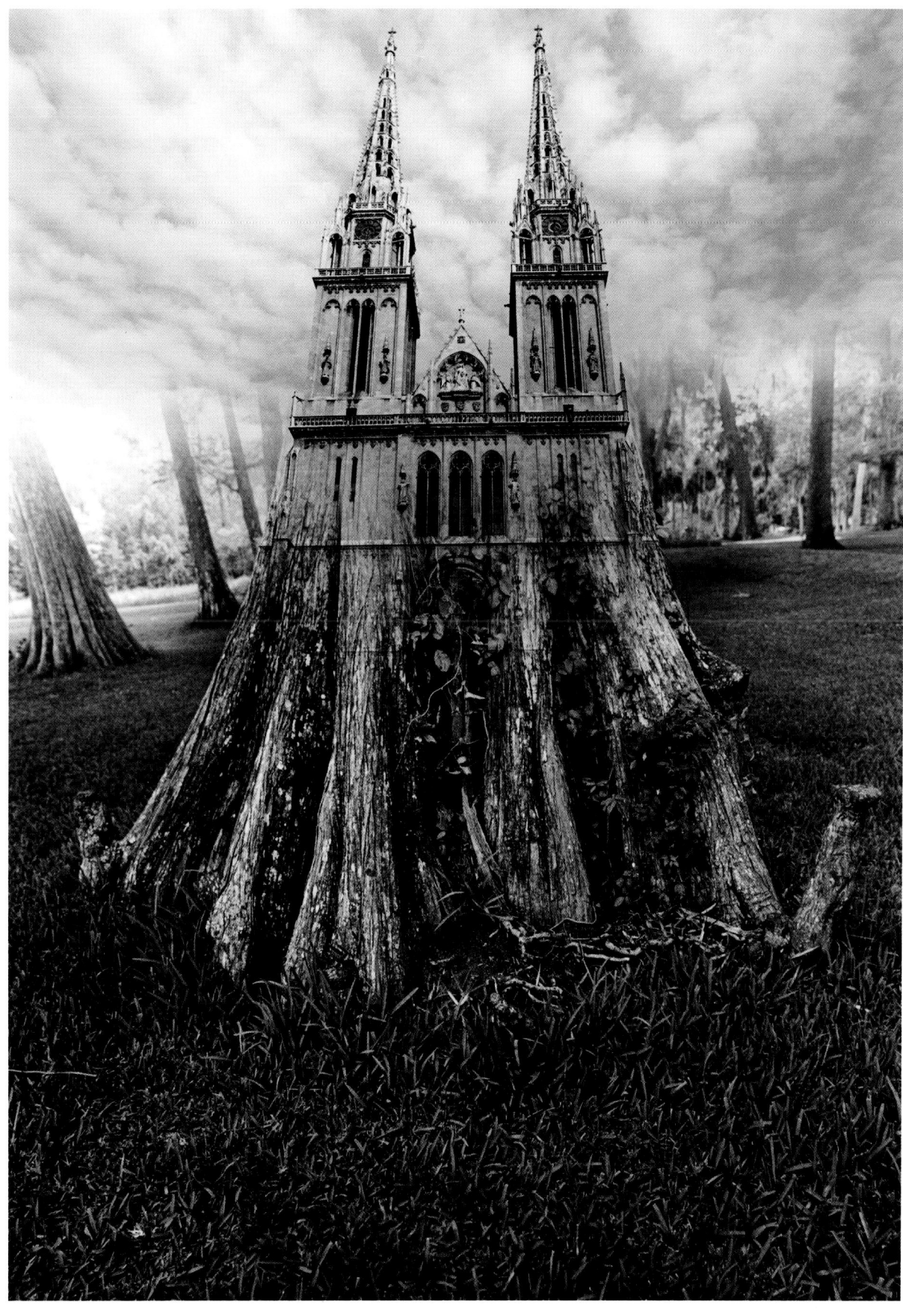

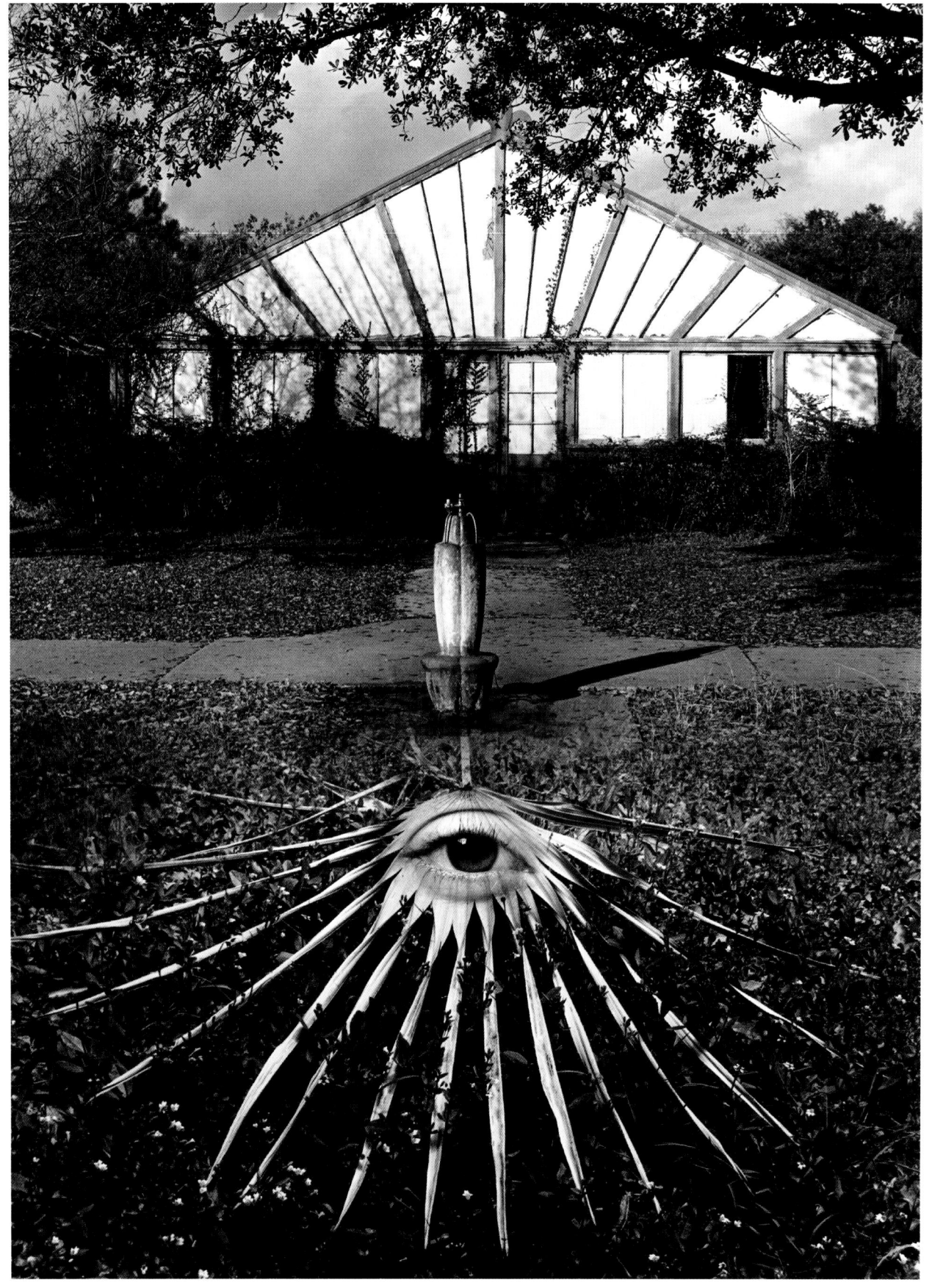

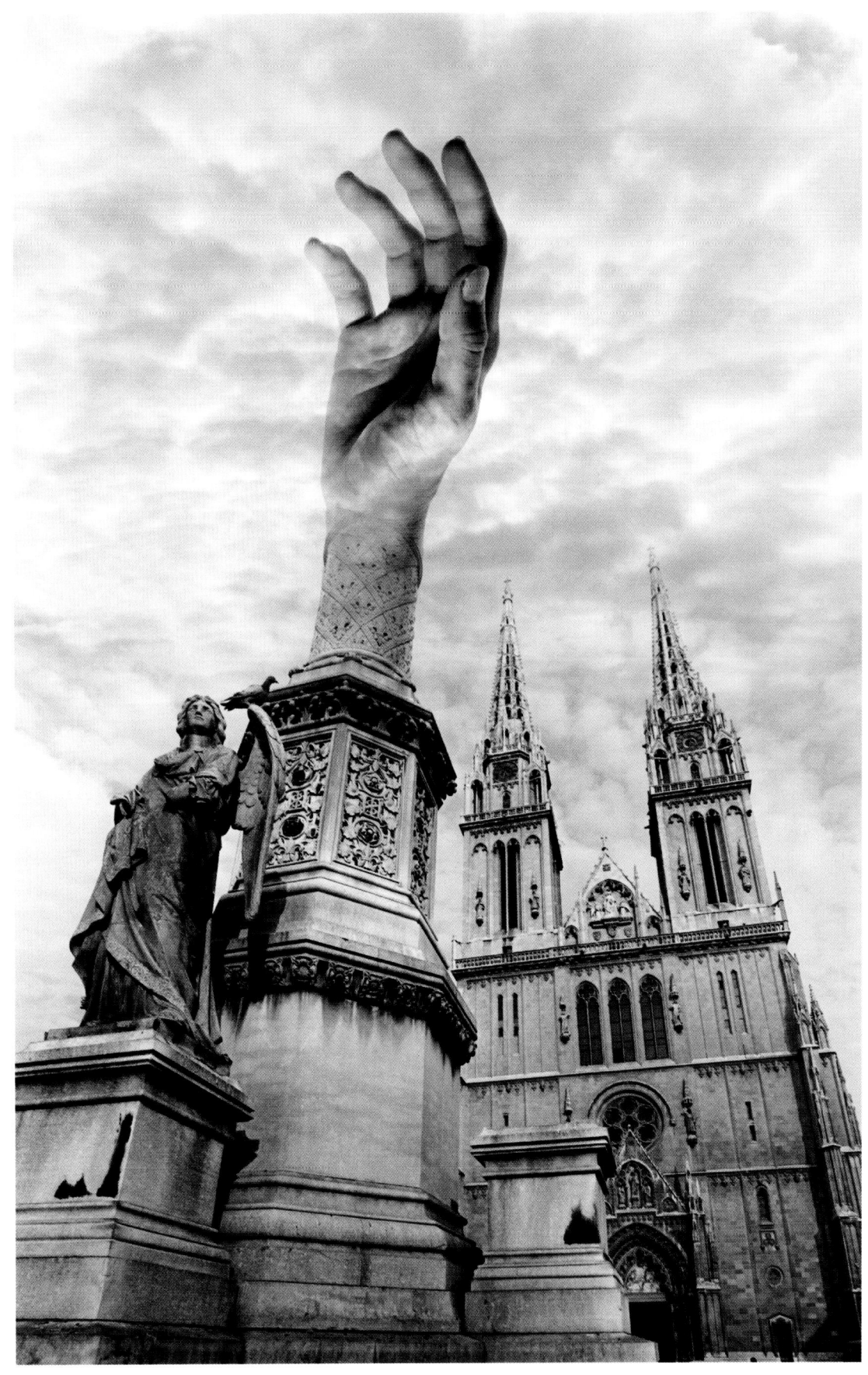

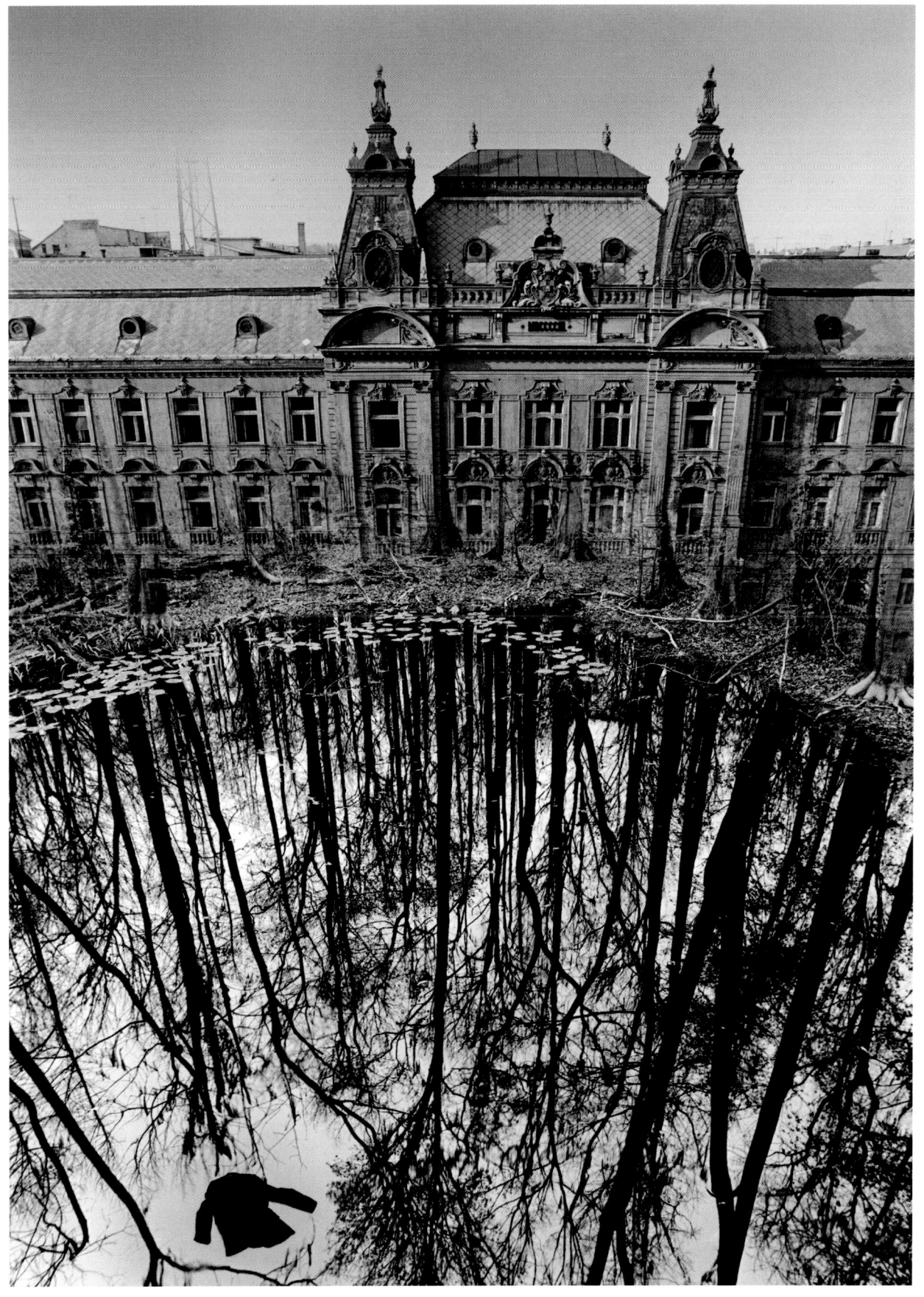

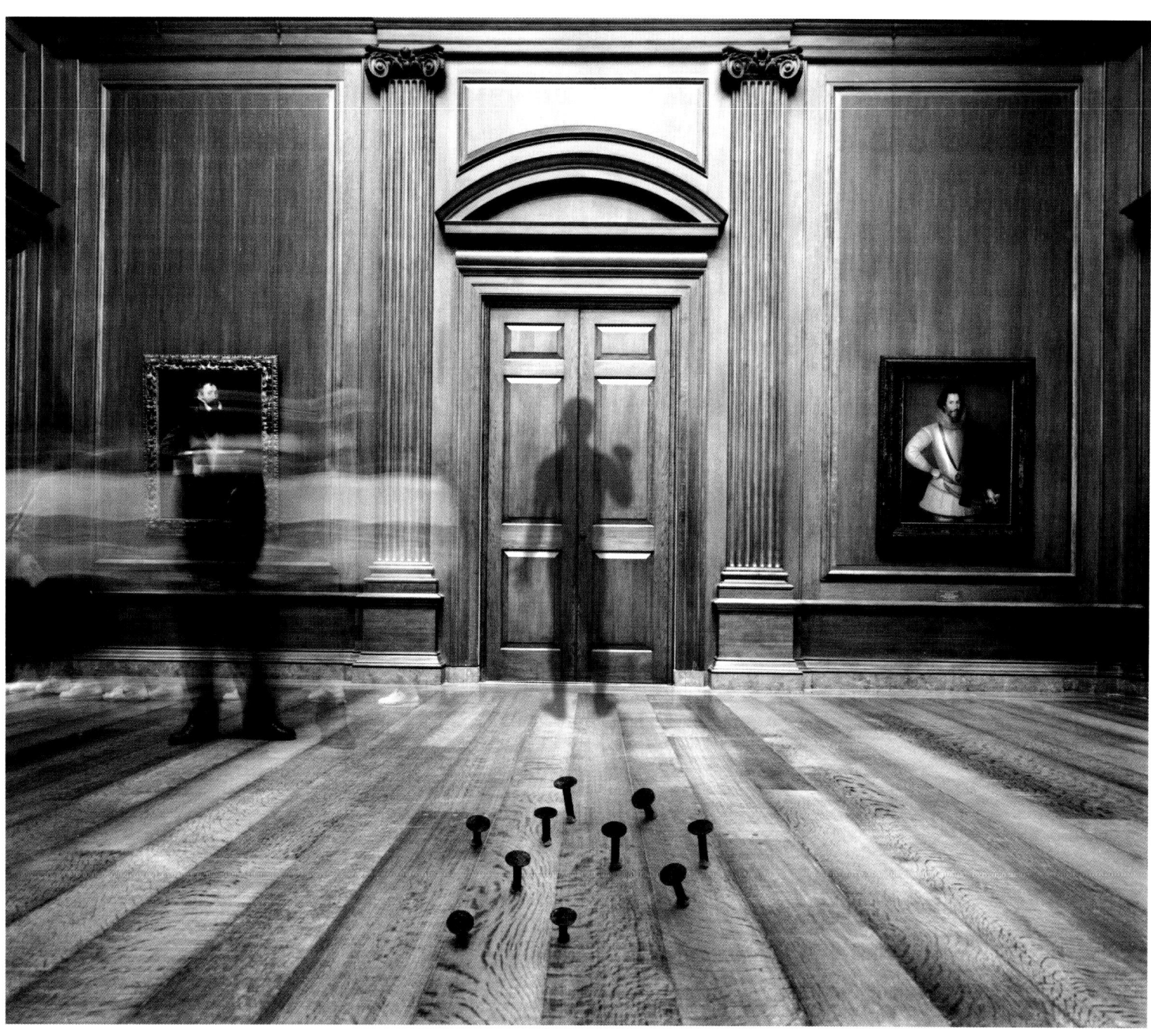

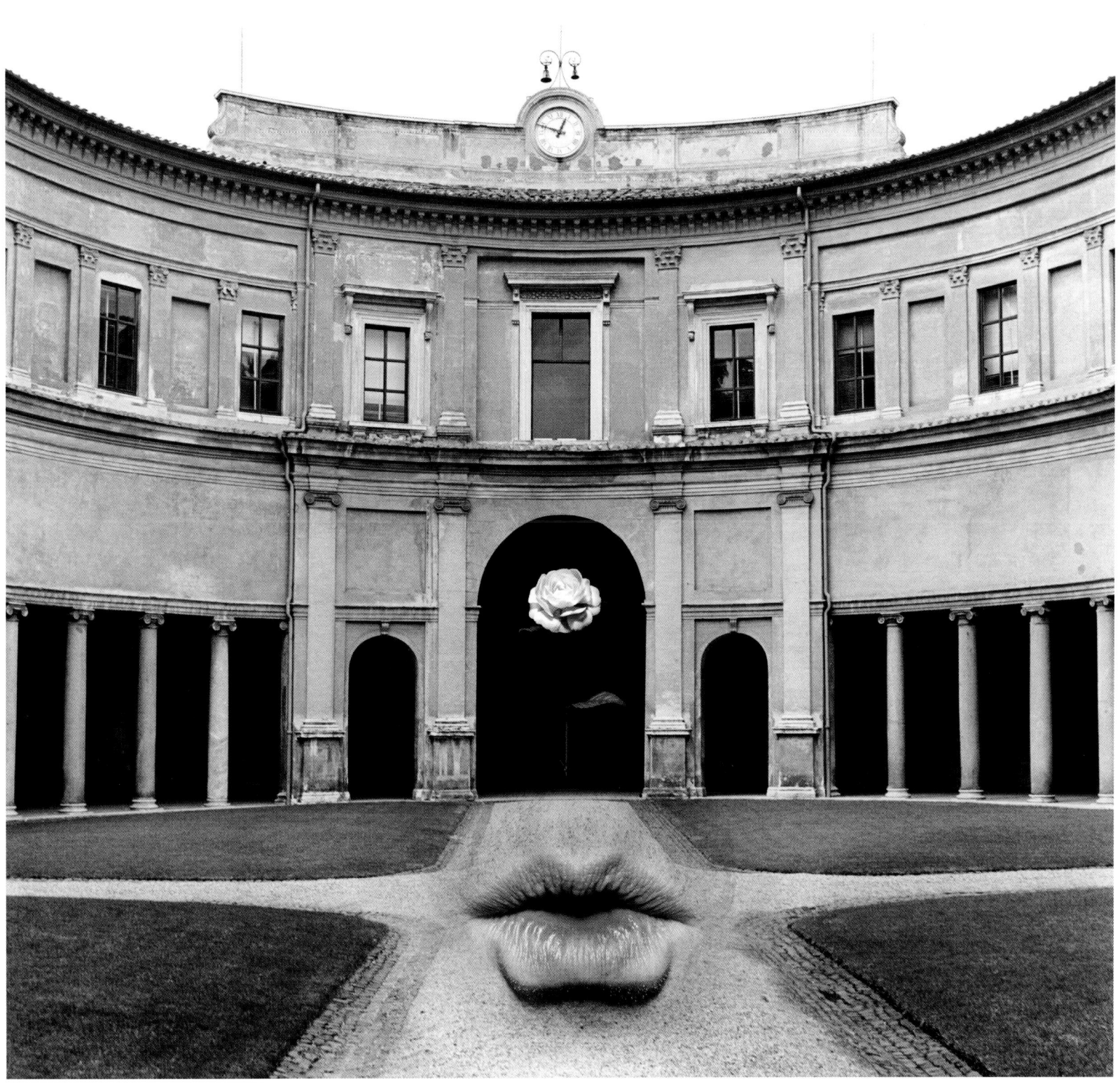

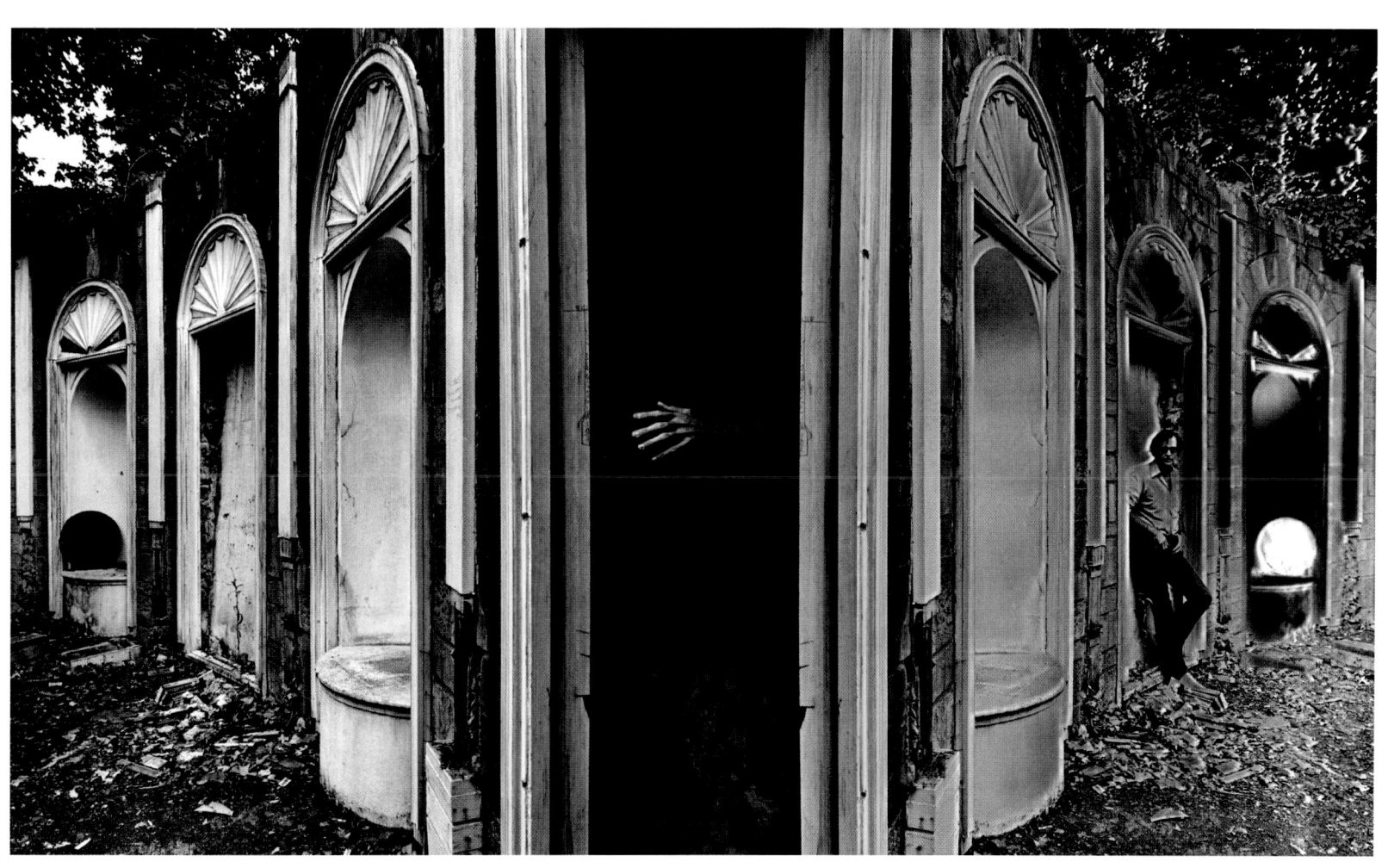

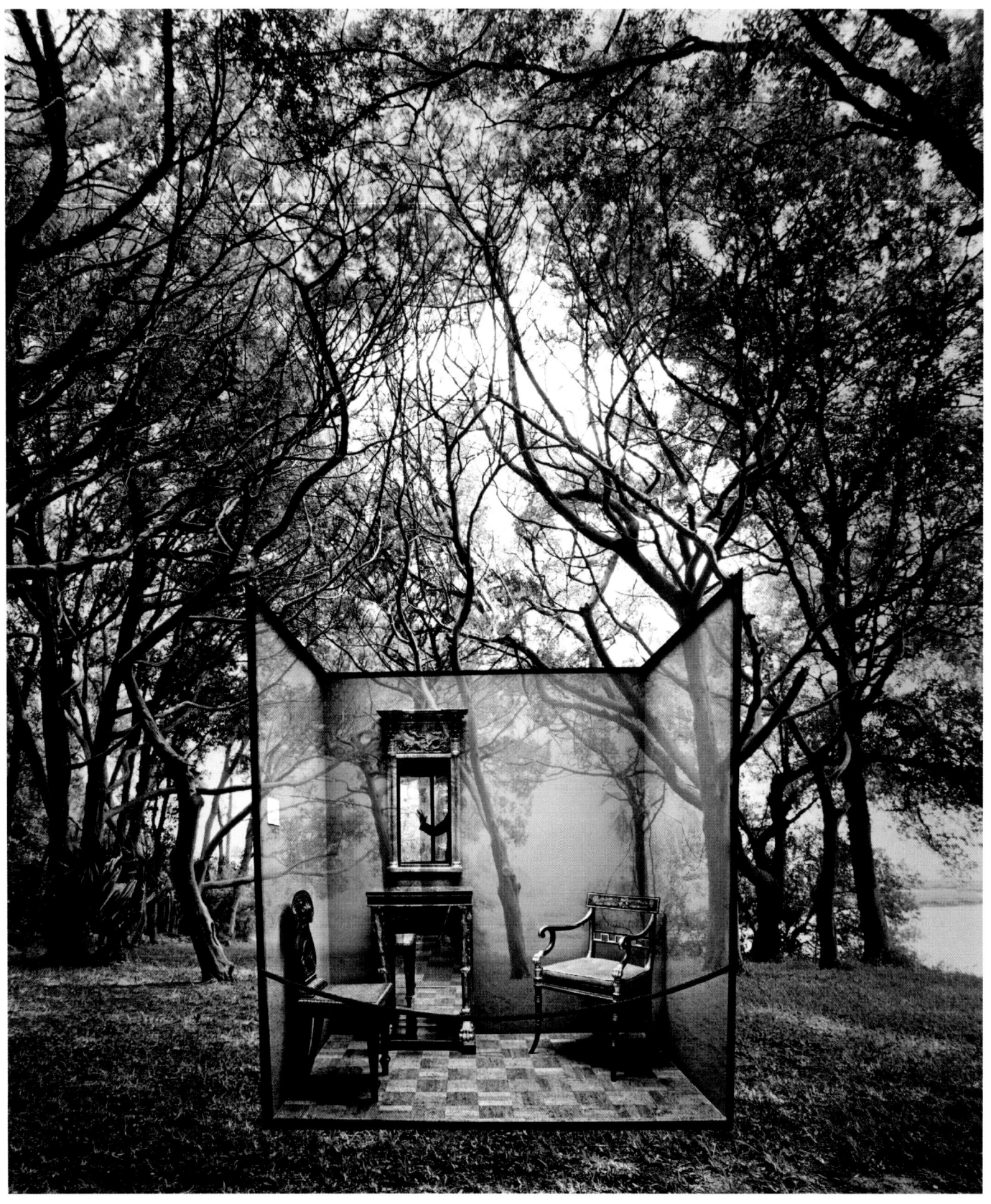

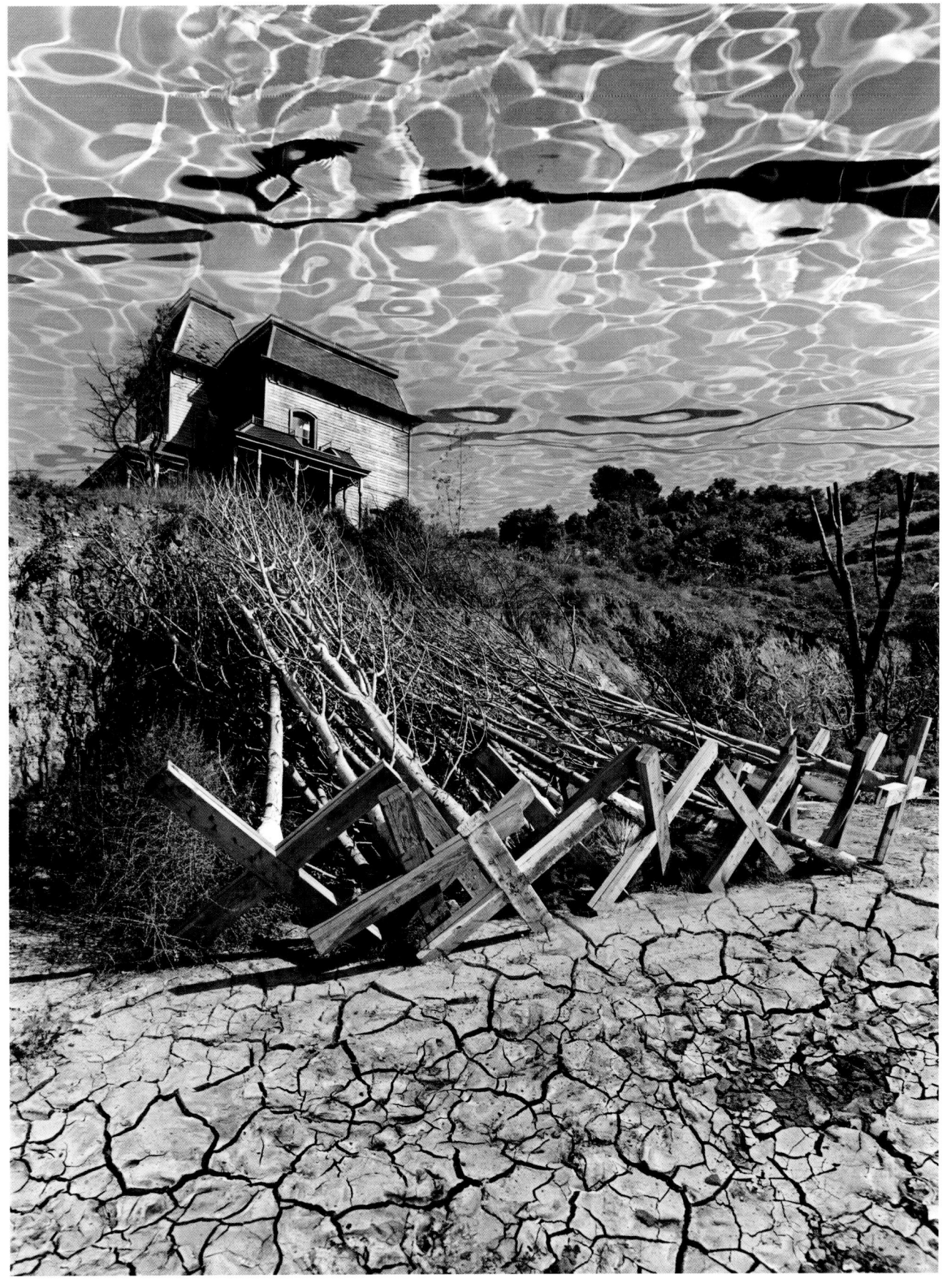

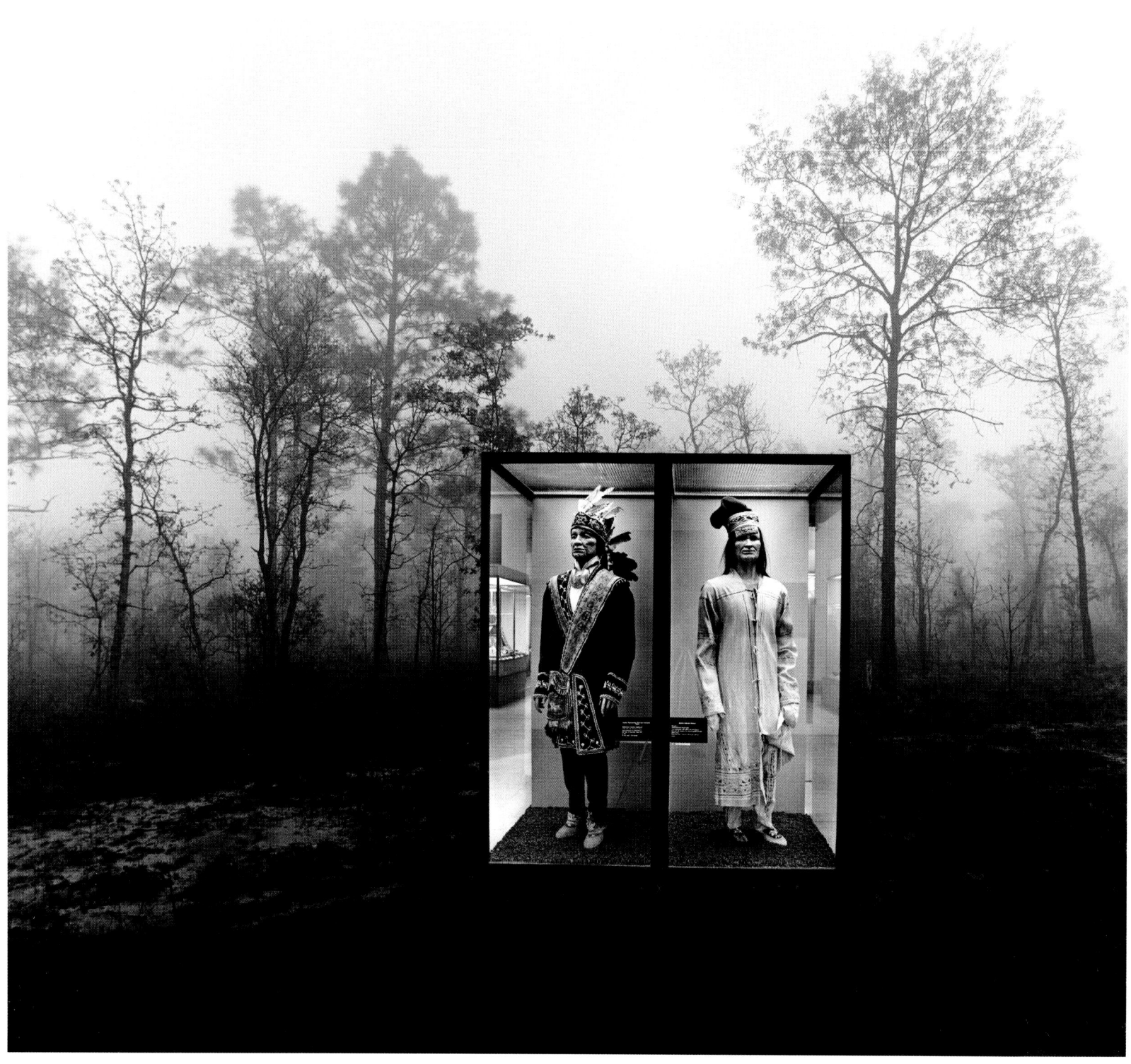

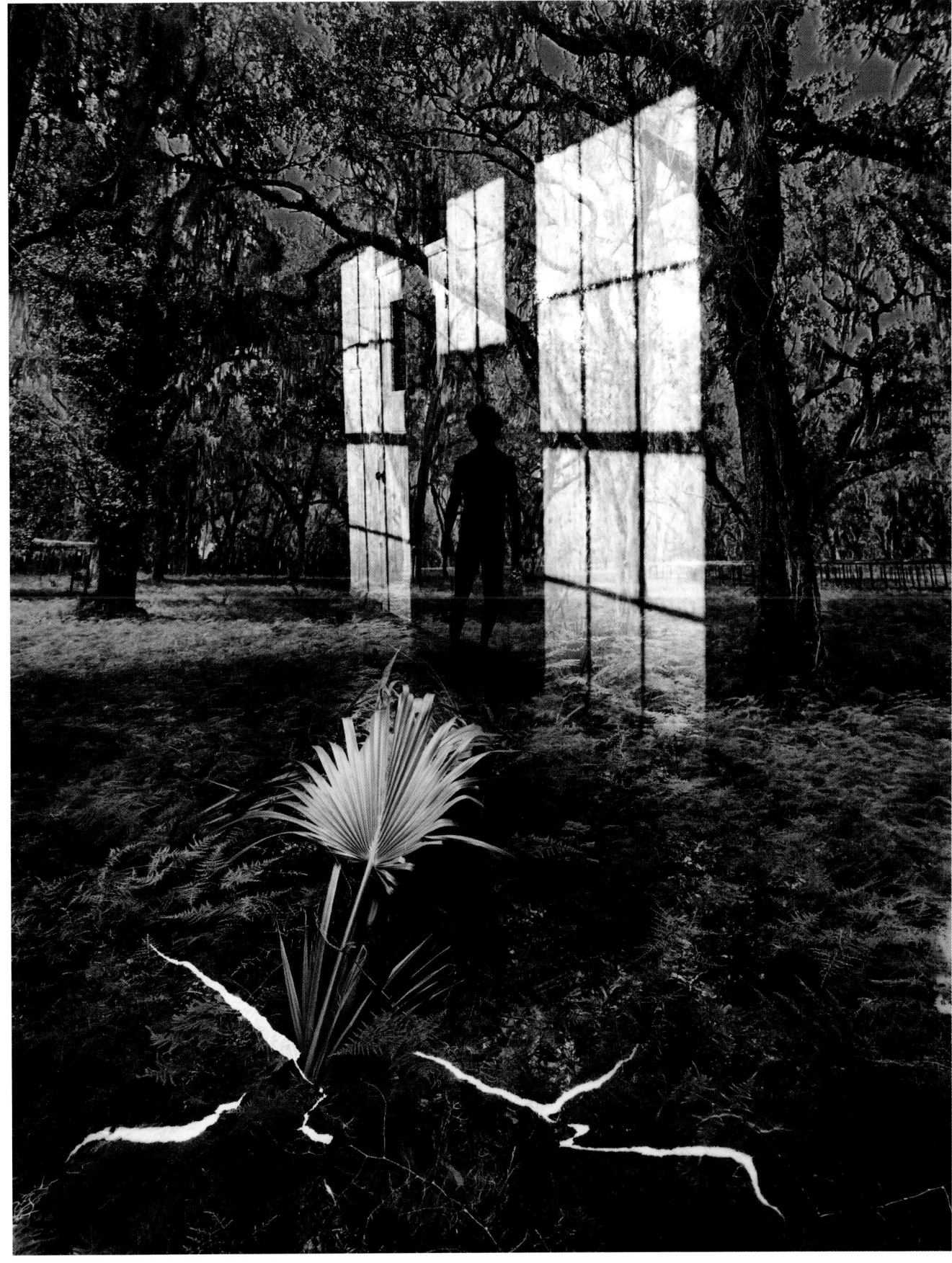

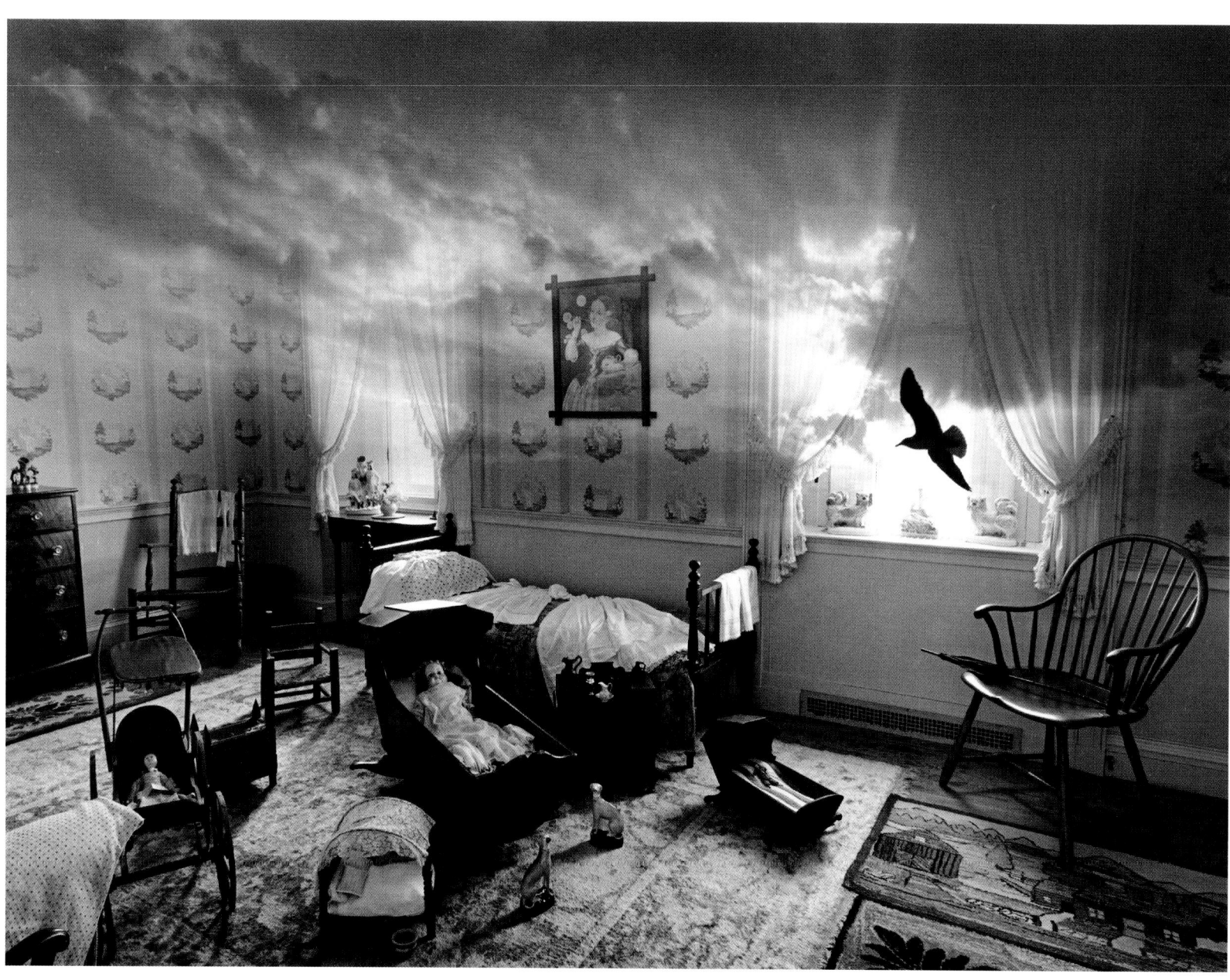

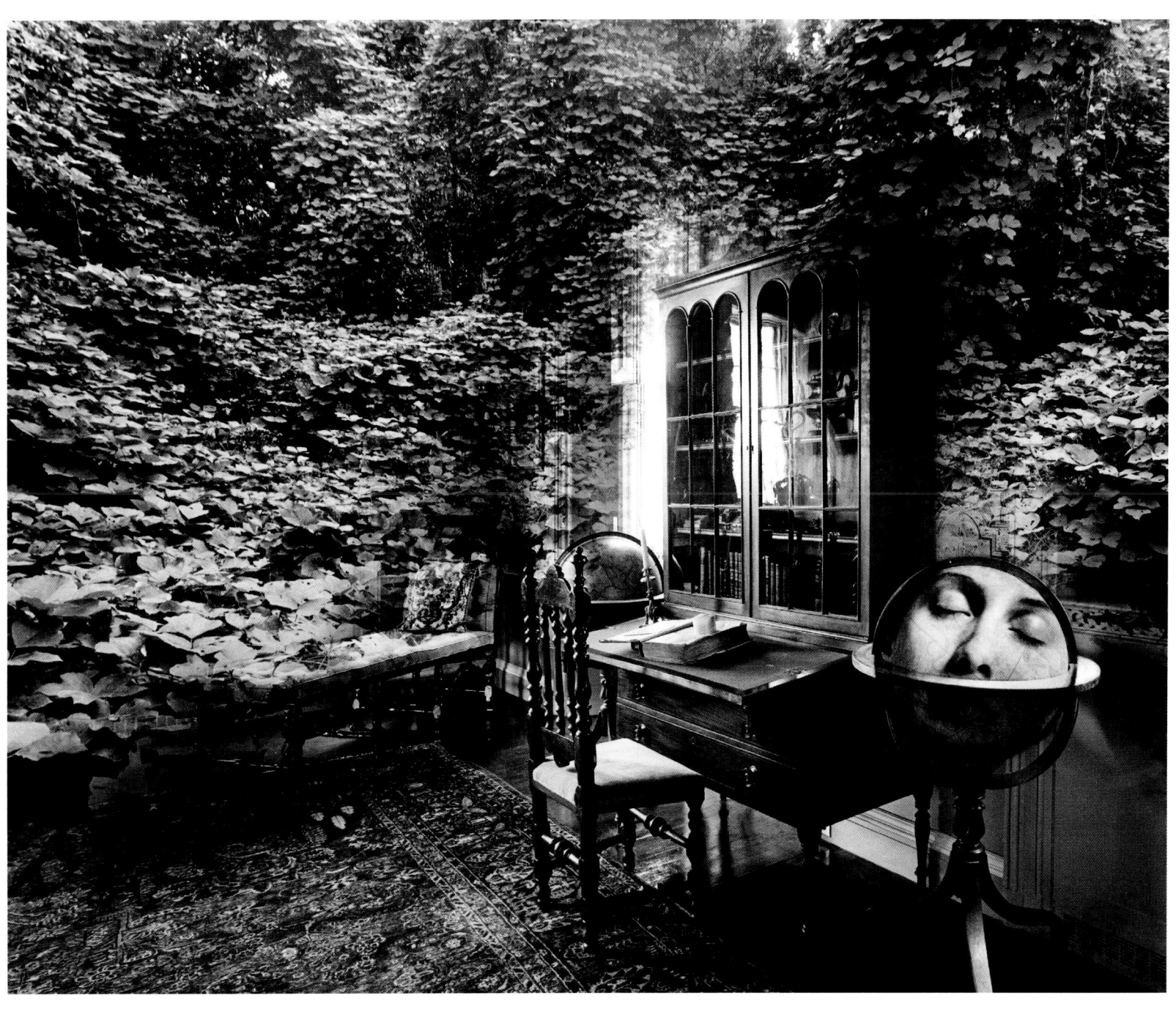

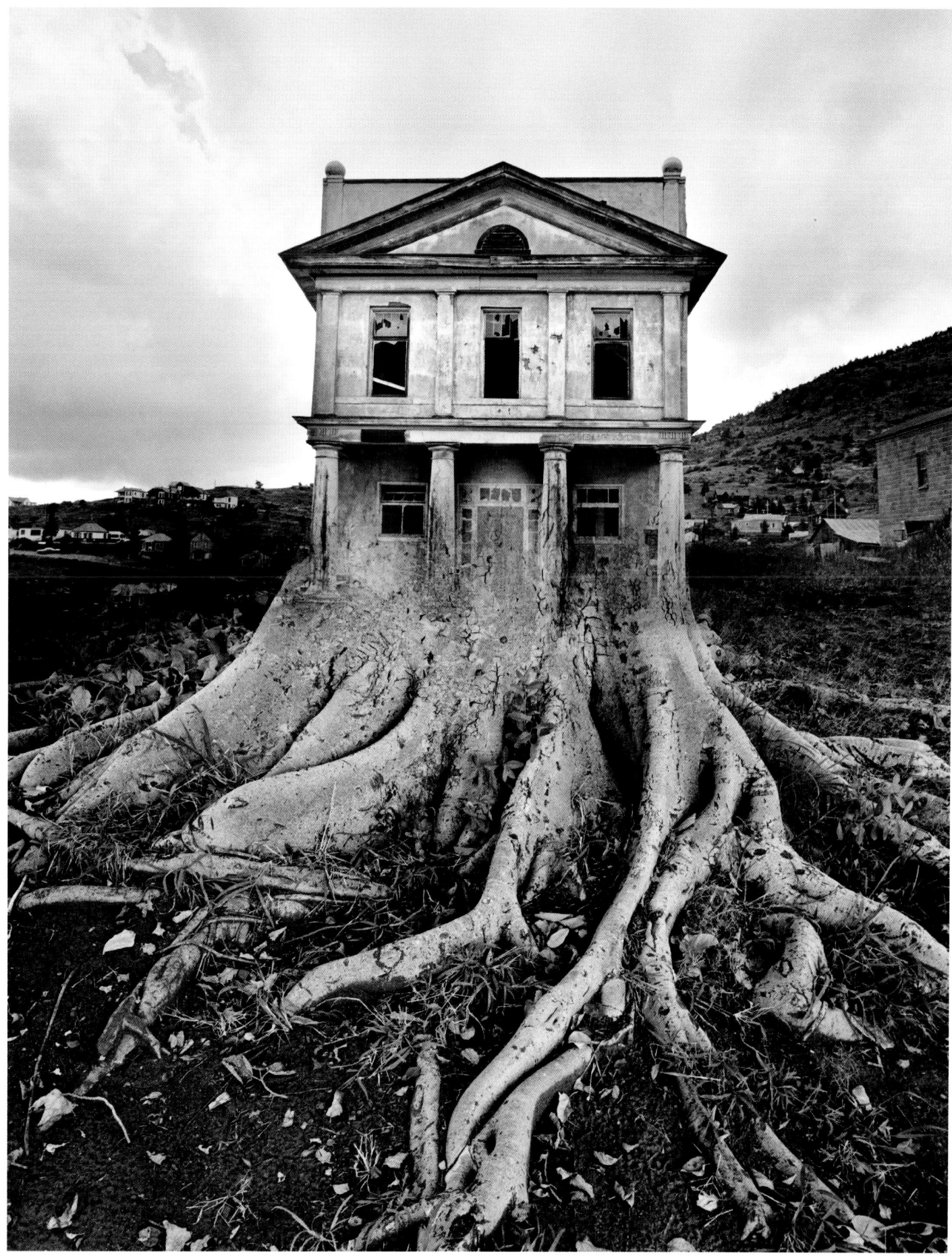

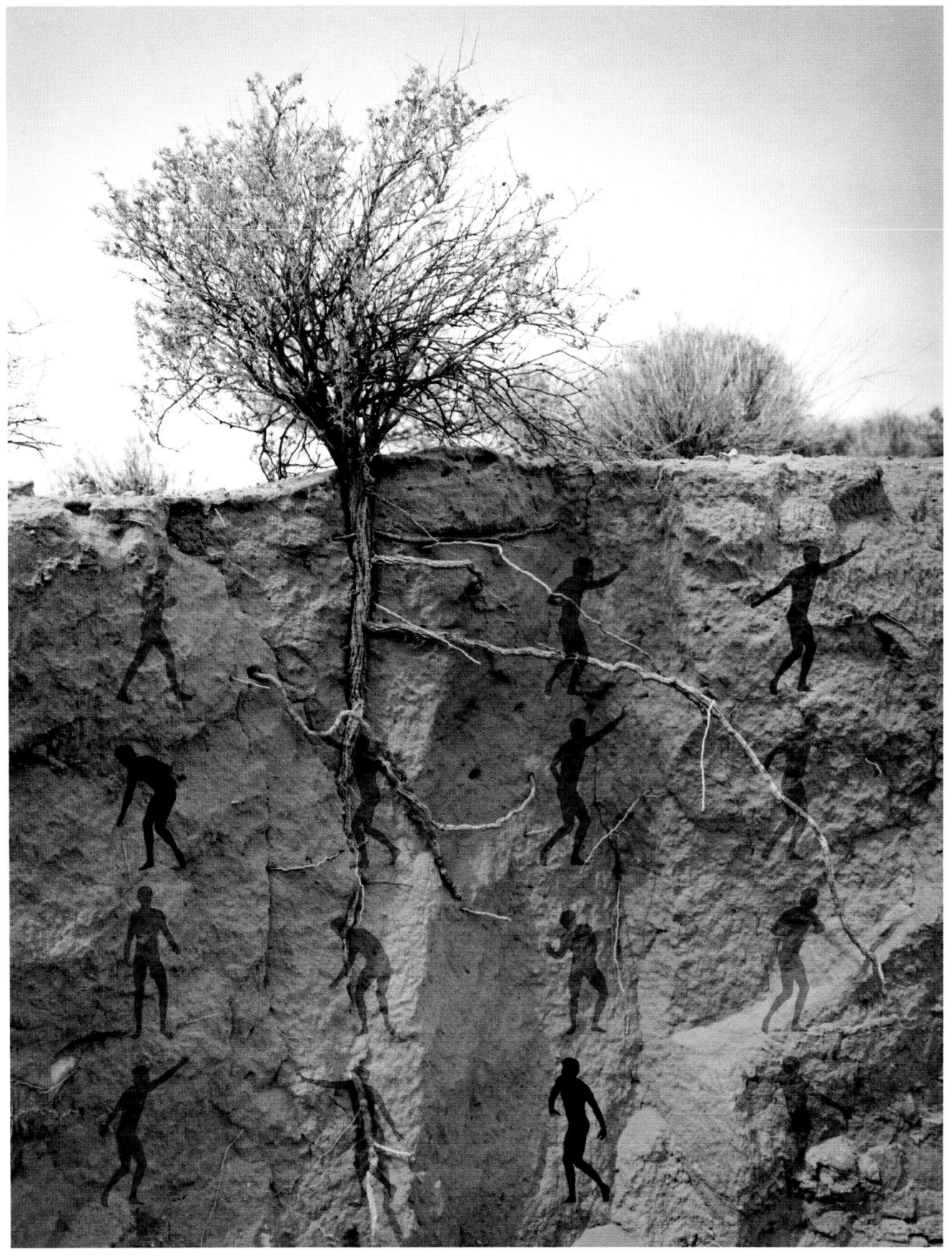

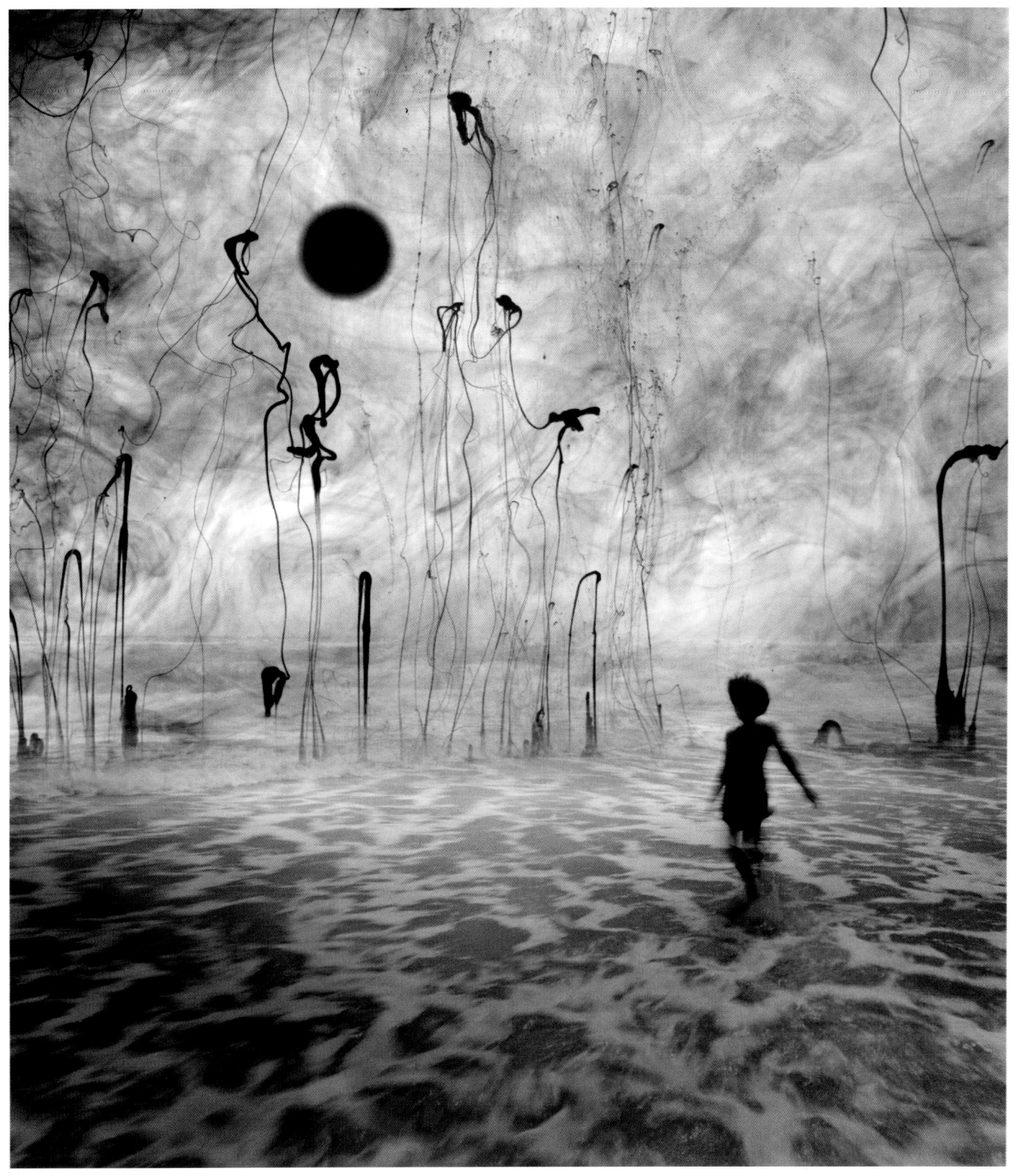

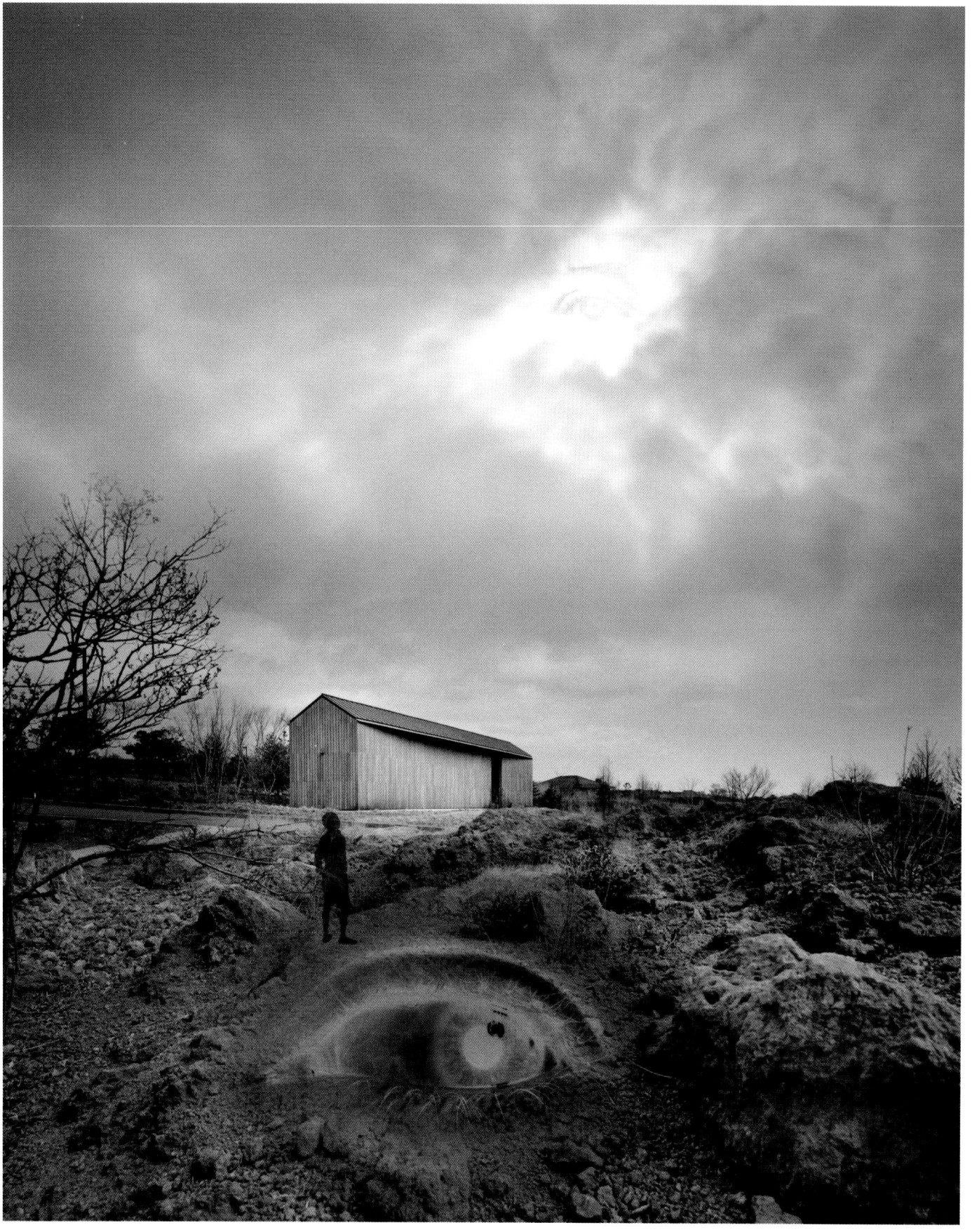

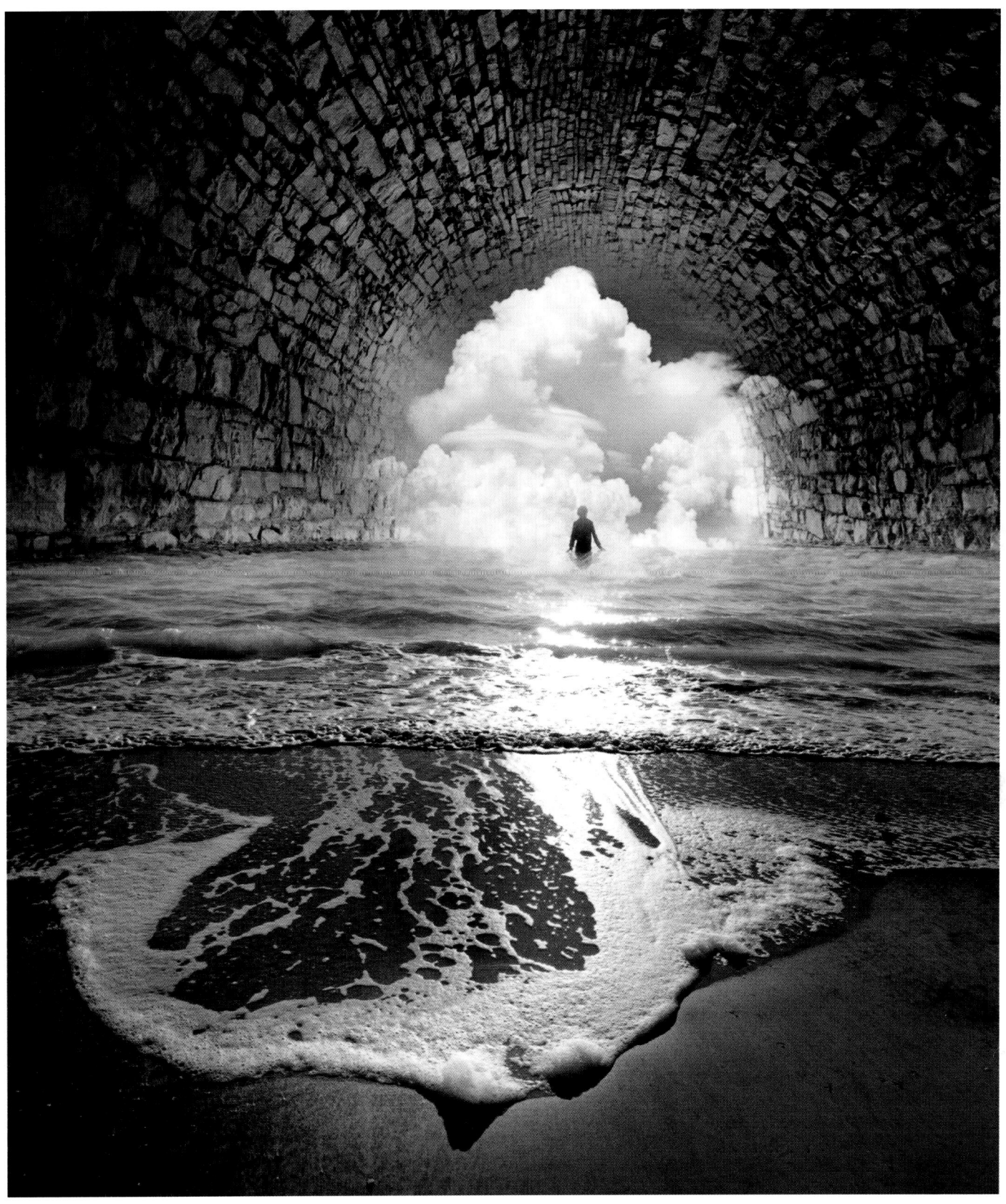

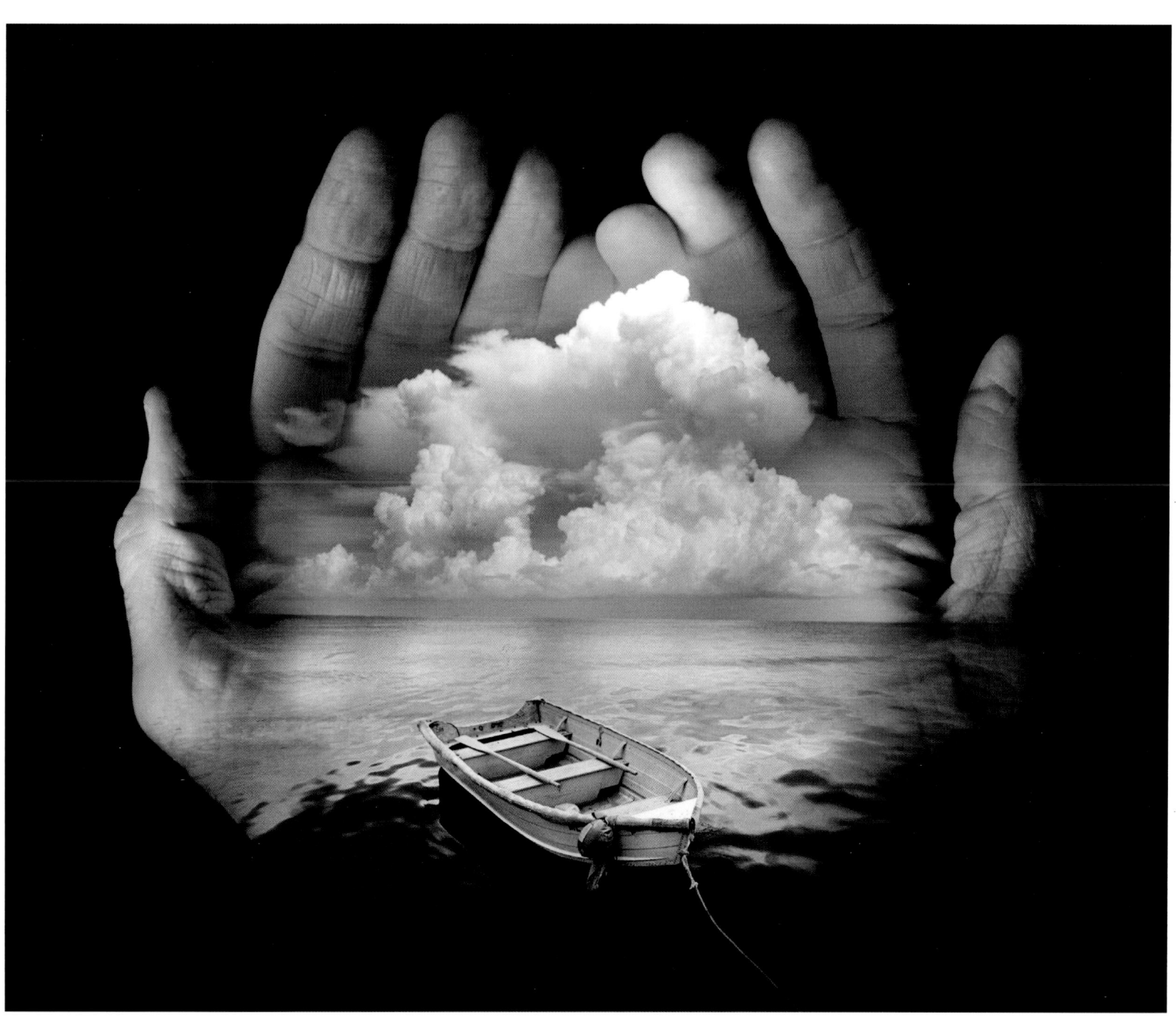

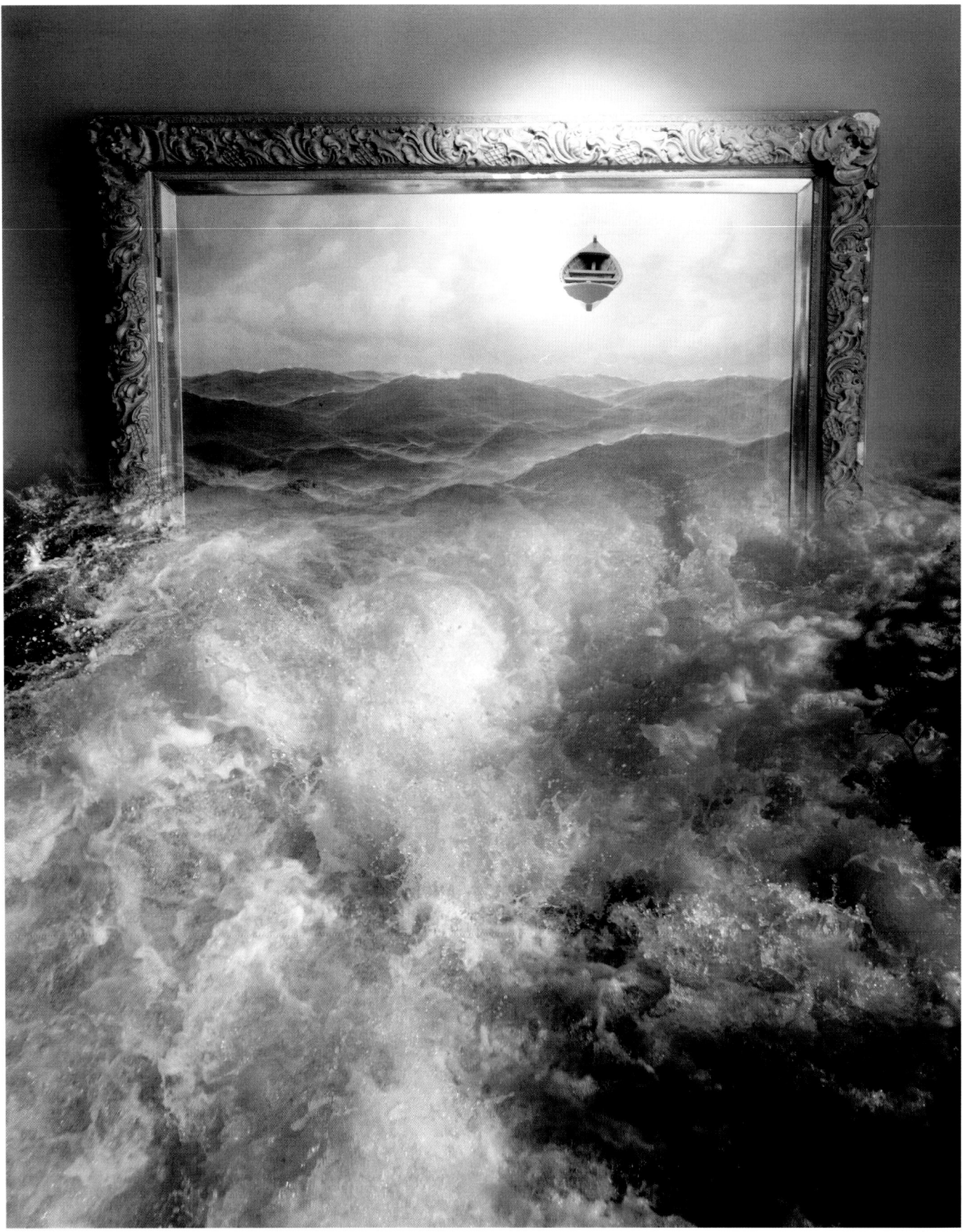

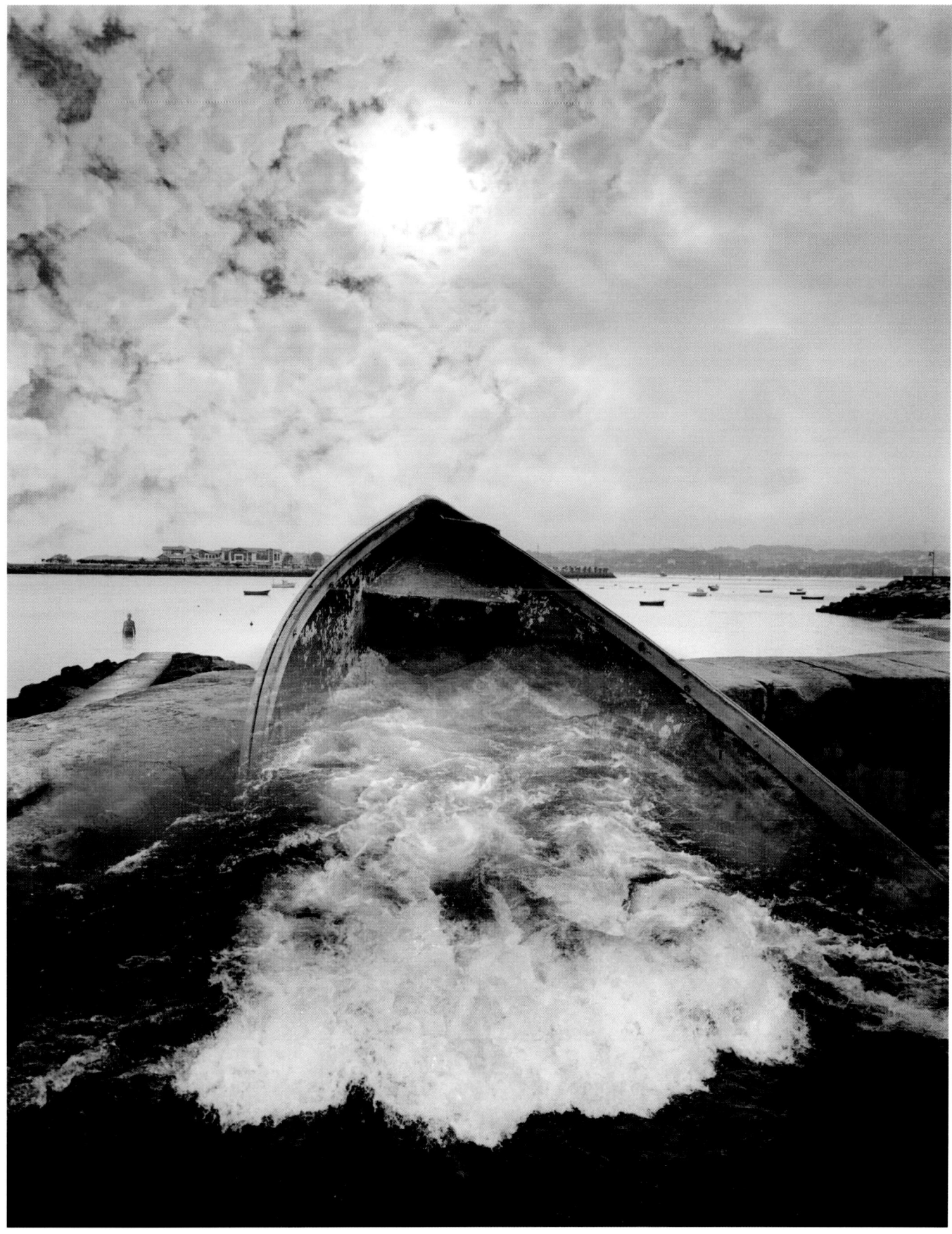

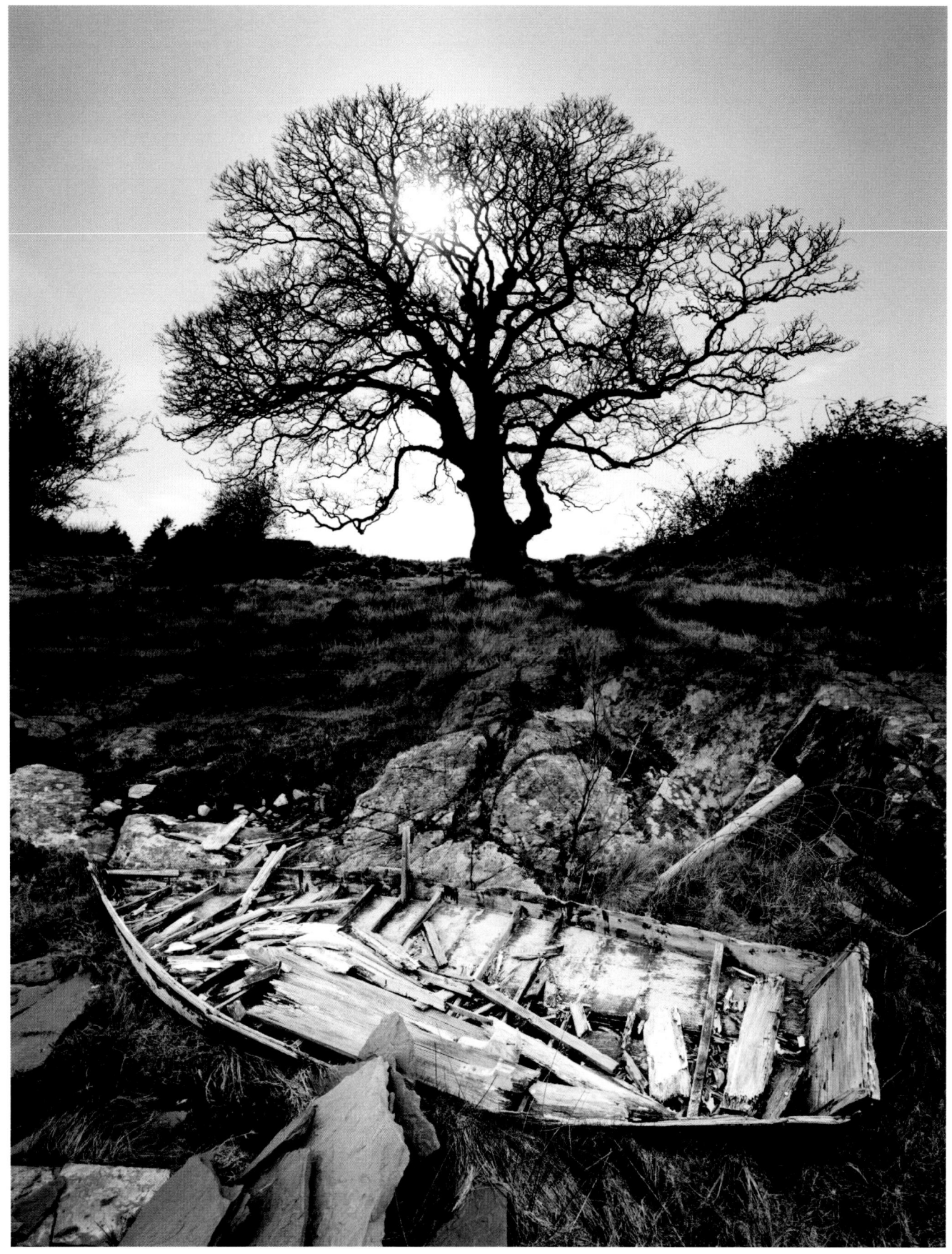

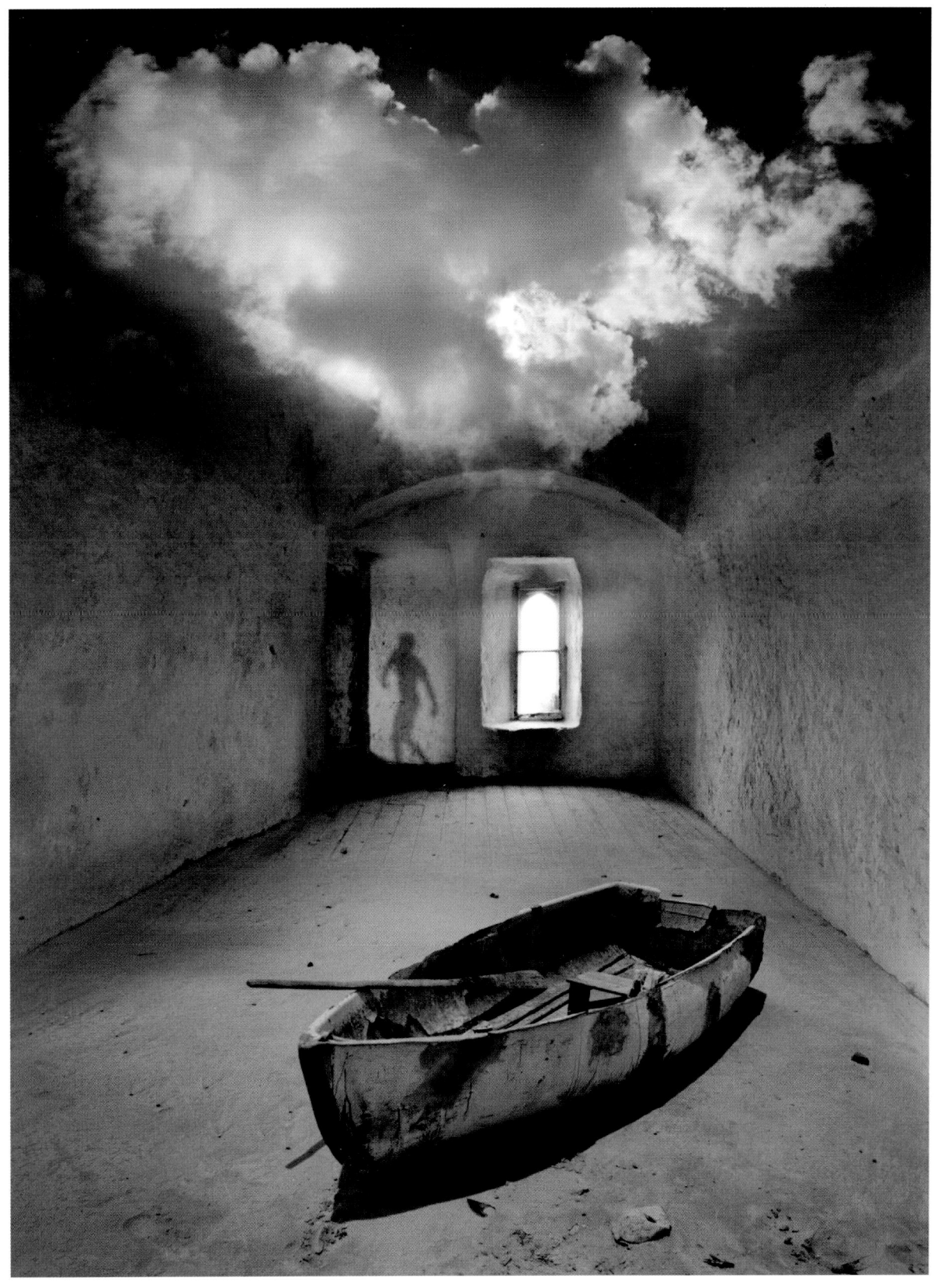

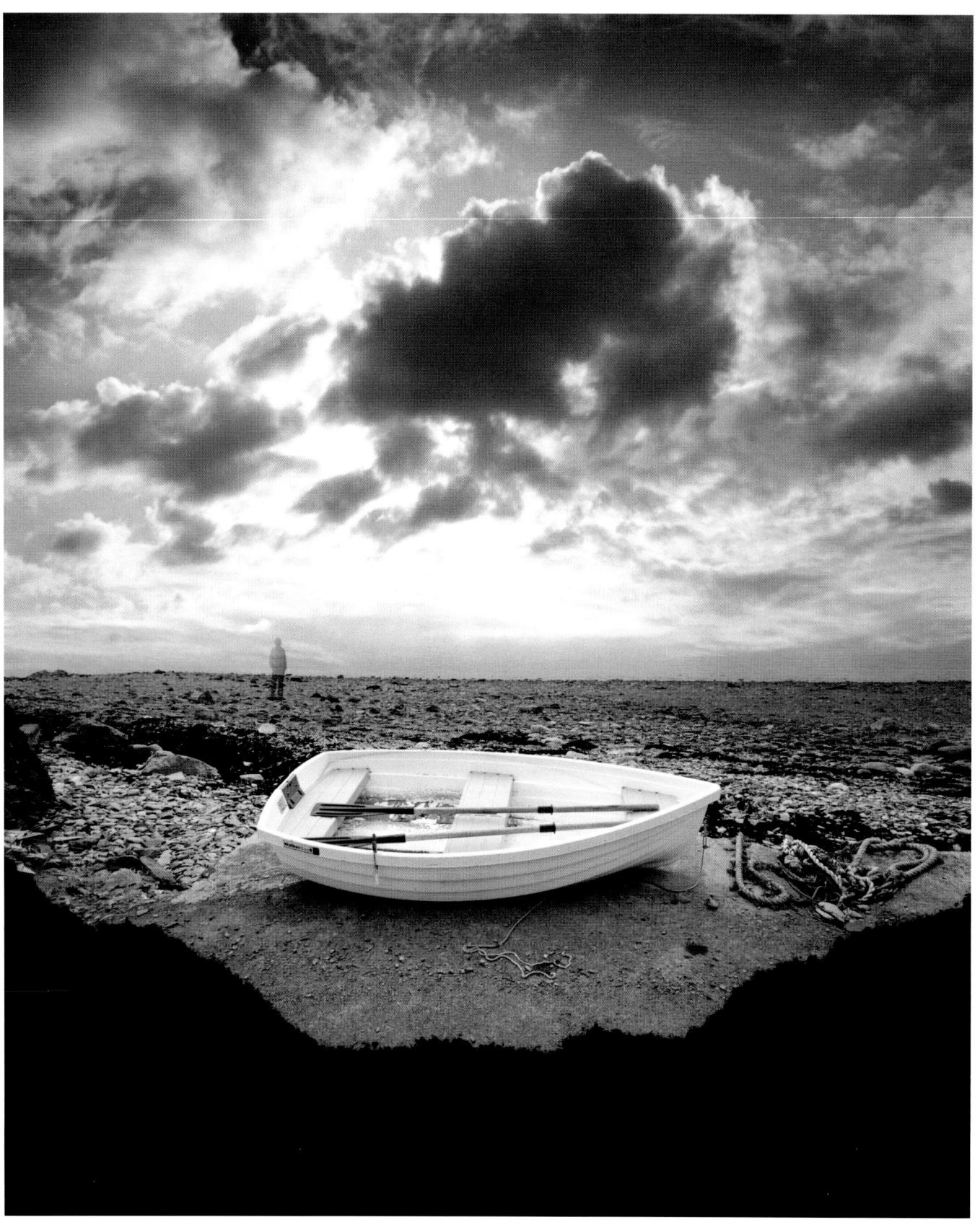

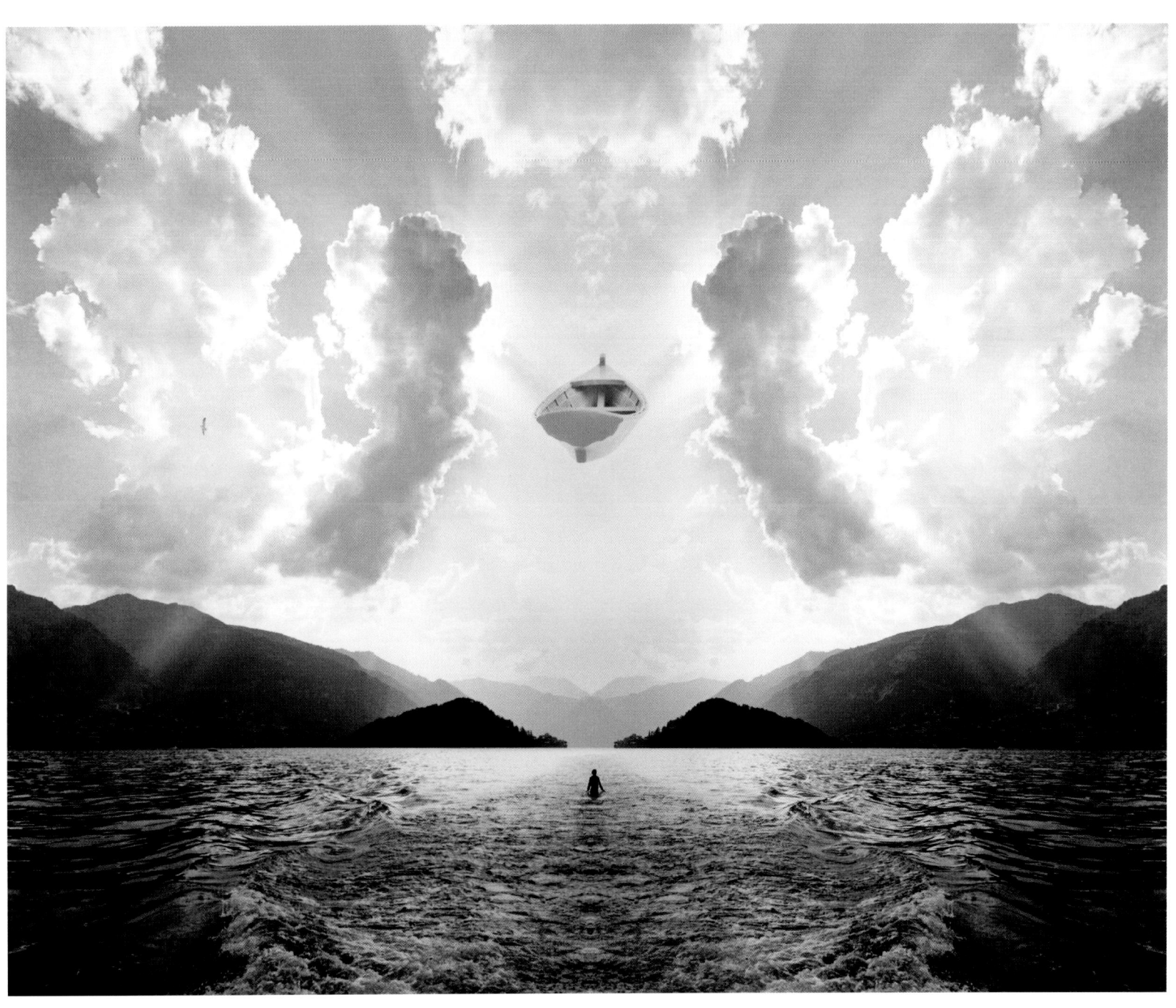

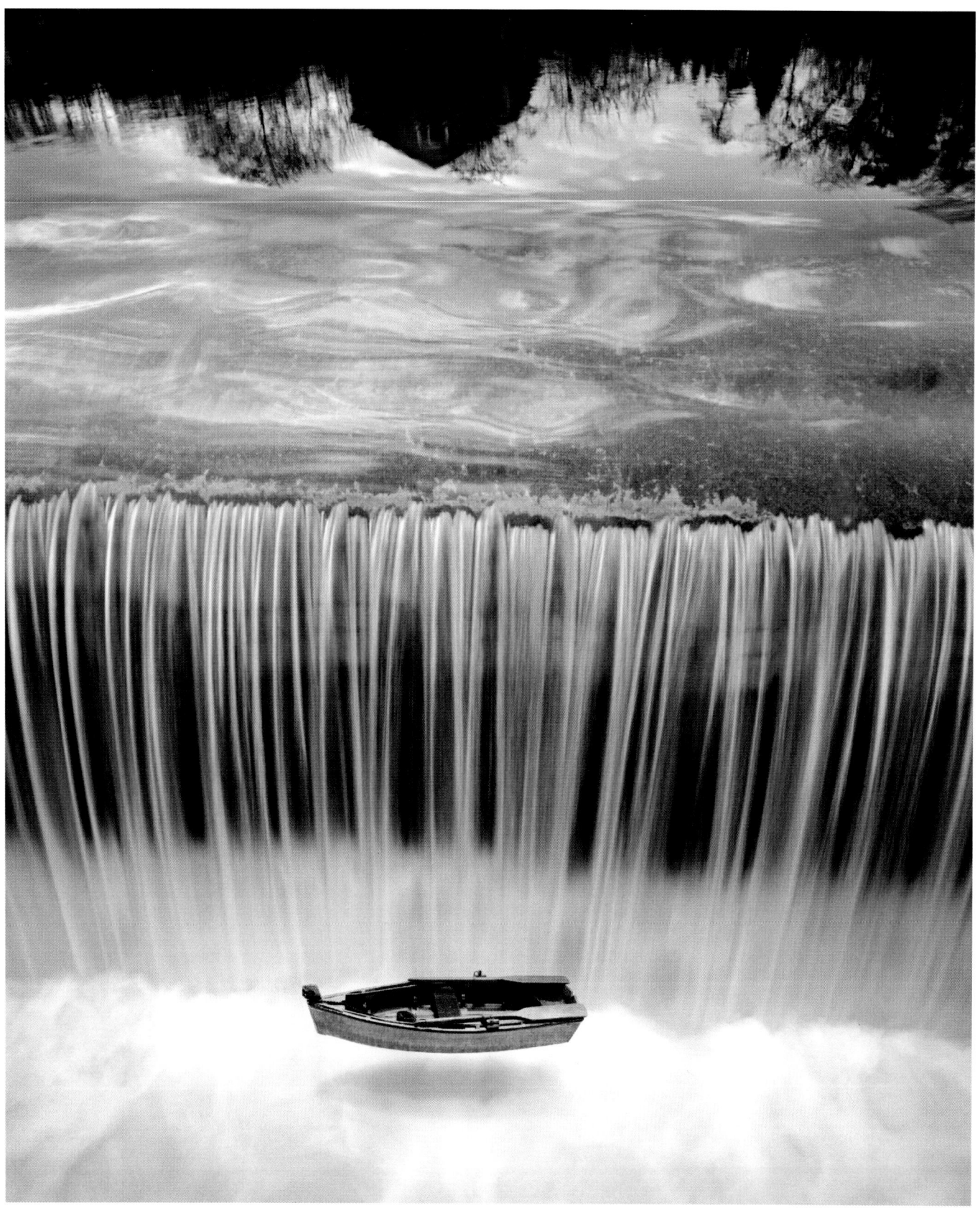

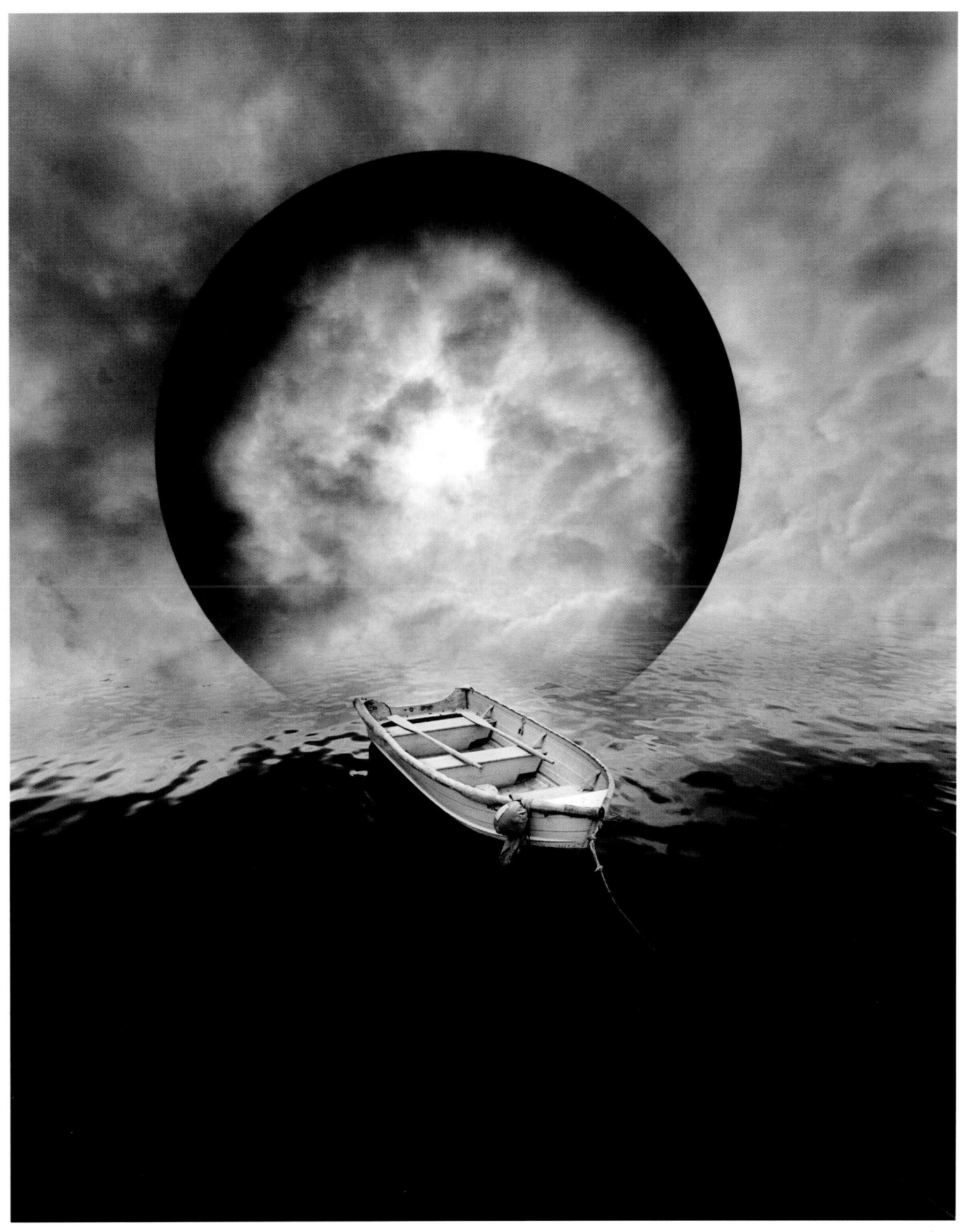

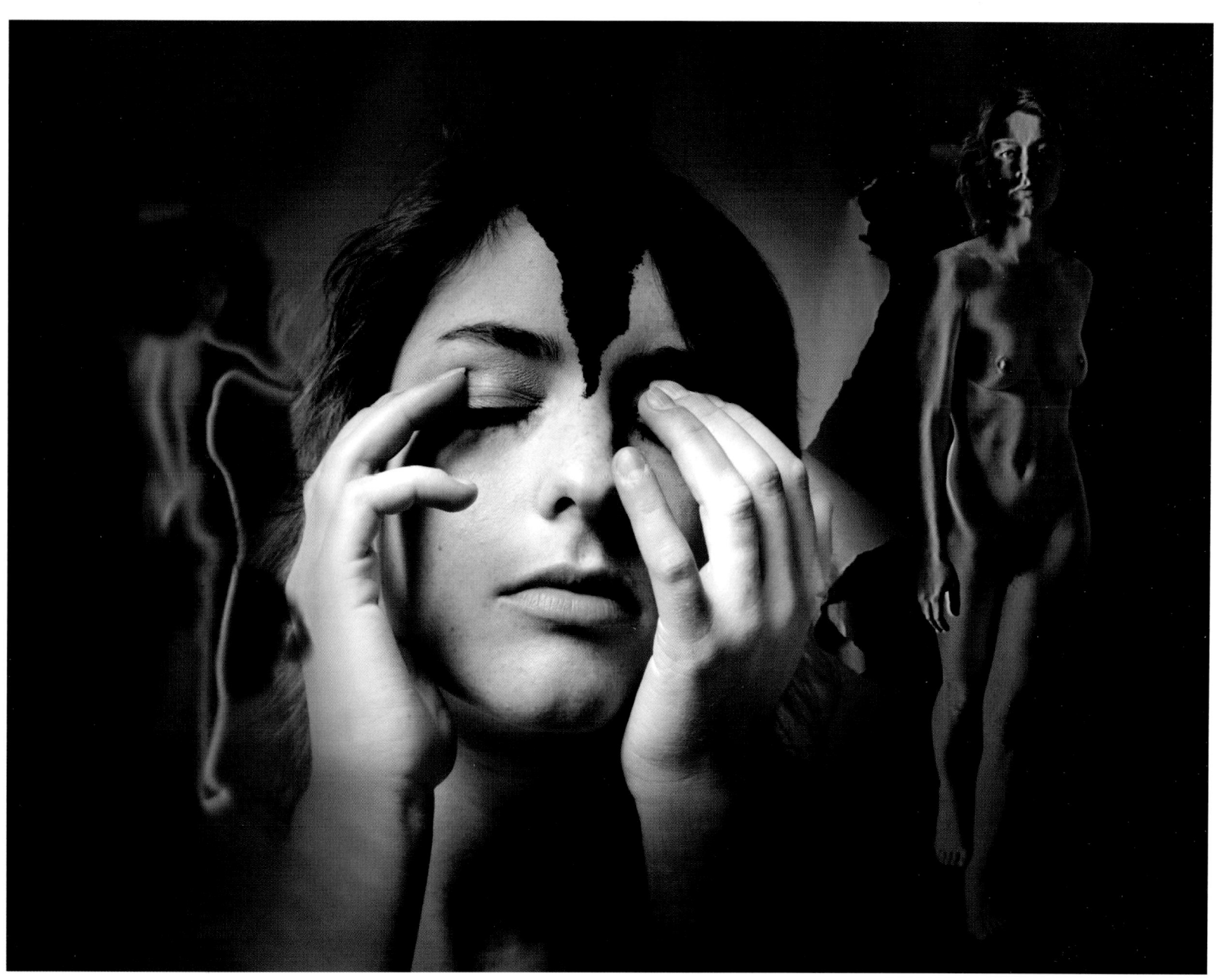

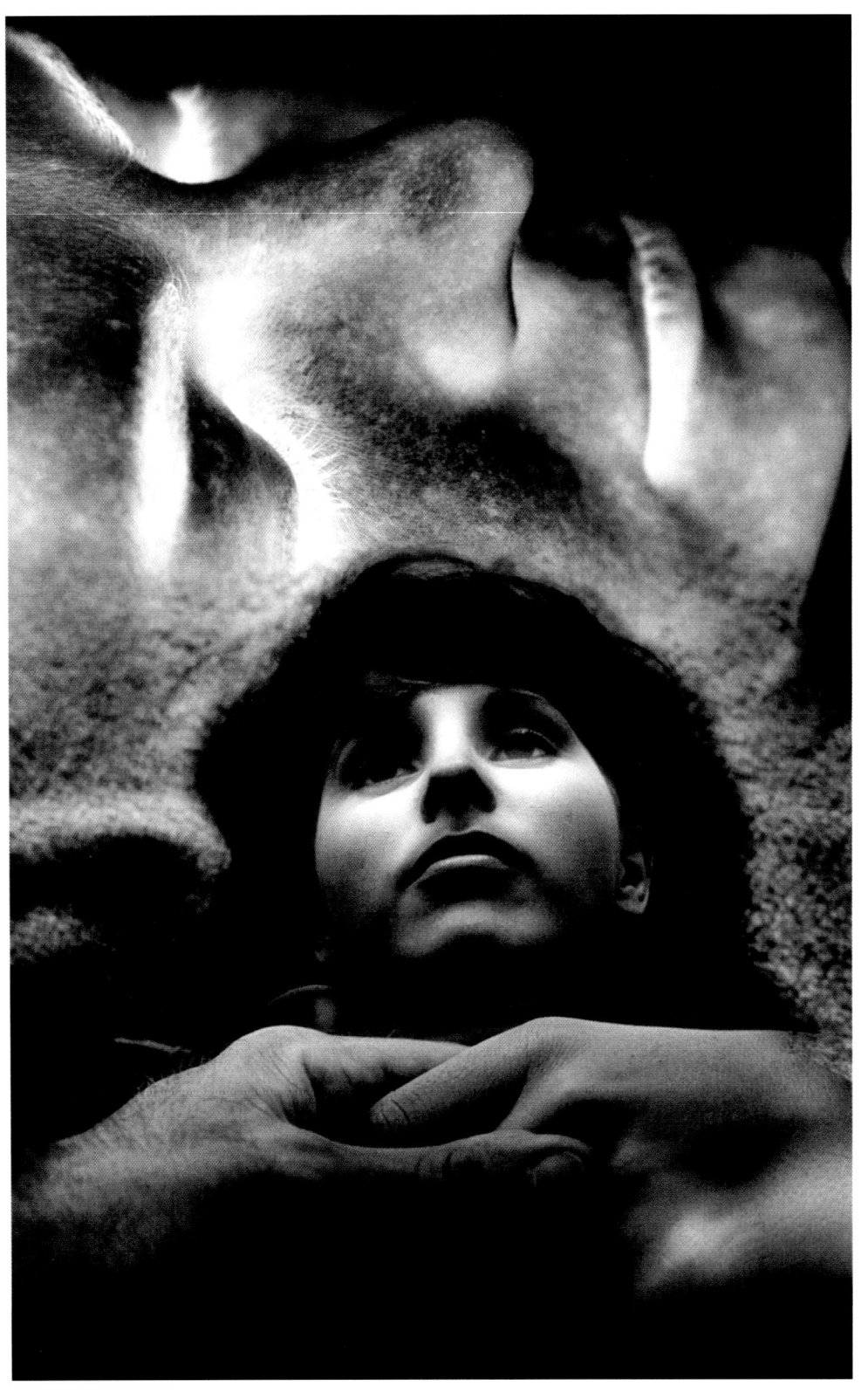

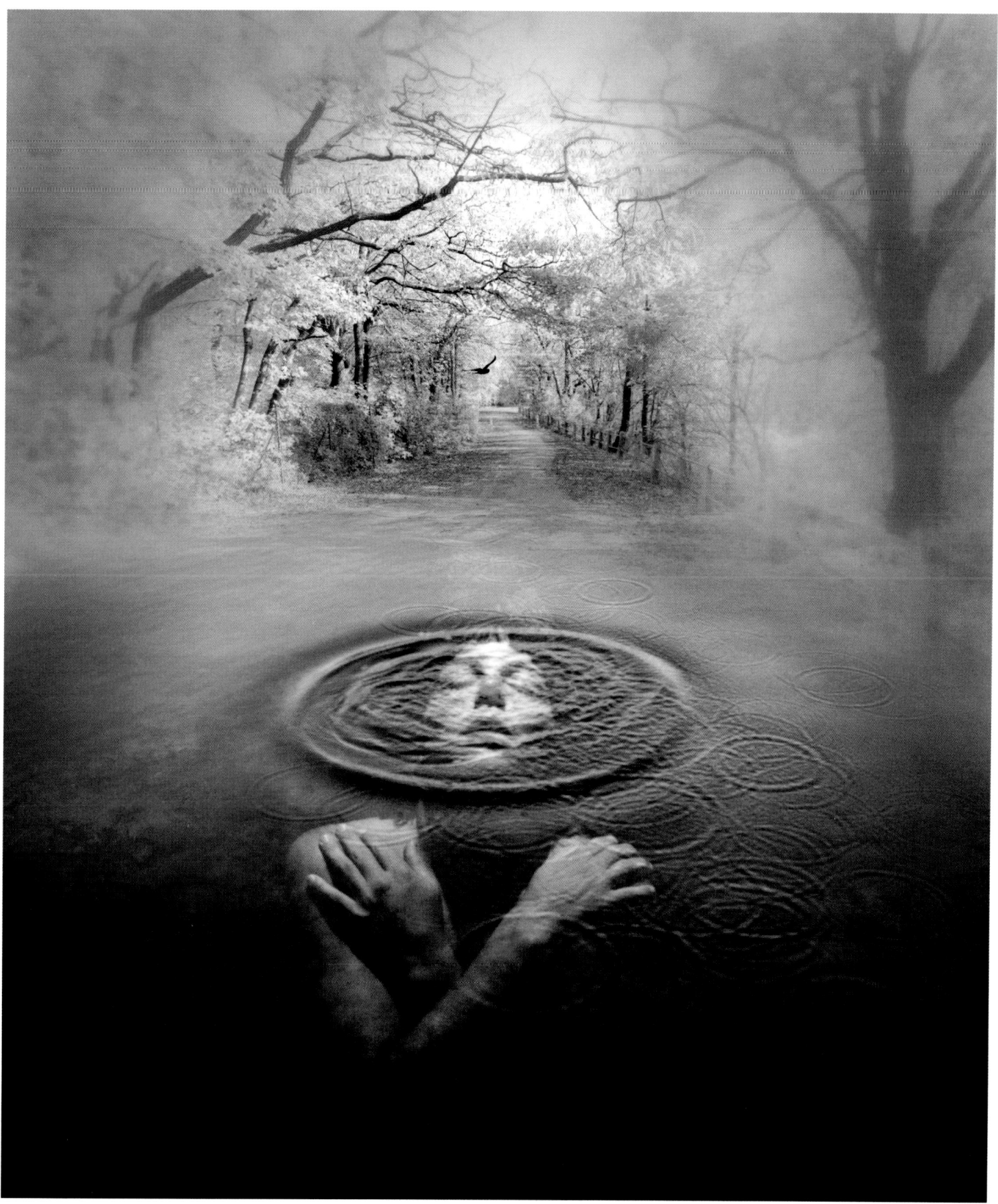

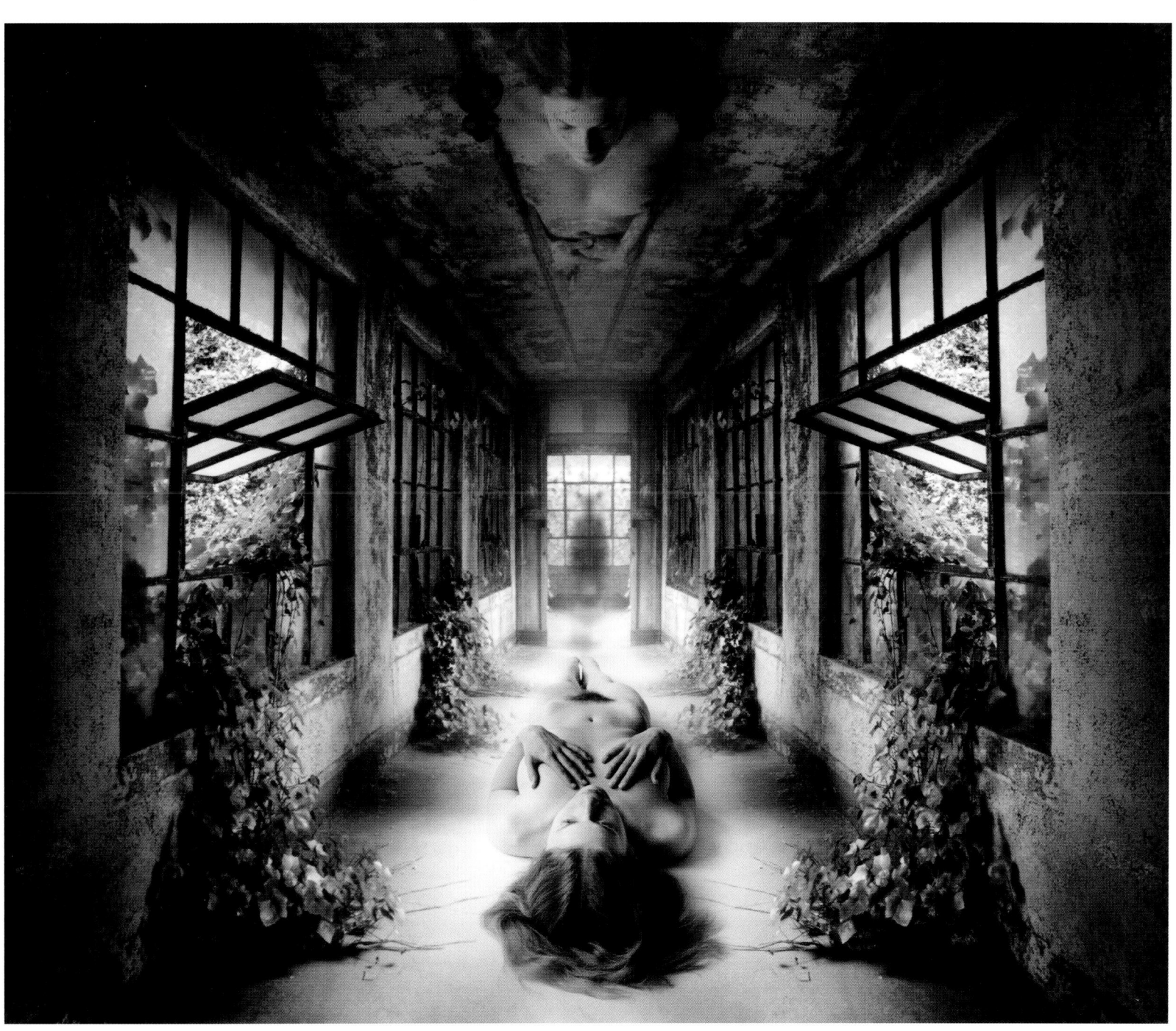

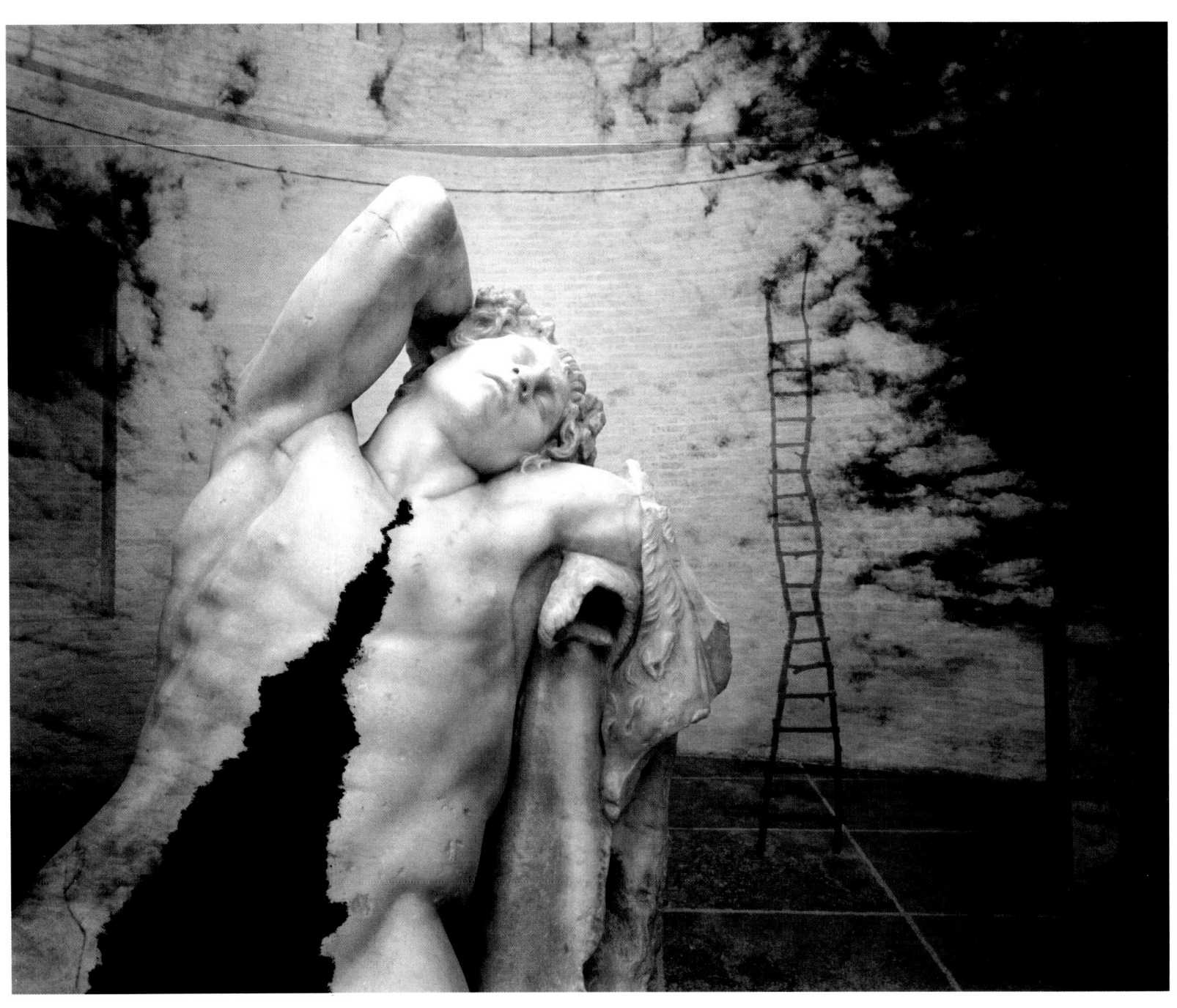

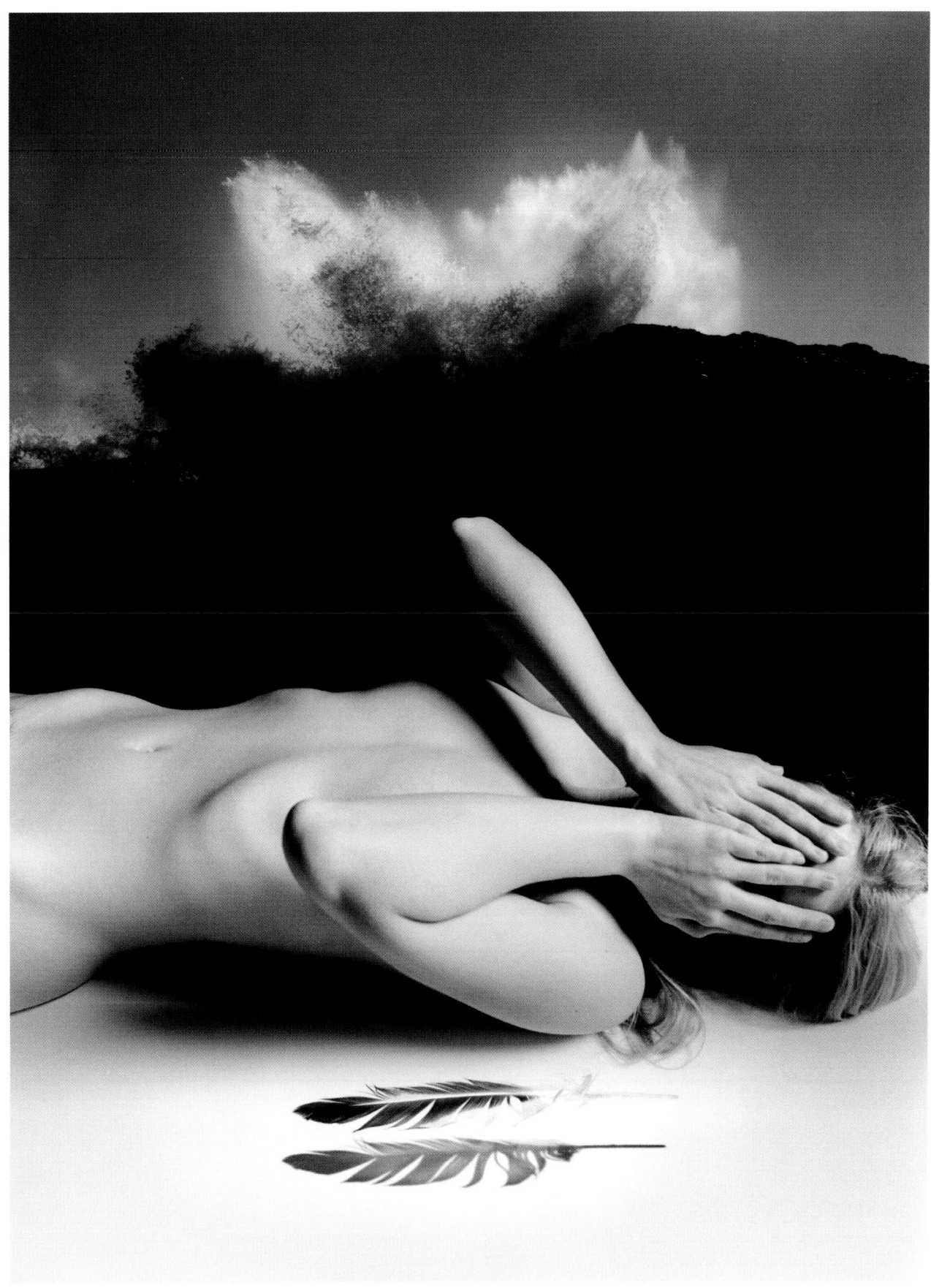

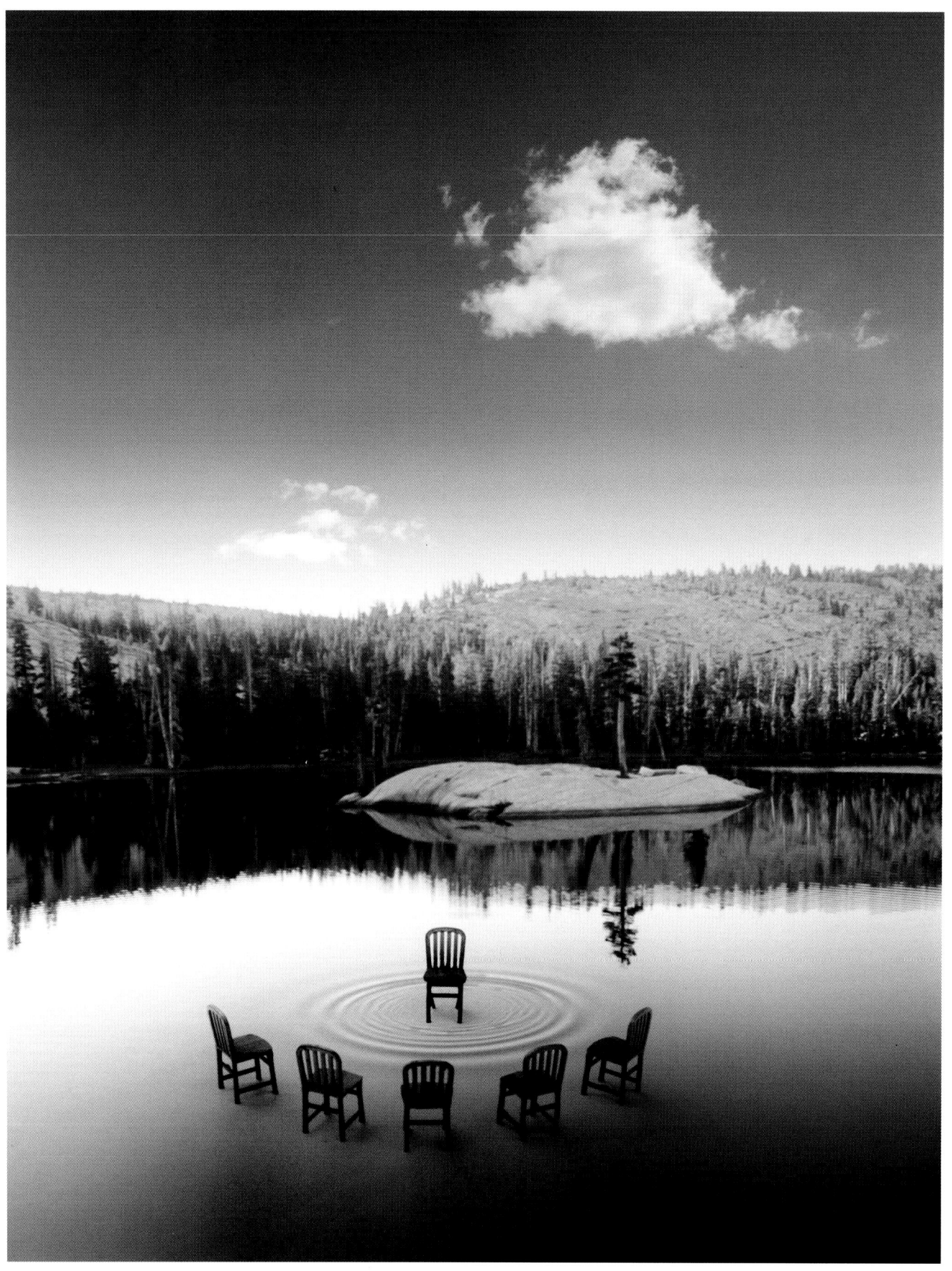

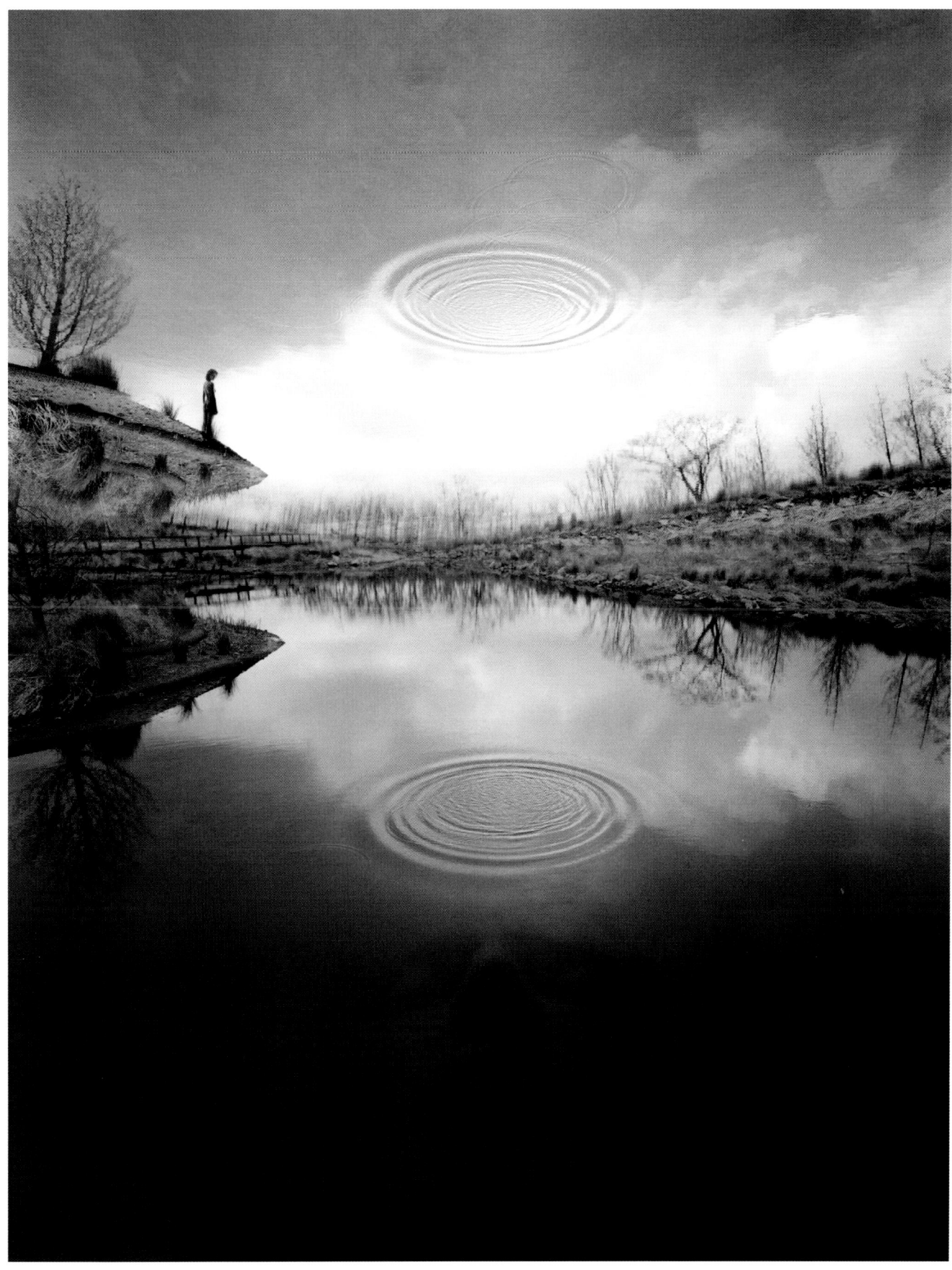

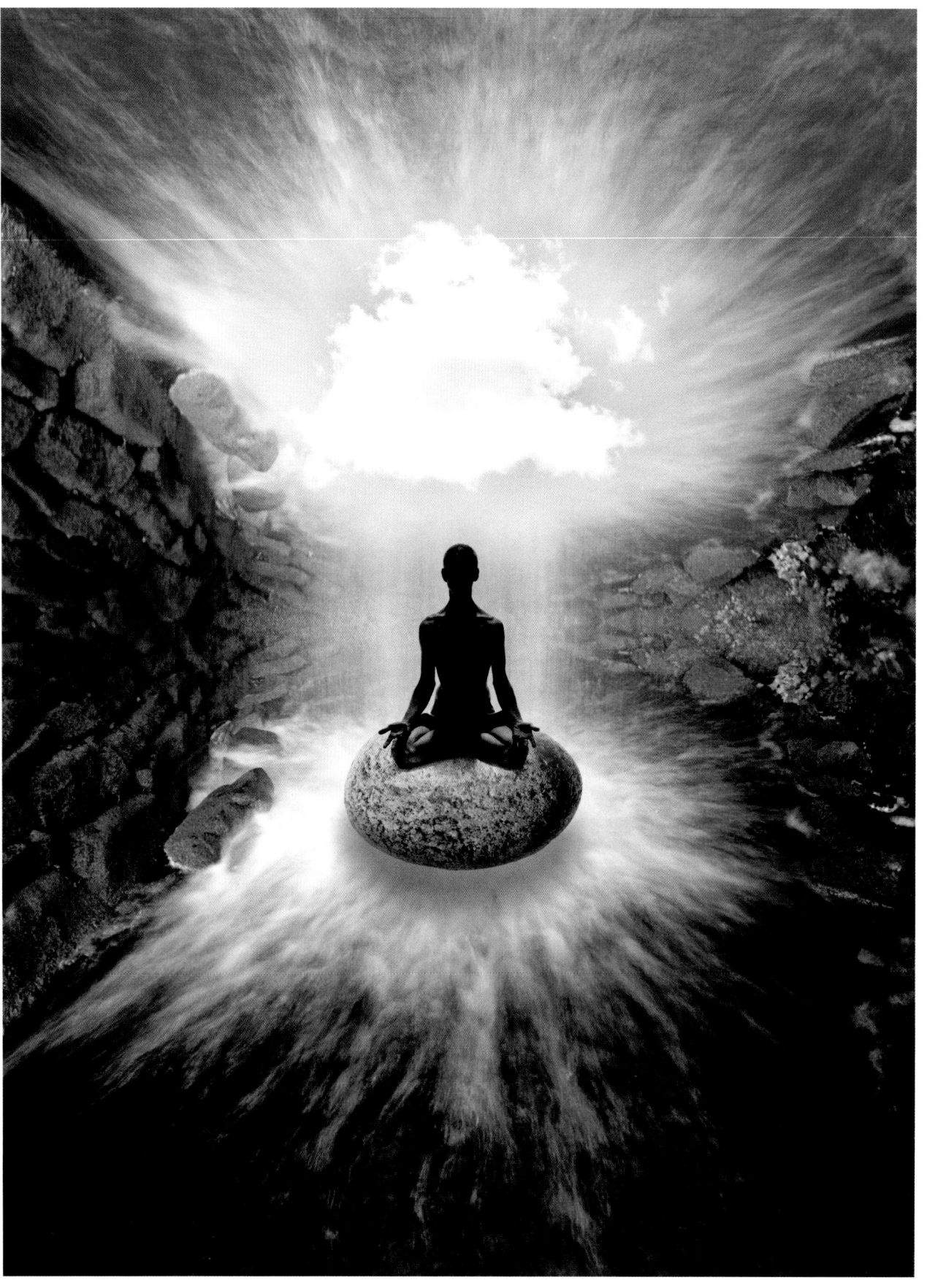

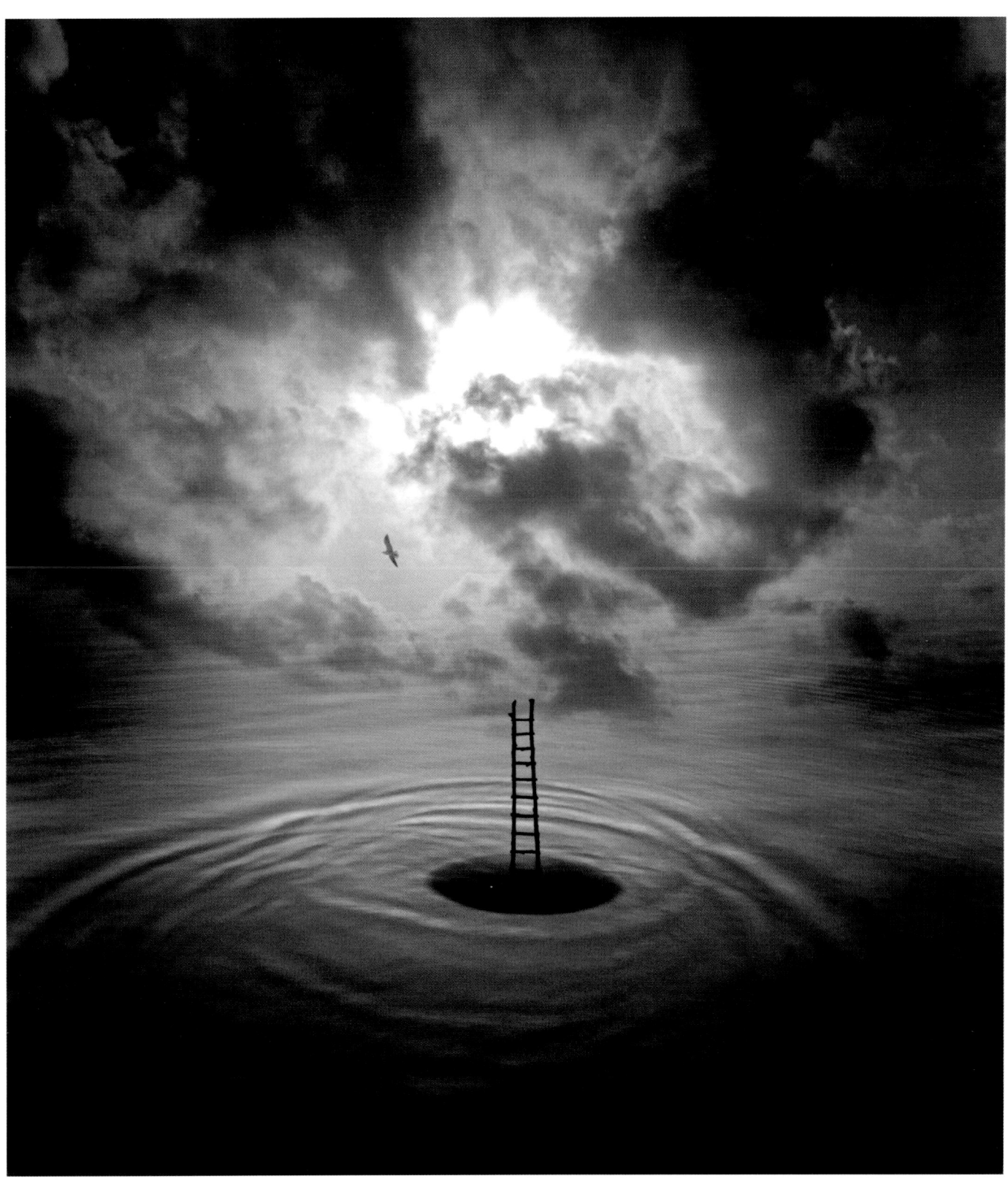

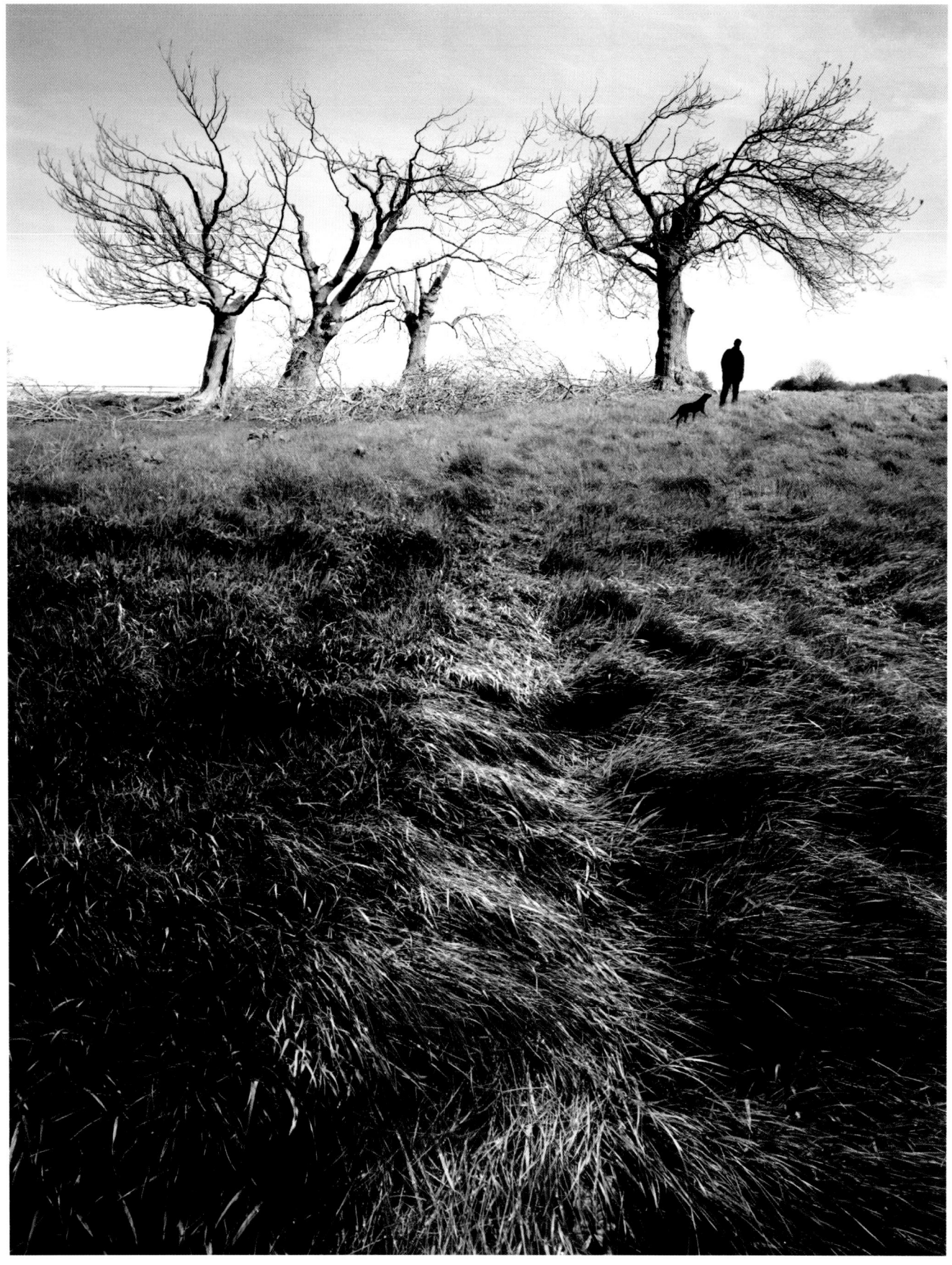

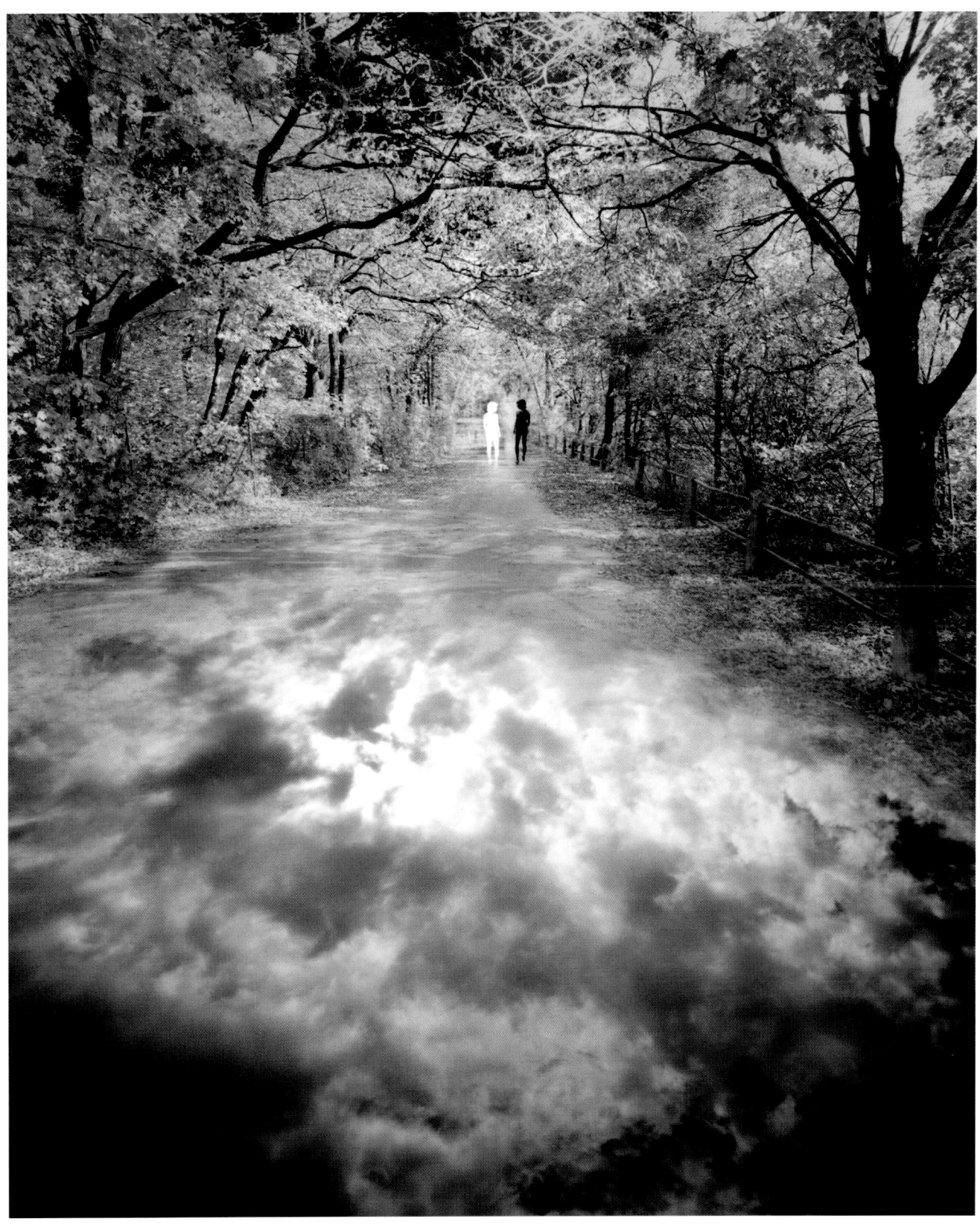

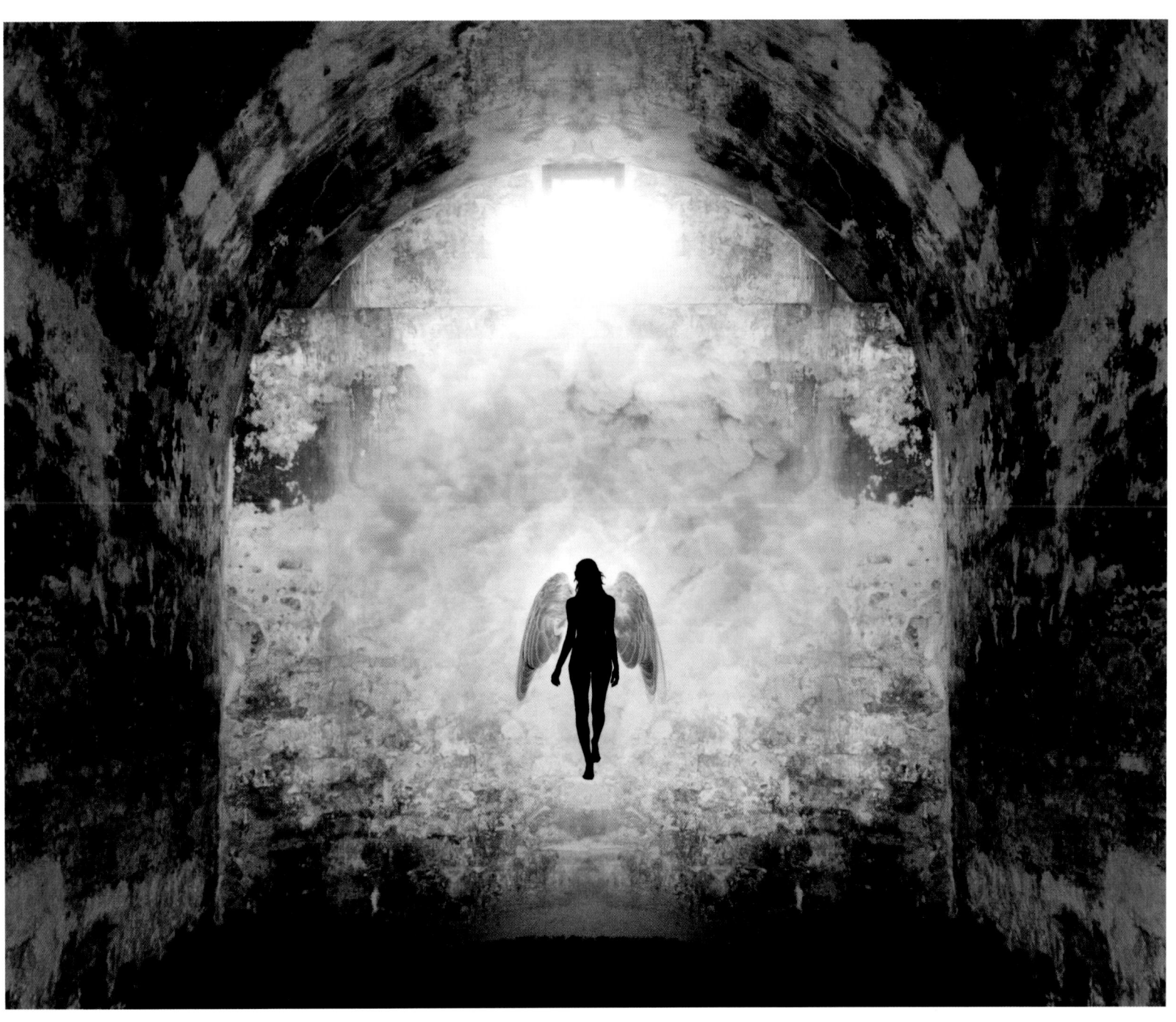

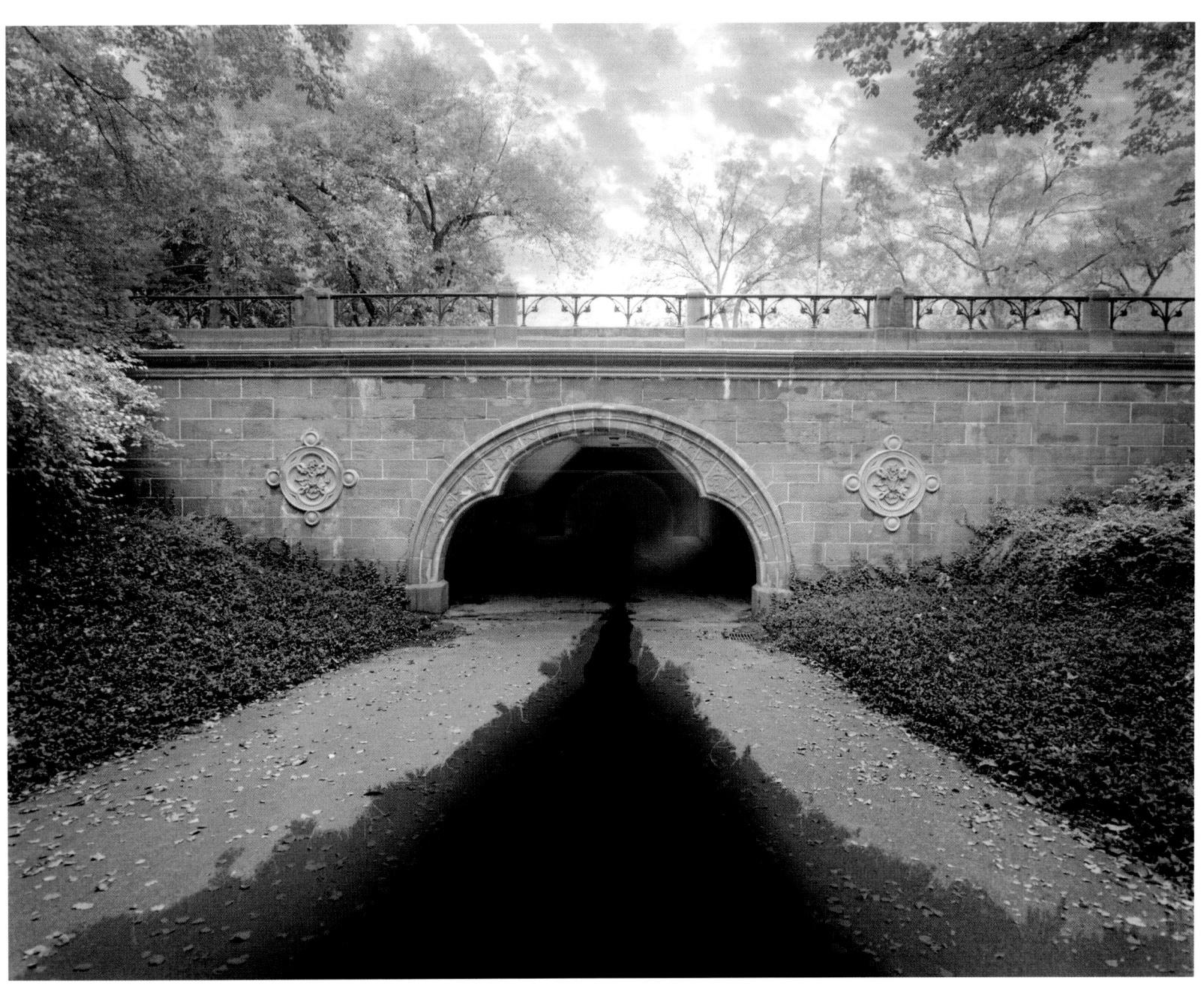

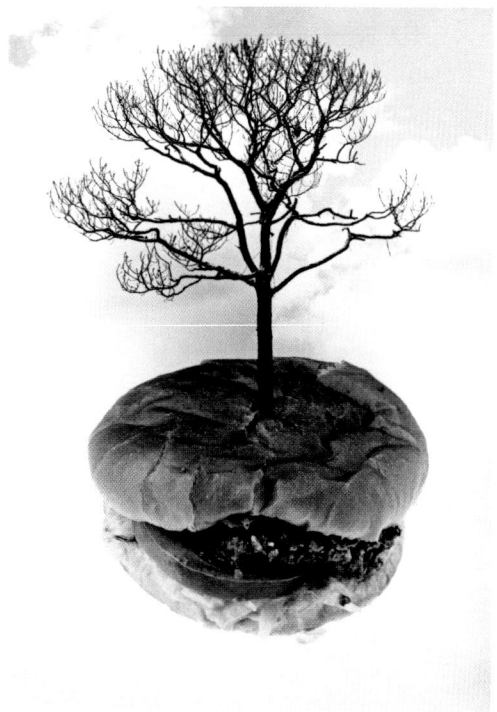

Born in Detroit on June 11, 1934, Jerry N. Uelsmann received his B.F.A. degree at the Rochester Institute of Technology in 1957 and his M.S. and M.F.A. at Indiana University in 1960. He began teaching photography in the Art Department at the University of Florida in 1960. He became a Graduate Research Professor of Art in 1974 and is now retired from teaching. He lives in Gainesville, Florida, with his wife, artist Maggie Taylor.

Uelsmann received a Guggenheim Fellowship in 1967 and a National Endowment for the Arts Fellowship in 1972. He is a Fellow of the Royal Photographic Society of Great Britain and a founding member of the Society for Photographic Education. In 2012, he was awarded an Honorary Doctor of Fine Arts from the University of Florida.

Uelsmann's work has been exhibited in more than 100 individual shows in the United States and abroad over the last fifty years. His photographs are in the permanent collections of many museums worldwide, including the Metropolitan Museum of Art, the Museum of Modern Art, and the Whitney Museum of American Art in New York, the Chicago Art Institute, the International Museum of Photography at the George Eastman House, the Nelson-Atkins Museum of Art in Kansas City, the Museum of Fine Arts in Boston, the National Museum of American Art in Washington, D.C., the Center for Creative Photography at the University of Arizona, the Harn Museum of Art in Gainesville, the Victoria and Albert Museum in London, the Bibliotheque National in Paris, the Moderna Museet in Stockholm, the National Gallery of Canada, the National Gallery of Australia, the National Galleries of Scotland, the Tokyo Metropolitan Museum of Photography, the National Museum of Modern Art in Kyoto, Taipei Fine Arts Museum, and the Museum of Photography in Seoul.